Breadtime

Breadtime

A Down-to-Earth Cookbook
for Bakers and Bread Lovers

Susan Jane Cheney

Illustrated by Kathy Miller-Brown

Ten Speed Press
Berkeley, California

Ten Speed Press
P.O. Box 7123
Berkeley, CA 94707

Distributed in Australia by Simon & Schuster Australia; in
Canada by Publishers Group West; in New Zealand by Tan-
dem Press; in South Africa by Real Books; in the United
Kingdom and Europe by Airlift Books; and in Malaysia and
Singapore by Berkeley Books.

Text design by Tasha Hall
Cover design by Gary Bernal
Cover illustration by JoAnna Roy

Printed in the United States of America

Library of Congress Cataloging-in-Publication Data
on file with publisher

1 2 3 4 5—02 01 00 99 98

*To the memory of my mother, Jane E. Cheney,
and her mother, Emma M. Ettinger, in whose
kitchens my culinary odyssey began.*

Contents

Preface to the New Edition

WHEN I WROTE THE ORIGINAL *Breadtime Stories*, I WAS EAGER to share my conviction that breads provide a wholesome and supremely appealing foundation for meals in a variety of ways. Consequently, the book included quite a number of recipes for things that complement breads, especially soups and salads and even a selection of favorite desserts. This time around, I've tethered my focus a bit and stuck to more strictly bread-related formulas like spreads, sandwiches, and pizzas. I also revised text and recipes either to reflect changes in my own cooking and baking or to simplify or clarify explanations. The paring-down process allows room for a new section on bread-machine baking.

The food world has changed dramatically since *Breadtime Stories* first appeared and so has my more personal culinary landscape. I now gaze out at a central Minnesota scene, having moved from deep in the heart of Texas to this northern edge of the American heartland. I'm eating root vegetables and sustaining soups and stews more of the year now, and less tiny tender leafy greens, guacamole, and salsa. But whatever the season, temperature, and meal plan, I still often include breads to match and enhance the menu.

Prevailing national culinary trends are more supportive than ever of my views about the inherent appeal of good breads and basic principles for producing them. Healthful breads have a natural niche in today's "dietary pyramids," which affirm the important role of grains, especially whole grains, in the human diet. Aesthetic factors play an important role in bread making on this side of the Atlantic now too. There's been an upsurge in small local bakeries using traditional techniques. And I've noticed with great pleasure that more commercially made breads resemble European-style, artisan loaves: carefully shaped, freestanding, and wonderfully crusty. Many of these breads taste good too, reflecting their makers' knowledge of and commitment to high quality ingredients.

Beautiful, flavorful loaves also are appearing in natural foods supermarkets popping up all over the country. These avant-garde groceries contribute substantially to the availability of foods I've long sought out: organic whole grains and whole grain flours and other unadulterated products. They also foster greater acceptance of ingredients such as soy products and sea salt.

Although no substitute for handmade techniques, automatic bread machines have increased appreciation of freshly made bread. While the earliest bread machines were capable only of producing light breads, many can now manage the whole grain breads I favor. My new section on bread-machine baking is designed to bolster the scanty repertoire of truly whole grain recipes that already exists. Yet, I'm hoping that the bread machine's popularity ultimately will arouse interest in hands-on methods, which I still find most satisfying in both process and product.

As was true of the original *Breadtime Stories,* this book, now simply *Breadtime,* is again dedicated to all creative cooks and innovative bakers. It's my sincere hope that this revised edition continues to inspire readers of the first volume, many of whom have shared their enthusiasm with me, and that it engages the interest of new bread fans. To all of you, I extend warmest wishes for baking happily ever after!

SUSAN JANE CHENEY
St. Paul, Minnesota
February 1998

Acknowledgments

I WISH TO THANK DAVID ARBEIT, MY HUSBAND AND DEAREST friend, for his willingness to taste anything and everything, his careful and honest critiques, and his invaluable technical assistance. His unwavering support and confidence in me made this book possible.

I would also like to express my appreciation to my father, Lee C. Cheney, for teaching me by example how to work hard at the things I find interesting and for reminding me to "have a little fun every day."

My sincere thanks, too, to other family members and to friends scattered far and wide; their enthusiasm and encouragement spurred me on far more than they know. Special thanks to Sue Taylor for her editorial aid at a critical juncture and to Ray Bard for his help in getting this project off the ground.

I am grateful to Jackie Wan, my editor. Her expertise and considered advice have greatly enhanced the book.

Many thanks to Kathy Miller-Brown for lending her creative spirit to the artwork and for translating my mental images of illustrations into the fine drawings in the book.

This revised edition of the book calls for further acknowledgments. Clancy Drake and Mariah Bear were especially instrumental in setting the revision process in motion and keeping it on track; many thanks to both of them for their ideas and energy. I greatly appreciate Tasha Hall's work in developing and masterfully executing a challenging design. And finally, heartfelt thanks to Jason Rath for so competently seeing the project through to completion.

Once Upon a Time

THE LITTLE RED HEN WAS ONE OF MY FAVORITE CHILDHOOD stories. IT tells the tale of bread making to illustrate that those who work will receive their just rewards and those who don't won't. On her own, the Little Red Hen sows, grows, harvests, and mills a crop of wheat and prepares a batch of bread. Her barnyard friends ignore her requests for assistance until she asks: "And who will help me eat this bread?" Then everyone is eager to participate, but the Little Red Hen keeps all the bread for herself. I was not so much impressed by the story's moral as I was fascinated by the activities described, and age hasn't quelled my enthusiasm. Fresh grains and flour, thick ceramic bowls, wooden spoons, smooth marble work surfaces—all the ingredients and implements for baking—enthrall me. Mixing and kneading invigorate rather than tire me. I faithfully peruse cookbook sections of bookstores and libraries, ponder uses for every new discovery in cookware shops, and make pilgrimages to bakeries as though they contained rare works of art.

Are people born with compelling interests? As a toddler, I was caught sprinkling flour throughout the first floor of the house. I think I recall the shocked expression on my mother's face before she broke into laughter. I no doubt enjoyed the soft, satiny feel of Pillsbury's All-Purpose Blend sifting through my fingers, and perhaps this incident foretold my intensely "breadridden" years to come. I have been known to cart a bowl of dough around in my car to punch down at appropriate times and have often hurried home from restaurant kitchens to cook in my own.

I'm sure I was influenced by my grandmother, whom I shadowed at her kitchen counters, sink, and stove. I still feel her presence as I use her finely crocheted pot holders, flowered china, and shiny copper-bottomed pans. Granny took pride in her excellence as a homemaker, but didn't pursue baking and cooking as sciences and arts as I do. I'm always pleased by turning out attractive, delicious products but also want to know why they were successful. When something flops, I want to understand what went wrong.

This book reflects my years in the kitchen. Its primary focus is baking, but it is not just another bread book. My special interest is the intermingling of baking and cooking, whereby breads fit into a healthful yet satisfying pattern of eating. I view baking and cooking as a cooperative adventure and like to explore the synergy between them.

The recipes, inspired by loaves and dishes I have tasted or read, heard, dreamed about, or just imagined, were devised and refined in "the lab," as my husband long ago labeled our kitchen. They incorporate grains, legumes, soy foods, vegetables, fruits, nuts, seeds, and occasionally eggs. Meat, fowl, and fish are absent, and milk products appear only as options. These recipes are for you bread lovers resolute about consuming a wholesome diet. They are for you whole grain enthusiasts weary of adjusting recipes with refined flours. And those of you who avoid animal products or refined sweeteners for any reason will happily discover answers to your special needs without going through a tedious translation process. Yet these recipes will appeal to anyone who savors wholesome food and the art of preparing it.

Regardless of dietary persuasion, most everyone is increasingly cognizant of the close relationship between diet and health. Many of my meat-eating and dairy-loving friends are heeding the advice of health professionals by cutting down on fatty, high-cholesterol foods and consuming more fiber. Vegetarians too are reevaluating their diets, since many traditional meat substitutes, notably cheese and eggs, are high in cholesterol and don't jive well with new dietary guidelines. Whole grains, beans, and soy products are healthier choices. Tofu and tempeh in particular can fill the role of meat. Tofu readily stands in for ricotta and cottage cheese and can serve the binding function of eggs in baked goods. Blended with a bit of lemon juice and oil, it substitutes for sour cream. Soy milk replaces milk. Once you've incorporated these ingredients into your culinary repertoire, you may well wonder how you've managed without them.

By far the most difficult aspect of writing this book was capturing recipes at a point in time before some new idea inspired me to alter them yet again. Though I usually refer to recipes casually, as skeletal outlines, and toss in intuitive rather than carefully measured quantities, I clearly specify amounts here. Still, I view baking and cooking as flexible, expressive mediums, and encourage you to do so too. Once you have the gist of a recipe, you can substitute seasonings and make alterations to reflect your personal taste. With *Breadtime* my goal is to build a foundation for creative bakers and cooks as opposed to rote recipe followers, to provide a guide for a new breed in the kitchen.

The book is organized into three major parts. Part One: Getting Ready for Bread lays the groundwork for all that is to follow. It introduces grains and other key bread ingredients, describes helpful utensils, and offers tips on organization. Consider this a storeroom of ideas to refer back to periodically. Part Two: The Breadroom covers bread-making techniques and includes a large selection of bread recipes. Part Three: Getting into Bread explores collaborative possibilities between baking and cooking, combining toppings and fillings with breads in numerous ways.

I suggest you read a recipe through completely before assembling ingredients and getting to work. Yield and preparation times are approximate, depending upon appetites and individual working pace, respectively. Notes with recipes explain uncommon ingredients and techniques and suggest possible substitutions. So, grasp the fundamentals, explore the recipes, exercise your imagination, and you'll be ready for breadtime in no time at all.

PART ONE

Getting Ready for Bread

I ONCE TAUGHT KINDERGARTEN IN NEW YORK CITY AND WAS amazed to discover that the children didn't have the slightest idea where bread came from. The only child who ventured a guess suggested that slices grew on trees! Needless to say, our next lesson was about bread. We mixed and kneaded a dough, baked and sliced a loaf, and enjoyed our just rewards. Sometimes I imagine the children of those children pondering the mystery of bread—and learning the answer from their enlightened parents who remember their kindergarten project. Regardless of age, every baker benefits from a basic understanding of bread, its components, and tools of the trade.

Bread undoubtedly evolved as a series of happenstances, the consequences of early peoples' attempts to make grains palatable and digestible. I picture these people pounding and soaking grains to soften the seed coats. At some point, pulverized, soaked grain was left out in the sun or near a fire and was baked into a solid chunk that tasted somewhat different, maybe better, than its wetter form. Risen bread was probably also a chance happening: moist grain sat around in a warm place long enough to attract airborne wild yeast, and these organisms initiated fermentation, causing the doughy mass to expand.

Though the specific history of bread making remains obscure, countless breads and bread-making techniques have evolved over time. Breads around the world reflect regional grains, different culinary methods and customs, and, especially, the diversity of individuals—their tastes and creative impulses. Yet the fundamental nature of bread hasn't changed much at all. In its most elementary form, bread remains a mixture of grain and liquid cooked in some way to form a compact whole.

Most modern bread originates far from human hands and homes—hence the ignorance of my kindergartners. In Western society at least, technological developments have transformed most bakeries into factories and most breads into the crustless, squishy pale loaves that line store shelves today. High-tech bread is typically tasteless and short on nutrients and character.

Many Americans have never tasted really good bread, making their take-it-for-granted and take-it-or-leave-it attitudes toward bread understandable. Furthermore, we have become so used to the appalling absence of sustaining qualities in modern bread that we consider it to be dispensable high-calorie starch rather than a valuable contribution to health. No wonder we regard bread as little more than an accessory to a meal rather than an integral part of it. Yet the word "bread" is synonymous, at least in English, with food in general, and even with livelihood: a breadwinner is a provider, and the term connotes nurture.

The timing seems right for an upgrading of bread and its image among modern consumers. Not all of us are sold on soft white bread, and recently, as health professionals have recognized the value of complex carbohydrates, their dietary recommendations for whole grain products are on the upswing. Whole grain bread appears to be gaining a new respect in the American diet.

Still, good and good-for-you commercial bread isn't always easy to find. One solution is to make it yourself. You'll discover rewards even beyond a delicious, nutritious final product. Bread dough is an artistic medium, a means of personal expression. Manipulating it affords sensual pleasure comparable to working with clay or playing with mud. Bread making can be an engrossing, calming, meditative activity. This may be stretching it, but I think that by making your own bread rather than buying bread that you don't really care much for, you may eventually improve the quality of society as a whole.

Whatever your particular motivations, a thorough baking education will dispel the mystique shrouding bread making without doing away with its delights. The mystery functions primarily as a handicap; an ignorant baker is at the mercy of the dough. Comprehending baking principles won't squelch your wonder at the process or your appreciation of the finished product, just as a grasp of biology doesn't preclude awe at the miracle of birth. Baking knowledge drives away apprehension, inhibition, and anxiety—major stumbling blocks to the adventures awaiting you in bread making.

Begin your education by taking a close look at grains—the staff of the "staff of life." Move on to other bread components, including liquids, leavens, salt, fats, and sweeteners. Then collect the appropriate utensils. Baking implements aren't particularly specialized, so you don't have to make a large dollar investment to get going. One thing you do need is some time, but baking isn't too demanding in this respect either. Let's get started.

ONE

Grains

Glass jars of grains form an earthy colored collage in my
kitchen cupboards. In them I store everything from whole wheat
berries to rye, barley, oats, millet, and rice. In a sense, I have the
whole world in my cupboard, because grains just like these have
nourished people all over the world for eons.

Grains are the primary raw materials of bread and largely determine its character. And bread, of course, is virtually a universal
food. As you stock your kitchen to get ready for baking, look to this
primer for information on buying, storing, and cooking grains, as
well as a rundown on the grains most commonly used in making
bread, from ancient wheat and barley to high-tech triticale.

In my cooking, I favor unrefined whole grains for their superior
flavors and textures. A taste test comparing white and brown rice,
white and whole wheat pasta, or pearled and hull-less barley dramatically reveals the impact of refinement on grains. Anyone accus-
tomed to refined grains is usually astounded at whole grains'

distinct flavors and textures. These aren't just vehicles for sauces and spreads; they have personalities of their own. I remember the first time my father-in-law, a notorious natural foods skeptic, tasted brown rice. After the first bite, he exclaimed: "How come our rice at home doesn't taste this good!"

The other reason I prefer whole grains is because of their higher nutritive value. You've probably been hearing a lot lately about complex carbohydrates. Grains are loaded with them, which makes grains of all types superb energy sources. But unrefined grains provide other valuable nutrients as well, including proteins, fats, vitamins, and minerals. Also, whole grains supply fiber or roughage, which benefits us all the way from our teeth and facial muscles to our large intestines.

Despite their different looks and tastes, all grains have basically the same makeup, and understanding their components helps us to comprehend what refinement takes away. Each kernel contains a nutrient-packed minuscule seed for a rudimentary plant, called the germ. Adjacent to this is the much larger endosperm, consisting mostly of complex carbohydrates encased in protein and designed to sustain the germ in the early stages of its growth. A multilayered hard covering, the bran, protects the grain embryo and its storehouse until moisture and light bring it to life. The innermost bran layer contains minerals, vitamins, oil, and additional proteins, including enzymes, special proteins that act as catalysts for accessing nutrients. In essence, each grain kernel is a system unto itself, including, in the correct proportions, both nutrients and the agents required to release them.

Early milling technology consisted of the simple process of rubbing whole grains between two stone surfaces to a desired fineness—grits, meal, or flour. Small-scale, mechanized stone-wheel milling is still used to produce some of today's whole grain flour. This technique maintains a low temperature and low humidity in the grain, conditions thought to preserve its flavor, nutrients, and freshness. Stone milling also disperses natural oils quite evenly throughout the flour, retarding spoilage. Vitamin E in ground grain serves as a preservative, but only for a couple of months.

Modern mills use steel rollers. For 100% whole grain products, grains entering the mill are merely pulverized and leave the mill changed only in physical form. However, modern milling is capable of much more sophisticated processes in which grain is ground and select portions are removed. The flour is then generally subjected to various treatments, such as bleaching with chemical gases. It is often enriched with vitamins and minerals, but many more substances are removed than are added back, and those replenished aren't done so in their original proportion in the whole grain. Refinement also robs grains of their wonderful capacity for natural fermentation. To remedy this, chemical conditioners are added to white flour. My big objection to grain refinement can be summed up in one phrase: "If it isn't broken, why fix it?" Why not leave grains intact in the first place?

Historically, attraction to refined flour is threefold. First, the color white has been associated with cleanliness and purity for ages. Early flour was simply picked free of dirt and other foreign matter—an expensive, tedious task. Later, sifting or "bolting" removed the darker portions of the grain (the bran and germ) and whitening agents—even chalk—were added to lighten the flour. Only the wealthy could afford refined flour, so the color of one's flour came to signify social position. Finally, white flour's diminished vulnerability to spoilage enabled early travelers to carry it long distances and shopkeepers to stock it for extended periods. The difference between then and now is—or should be—awareness that long-storage convenience is paid for with lost nutrition and taste.

Storing Grains

I KEEP GRAINS IN TIGHTLY CLOSED JARS ON LOW, COOL shelves, and I enclose a few fresh bay leaves in each container or affix a cotton swab dipped in bay oil to the underside of lids to discourage insects, notably Indian meal moths. Careless grain storage can result in expensive disasters. Some friends suddenly realized they had a "living" cupboard: The bugs went after everything, from grains and flour to raisins and shelf paper!

Pick a dry, cool, dark spot for grain storage. In cold climates, use an unheated dry room or porch, but make sure containers are impervious to mice, squirrels, and other predators. In warm areas and where temperature and humidity fluctuate a lot, buy small quantities of grains and use them up quickly, or store them, well wrapped, refrigerated or frozen. Whatever your storage strategy, always use up the oldest grains first.

Intact kernels with hard protective coats keep much better than broken or pulverized grains do. As soon as a grain is cracked open and its natural oils are exposed to air, oxidation sets in, making it susceptible to rancidity. Corn and oats are especially vulnerable. Rancid grain tastes bitter, while the flavor of freshly ground grains is truly incomparable! For enthusiastic bakers, an effective, efficient home grain mill is a wise investment.

Shopping for Grains

ORGANICALLY GROWN GRAINS ARE A PRIORITY FOR ME because they are more nutritionally sound and their production isn't detrimental to farm workers or the environment. I look for merchants who share that concern and are committed to quality. I'm fortunate to live near a quality-conscious natural foods supermarket. Smaller natural foods stores, food cooperatives, and natural foods sections in regular supermarkets are other good sources for quality grains.

Bulk bins may give stores an appealing, old-time country store ambiance, but they can be risky in the insect department. Many markets are switching to lim-ited-access Plexiglas chute-style bins. If you do see any tiny moths fluttering around anywhere, buy your grains elsewhere. Heat suspect grain for about 30 minutes in a 140° to 150° oven and cool it thoroughly before storing. Freezing grain is another way to both prevent and rem-edy insect infestation. Many quality grains are also sold in hermetically sealed bags.

A major problem in shopping for grains is not know-ing how old they are. Unless unpackaged grains (cracked and ground ones in particular) turn over quickly, they should be refrigerated. To ensure fresh-ness, you might consider mail-order sources of grains. Reputable companies I'm most familiar with include Walnut Acres Natural Foods (Penns Creek, PA 17862; 1-800-433-3998); Mountain Ark Trading Company (120 South East Avenue, Fayetteville, AR 72701; 1-800-643-8909); and Goldmine Natural Foods (3419 Han-cock Street, San Diego, CA 92110; 1-800-475-3663).

Next, let's go over the different grains used in baking, beginning with the most common of all: wheat.

WHEAT

Without a doubt, wheat is the most important bread grain. A high proportion of wheat flour is generally incor-porated into yeast-leavened bread because of a particu-lar gluten protein pretty much unique to wheat. When activated by beating and kneading, wheat gluten forms an elastic network that expands with the carbon dioxide produced by yeast activity. Heat solidifies this gas-filled structure, maintaining the shape of a loaf.

Wheats for baking differ and are classified on the basis of hardness or strength as determined by gluten content: the more gluten, the "harder" or "stronger" the wheat. High-gluten or hard wheat flours give bread a springy, resilient texture. Low-gluten or soft wheat flours contain less protein and produce a tender, cakey crumb.

Hard wheats are often referred to as bread wheats and soft wheats as pastry wheats. Bread flours are slightly granular in texture; pastry flours have a soft, silky feel. Gluten content can be too high for breads. Durum wheat, an exceptionally high-gluten variety, is too hard for most bread making, though superlative for pasta.

There are several other terms regarding wheat that should be explained: Spring wheats are planted in spring and harvested in fall. Winter wheats are sown in autumn and are reaped late the following spring. Spring wheats are generally higher in gluten than winter wheats are. Wheats are also identified as "red" or "white," based on kernel color. Red wheats are higher in gluten than white wheats are. I find hard, red, spring wheat flour ideal for kneaded breads.

I also prefer finely ground flour for kneaded breads because the bran in any whole grain flour tends to abrade the gluten strands that form as dough is mixed and kneaded. Mixing and kneading strengthen gluten, but the finer the bran fragments in flour, the less damage they will do to developing gluten. Finely ground high-gluten whole wheat bread flour yields the lightest, highest-rising whole grain loaves.

All-purpose flour is a hard- and soft-wheat blend advertised as suitable for all types of baking. However, the label doesn't specify the relative proportions of hard and soft wheats present. I find selecting identifiably strong flour for kneaded breads, and weak flour for quick breads and pastries, a better way to ensure success in baking. All-purpose flour simplifies the pantry but may compromise the excellence of baked goods.

One more thing about wheat flour: You've probably heard of gluten flour. Gluten can be isolated by washing everything else out of wheat flour—refined wheat flour, in the case of commercial gluten flour. The pure gluten is dried, ground, and usually mixed half and half with refined white flour to produce gluten flour. Combined with low-gluten flours, gluten flour will enhance bread rise—but at the expense of flavor, texture, digestibility, and keeping quality. So, I don't recommend using this highly refined product.

The nutty flavor of whole wheat comes through no matter what its form. Cooked whole berries add chewiness to breads. Cracked wheat and bulgur (whole wheat that has been steamed and dried before cracking) require only a soaking in boiling water before going into a bread mix. Uncooked wheat flakes add texture. Wheat sprouts are surprisingly sweet tasting and add flavor, texture, and moistness to breads; they also contain active enzymes that enhance rising.

Whole wheat products are rich in iron, magnesium, calcium, phosphorous, many trace minerals, vitamin E, and B vitamins. Since wheat germ and bran contain concentrated nutrients, extra amounts of these augment baked goods' nutritive value. Bran contributes extra fiber as well.

SPELT AND KAMUT

Spelt and kamut are particularly high-protein unhybridized ancestors of modern-day wheat. Though these ancient grains both contain gluten, wheat-sensitive individuals can often tolerate them. Spelt, known as *farro* in Italy and *dinkel* in Germany and Switzerland, tastes and appears similar to wheat but has a reddish cast. Substitute spelt flour for high-protein wheat flour, but you may have to reduce the recipe's liquid by as much as one-quarter. Spelt gluten is fragile, so knead gently and minimally and rise only once. Kamut has a rich, buttery flavor. Kernels are lighter in color and two to three times larger than wheat kernels are. Because kamut most closely resembles durum wheat, used primarily for pasta, kamut flour is best combined with lower-gluten flours in baked goods.

BARLEY

My first taste of barley was probably in canned Scotch broth soup: I remember the mushy white grains as bland and undistinguished. The distinctive, sweet flavor of whole grain barley was a tremendous surprise. Most commercial barley is run through a sander-type device called a pearler, which strips off the chaff and most of the nutrient-filled, fiber-rich germ and bran with it. Hull-less barley with only the chaff removed is far superior. Look for it in natural foods stores. Whole barley takes longer to cook, but presoaking shortens cooking time somewhat. You can also pressure-cook it.

Barley flour lends a wonderfully sweet flavor, which prior roasting intensifies. It also contributes moistness and a cakelike texture to baked goods, but don't include too much or you'll have dense loaves. Grind your own flour from hull-less barley or buy the darkest barley flour you can find to ensure it was ground from whole or minimally pearled grain. For chewy sweetness, add cooked whole barley to bread dough. Barley is my favorite grain for natural-rise breads (see pages 192 and 201).

BUCKWHEAT

I don't think anyone is lukewarm about buckwheat, or kasha (its Russian name). You're either drawn to or revolted by its distinctive flavor and aroma. I'm one of its most enthusiastic fans!

Though used as a grain, buckwheat is actually a member of the rhubarb family. Hulled buckwheat groats are cream-colored and turn reddish-brown when toasted. Roasting accentuates buckwheat's flavor.

Nutritionally, buckwheat resembles wheat and contains generous amounts of iron, B vitamins, and calcium. Darker buckwheat flour has retained more of its lysine-rich hull. Lysine, scarce in most grains, is one of several amino acids, the building blocks of proteins, that the human body cannot synthesize and must obtain from diet; these are called essential amino acids.

Gluten-free buckwheat flour contributes heft and compactness, as well as its unusual flavor, to baked goods. A little bit goes a long way in both respects. I like to add softened, toasted buckwheat groats to breads and muffins. Cooked groats lend flavor and moistness, but not much texture. Buckwheat flour also makes fine thin crepes.

CORN

Corn is indigenous to the Americas, though its cultivation spread throughout the world long ago. I was treated to *mamaliga*, a traditional cornmeal porridge, in a Romanian village and first relished polenta (cornmeal mush) in northern Italy. In North America, we eat sweet corn as a vegetable and we cook dried field corn whole or, more often, grind it into grits, meal, or flour.

Corn varieties differ in protein and starch content, and in color—from familiar yellow and white to red, blue, brown, and black. Corn (especially the yellow varieties) is high in carotene, a compound our bodies transform into vitamin A. Phosphorous and potassium are also abundant in corn.

Freshly ground corn is sweet; stale meal has a strong bitter taste. Buy cornmeal as freshly ground as possible in small quantities and keep it tightly wrapped in the freezer. Add whole corn kernels to breads for chewy sweet spots. Cornmeal produces a somewhat crunchy and crumbly texture. Sprinkle cornmeal on baking sheets to keep pizzas, freestanding loaves, and rolls from sticking.

MILLET

A common ingredient in birdseed, millet is likely more familiar to birds than humans in the United States. Millet for both birds and people is sold hulled; each grain is a tiny yellow sphere.

Millet's protein is particularly well endowed with the scarcer essential amino acids, and it contains an abundance of iron. This grain cooks quickly to a light, fluffy consistency and has a delicately nutty flavor, enhanced by light toasting.

Cooked millet adds moistness, a slight chewiness, and subtly sweet flavor to bread. Uncooked millet contributes a pleasant crunch and appealing speckled pattern to bread. Millet flour doesn't promote rise, but it gives baked goods a soft, cakelike crumb.

OATS

In this country, oats connote breakfast: steaming bowls of hot oatmeal, Cheerios, crunchy granola. The abundance of polyunsaturated fats in oats makes them a good source of long-lasting energy, but it also makes them especially vulnerable to rancidity. Store milled oat products with care—in the freezer if possible. Oats are high in protein, B vitamins, iron, phosphorous, and calcium. Oat bran is a new dietary hero because of its ability to absorb cholesterol and transport it out of the body.

Steel-cut oats are made by slicing whole oats into smaller pieces. Rolled oats are flattened oat grains, and quick oats are presteamed, particularly thin flakes. Instant oats, super-thin flake fragments, are even quicker to prepare. Grind rolled oats to a flour in your blender.

All forms of oats taste good in breads. Cooked oats give bread a moist and chewy, yet light texture and a slightly sweet flavor. Uncooked flakes appear as light-colored specks in breads and add chewiness. Oat flour contributes moistness and sweetness to breads. Oat breads keep well and make superlative toast.

RICE

Rice sustains more people worldwide than any other grain or food. In some Oriental languages, the words for rice and meal are synonymous. Rice is a familiar though not particularly important food for most Americans, and much of the rice eaten here is refined. Polished rice is depleted of most of its protein, fat, minerals, vitamins, and fiber. Brown rice tastes mildly sweet and chewy, while white rice is almost characterless in both respects. Since rice plants are particularly susceptible to diseases and pests, in the United States all but organically grown rice is typically doused with pesticides.

Rice varieties are differentiated by grain length and classified as short-, medium-, or long-grain. These cook up a bit differently but are similar nutritionally. The starch in short-grain rice causes it to cook slightly stickier and chewier than medium- or long-grain rices. These cook to a fluffier consistency because individual grains remain more separate. Short- and medium-grain rice tend to have a more pronounced flavor than does regular long-grain rice. Basmati rice, a long-grain Indian variety, has an exotic, alluring flavor and aroma. Short-grain sweet rice, also known as glutinous rice, cooks to an almost gluey consistency—an advantage for certain preparations but not for general cooking.

Any whole grain rice contributes its subtly sweet flavor to baked goods. Cooked whole brown rice adds a moist and chewy texture to breads; I think it's best in sourdough and natural-rise breads (see pages 195, 197, and 200). Rice grits produce crunchiness. Rice flour fosters a moist, compact, smooth crumb, and pretoasting augments its flavor. It doesn't contain gluten, so go easy on the amount you add to yeasted breads. Most commercial rice flour is ground from polished rice; for a more nutritious and tasty alternative, look for brown rice flour or grind your own from the whole grain. Like wheat bran and germ, rice bran and polishings (the inner bran layers) provide extra fiber and enrichment.

RYE

Rye berries are darker and slightly longer and narrower than wheat grains. Rye has a unique, hearty flavor. Somewhat intense by itself, it mingles agreeably with whole wheat's nutty taste. Nutritionally, whole rye resembles wheat. It is especially rich in minerals, notably potassium, and in B vitamins, particularly riboflavin.

Rye gluten differs from wheat gluten and can't be developed into a strong, elastic structure in dough. Predominantly rye doughs tend to be soft and sticky, and rye breads have a fine-grained, compact crumb. Rye ferments readily, producing a desirable sourness in breads. Molasses, orange, caraway, fennel, and anise seeds all blend well with the flavor of rye and are frequently included in rye baked goods.

TRITICALE

Triticale is a 20th century, manmade grain, created by genetically manipulating and crossing wheat and rye. Its name derives from the Latin terms *triticum*, meaning wheat, and *secale*, rye. This hybrid marries the plentiful protein and gluten content of wheat with the heartiness and prolific nature of rye. Triticale berries are the color of wheat and the shape of rye. The grain is also available as rolled flakes and as flour.

Triticale tastes milder than rye but not quite as nutty as wheat. This new grain is higher in protein than either of its parent plants and is particularly well endowed with the amino acid lysine. Triticale contains gluten that differs from both wheat and rye glutens. Predominantly triticale doughs do best with minimal handling and one rather than multiple rising periods. A small amount of triticale in any form is an agreeable addition to wheat doughs.

Cooking Grains

SPECIFIC COOKING DIRECTIONS FOR DIFFERENT GRAINS vary, but some fundamental principles apply to all:

∽ In general, the more finely ground a grain, the quicker it cooks: whole grain berries take the most time, grain meals the least.

∽ Most packaged grains are quite clean, but bulk grains may be intermingled with small twigs or stones. Spread suspect grain in a single layer on a tray or baking sheet and check carefully for inedible particles. Before cooking whole grains, swirl them in a bowl of cool water and then drain them in a fine-mesh strainer.

∽ Match pot size and the quantity of grain to be cooked as closely as possible. Grains require sufficient room to expand, but a small amount of grain in a large pot won't cook evenly and thoroughly no matter how long it simmers. Use a 1- to 2-quart pot for 1 cup of dry grain.

∽ When increasing the quantity of grain to be cooked, you won't need to increase the liquid proportionately. For example, use $1^3/_4$ to 2 cups water for 1 cup of rice and 3 cups water for 2 cups rice.

∽ Grains continue to cook after the heat is turned off. Leave the pot covered for at least 10 minutes and preferably longer while the grain finishes steaming. It will be fluffier and less sticky than if uncovered immediately.

∽ It's difficult to give an absolute ratio of liquid to grain or an exact cooking time, because a number of factors influence the cooking process. Older grain may require a bit more liquid and take a little longer to cook. Grains cook more efficiently in heavy, well-insulated pots with snug lids. Finally, "just right" for you might be underdone or overdone for me, and vice versa. Tune in to your particular supplies, utensils, and personal taste preferences, and use the following cooking directions as a guide.

WHOLE GRAINS

Soaking cuts down cooking time for wheat, spelt, kamut, hull-less barley, whole oats, and rye and triticale berries. After rinsing the grain, pour boiling water over it in a pot (see chart), cover, and soak at least until the water cools and preferably for several hours or overnight. Bring to a simmer, cover, reduce the heat to low, and cook until the grain has absorbed the liquid and is tender (see approximate times). Add more water if it cooks away before the grain is done. If liquid remains when the grain is tender, drain and reserve it for stock. If it's just a bit of liquid, uncover and cook to dryness.

Rice, millet, and buckwheat cook relatively quickly without presoaking. To enhance flavor, dry-roast or sauté these grains in a small amount of oil before cooking. Add water (see amounts) and a pinch of salt and bring to a boil. Reduce the heat to low, cover tightly, and cook (see times). Remove the pot of cooked grain from the heat but leave the lid in place for 10 minutes or longer.

CRACKED GRAINS

Cracked grains are generally cooked either as a pilaf with a light, fluffy texture or as a thick, creamy porridge. Coarse particles of grain are best for pilaf. Use finely cracked grain (grits) for a smooth porridge.

Cook cracked wheat, rye, or triticale pilaf-style using the method described for rice, millet, and buckwheat. Cook grits by slowly sprinkling them into boiling water, stirring constantly. Simmer over low heat, stirring often, until the mixture is smooth and has reached the desired consistency.

ROLLED GRAINS

Cook rolled grains using the method described for grits. Or, combine the flakes and water in a pot, bring to a simmer, and cook, stirring occasionally, until done.

Remove from the heat and let sit, covered, for several minutes; the cereal will hardly stick to the pot. Use 1 part grain to 2 to 3 parts water, depending on the consistency you desire: more liquid produces a creamier texture. Pretoast flakes in a dry pan or with a little oil for a nuttier flavor.

GRAIN MEALS

For mush (corn, for instance), slowly sprinkle the grain meal into rapidly boiling water while stirring constantly. Reduce the heat to low and cook, stirring constantly or at least frequently, until it reaches the desired consistency. The longer the grain cooks and the more vigorously you stir, the smoother and creamier the mush will become. Alternatively, stir the meal with an equal amount of cold water, then gradually add the resulting paste to 3 parts boiling water, stirring constantly. Either technique prevents a lumpy texture.

GRAIN PREPARATION CHART

GRAIN	WATER PER CUP OF GRAIN	COOKING TIME	APPROXIMATE YIELD
Whole Grains			
Wheat/spelt	3 cups	About 1 hour	2¼ cups
Kamut	3 cups	30 to 40 minutes	2¾ cups
Rye	3 cups	45 to 60 minutes	2½ cups
Triticale	2½ cups	About 40 minutes	2½ cups
Whole oats	2 to 3 cups	30 to 40 minutes	3 cups
Barley	3½ to 4 cups	45 to 60 minutes	3 cups
Brown rice	1¾ cups	40 minutes	4 cups
Millet	2 cups	20 minutes	4 cups
Buckwheat	1½ cups	15 minutes	4 cups
Cracked Grains			
Cracked wheat or rye	2 cups	25 to 30 minutes	4 cups
Grits (any grain)	4 cups	15 to 30 minutes	3 to 4 cups
Rolled Grains			
All grains	2 to 3 cups	10 to 20 minutes	2 to 3 cups
Grain Meals			
All grains	3 to 5 cups	10 to 20 minutes	3 to 6 servings

Two

Other Bread Ingredients

WHEN I DISCOVERED A DELICIOUS, WONDERFULLY CRUSTY, naturally leavened bread in a market in Amherst, Massachusetts, I was eager to visit its creators and learn some of their secrets. I found the bakery in a rural area west of Boston, and one of the two baker/owners showed me around. Brick oven baking explained the superb crusts of their loaves. These bakers had learned their craft from a Belgian master baker who stressed top-quality ingredients above all else. Heeding his advice, they chose this site on the basis of water quality studies. Before this visit, I had taken water pretty much for granted. Now I began to take a closer look at everything in my baking larder.

Without water or another liquid to bind everything else together, there wouldn't be bread. Other more or less key bread components aside from grains include leavens, salt, fats, and sweeteners. Dried fruits, nuts, seeds, herbs, spices, and citrus zest enhance bread's texture and flavor.

PLAIN WATER IS THE LIQUID COMPONENT FOR MANY FINE breads but, depending on its source, differs considerably in flavor, due to minerals and other dissolved substances. Most public utilities treat water with chemicals like chlorine and fluorine, and tap water is increasingly contaminated. I use reputable spring water or filtered water. Pure water is especially important for sourdough and natural-rise doughs. You can remove chlorine by boiling water and leaving it uncovered for several hours.

Some minerals are beneficial to bread dough, but both exceedingly hard and soft water can interfere with dough development. Since distilled water is the softest water there is, it's undesirable for bread dough.

Many bread recipes call for milk. Always scald it to destroy proteins that might hinder gluten development. Compared to water, milk and other dairy products, such as yogurt, buttermilk, and cottage cheese, impart a lighter, softer character to a bread's crumb and crust and also prolong freshness. This is particularly true of higher-fat products. If you substitute milk for water, still use water for proofing the yeast.

I generally avoid milk products and use plain, unsweetened soy milk instead. Scald fresh soy milk before adding it to bread mixes to destroy any undesirable bacteria; packaged soy milk has already been heated. Soy milk produces a lustrous dark brown crust and light crumb.

Nut "milks" can also be substituted for milk. Blend 1 part cashews or blanched, peeled almonds with 4 parts water and a pinch of salt. Like whole dairy products, these contain significant fat.

Teas, coffee, beer, roasted grain beverages, fruit or vegetable juices, grain or noodle cooking water, vegetable or bean stocks, and even blended leftover soups are other possible bread liquids. Mildly acidic liquids, such as potato water and some fruit juices, accelerate

Liquids

Soy milk is a godsend to anyone who's allergic to cow's milk, and a number of aseptically packaged commercial brands are now readily available. Use soy milk as you would milk, for drinking, cooking, and baking. Cholesterol-free and lower in fat than cow's milk, soy milk has about the same amount of protein and more iron, niacin, and thiamine. Cow's milk is richer in calcium, riboflavin, and vitamins A and B-12.

Making soy milk from scratch is a production but becomes routine if you do it regularly. Measure out 1 cup of dried beans, sort through them, and pick out foreign matter. Rinse the beans and soak them in cool water to cover and then some, because they will expand considerably, for several hours or overnight. Refrigerate the soaking beans if the room is warm. Drain the beans and blend them, in batches, with a total of 6 cups boiling water for 2 to 3 minutes. Be sure to preheat the blender jar with hot water to keep the temperature up and, in the case of a glass jar, to guard against cracking. Swathe the blender jar in a towel to hold in the heat. Line a strainer with a piece of muslin and set it over a bowl. Pour the blended mixture into the muslin and stir to urge the liquid through the strainer, then gather up the muslin and squeeze out as much liquid as possible. Measure the liquid and pour it into the top of a double boiler. Cook over gently simmering water, stirring occasionally, for about 30 minutes. This step makes the bean protein digestible by destroying the enzymes. Again measure the soy milk and add water to equal the uncooked amount to compensate for evaporation. Cool the hot liquid quickly and store it in sterile jars in the refrigerator; it will keep for several days to a week. You may flavor soy milk with a sweetener, vanilla extract, or a sweet spice such as nutmeg.

yeast activity somewhat. Cooked grains and beans and raw or cooked fruits and vegetables add moisture as well as flavor to breads. Some of the latter double as sweeteners, too.

Eggs count as a liquid ingredient in bread. They serve a binding function and add loft and richness. A high proportion of whole eggs causes bread to dry out quickly; extra fat is often added to egg breads to compensate. I recommend fresh eggs from free-range hens: the yolks are bright yellow, whites firm rather than watery, and the flavor is wonderful. Test for freshness by putting eggs into water: Eggs that float aren't fresh. My dad taught me to break each individual egg into a cup before combining it with other ingredients—including other eggs.

Leavens

A LEAVEN IS ANYTHING THAT PROMOTES RISING. THE SIMplest is steam, produced by oven or pan heat encountering moisture in dough or batter. Other leavening agents include yeast, beaten eggs, baking soda, and baking powder.

YEAST

Yeast is a fungus that thrives and proliferates in a warm, wet environment if starch is available for nourishment. As yeast feeds on sugars, it multiplies and produces alcohol and carbon dioxide, making bread dough balloon. In a cold, dry state, yeast remains dormant. Too much heat, over about 130°, will kill it.

There are yeasts in the air all the time. These random organisms leaven natural-rise breads. Saved sourdough starters perpetuate the life of particular yeast strains.

Commercial baking yeast is an isolated yeast strain, available as compressed solid cakes or dried granules. Freezing is the best way to keep either type. Wellwrapped frozen compressed yeast remains viable for three or more months, dried yeast for three years or longer. Thawed, compressed yeast should appear tan, smell fresh, and be moist, compact, and smooth; it is probably inactive if dry, crumbly, and gray. To test the yeast's viability, dissolve a teaspoonful in 2 tablespoons lukewarm water sprinkled with a teaspoon of flour, cover, and place in a warm spot. If it foams up within 10 minutes, the yeast is still alive. This is known as proofing the yeast, and I recommend you do it for every batch of bread.

For convenience, I use active dry yeast, usually the Red Star brand. It's available in ¼-ounce packets, 4-ounce jars, and sometimes in bulk. Some brands contain unnecessary preservatives or accelerators, so check before you buy them. Purchase yeast stored in a cool, dry location and, if it isn't stamped with an expiration date, buy it from a source with relatively quick turnover.

BAKING SODA AND BAKING POWDER

Liquid activates baking soda and baking powders, and most baking powders have a secondary reaction when warmed. Baking soda requires an acidic liquid, such as sour milk or fruit juice, while any liquid prompts leavening with baking powder.

You shouldn't need more than 1 teaspoon of baking soda or baking powder per cup of flour. Overuse of these leavens causes a bitter flavor in baked goods and diminishes nutritional worth. Despite the surer effectiveness of baking powders containing aluminum compounds, I avoid them because of the questionable impact of aluminum on health. Instead, I use Rumford Baking Powder, an all-phosphate type. Replace your supply of baking soda and baking powder periodically to ensure a fresh flavor and effective rise. If you can't find nonaluminum baking powder, prepare your own by combining 2 parts cream of tartar, 1 part baking soda, and 2 parts arrowroot powder. If you're trying to cut down on sodium, substitute potassium bicarbonate (from your pharmacist) for the baking soda.

Due to decreased barometric pressure, chemical leavens possess more leavening power at high altitudes. To counteract this effect, decrease the quantity of baking soda or baking powder approximately $1/4$ teaspoon per teaspoon in the recipe for every 2500 feet over 5000 feet of altitude.

EGGS

Vigorously beaten whole eggs leaven popovers and oven pancakes. They puff up dramatically upon contact with high oven heat. Stiffly beaten egg whites leaven spoonbread and give pancakes and other quick breads an extra boost.

Salt

ALTHOUGH SALT IS SCANT IN BREAD DOUGHS, IT SERVES several significant functions. Salt brings out the flavors of the other ingredients and promotes moisture retention and a crisp crust. It also helps prevent the growth of unwelcome bacteria in bread dough.

Regular table salts all look and taste pretty much alike. Refinement removes everything other than pure sodium chloride, and then substances are added to make the salt pure white in color and to prevent clumping. Most table salt is fortified with potassium iodide, since iodine may be lacking in a typical daily diet in certain geographical regions.

Minimally refined natural salts retain more minerals and trace elements than table salt and taste milder. Sea salts result from evaporation of salt water; other salts are mined on land. Natural salts vary in color, crystal size, and saltiness; they also differ somewhat in composition.

Lima Sea Salt, imported from Belgium, is a good brand. Look for it in natural foods stores and mail-order sources. To minimize caking, store salt in a tightly closed container in a cool, dry spot.

The amount of salt to add to bread depends somewhat on individual taste preferences. However, keep in mind that salt slows yeast activity and, consequently, dough development. Also, be sure to take into account other ingredients' saltiness. Fine-grained salt can go in directly with the flour, but predissolve large-crystal salt before adding it.

Fats

FATS ARE OPTIONAL IN MOST BREADS, AND SOME, SUCH AS French bread, are traditionally fat-free. Fat contributes to a rich, tender, smooth crumb and prevents bread from drying out quickly. Too much fat, however, gives bread a heavy, sticky texture and greasy taste.

All fats have much the same effect on dough, but health is an important selection criterion. For most recipes, vegetable oils are preferable to butter and margarine, which contain a greater proportion of saturated fats. However, these solid fats do excel at producing flakiness in biscuits and pastries.

I use minimally refined, mechanically extracted or "cold-pressed" oils, because the high heat and chemicals involved in extensive refinement deplete nutrients. Choose oils mainly on the basis of taste: a light, delicate oil for a subtle flavor; a full-bodied oil for a more pronounced effect, such as olive oil in Italian bread. For solid fat, I favor unsalted butter or preservative-free, unsalted soy margarine. Regular butter and margarine tend to be too salty for my taste. If you substitute salted butter or margarine in a recipe that specifies unsalted fat or vice versa, remember to adjust the salt in the recipe accordingly.

Whatever fat you use, freshness is absolutely essential. Rancid fat cannot hide in bread more successfully than it can anywhere else. Buy oils in relatively small quantities and keep them securely closed in a consistently cool pantry or in the refrigerator. Freeze surplus butter and margarine.

Sweeteners

FRESH WHOLE GRAINS HAVE SUBTLY SWEET FLAVORS. THE fermentation that takes place in yeasted breads enhances this intrinsic sweetness. Sweeteners do promote browning and a tender crumb but tend to mask the natural sweetness of grains and counteract the flavor-inducing effects of fermentation. Since yeast feeds on simple sugars before breaking down grain starch, added sweeteners accelerate yeast activity and promote swift rising of dough, causing underdeveloped bread texture and flavor. For a sweet effect, I usually combine doughs and breads with sweet fillings and toppings.

The practice of adding sweeteners to breads likely paralleled the escalation of grain refinement, which both strips grains of much of their intrinsic sweetness and hinders fermentation. Quick breads don't have the benefit of fermentation for flavor, so sweeteners play a more significant flavor role in these. Even so, I often add sweet-tasting spices, dried and fresh fruits, or vegetables in lieu of a lot of sweetener.

When you add sweetener to bread, consider flavor first. Even a modest amount of a strong-flavored sweetener like molasses or buckwheat honey will dominate. I favor honey, maple syrup, molasses, barley malt, or rice syrup over refined sugar, which I keep on hand only for feeding hummingbirds and for freshening cut flowers. I recently discovered a totally unrefined sugar called Sucanat, short for "sugar cane natural," which is simply granulated dehydrated sugar cane juice. Processed without chemicals and often organic, this light brown sweetener is less refined than white sugar and retains some trace elements. Substitute it in equal amounts for standard white or brown sugar. I like to use Sucanat or date sugar (ground dried dates) for streusel toppings and cinnamon buns.

HONEY AND MAPLE SYRUP

There's a lot more to honey than clover: Honeys vary in color and flavor, and these characteristics come through in baked items. Honey helps maintain moistness, and unrefined honey supposedly functions as a natural preservative in bread. Store honey in tightly closed jars in a cool cupboard. To decrystallize honey, remove the lid and place the jar in a pan of water over low heat. Honey and other liquid sweeteners are easier to measure accurately when heated first.

Unlike honey, maple syrup retains all of its nutrients even at high temperatures. Less expensive Grade B syrup has a more assertive flavor than Grade A, and I prefer Grade B for all uses. Keep opened containers of maple syrup in the refrigerator to prevent fermentation or molding.

MOLASSES AND GRAIN SYRUPS

I favor unsulfured molasses because sulfur, an agent of sugar refinement, is questionable healthwise. Blackstrap molasses contributes little sweetness but a dark color and unique flavor to breads.

Barley malt syrup is made from whole barley that has been sprouted, then roasted and extracted as a liquid. It is thick and sticky with a somewhat sweet, rich flavor. Rice syrup, also viscous, tastes mildly sweet. Neither syrup will crystallize but may harden if cold; warm them for easier pouring. Barley and rice syrups contain a high proportion of complex carbohydrates and won't cause a sugar rush like sweeteners composed of simple sugars do. Store molasses and grain syrups in a cool, dark cupboard.

DRIED FRUITS

Dried fruits contribute moisture as well as flavor, sweetness, and texture. Add them diced or as smooth purées.

*Special
Ingredients
for Breads*

Save any fruit's soaking or cooking water to use as part of the liquid in a bread recipe. Some dried fruits are preserved with sulfur, but many unsulfured, even organically grown, dried fruits are readily available. Store dried fruits in a cool pantry or in the refrigerator.

HERBS AND SPICES

Flavoring with herbs and spices requires a careful hand and nose: A little bit goes a long way. While the right amount may be sublime, too much can be dreadful. Combining different herbs and spices is an aspect of the art of seasoning best learned through experience and experimentation. Indian curry powders are examples of intricate, subtle spice blends. In addition to flavor and aroma, whole herbs and spices contribute a bit of texture to baked goods.

I generally use two to three times the amount of a fresh herb as I would its dried counterpart, since drying concentrates flavor. Mince fresh herbs to release their oils; crush or grind dried seasonings. Sautéing or toasting herbs and spices intensifies their flavor; I like to dry-roast cumin, coriander, fennel, and other seeds before adding them to doughs or batters.

To prolong freshness, stand cut herbs in a jar of water, cover loosely with a plastic bag, and refrigerate. Dried herbs and spices keep best in tightly closed jars in a dry, cool, dark location. Unground herbs and spices maintain zestiness longer than ground ones do. Buy small amounts and use them up within a few months.

NUTS AND SEEDS

Add nuts and seeds to doughs and batters whole, chopped, ground, or as smooth nut or seed butters or "milks" (see page 21). It's usually best to knead nuts and seeds into yeasted dough after a sponge stage and perhaps a bowl rise, because by then the dough is strong and elastic enough to rise well despite these additions.

Nuts add crunch to bread fillings, and seeds are attractive, tasty garnishes on loaves and rolls.

Light roasting amplifies the flavor of nuts and seeds and renders them more digestible. Toast nuts on a baking sheet in a 300° to 350° oven. Roast seeds in an ungreased heavy skillet over low to moderate heat, stirring frequently. In either case, watch closely to prevent burning!

Like other high-fat ingredients, nuts are especially prone to rancidity. Unshelled, they keep fresh for a long time, particularly if stored in a cool, dry spot. Refrigerate or freeze shelled nuts.

Bleaching and other processes improve nuts' cosmetic appeal but diminish their flavor and nutritional value. Organically grown, mechanically hulled nuts and seeds are increasingly available.

Flaxseeds can serve the binding function of eggs in recipes. Blend 1 part flaxseeds with 3 parts water until the seeds are thoroughly pulverized. Substitute $1/4$ cup of this mixture for each egg. Be sure to keep flaxseeds in the freezer, as they are particularly vulnerable to rancidity.

CITRUS ZEST

The outermost rind of citrus fruits—the zest—adds piquancy. Since these fruits are often injected and sprayed with various chemicals, choose organically grown ones. To prepare zest with least fuss: Press a piece of baking parchment or plastic wrap onto the finest grater surface and rub the peel lightly over it.

THREE

Breadtime Tools

WITHIN A SHORT PERIOD OF TIME, I experienced the two extremes of a faulty oven. First, visiting friends, I planned a special meal, including homemade yeasted rolls. Just before dinner, I popped them into the preheated oven. When the timer went off, grapefruit-sized balloons of semi-raw dough filled the oven! Unbeknownst to my hosts, one of their range's electric elements had failed.

Not long after, I moved into a new apartment and was eager to make my first batch of bread. After preparing and shaping the dough, I waited for the oven to reach the appropriate temperature, arranged the risen loaves inside and set the timer. Moments later, I heard a small explosion and whirled around to see flames leaping out from under the gas burners. The oven had never stopped heating! The simple moral of these accounts: Ovens do fail, and a malfunctioning oven throws a severe kink into a baking day.

As my anecdotes illustrate, **a reliable oven** is something you cannot happily manage without. Keep tabs on your oven's accuracy with **a high-quality oven thermometer.** Compare its reading to the temperature you set. It isn't unusual for ovens to fail gradually, and a thermometer will indicate when something is out of kilter.

A large, thick-sided ceramic bowl retains warmth and insulates dough from drafts, and its heft is stabilizing during mixing. You don't have to invest a lot; I found my three "Real McCoy" bowls in graduated sizes at a hardware store. Stainless steel bowls are another alternative, though they don't insulate as effectively. Be sure your bowl will sufficiently accommodate dough expansion. I use a 5-quart bowl for two- to three-loaf batches.

At least one **large, sturdy wooden mixing spoon** is essential for stirring bread dough. Reserve a few wooden implements for non-garlic and non-onion projects, as these flavors persist in wood.

Measuring cups and spoons for dry and liquid ingredients are necessary for precise quantities, especially for quick breads and bread-machine baking. It's handy to have 1-, 2-, and 4-cup glass measures, at least one set of 1/4- to 1-cup stainless steel measuring cups and multiple measuring spoons. Separate cups or spoons fastened to a ring for easier use and washing.

A dough scraper is a simple yet invaluable baking tool. The rounded edge of a plastic U-shaped scraper is especially effective for removing bread dough and scraps from the bowl. Use the straight edge to clear off the work surface while kneading dough and rolling pastry. A metal dough scraper, a square of sheet metal with a wooden grip along one side, is an alternative for cleaning off wooden and marble surfaces. It's likely to scratch corion and other such surfaces.

A kneading surface, ideally at least 2 feet square, is indispensable for kneaded breads. I prepare dough on a small, sturdy, maple table topped with marble, cut from a large slab that was formerly the front panel of an elegant soda fountain. I suspect many old pharmacies have these valuable remnants of past lives collecting dust in their basements.

On National Public Radio, Katherine Tucker Windham related a charming account of the marble pastry slab in her Southern childhood home. She recalled that most kitchens in town were equipped with marble salvaged when the decor of the drug store's old soda fountain was updated. Her family's marble surface was unique because it was a tombstone! For everyday projects—bread, biscuits, and pie dough—the stone's smooth back faced up. But when a special occasion came along, the intricately carved rosebuds, leaves and doves on the flip side were used for decorating purposes.

Smooth cool marble is splendid, but any stable surface is fine for kneading dough and rolling out pastry, as is a large wooden breadboard. Temporarily anchor it to a table or counter by placing a damp towel or rubber mat underneath. Avoid chopping onions and garlic on a wooden surface, unless you don't mind these flavors permeating your breads. Rub oil into the wood periodically to prevent it from drying out.

A kneading surface should just fit under your fully outstretched arm: Measure to the heel of your hand, not to your fingertips. You want to be able to work from above the dough without bending much at the waist. If the only available surface is too high, find something to stand on that puts you at the appropriate height. A too-low surface is more of a problem because it is difficult to adjust and adjust to and may strain your lower back.

A medium-sized **stainless steel fine-mesh strainer** works well for sifting and is much easier to clean than a regular flour sifter. I use a tea strainer for sifting lumps out of small measures of salt, baking powder, baking soda, and spices.

You'll need **a rolling pin** for biscuits, English muffins, kneaded flat breads and filled doughs. My special rolling pin is slender and graceful but surprisingly heavy, fashioned from rosewood by a Vermont woodworker.

A blender is just about unbeatable for achieving smooth popover and crêpe batters. A really basic machine is fine. Until recently, I used my mother's original, one-speed Waring model that began its long career making milkshakes in the early 1950s.

You'll need **several unnapped muslin or linen tea towels** for covering doughs to keep them from drying out. Look for this kind of toweling sold by the yard in fabric stores and mill-end outlets.

You may exercise a lot of flexibility with **baking pans.** There is nothing mandatory or magical about rectangular bread pans; they simply mold loaves that cut easily into traditional four-cornered slices. Several rectangular pans may fit more efficiently into the oven than those of other shapes, but bread can be baked in a wide variety of containers, including pottery or Pyrex casseroles and stainless steel or enamel mixing bowls. Springform cake pans permit especially easy removal, though an adequately baked loaf in a sufficiently greased pan should slip out readily anyway.

Breads baked in sided containers have straighter softer sides than freestanding loaves. For crustier results, bake loaves and rolls on tinned or blackened steel sheets. Clay oven tiles and baking stones produce especially wonderful bottom crusts.

My prize loaf pan is long and narrow, made of tinned steel by my great-great-grandfather, a Midwestern tinsmith. Well-seasoned tinned steel pans conduct and hold heat well, promoting desirable browning on loaves' bottoms and sides. Allow these pans to darken with age;

wash them minimally and dry in a warm oven. Aluminum is an excellent heat conductor, but tends to reflect heat when new and shiny, causing burned bottoms on freestanding breads and poor browning on panned ones. Tin cans are sometimes recommended for baking and steaming breads, but avoid those with lead-soldered seams.

You may want to invest in some specialized baking pans. **Muffin tins** are useful for yeasted rolls and small popovers as well as regular muffins; I prefer tinned steel tins with six or twelve 3-inch cups. Tinned or blackened steel **popover pans** make the best popovers and also work well for large muffins. **A decorative tube pan** makes sweet breads or coffee cakes even fancier. **A 14- to 15-inch round blackened steel pizza pan** is just right for large round loaves and turnovers too.

Baking on a preheated **pizza stone**—or **oven tiles**—produces a wonderful bottom crust. When a loaf or pizza is ready to bake, transfer it to the stone in the oven with a flat wooden implement called **a peel.** You can assemble a pizza or let a loaf rise directly on the peel.

Baking parchment eliminates the need for greasing pans—and scrubbing them later. Freestanding loaves, rolls, biscuits and cookies bake directly on the paper without sticking. One piece of parchment can be re-used for several bakings. Look for it in cookware shops.

For stove-top breads such as pancakes, crumpets, tortillas, and chapatis, you'll need **a griddle** or **shallow skillet** or two. I prefer cast-iron pans, because they are economical, even-heating, ovenproof and require little greasing once well seasoned. **An electric frying pan** is useful for cooking English muffins.

Waffle irons come in many makes and models. My favorite is a round Scandinavian cast-iron type which heats on top of the stove.

A long, sturdy serrated bread knife with a wavy rather than toothed cutting edge is best for cutting bread. My oak-handled stainless steel knife still slices well after more than ten years of daily use. **A heavy Chinese-style cleaver** is my preference for cutting pizza and flat breads; slide them onto a cutting board first.

A baking cloche functions as a pan and miniature brick oven rolled into one. Mine consists of two pieces of unglazed earthenware: a 10-inch round base with an inch-high lip and dome that rests on it to form a closed container. Although its dimensions limit the size and shape of loaves it can accommodate, this is a terrific contraption. Every loaf emerges superbly browned and crusty.

You can improvise a baking cloche by inverting an earthenware bowl over a loaf on a sheet or baking tiles, but a glazed bowl may suffer from the high oven heat. Another improvisational possibility is a large inverted unglazed plant pot without a drainage hole. Still, a secure handle on the commercial cloche's dome is a distinct safety feature, and the snug fit of its top and bottom are advantages over alternatives. When not in use for baking, the cloche can serve as a breadbox.

An electric mixer is most efficient for beating egg whites and mixing batters in quantity, and **a food processor** is invaluable for quickly preparing biscuit and pastry doughs and puréeing practically anything. I don't make yeasted doughs in either one, but not because I'm philosophically opposed to mechanical mixing; in fact, I think it is the only sensible approach to large-quantity baking. For home baking, I prefer hand kneading. Neither machine can handle more than a small batch of dough, but more to the point, using them for kneading deprives me of one of the bread-making activities I most enjoy. If you do try machine kneading, take care not to overwork the dough and handle it at the end to check its condition.

Other Useful Tools

A NUMBER OF OTHER GADGETS ARE LESS ESSENTIAL FOR successful baking but play significant bit parts in bread making. These are mostly common kitchen or household utensils that you may already have around.

A food or "chef's" thermometer consists of a thin metal spike with a round temperature dial on one end. It gives an almost instant reading and can reassure you about water temperature for yeast.

A portable room thermometer may sound like a strange bread-making tool, but room temperature is a key factor in the making of yeasted doughs. By moving dough to warmer or cooler spots, you can regulate rising time.

A scale (up to at least 5 pounds) is useful for portioning dough for loaves and rolls—as well as for weighing pasta and vegetables. I often wonder how I managed without one.

A timer helps keep track of baking times. You may have one built into your oven already, but a portable timer is even better. Multiple timers are an asset when more than one project is underway at the same time.

A ruler is useful for checking pan and rolled dough dimensions. Look for an easily washed plastic one.

An atomizer or plant mister is handy for dampening towels and spraying loaves during baking to promote crisp crusts. Be sure to use one that hasn't had anything toxic in it.

Plastic or rubber spatulas in different sizes make it possible to retrieve everything to the last drop. Use only heat resistant scrapers for hot substances to avoid consuming plastic compounds.

Long **tongs** are the safest way to hold chapatis over a burner to encourage their puffing up.

A ladle is my favorite tool for transferring batter from bowl to griddle.

A **pancake turner** or **metal spatula** is necessary for turning griddle- baked items.

A **pastry brush** works best for glazing breads and rolls and oiling hot griddles. Use soft bristles or feather brushes on risen dough.

A **wire whisk** combines liquid ingredients and whips up egg whites in a jiffy. Collect whisks in assorted sizes.

Aside from a food processor, **a pastry blender** is most efficient for cutting fat into flour for biscuits or pastry dough.

A **cake tester,** a fine, long rigid wire with a loop on one end, is a reliable way to determine doneness of quick loaves, muffins, biscuits, and scones. Insert it into the center of a baked item and see if it comes out without any adhering batter or dough. A clean broom straw serves the same purpose.

A **stainless steel grater** with a variety of grating surfaces is effective for preparing citrus zest, fresh ginger, nutmeg, raw vegetables, and fruits for bread doughs and batters.

Sharp-edged metal cutters give biscuits and English muffins a clean edge which promotes even rising. Biscuits are usually 2 to 3 inches in diameter and English muffins typically 4 inches across.

Crumpet rings are necessary for making these teatime treats. Look for stainless steel ones in cookware shops or improvise by cutting both ends out of squat 4-inch cans without lead-soldered seams.

A **mortar and pestle** or **spice grinder** release the flavors of dried herbs and spices.

Razor blades are best for slashing loaves and rolls before baking. Take care with double-edged blades.

Wire or slatted wooden cooling racks are ideal for cooling breads as they allow air circulation on all sides.

You'll need an actual or makeshift **steamer** for

steamed breads. Steaming is also the best way to warm bread and replenish moisture too.

Lastly, keep **pot-holders** handy for hot pans.

Perhaps the Most Critical Tool of All

So, BREAD MAKING DOESN'T REQUIRE MUCH IN THE WAY of specialized equipment, though certain items are almost indispensable. Others make baking tasks easier or more enjoyable or the final product more aesthetically pleasing. Still, no amount of equipment can make up for a lack of forethought, which may be the most important tool of all.

Because many utensils serve multiple purposes in the kitchen, check to be sure that necessary or preferable items are in good condition and available for bread making. Your large, ceramic bread bowl may be filled with a mixture of grains for a batch of granola; the casserole that molds such a nicely shaped loaf may be in the refrigerator holding last evening's leftovers; your kneading surface, alias the kitchen table, may be littered with breakfast dishes, library books, and assorted mail....

A small amount of planning and preparation may prevent annoying interruptions and delays and keep your bread making moving along smoothly. Properly equipped and organized, you will be freer to enjoy the activities and approach it more creatively.

PART TWO

The Breadroom: Breads and Bread Making

I DIDN'T GROW UP EATING SPLENDID, WARM-FROM-THE-OVEN, yeasted loaves or even fresh bakery bread, but because of my parents' preferences, was spared an exclusive diet of the white balloon bread that became prevalent in the '50s and '60s. There was always some whole wheat bread in our house, often Monks' Bread, a coarse-grained, nutty-flavored loaf that somehow seemed less commercial than other packaged brands. Its name alone held exotic appeal: I envisioned silent, heavily robed men kneading, shaping, and baking the dough in a secluded monastery.

Over the years, I've experienced a multitude of breads from bakeries, restaurants, and cafes, at friends' and friends of friends' homes, and of course in my own kitchen. The most memorable of these have all added something to my understanding of bread. In the following chapters, I'll retrace my experiences and share what I've learned with you.

The homemade breads of my childhood were quick breads. We had pancakes or waffles for breakfast on weekend mornings, hardly thinking of them as breads at all. Economical dinners paired corn-bread with hearty soups. Biscuits with honey accompanied beef stews. Banana and date-nut breads served as desserts or Sunday night suppers. These breads became my first baking projects.

The summer after high school, I worked in an Italian restaurant on Mackinac Island, a picturesque resort in northern Michigan. A large family from Chicago owned and operated the business. Iggy Palermo, the patriarch, and eldest son Frank made the pizza dough for the Sunday night special. On Wednesday evenings, the locals gathered for hoagies on fresh rolls. The aroma of the just-baked dough was overwhelmingly enticing, and we waitresses always managed to sneak a few warm loaves, butter, and jam back to our rooming house quarters. This was my introduction to fresh home-made yeasted bread.

The next year, my eyes were opened wide to the extraordinary variety and exquisite flavors possible in baked goods as I journeyed about eastern and western Europe for several months. I traveled from one baked marvel to another: chewy robust sour ryes and pumpernickels, crisp skinny baguettes, flaky croissants and golden brioches. There were paper-thin crêpes folded around delectable fillings and even East Indian flat breads in London.

My initial hands-on experience with yeasted doughs came a cou-ple of years later, while spending several weeks with my college roommate on her parents' farm, where making yeasted coffee cakes or "buns" was routine. Ann and her mother showed me how to pre-pare yeasted dough and, along with her father and brother, pro-vided my first critiques.

Settled in my own post-college apartment, I began to explore baking in earnest, and my repertoire of both quick and yeasted breads expanded. At the same time, the emerging health foods movement changed the way I thought about ingredients. I was amazed by the natural food supermarkets and whole grain bak-eries I discovered on a trip to California. Back home, I became involved with the newly organized Ithaca Real Food Co-op.

A friend shared her sourdough starter, catapulting me into yet another baking realm. First, I incorporated starter into quick and yeasted breads for added flavor. Gradually, I began using sourdough for leavening and learned I was perpetuating a family legacy: My father's mother maintained a "sour" for the bread she regularly baked on their fruit farm in Utah.

A move to western Massachusetts introduced me to even wilder yeasts. A tiny Amherst restaurant served sandwiches on thin slices of natural-rise rice bread. This bread had a pleasant, slightly sour flavor and satisfying substance and chewiness, and unlike the bricklike unleavened breads I had tasted in the '60s, it had risen. When a friend brought back even better natural-rise rice bread from a bakery in Boston, I arranged to spend a day with the baker. Then I began experimenting. First I developed a cider and rice bread; the unpasteurized liquid gave the fermenting grain an extra boost. Eventually, I devised breads that rely solely on the natural fermentation of whole grain doughs for rise. More recently, I've been leavening breads with a special cultured grain.

Flat breads haven't fit into my personal baking time line quite so neatly. They've slipped in around the edges. But I've made them especially often since moving south, because they require minimal baking or can be cooked on top of the stove.

Looking back, I see a clear pattern: My bread making evolved from breads requiring modern-day leavenings to those that are fundamentally primitive. I began with quick breads, then progressed to commercially yeasted, sourdough, natural-rise, and flat breads. Perhaps ironically, my first breads, quick breads, depend more upon advances in bread-making technology than technique, while later natural-rise breads rely much more on technique than technology. Yet, this is a logical learning sequence. The next five chapters follow the course of my own learning and are designed to gradually develop the technical proficiency necessary for you to master each successive bread-making challenge.

As you add to your own baking skills, don't feel you must drop earlier techniques in favor of new ones. Enjoy all kinds of breads—

and remember that masterful baking requires more than recipes. In a modest Greek restaurant in Toronto, I was served heavenly tasting baklava and excitedly asked for the recipe. The cook sent out a written formula, along with the admonition: "It won't come out the same." A skilled professional baker I met rarely shares her recipes because, like the Greek baker, she knows that lists of ingredients and instructions won't guarantee quality replications of her fine breads and pastries.

Rest assured, you'll gradually feel at home with bread making. For genuine understanding, delve beyond the physical methods and ask questions. What is happening in the bread batter or dough to make it rise? What are the effects of including particular ingredients, using certain utensils and methods? How do external factors such as time, temperature, humidity, and altitude affect bread making? The answers will draw the various aspects of baking together into a meaningful whole and, on a tangible level, may move you from mediocre to truly remarkable baked goods. So, try out these recipes, but keep attuned to the larger context of information accompanying them. Hopefully, it will both assure your success with these particular breads and serve as a springboard for your own creative baking.

FOUR

Quick Breads

*A*s a small child, I helped my mother and grandmother measure and sift ingredients, stir up batters and spoon them into loaf pans and muffin tins, roll and cut out biscuits, and ladle batter onto the griddle for pancakes. Sometimes they gave me leftover batter and bits of dough to make miniature muffins and biscuits in my toy baking tins. Later, I made the life-sized items on my own from start to finish and basked in my family's praise.

My first breads were all quick breads because these were the only ones made in my childhood home. Quick breads are a good starting point for any beginning baker because they can be made in a hurry, entail only simple and straightforward processes, and provide almost immediate gratification. But even experienced bakers find it pays to have quick breads in their repertoires for breads on short notice.

Most quick loaves, muffins, pancakes, waffles, biscuits, and scones are leavened with baking soda and/or baking powder. These chemically leavened breads are the youngsters in baking history. They became popular in the United States in the last half of the nineteenth century when baking powders became readily available. Long-keeping and easy to use, these leavens obviated the need for maintaining starters and fussing with live yeasts. No doubt their time-saving features were highly appealing. Quick breads have since carved out a permanent niche in home baking.

INGREDIENTS FOR QUICK BREADS

Low-gluten or pastry wheat flour is preferable for quick breads. Other low-gluten flours, ground from oats, corn, barley, buckwheat, rice, and millet, are appropriate as well and provide variety in flavors and textures. Bread flour may be included but produces a tough texture if used exclusively. If you can't find whole wheat pastry flour, an all-purpose whole wheat flour is the best alternative.

You may use any liquid for quick breads leavened with baking powder but must combine baking soda with an acidic liquid for effective leavening. Fruit juices are one option. Try to find organically grown citrus fruits, particularly if you are using the zest as well as the juice. Eggs count as liquid ingredients and add richness and cohesiveness. They are leavening agents too, especially when the whites are separated from the yolks, beaten and folded into a batter. If you add extra fresh fruits, vegetables, and cooked grains, take into account their moisture content and reduce the amount of liquid specified in the recipe. Conversely, add a bit more liquid if you increase the proportion of solids by adding extra nuts or other dry ingredients.

Salt's only role in quick breads is enhancing flavor. Chemical leavens containing sodium also taste salty, so a small amount of salt suffices. One teaspoon baking soda or baking powder per cup of flour is adequate for leavening purposes and isn't likely to produce the bitter or metallic taste that results from adding too much.

Through much experimentation, I've discovered that it's possible to make healthful yet still delicious quick breads. They don't have to be laden with fat and refined sweeteners to taste good. I generally use liquid vegetable oils rather than butter and other solid fats, and find modest amounts are sufficient for good flavor and texture. Judicious quantities of honey, maple syrup, molasses, rice syrup, barley malt, and Sucanat produce pleasing but not cloyingly sweet quick breads. Fresh and dried fruits, fruit juices, and vegetables such as carrots, winter squash, and yams also contribute sweetness. Nuts and seeds add richness and crunch. I sometimes use tofu or a blended flaxseed and water mixture instead of eggs for binding, and unsweetened soy milk in place of milk; these ingredients provide nutrients yet cut down on fat and cholesterol. Yogurt, buttermilk, and low-fat milk are healthier dairy choices than sour cream or cream. Keep these things in mind when you want to modify traditional quick bread recipes to make them more wholesome.

MIXING THE BATTER

Precise measurements are important for successful quick breads, and improvising is best limited to simple substitutions of like ingredients. Bring all ingredients to room temperature before mixing to ensure breads bake evenly.

Putting together most quick breads involves three swift steps. First, sift the salt, baking soda and/or baking powder, and any ground spices through a small fine-mesh strainer before sifting them along with the flour, and then stir in any bran that separated and coarse ingredients like grain flakes. Next, blend or beat together the liquid ingredients. Finally, combine the dry and wet mixtures all at once and stir gently just enough to form a slightly lumpy batter. Overmixing makes quick breads heavy and tough.

Loaves and Muffins

Once the batter or dough is mixed, bake it at once, because leavening begins as soon as the dry ingredients are moistened and quickly runs its course. For almost-instant quick breads, prepare dry and wet ingredients separately ahead of time and combine them just before baking.

QUICK LOAVES AND MUFFINS ARE MADE FROM RELATIVELY thick, generally interchangeable batters. Follow the basic three-step sequence outlined above. Add dried fruits and nuts as you mix the dry and wet mixtures together. The batter should resemble a medium-thick porridge; correct the consistency by adding a little extra liquid or flour.

Immediately spread the mixture evenly in a greased loaf pan or divide it among greased or paper-lined muffin tins. Loaf pans should be two-thirds to three-quarters full to allow for rising. For particularly high-capped muffins, fill cups level with the top, but be sure to grease the surface of the tin around the muffin cups. I use a tin with $2^3/_4$-inch cups, and recipes refer to muffins this size. If there isn't enough batter to fill all the cups, partially fill empty cups with hot water. This prevents unfilled greased cups from burning, and extra steam benefits the muffins' texture.

Deep rectangular pans are not essential for loaves; any ovenproof pan with about the same volume will do. Corn bread is traditionally baked in a square or round cake pan or a cast-iron frying pan. Other batter breads can be nonconformists too.

Put filled pans directly into a preheated oven. Loaves require a moderate temperature (325° to 350°) and bake in about an hour, depending on pan size. Bake muffins at a higher temperature (400°) for about 20 minutes.

To check for doneness, insert a cake tester, broom straw, or skewer into the center and see if it comes out

without any adhering uncooked batter. Loaf and muffin tops should be browned and firm yet resilient to a light touch, and their sides shrunken slightly from the pan sides. An exemplary quick loaf or muffin has a moist, tender, cakelike crumb.

Quick loaves and muffins are rather fragile, especially when still hot, and become firmer as they cool. Cool these in the pan for a few minutes before turning them out onto a rack. You may eat muffins right away. Quick loaves slice much better when thoroughly cooled.

Both loaves and muffins keep quite well. Wrap and store them in a cool, dry location when completely cool. Refrigerate particularly moist, fruity items after a couple of days to prevent an off flavor. Slices are good heated, toasted, or steamed even when a loaf is a bit past its prime. Perk up muffins with a light steaming or by warming them in the oven in a covered container.

Corn Bread

HOT CORN BREAD IS WONDERFUL WITH BEAN OR PEA soups. It's also a perfect partner for chilies, baked beans, or marinated bean salads. Warm up leftovers and serve with apple butter for breakfast.

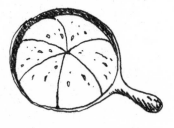

YIELD: 1 8-inch square or 9-inch round bread

PREPARATION TIME: 20 minutes to prepare; 20 minutes to bake

2 tablespoons wheat germ, bran, or sesame or poppy seeds
1¹/₂ cups milk or unsweetened soy milk
1¹/₂ tablespoons lemon juice or vinegar
1¹/₂ cups whole wheat pastry flour

1¹/₂ cups cornmeal
³/₄ teaspoon sea salt
1¹/₂ teaspoons baking soda
3 tablespoons vegetable oil
3 tablespoons maple syrup, mild-flavored honey, or rice syrup (optional)
2 eggs

Preheat the oven to 400°. Grease the pan and coat the inside with the wheat germ or bran or seeds. Combine the milk and lemon juice and set it aside to curdle.

Notes
• For a slightly finer-grained corn bread, substitute rye flour for all or part of the whole wheat pastry flour.
• For especially crusty bread, bake it in a preheated, greased 9-inch cast-iron frying pan.
• Stir 1 cup fresh corn kernels into the batter.
• If you don't have lemon juice or vinegar to sour the milk, substitute 1¹/₂ cups buttermilk or beaten yogurt; or use uncurdled milk or unsweetened soy milk and substitute either 1¹/₂ teaspoons baking powder or ³/₄ teaspoon baking soda plus ³/₄ teaspoon cream of tartar for the baking soda in the recipe.

(continued)

Notes (cont.)

- For a different flavor, add the finely grated zest of an orange to the liquid mixture; substitute orange juice for all or part of the milk or unsweetened soy milk and omit the lemon juice.
- Use this batter to make about 10 muffins. Omit the wheat germ or bran or seeds. Bake at 400° for 20 minutes, or until done.
- Add minced fresh thyme or sage to the batter before baking.
- For eggless cornbread or muffins, substitute $1/2$ cup of 1 part flaxseeds thoroughly blended with 3 parts water for the eggs.

YIELD: 1 loaf

PREPARATION TIME: 25 minutes to prepare; 1 hour to bake.

Notes

- Use the batter to make 8 to 10 muffins. Omit the poppy seeds. Bake at 400° for 20 minutes, or until done.
- For eggless bread or muffins, substitute $1/4$ cup of 1 part flaxseeds thoroughly blended with 3 parts water for the eggs. Or omit the milk or soy milk, lemon juice, and egg, and thoroughly blend 4 ounces tofu with $3/4$ cup unsweetened apple juice; whisk this mixture with the oil and syrup.

Sift the flour, cornmeal, salt, and baking soda into a medium-sized bowl.

In a second bowl, whisk the oil and sweetener. Beat in the eggs. Whisk in the curdled milk.

Make a well in the center of the dry ingredients. Pour in the wet mixture and stir gently, just until the two are combined. Spread the batter in the prepared pan. Bake in the preheated oven for 20 minutes, or until the top is browned and a tester inserted in the center comes out clean. Cool the bread briefly and serve it warm.

BANANA BREAD

I ASSOCIATE BANANA BREAD WITH MRS. WILSON, AN elderly baby-sitter from my childhood. The four of us often gave other sitters a tough time, but never this surrogate grandmother; her stays with us were special. Though firm, she exercised some practical indulgence, such as her homemade banana bread.

2 tablespoons poppy seeds	2 cups whole wheat pastry flour
$2/3$ cup milk or unsweetened soy milk	$1/2$ teaspoon sea salt
2 teaspoons lemon juice or vinegar	1 teaspoon baking soda
2 tablespoons sunflower or other vegetable oil	1 teaspoon baking powder
$1/3$ cup maple syrup	1 cup mashed ripe banana
1 egg	1 cup lightly toasted walnuts or pecans, coarsely chopped

Preheat the oven to 350°. Grease an $8^1/_2$ x $4^1/_2$-inch loaf pan. Sprinkle in the poppy seeds and tilt the pan to coat the bottom and sides.

Combine the milk and lemon juice, and set it aside to curdle.

In a medium-sized bowl, whisk the oil and syrup. Beat in the egg. Stir in the curdled milk.

Sift the flour, salt, baking soda, and baking powder.

Add half this mixture and half the banana to the bowl and stir gently. Add the remaining dry ingredients and banana and stir just until a thick batter forms. Fold in the nuts with a few strokes. Spread the batter in the prepared pan. Bake in the preheated oven for 1 hour, or until a tester inserted in the center comes out clean. Cool the bread in the pan for 10 to 15 minutes, then turn it out onto a rack. The loaf will slice best when it has thoroughly cooled.

Peanut-Banana Bread

PEANUT BUTTER CONTRIBUTES TO THE FLAVOR AND MOIST-ness of this subtly spiced, fine-grained quick bread.

YIELD: 1 loaf

PREPARATION TIME: 20 minutes to prepare; 50 to 60 minutes to bake

3 tablespoons sesame seeds	1 cup mashed ripe banana
1/2 cup unsalted peanut butter	2 cups sifted whole wheat pastry flour
2 tablespoons peanut or sesame oil	1/2 teaspoon sea salt
6 tablespoons mild-flavored honey	1 teaspoon baking powder
	1 teaspoon baking soda
2 eggs	1 teaspoon ground coriander
	1 teaspoon ground ginger

Preheat the oven to 325°. Grease an 8^1/$_2$ x 4^1/$_2$-inch loaf pan and coat the inside with 2 tablespoons of the sesame seeds.

In a medium-sized bowl, whisk the peanut butter, oil, and honey. Thoroughly whisk in the eggs. Whisk in the mashed bananas.

Sift the flour, salt, baking powder, baking soda, coriander, and ginger. Add to the wet mixture and stir gently, just until a thick batter forms. Spread it in the prepared pan and sprinkle the remaining sesame seeds on top. Bake in the preheated oven for 50 minutes, or until it tests done. Cool in the pan for 10 to 15 minutes, then turn it out onto a rack.

Notes
• Use this batter to make 8 to 10 muffins. Omit the 2 tablespoons sesame seeds for coating the pan. Bake at 400° for about 20 minutes.
• For eggless bread or muffins, substitute 1/2 cup of 1 part flaxseeds thoroughly blended with 3 parts water for the eggs.

FRUIT SAUCE–RAISIN BREAD

YIELD: 1 loaf

PREPARATION TIME: 20 minutes to prepare; about 1 hour to bake

SET ASIDE A CUP OF APPLE SAUCE OR PEAR SAUCE TO MAKE this wonderfully spicy loaf. Serve it for tea, dessert, or breakfast.

2 tablespoons bran or wheat germ	¹/₄ teaspoon freshly grated nutmeg
1 cup milk or unsweetened soy milk	2 tablespoons walnut or other vegetable oil
1 tablespoon lemon juice	¹/₄ cup maple syrup
2 cups whole wheat pastry flour	1 egg
¹/₂ teaspoon sea salt	1 cup **Apple Sauce** or **Pear Sauce** (page 256)
1 teaspoon baking soda	²/₃ cup raisins
1 teaspoon baking powder	²/₃ cup lightly toasted pecans or walnuts, coarsely chopped
¹/₂ teaspoon cinnamon	
¹/₄ teaspoon ground cloves	

Preheat the oven to 350°. Grease an 8¹/₂ x 4¹/₂-inch loaf pan and dust the inside with the bran or wheat germ.

Combine the milk and lemon juice, and set it aside to curdle.

Sift the flour, salt, baking soda, baking powder, cinnamon, cloves, and nutmeg.

In a mixing bowl, whisk the oil and syrup. Whisk in the egg. Stir in the fruit sauce, curdled milk, and raisins. Add the dry mixture and stir gently, just until a thick batter forms. Fold in the nuts.

Spread the batter in the prepared pan. Bake in the preheated oven for about 1 hour, or until a tester inserted in the center comes out clean. Let cool in the pan for about 10 minutes, then turn out onto a rack to finish cooling.

Notes
- Use this batter to make about 10 muffins. Omit the bran or wheat germ. Bake at 400° for 20 minutes, or until they test done.
- For eggless bread or muffins, substitute ¹/₄ cup of 1 part flaxseeds thoroughly blended with 3 parts water for the eggs.

Date Bread

DAINTY DATE-NUT BREAD SANDWICHES HAVE ALWAYS seemed to me like the ultimate in tearoom fare. Medjool dates are my favorite. Spread thin slices of this loaf with **Tahini-Miso Spread** (page 249).

2 tablespoons bran or wheat germ	1 cup chopped dates
1 orange	2 cups whole wheat pastry flour
1 cup unsweetened apple juice, or as needed	1 teaspoon baking soda
4 ounces tofu	1 teaspoon baking powder
1/4 cup sunflower or other vegetable oil	1/2 teaspoon sea salt
1/4 cup maple syrup, rice syrup, or mild-flavored honey	1 cup lightly toasted pecans, coarsely chopped

Preheat the oven to 350°. Grease and lightly dust the inside of an 8 1/2 x 4 1/2-inch loaf pan with the bran or wheat germ.

Grate the zest from the orange into a medium-sized bowl. Juice the orange and measure the juice. Add apple juice to equal 1 1/4 cups. In a blender, thoroughly blend the juice with the tofu. Whisk the oil, syrup, and blended mixture with the zest. Stir in the dates.

In another bowl, sift the flour, baking soda, baking powder, and salt. Add this mixture to the wet mixture and stir gently, just until a thick batter forms. Fold in the pecans.

Spread the batter in the prepared pan. Bake in the preheated oven for 1 hour, or until the bread tests done. Cool the bread in the pan for 10 to 15 minutes, then turn it out onto a rack.

YIELD: 1 loaf

PREPARATION TIME: 25 minutes to prepare; about 1 hour to bake

Notes
• Substitute walnuts or other nuts for the pecans.
• For an egg/milk variation of this recipe, omit the tofu. Substitute milk or unsweetened soy milk for the apple juice. Beat 1 egg and the milk/orange juice mixture with the oil and syrup.
• Bake the bread in an 8 x 8 x 2-inch pan at 350° for 40 minutes. Top the cooled bread with **Lemon Sauce** or **Orange Sauce** (page 213).
• Use the batter to make 8 to 10 large muffins. Omit the bran or wheat germ. Bake at 400° for about 20 minutes.

CRANBERRY-NUT BREAD

YIELD: 1 loaf

PREPARATION TIME: 25 minutes to prepare; 50 to 60 minutes to bake

MY FEET WERE COLD AND DAMP, MY FINGERS WERE numb, I was chilled all over, yet I still felt honored to be sharing the secret of a New York cranberry bog. We had chosen to go on a late autumn afternoon when we figured the berries would be ripe to pick. Dismal gray clouds hung over us and daylight was rapidly waning as we squatted in our rubber boots and combed our fingers through the icy water, feeling for firm berries. Only mental images of the cranberry-nut bread that would soon follow this expedition kept my sense of adventure from freezing over.

Red cranberries interspersed throughout this bread provide a pleasant contrast in flavor as well as bright spots of color. Make this one for winter holidays.

2 tablespoons bran or wheat germ	2 cups whole wheat pastry flour
1 orange	1/2 teaspoon sea salt
2/3 cup unsweetened apple juice, as needed	1 teaspoon baking soda
4 ounces tofu	1 teaspoon baking powder
1/3 cup sunflower or other vegetable oil	1 cup fresh cranberries, picked over, rinsed, and well drained
1/3 cup mild-flavored honey (orange blossom honey is especially good in this bread)	1 cup lightly toasted walnuts or pecans, coarsely chopped

Preheat the oven to 350°. Grease an 8 1/2 x 4 1/2-inch loaf pan and dust the inside with the bran or wheat germ.

Finely grate the zest of the orange into a medium-sized bowl. Juice the orange and measure the juice. Add apple juice to equal 1 cup. In a blender, blend the tofu and a small amount of the juice. With the machine running, gradually add the remainder of the juice and blend until the mixture is thoroughly smooth. Whisk the oil and honey with the zest. Whisk in the blended mixture.

In another bowl, sift the flour, salt, baking soda, and baking powder. Add to the wet mixture and stir gently, just until a batter forms. Fold in the cranberries and nuts.

Spread the batter in the prepared pan. Bake immediately in the preheated oven for 50 to 60 minutes, or until the bread is well browned and a tester inserted in the center comes out clean. Cool the bread in the pan for 10 minutes, then turn it out onto a rack.

St. Patrick's Irish Soda Bread

THIS BREAD IS MADE FROM A BISCUIT-TYPE DOUGH. Cutting the top allows for even expansion as the bread rises in the oven. One St. Patrick's Day, I delivered fresh, warm loaves of this bread to three generations of Ryans and Kellys.

1 1/4 *cups milk or soy milk*	1 *teaspoon baking soda*
4 *teaspoons lemon juice*	1 *teaspoon baking powder*
or vinegar	1 *tablespoon caraway*
3 *cups whole wheat*	*seeds, coarsely ground*
pastry flour, plus extra	*(optional)*
for shaping	1/2 *cup currants or raisins*
1/2 *teaspoon sea salt*	*(optional)*

Preheat the oven to 375°. Lightly grease or line a baking sheet with baking parchment.

Combine the milk and lemon juice; set it aside to curdle.

In a mixing bowl, sift the flour, salt, baking soda, and baking powder. Stir in the caraway seeds and currants. Make a well in the center of the dry mixture. Pour in 1 cup of the curdled milk and stir gently to form a soft dough; add more of the milk as needed. Turn the dough out into a lightly floured surface and knead it gently and briefly—just a few turns.

Notes
• Substitute unthawed frozen cranberries for the fresh ones.
• Substitute 1/2 cup raisins for half the nuts for a loaf with sweet and tart spots throughout.
• For an egg/milk variation, see Date Bread notes (page 51).
• Use the batter to make 8 to 10 muffins. Omit the bran or wheat germ. Bake about 20 minutes at 400°.

YIELD: 1 round loaf

PREPARATION TIME: 20 minutes to prepare; 35 to 45 minutes to bake

Notes

• Add the grated zest of a lemon or orange to the liquid ingredients before combining them with the dry mixture. If you add orange zest, you may also juice the orange and combine the juice with enough milk or soy milk to equal 1¼ cups of liquid; omit the lemon juice.

• Substitute buttermilk for the milk or soy milk and omit the lemon juice.

• For an especially moist yet crusty bread, bake it in a baking cloche.

YIELD: 1 8-inch square or 9-inch round coffee cake

PREPARATION TIME: 25 minutes to prepare; 40 minutes to bake

Shape the dough into a ball, pat it into a somewhat flattened round, and place it on the prepared sheet. Dip a razor blade or sharp knife in flour and cut a cross on top.

Bake the bread in the preheated oven 35 to 45 minutes, until a tester comes out clean. Cool at least 30 minutes before slicing.

STREUSEL COFFEE CAKE

QUICK COFFEE CAKES ARE USUALLY LOADED WITH BUTTER, sour cream, eggs, and sugar. Here's an eggless, nondairy alternative that is still plenty rich and sweet. Serve it for breakfast or dessert.

4 tablespoons lightly toasted fine whole grain bread crumbs	⅓ cup sunflower or other vegetable oil
1 teaspoon cinnamon	⅓ cup maple syrup
2 tablespoons date sugar or Sucanat	1 teaspoon pure vanilla extract
½ cup lightly toasted chopped pecans	2 cups sifted whole wheat pastry flour
4 ounces tofu	½ teaspoon sea salt
1 cup unsweetened apple juice	1 teaspoon baking soda
	½ teaspoon freshly grated nutmeg

Preheat the oven to 350°. Grease an 8-inch square or 9-inch round baking pan and lightly dust the inside with 2 tablespoons of the bread crumbs.

In a small bowl, thoroughly mix the remaining 2 tablespoons crumbs, ½ teaspoon cinnamon, the sugar, and pecans with a fork. Set this streusel mixture aside.

In a blender, blend the tofu, gradually adding the apple juice, until the mixture is thoroughly smooth. Whisk the oil, syrup, and vanilla together in a medium-sized bowl. Whisk in the blender mixture.

In another bowl, sift the sifted flour, salt, baking soda,

remaining ¹/₂ teaspoon cinnamon, and nutmeg. Add this to the wet mixture and stir gently, just until a batter forms. Spread half the batter in the prepared pan and sprinkle half the streusel mixture over it; repeat these two layers.

Bake immediately in the preheated oven for 40 minutes, or until a tester inserted in the center comes out clean. Serve the cake warm or at room temperature.

Oatmeal-Raisin Muffins

THESE MOIST, RAISINY MUFFINS ARE LOW IN FAT AND CHOlesterol and high in fiber—a great way to start your day.

YIELD: 10 to 12 muffins

PREPARATION TIME: 20 minutes to prepare; 20 minutes to bake

1¹/₂ cups unsweetened apple juice	*1¹/₄ cups whole wheat pastry flour*
³/₄ cup raisins	*1 cup rye flour*
6 ounces tofu	*³/₄ teaspoon sea salt*
3 tablespoons vegetable oil	*1¹/₂ teaspoons baking soda*
3 tablespoons maple syrup	*³/₄ cup rolled oats*

Heat the apple juice just to a simmer and pour it over the raisins. Preheat the oven to 400°. Grease 10 to 12 muffin cups.

When the juice has cooled to lukewarm, drain the raisins, saving the liquid. In a blender, thoroughly blend the reserved liquid with the tofu. In a medium-sized mixing bowl, whisk the oil and syrup. Whisk in the blended mixture and stir in the raisins.

In another bowl, sift the flours, salt, and baking soda. Thoroughly stir in the oats. Add to the liquid mixture, stirring gently just until a thick batter forms.

Fill the prepared muffin cups. Bake immediately in the preheated oven for 20 minutes, or until the muffins are lightly browned and test done. Cool the muffins for about 5 minutes in the tin, then run a small metal spatula around each one and turn them out onto a rack. Serve them warm.

Notes
- For a finer texture, grind the oats to a flour and sift with the other dry ingredients.
- For variety, fold ³/₄ cup lightly toasted, coarsely chopped walnuts or pecans into the batter.
- To make a loaf, spread the batter in an 8¹/₂ x 4¹/₂-inch loaf pan and bake at 350° for about an hour.

YIELD: 8 to 9 muffins

PREPARATION TIME: 25 minutes to prepare; 20 minutes to bake

MELLOW MUFFINS

ON SUMMER SUNDAY MORNINGS, I LIKE TO MAKE A BATCH of these muffins, cut up juicy seasonal fruits, grab the newspaper, and head for the natural spring pool in my town for a swim and breakfast picnic. **Tahini-Miso Spread** (page 249) goes well with these muffins.

1 orange
2/3 cup milk or
    unsweetened soy milk,
    or as needed
1 cup whole wheat
    pastry flour
1/2 cup barley flour
1/2 teaspoon sea salt
1 teaspoon baking soda

1/2 cup rolled oats
2 tablespoons sunflower or
    other vegetable oil
1/4 cup maple syrup
1 egg
1/2 cup chopped dates
1/2 cup lightly toasted,
    coarsely chopped pecans

Preheat the oven to 400°. Grease the muffin cups.

Grate the zest from the orange into a medium-sized mixing bowl. Juice the orange. Measure the juice and add milk to equal 1 cup of liquid, and set aside to curdle.

In another bowl, sift the flours, salt, and baking soda. Stir in the oats.

Add the oil and syrup to the zest and whisk thoroughly. Whisk in the egg and curdled milk. Stir in the dates. Add the dry mixture and stir gently, just until a thick batter forms. Fold in the nuts.

Fill the prepared cups. Bake in the preheated oven 20 minutes, or until the muffins test done. Cool the muffins for about 5 minutes in the tin, then run a small metal spatula around each one and turn them out onto a rack. Serve them warm or at room temperature.

Notes
• For finer-textured muffins, grind the rolled oats to a coarse flour (in a blender, for example) before mixing them with the other dry ingredients.
• Omit the orange zest and juice; add the zest of one lemon and 1 tablespoon lemon juice plus milk or unsweetened soy milk to equal 1 cup.
• For eggless muffins, substitute 1/4 cup of 1 part flaxseeds thoroughly blended with 3 parts water for the egg.

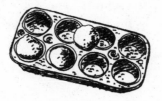

Got the Blues Muffins

Blue cornmeal, ground from blue corn, has long been a staple for the Pueblo Indians of the Southwest. I became acquainted with the unique flavor and unusual color it imparts to quick breads and tortillas a decade ago when a friend brought me several pounds from New Mexico. Now it is not so difficult to find in other regions of the country. Substitute yellow or white cornmeal if you don't have the blue variety. Frozen blueberries can replace the fresh ones in these muffins; use them straight out of the freezer.

Yield: 8 muffins

Preparation time: 20 minutes to prepare; 20 minutes to bake

¹/₃ cup blue cornmeal
1¹/₃ cups whole wheat
   pastry flour
¹/₄ teaspoon sea salt
1 teaspoon baking soda
4 ounces tofu

²/₃ cup unsweetened
   apple juice
2 tablespoons sunflower or
   other vegetable oil
¹/₄ cup maple syrup
1 cup blueberries

Preheat the oven to 400°. Grease 8 muffin cups.

Sift the cornmeal, flour, salt, and baking soda.

In a blender, blend the tofu and gradually add the apple juice. Add the oil and syrup and blend until the mixture is thoroughly smooth. Pour it into a medium-sized mixing bowl. Add the dry mixture and stir gently, just until a thick, slightly lumpy batter forms. Fold in the blueberries.

Fill the prepared muffin cups. Bake in the preheated oven for 20 minutes, or until a tester inserted in the center comes out clean. Cool the muffins for about 5 minutes in the tin, then run a small metal spatula around each and turn them out onto a rack. Serve them warm.

Maple Bran Muffins

Yield: 9 muffins

Preparation time: 20 minutes to prepare; 20 to 25 minutes to bake

These basic bran muffins are wide open for variation. Look at the notes for some possibilities or try out some of your own ideas.

1½ cups milk or
   unsweetened soy milk
1½ tablespoons lemon
   juice
3 tablespoons vegetable oil
3 tablespoons maple syrup
2 eggs

¾ cup raisins
1½ cups whole wheat
   pastry flour
¾ teaspoon sea salt
1½ teaspoons baking soda
1½ cups bran

Preheat the oven to 400°. Grease the muffin cups.

Combine the milk and lemon juice and set it aside to curdle.

In a mixing bowl, beat the oil and syrup. Thoroughly beat in the eggs. Stir in the curdled milk and the raisins.

In another bowl, sift the flour, salt, and baking soda. Stir in the bran. Add to the wet mixture. Fold gently, just until a thick batter forms.

Fill the prepared muffin cups. Bake in the preheated oven for 20 to 25 minutes, or until a tester inserted in the center comes out clean. Cool the muffins for about 5 minutes in the tin, then run a small metal spatula around each one and turn them out onto a rack.

Notes
• Substitute honey or unsulfured molasses for the maple syrup.
• Substitute chopped dates, prunes, or soaked dried apricots for the raisins.
• Substitute lightly toasted, coarsely chopped walnuts or pecans for all or half of the raisins.
• Substitute buttermilk or yogurt for the milk or unsweetened soy milk and omit the lemon juice.
• For eggless muffins, substitute ½ cup of 1 part flaxseeds thoroughly blended with 3 parts water for the eggs.

Buckwheat Muffins

Yield: 8 muffins

Preparation time: 20 minutes to prepare; 20 minutes to bake

At our house, we refer to these moist muffins as "Gussie muffins" after my husband's Grandma Gussie, who always stuffed him with kasha when he visited. Buckwheat is one of my favorite grains too, and I relish its unique flavor in breads.

²/₃ cup milk or
    unsweetened soy milk
2 teaspoons lemon juice
    or vinegar
2 tablespoons vegetable oil
3 tablespoons honey
1 tablespoon blackstrap
    molasses
1 egg

1 cup cooked toasted
    buckwheat groats (see
    pages 17-19)
¹/₂ cup raisins
1¹/₂ cups whole wheat
    pastry flour
¹/₂ teaspoon sea salt
1 teaspoon baking soda
¹/₂ teaspoon baking powder

Preheat the oven to 400°. Grease 8 muffin cups.

Combine the milk and lemon juice and set it aside to curdle.

In a medium-sized bowl, beat the oil, honey, and molasses. Thoroughly beat in the egg. Stir in the curdled milk, buckwheat groats, and raisins.

In another bowl, sift the flour, salt, baking soda, and baking powder. Add to the wet mixture all at once and stir gently, just enough to form a thick batter.

Fill the prepared muffin cups. Bake in the preheated oven about 20 minutes, or until the muffins have browned and a tester inserted in the center comes out clean. Cool the muffins for about 5 minutes in the tin, then run a small metal spatula around each one and turn them out onto a rack. Serve them warm.

Notes

• Substitute ¹/₄ cup lightly toasted chopped walnuts for half the raisins.

• Substitute barley malt or rice syrup for the honey and molasses.

• Substitute buttermilk or yogurt for the milk or unsweetened soy milk and omit the lemon juice.

• For eggless, nondairy muffins, omit the egg, milk, and lemon juice; blend 4 ounces tofu with ³/₄ cup unsweetened apple juice, and whisk this mixture with the oil, honey, and molasses. Or, simply substitute ¹/₄ cup of 1 part flaxseeds thoroughly blended with 3 parts water for the egg.

Pancakes and Waffles

THOUGH USUALLY INTERCHANGEABLE WITH WAFFLE BATTER, pancake batter may require more fat to prevent sticking in the waffle iron, and you may want to add an extra tablespoon of oil. For both pancakes and waffles, follow the basic instructions for making quick bread batters on page 45.

Bake pancakes on a hot, lightly greased griddle. My cast-iron one is well seasoned and requires little greasing. As I learned from *The Laurel's Kitchen Bread Book*, a combination of one part liquid soy lecithin to two parts vegetable oil is especially effective for pan-greasing, though oil alone will do. In either case, use an oil with a high smoke point. High-quality refined canola, peanut, or high-oleic sesame and sunflower oils are good choices.

Turn a pancake when the top is well bubbled and edges are beginning to firm up. When you lift the edge, the bottom should appear golden. Cook it for a shorter time on the second side. Cooking time will vary for different batters. A pancake is ready when it's puffy and browned on both sides.

Specific directions for waffles depend on the particular waffle iron. My cast-iron, top-of-the-stove type makes circular waffles composed of five little hearts which meet in the middle. You will soon tune in to the appropriate amount of batter and timing for your waffle iron. Always preheat and lightly grease it before ladling in the first batch of batter; try the lecithin and oil formula above. Merely closing the lid will spread the batter evenly. A waffle is done when golden and crisp on both sides. If the iron was preheated and greased sufficiently, the waffle should lift out easily. Avoid opening the iron before the waffle is likely to be ready or you may tear it apart.

Pancakes and waffles are best eaten hot off the griddle but can be kept warm in a low oven. To keep waffles crisp, place them directly on the oven rack; they become soggy on a plate. If you have extra batter, make up waffles and freeze them. They'll warm quickly in a moderate oven or toaster oven.

LIGHT LEMONY PANCAKES

YIELD: About 1 dozen 3-inch pancakes

PREPARATION TIME: 15 minutes to prepare; about 5 minutes to cook each batch

LEMON ZEST AND NUTMEG ADD A SPECIAL TOUCH TO these basic whole wheat pancakes, and a beaten egg white makes them extra light. Serve fresh berries or other seasonal fruits alongside.

Grated zest of 1 lemon

1 tablespoon sunflower or
   other vegetable oil

1 tablespoon maple syrup

1 egg, separated

1 cup milk or
   unsweetened soy milk

1 tablespoon lemon juice

1 cup whole wheat pastry
   flour

1/4 teaspoon sea salt

1 teaspoon baking soda

1/4 teaspoon freshly grated
   nutmeg

Heat a griddle until water dripped on it sizzles immediately.

In a medium-sized bowl, whisk the lemon zest, oil, and syrup. Thoroughly beat in the egg yolk.

Combine the milk and lemon juice; set it aside to curdle.

Sift the flour, salt, baking soda, and nutmeg.

Beat the egg white until it is stiff but not dry.

Whisk the curdled milk into the yolk mixture. Add the dry ingredients and stir gently to form a batter. Gently fold in the beaten egg white.

Lightly grease the hot griddle and ladle on batter. Cook until bubbles appear on the tops of the pancakes and their undersides are golden brown. Flip the pancakes and cook briefly, until light brown on the bottom. Serve them hot off the griddle, drizzled with a bit more maple syrup.

ORANGE–POPPY SEED PANCAKES

TOASTED POPPY SEEDS ADD FLAVOR AND CRUNCH TO these zesty pancakes.

2 tablespoons poppy seeds

1 orange

2/3 cup milk or
   unsweetened soy milk,
   or as needed

1 tablespoon sunflower or
   other vegetable oil

1 tablespoon maple syrup

1 egg, separated

1 cup whole wheat pastry
   flour

1/4 teaspoon sea salt

1 teaspoon baking soda

YIELD: About 1 dozen 3-inch pancakes

PREPARATION TIME: 20 minutes to prepare; about 5 minutes to cook each batch

Heat a dry skillet over medium heat. Add the poppy seeds and cook, agitating the pan or stirring often, until the seeds are lightly toasted; set them aside.

Heat a griddle until water dripped on it sizzles immediately.

Grate the zest of the orange into a medium-sized mixing bowl. Juice the orange and measure the juice. Add milk to equal 1 cup of liquid; set it aside to curdle. Add the oil and syrup to the zest and whisk thoroughly. Beat in the egg yolk. Whisk in the curdled milk.

Beat the egg white until it is stiff but not dry.

Sift the flour, salt, and baking soda. Add this all at once to the wet mixture and stir gently to form a batter. Gently stir in the toasted poppy seeds, and fold in the beaten egg white.

Lightly grease the hot griddle and ladle on batter. Cook until the tops of the pancakes bubble and the bottoms are golden. Flip and cook briefly, until the other side has browned. Serve the pancakes hot off the griddle or keep them warm in a low oven until serving. Top them with maple or orange syrup.

CORNCAKES

THESE GRIDDLECAKES ARE DELICATE STEAMING ROUNDS of corn bread. Use blue cornmeal for purple pancakes!

YIELD: About 1 dozen 3-inch pancakes

PREPARATION TIME: 15 minutes to mix; about 5 minutes to cook each batch

1 cup milk or unsweetened soy milk	1 teaspoon baking soda
1 tablespoon lemon juice or vinegar	1/4 teaspoon sea salt
1/2 cup cornmeal	1 egg, separated
1/2 cup whole wheat pastry flour	1 tablespoon sunflower or other vegetable oil
	1 tablespoon maple syrup

Heat a griddle until water dripped on it sizzles immediately.

Combine the milk and lemon juice and set it aside to curdle.

Sift the cornmeal, flour, baking soda, and salt.

Beat the egg white until it is stiff but not dry.

In a medium-sized bowl, whisk the oil and syrup. Thoroughly whisk in the egg yolk. Whisk in the curdled milk. Add the dry ingredients all at once and stir just until a batter forms. Gently fold in the beaten egg white.

Lightly grease the hot griddle. Ladle on batter and cook until bubbles appear on the tops of the pancakes and the bottoms are golden. Turn and cook briefly, until the second side has browned.

Serve the pancakes hot off the griddle or keep them warm in a low oven. Top them with maple syrup or fruit butter.

Notes
• Substitute buttermilk or yogurt for the milk or unsweetened soy milk, and omit the lemon juice.

GOLDEN GRIDDLECAKES

SWEET BUTTERNUT SQUASH IS SUPERB IN THESE PANcakes, but you can substitute other varieties of winter squash or use pumpkin, carrot, sweet potato, or yam. Top the pancakes with **Pear Butter** (see page 255-256).

YIELD: About 1 dozen 3-inch pancakes

PREPARATION TIME: 15 minutes to mix; about 5 minutes to cook each batch

1 egg, separated
1 tablespoon sunflower or
   other vegetable oil
1/2 cup mashed cooked
   squash
1 cup milk or
   unsweetened soy milk

1 cup whole wheat pastry
   flour
1/4 teaspoon sea salt
1 teaspoon baking powder

Heat a griddle until water dripped on it sizzles immediately.

Beat the egg white until stiff but not dry and set it aside. In a mixing bowl, thoroughly whisk the egg yolk, oil, squash, and milk.

In a separate bowl, sift the flour, salt, and baking powder. Gently stir the dry mixture into the wet mixture, just enough to form a batter. Carefully fold in the beaten egg white.

Notes
• For a sweeter batter, whisk a tablespoon of maple syrup or another sweetener into the liquid mixture.

Lightly grease the hot griddle. Ladle batter onto it. Cook until bubbles form on the tops of the pancakes and their undersides are golden brown. Turn and cook briefly, until the other side has browned. Serve the pancakes hot off the griddle or keep them warm in a low oven.

APPLE FLAPJACKS

NUDGE YOUR HOUSEHOLD AWAKE WITH THE SPICY AROMA of these light pancakes. Nobody will miss the eggs and milk products.

YIELD: About 1 dozen 3-inch pancakes

PREPARATION TIME: 15 minutes to mix; about 5 minutes to cook each griddleful

4 ounces tofu
1 cup unsweetened
  apple juice
1 tablespoon vegetable oil
1 tablespoon maple syrup
1 cup whole wheat
  pastry flour

$^1/_4$ teaspoon sea salt
1 teaspoon baking soda
$^1/_4$ teaspoon freshly grated
  nutmeg
$^1/_4$ teaspoon cinnamon

Heat a griddle until water dripped on it sizzles immediately.

Put the tofu in a blender with about $^1/_4$ cup apple juice. Blend, and with the machine running, gradually add the remaining juice and the oil and syrup. Blend until the mixture is thoroughly smooth, then transfer it to a medium-sized bowl.

Sift the flour, salt, baking soda, nutmeg, and cinnamon. Add this mixture to the wet ingredients and stir gently, just enough to form a batter.

Lightly grease the hot griddle. Ladle tablespoons of the batter onto it. Cook until the tops of the pancakes bubble and dry a bit and the bottoms have browned. Turn the pancakes and cook briefly, until golden. Serve them immediately.

Three-Grain Waffles

Make these zesty, crisp waffles on a leisurely weekend morning and freeze extras for a breakfast treat during the week. Just pop them directly from the freezer into a preheated oven for a few minutes.

²/₃ cup yellow cornmeal	*Juice and zest of 1 orange*
²/₃ cup rye flour	*About 1¹/₃ cups milk or*
²/₃ cup whole wheat	*unsweetened soy milk*
pastry flour	*2 eggs, separated*
1 teaspoon baking soda	*2 tablespoons sesame or*
1 teaspoon baking powder	*other vegetable oil*
¹/₂ teaspoon sea salt	

YIELD: About 8 waffles

PREPARATION TIME: About 15 minutes to prepare; 3 to 5 minutes to cook each batch

Sift together the cornmeal, flours, baking soda, baking powder, and salt.

Pour the orange juice into a 2-cup measure. Add milk or soy milk to equal 1²/₃ cups and set it aside to curdle.

Beat the egg whites until stiff but not dry.

Preheat your waffle iron if necessary.

Whisk the egg yolks and curdled milk with the orange zest. Add the dry mixture and stir gently, just until the ingredients are combined. Gently fold in the beaten egg whites.

Lightly grease the waffle iron grids. Ladle on batter and bake, following directions for your particular waffle iron. Serve waffles immediately or keep them warm and crisp by placing them directly on the racks of an oven set on low heat.

Biscuits and Scones

Both biscuits and scones should be tender and flaky inside and browned and slightly crusty outside. They are much the same, though scone recipes often include more—and sometimes richer—ingredients. Also, scones are usually wedge-shaped.

The secret to making light biscuits and scones is to

follow the light-handed, rapid-mixing principles described earlier. If a recipe calls for cold fat, as many do, use a pastry blender or a food processor fitted with a metal blade to cut chilled butter, margarine, or oil into the dry mixture until it reaches an even, mealy consistency. If you use a food processor, transfer the mixture to a bowl. Add the liquid all at once and mix slowly with a long-tined fork, wooden spoon, or rubber spatula just enough to form a soft dough. Gently knead the dough on a lightly floured surface a few times until it holds together and isn't sticky. Too much handling will toughen and flatten the end product.

For biscuits, pat or roll the dough $\frac{1}{2}$ to $\frac{3}{4}$ inch thick. Cut out biscuits with a cutter of any shape or a sharp knife—biscuits do not have to be round! Dip the cutter or knife into flour before cutting each biscuit. Don't twist a round cutter or the biscuits will rise unevenly and bake up lopsided. To make traditional triangular scones, round the dough into a ball, flatten it to approximately 1 inch thick, then cut equal wedges. This is the easiest way to shape biscuits too, because it doesn't entail recombining and rerolling dough scraps.

Arrange biscuits or scones on an ungreased sheet: Put them close together for soft sides, an inch or so apart for crusty sides. Bake them immediately in a preheated 450° oven for 10 to 15 minutes. Or use a preheated, medium-hot griddle and turn them once the first side is browned and firm. Test by inserting a cake tester in the center.

Drop biscuits are prepared from a thick batter rather than a dough. Simply drop $\frac{1}{4}$-cupfuls onto a baking sheet. Bake these the same as regular biscuits and scones.

Biscuits and scones continue to cook after they come out of the oven or off the griddle. To avoid an uneven, doughy consistency, cool them on a wire rack, loosely covered with a dry towel, for 20 to 30 minutes before serving.

Basic Biscuits

THESE FLAKY LITTLE BREADS ARE TENDER AND FULL-flavored; dress them up with some spices, herbs, or lemon or orange zest. Handle the dough gently and as little as possible. They will be soft-sided if baked close together, crusty if spaced further apart.

*2 teaspoons lemon juice
  or vinegar
About ²/₃ cup milk or
  unsweetened soy milk
2 cups whole wheat
  pastry flour, plus extra
  for shaping*

*¹/₄ teaspoon sea salt
¹/₂ teaspoon baking soda
1¹/₂ teaspoon baking powder
3 tablespoons cold, unsalted
  butter or soy margarine,
  or vegetable oil*

Preheat the oven to 450°.

Combine the lemon juice with milk to equal ²/₃ cup and set it aside to curdle.

Sift the flour, salt, baking soda, and baking powder into a mixing bowl. Using a pastry blender, cut the butter, margarine, or oil into the sifted ingredients until the mixture resembles a coarse meal; or do this in a food processor fitted with the metal blade, and transfer the mixture to a bowl. Make a well in the center of the dry ingredients. Add the curdled milk all at once and stir gently with a fork just until a soft dough forms.

Turn the dough out onto a floured surface and gently knead a few times, until the dough comes together into a ball and is not sticky. Pat or roll the dough about ¹/₂ inch thick and cut rounds, wedges, or other shapes.

Arrange the biscuits on an ungreased or parchment-lined baking sheet. Bake them about 10 minutes, until the tops have browned and a tester inserted in the center comes out clean. Transfer the biscuits to a cooling rack and cover them loosely with a dry, unnapped towel for about 15 minutes before serving.

YIELD: About 8 biscuits (2¹/₂ inches in diameter)

PREPARATION TIME: 20 minutes to prepare; 10 minutes to bake

Notes

• If you don't have lemon juice or vinegar to curdle the milk, omit the baking soda and increase the baking powder to 2 teaspoons; or, substitute ²/₃ cup buttermilk or yogurt for the milk or soy milk and omit the lemon juice.

• For quick and still tender biscuits, simply whisk oil, melted butter, or margarine into the curdled milk and add this to the sifted dry ingredients to form a dough.

YIELD: About 8 biscuits (2½ inches in diameter)

PREPARATION TIME: About 20 minutes to prepare; 15 minutes to bake

SWEET POTATO PECAN BISCUITS

SWEET POTATOES OR YAMS BAKED IN THEIR SKINS, SPLIT open, and sprinkled with toasted pecans are superbly sweet. Bake an extra one and set it aside for this further treat. Serve the biscuits with apple butter or orange marmalade.

1 orange
⅓ cup milk or
    unsweetened soy milk,
    or as needed
2 cups whole wheat
    pastry flour
½ teaspoon sea salt
1½ teaspoons baking
    powder
½ teaspoon baking soda
½ cup lightly toasted
    pecans, coarsely chopped
¾ to 1 cup mashed baked
    sweet potato or yam
3 tablespoons sunflower or
    other vegetable oil
1 tablespoon maple syrup
Maple syrup for glazing

Preheat the oven to 450°.

Finely grate the orange zest into a medium-sized bowl. Juice the orange and measure the juice. Add milk to equal ⅔ cup of liquid; set it aside to curdle.

Sift the flour. Measure 2 cups of the sifted flour back into the sieve; set aside the remaining sifted flour for kneading and shaping. Sift the measured flour, salt, baking powder, and baking soda into another bowl. Stir in the chopped nuts.

Add the mashed sweet potato, oil, and syrup to the orange zest and mix thoroughly. Beat in the curdled mixture.

Make a well in the center of the dry ingredients. Pour in the wet ingredients all at once and mix gently, just until a soft dough forms. Turn the dough out onto a lightly floured surface and knead gently a few times. Pat or roll the dough about ½ inch thick. Cut out biscuits and arrange them on an ungreased or parchment-lined baking sheet.

Bake 15 minutes, or until the biscuits have browned and a tester inserted in the center comes out clean. Place them on a cooling rack and lightly brush the tops with maple syrup. Cool the biscuits about 15 minutes before serving.

Anita's Drop Biscuits

ANITA AND I LIVED IN A LARGE COOPERATIVE HOUSE BACK in the '70s and we did a lot of the cooking. Her multigrain drop biscuits were especially quick to prepare and go well with both sweet and savory spreads.

YIELD: 6 biscuits

PREPARATION TIME: 15 minutes to prepare; 10 to 15 minutes to bake

2/3 cup milk or
unsweetened soy milk
2 teaspoons lemon juice
or vinegar
1/2 cup rolled oats
1/2 cup whole wheat
pastry flour

1/2 cup rye flour
1/4 teaspoon sea salt
1/2 teaspoon baking soda
1 teaspoon baking powder
3 tablespoons cold unsalted
soy margarine, butter,
or vegetable oil

Preheat the oven to 450°. Lightly grease a baking sheet or line it with baking parchment.

Combine the milk and lemon juice; set it aside to curdle.

In a blender or a food processor fitted with the metal blade, grind the oats to a flour. Sift this with the other flours, salt, baking soda, and baking powder into a medium-sized bowl. Using a pastry blender, cut the margarine, butter, or oil into the dry mixture until it resembles a coarse meal. Or do this in a food processor fitted with the metal blade and transfer the mixture to a bowl. Make a well in the center and pour in the curdled milk. Stir gently with a fork just until a soft dough forms.

Drop equal-sized mounds of the dough onto the prepared baking sheet. Bake in the preheated oven for 10 to 15 minutes, or until the biscuits are browned and a tester inserted in the center comes out clean. Transfer them to a cooling rack, cover loosely with a towel, and cool 15 to 20 minutes before serving.

Notes
• Substitute buttermilk or beaten yogurt for the milk or unsweetened soy milk, and omit the lemon juice.

OAT-CURRANT SCONES

YIELD: 6 scones

PREPARATION TIME: About 20 minutes to prepare; 10 to 15 minutes to bake

THERE'S A FINE LINE BETWEEN BISCUITS AND SCONES, though scones are often sweeter and richer, and usually wedge-shaped. Serve these for breakfast or an impromptu tea party.

³/₄ cup milk or
    unsweetened soy milk
2¹/₄ teaspoons lemon juice
    or vinegar
1 cup rolled oats
2 cups whole wheat
    pastry flour, plus extra
    for shaping
¹/₂ teaspoon sea salt

³/₄ teaspoon baking soda
2¹/₄ teaspoon baking powder
¹/₃ cup vegetable oil or
    melted butter or soy
    margarine
Finely grated zest of 1 lemon
3 tablespoons maple syrup
³/₈ cup currants

Preheat the oven to 425°.

Combine the milk and lemon juice and set it aside to curdle.

Blend the oats to flour, then sift it with the 2 cups pastry flour, salt, baking soda, and baking powder. Transfer the mixture to a bowl and make a well in the center.

Whisk the oil, lemon zest, and maple syrup into the curdled milk. Add this mixture to the dry ingredients along with the currants. Stir gently with a fork to form a soft dough.

Turn the dough onto a floured surface and knead gently just a few times. Form it into a ball and pat it into a round about 1 inch thick. Cut it into 6 wedges. Arrange the wedges on a lightly greased or parchment-lined baking sheet. Bake the scones in the preheated oven for 10 to 15 minutes or until a tester inserted in the center comes out clean. Transfer the scones to a rack and cover them loosely with a dry, unnapped towel for about 15 minutes before serving.

Notes

• Substitute buttermilk or yogurt for the milk and omit the lemon juice.

• Omit the oats and use 3 cups pastry flour. Without the currants, these make good shortcakes.

• Use cold butter or margarine: cut it into the dry mixture with a food processor or pastry blender to the consistency of coarse meal before adding the wet mixture and currants.

Several other quick breads depend solely upon the combination of beaten eggs and high oven heat for leavening. Popovers, oven-baked pancakes, and spoonbread fall into this group.

Popovers

Popover batter should be thoroughly smooth and about the consistency of heavy cream. In a hot oven, this airy egg-rich mixture swells up into hollow rolls. These small bread balloons should be crusty outside and soft inside.

I find that a large proportion of bread flour works best for popovers. Used exclusively, pastry wheat and other low-gluten flours result in less puffy, muffinlike popovers. Prepare the batter with room temperature ingredients.

Though you can bake popovers in greased custard cups or muffin tins, special popover pans are particularly effective. Preheat and grease them before pouring in the batter. Fill pans one-half to two-thirds full.

Most popover recipes specify baking in a hot oven (425° to 450°) for 15 minutes and then lowering the temperature to 325° to 350° for 20 minutes more. This method works fine, but two-stage baking presents a problem if you want to start a second batch as soon as the first popovers come out of the oven. Baking at 450° for 25 minutes also produces good results, and a second batch can go directly into the oven; popovers are done sooner too.

Popovers are best right out of the oven. If you must wait to serve them, remove the popovers from the pan and puncture each one with the tip of a sharp knife to release the steam inside. Turn off the oven, put the popovers on the oven rack and prop the door partially open.

Egg-Leavened Quick Breads

Yield: 6 large popovers

Preparation time: 10 to 15 minutes to mix; 25 minutes to bake

Notes

- Blend herbs or spices into the batter; heavier additions, such as dried or fresh fruits or nuts, tend to interfere with rising.
- Substitute ¼ cup rye flour for ¼ of the cup whole wheat bread flour.
- Before baking, sprinkle about ¼ teaspoon sesame seeds on top of each popover.
- Sift ¼ teaspoon freshly grated nutmeg with the flour and salt and blend the finely grated zest from 1 lemon (about 1 teaspoon) into the batter.
- Blend 1 teaspoon finely grated orange zest into the batter and, just before baking, sprinkle about ¼ teaspoon poppy seeds on top of each popover.

Serve popovers with preserves and fruit for breakfast or with soup and salad for lunch or supper. Prepare a dainty entree by stuffing popovers with a savory filling.

1 cup whole wheat
   bread flour
¼ teaspoon sea salt
3 large eggs
1 cup milk or
   unsweetened soy milk

1 tablespoon vegetable oil
2 teaspoons unsalted soy
   margarine or butter

Preheat the oven to 450°.

Sift together the flour and salt onto a piece of waxed paper.

Break the eggs into a blender and blend, gradually adding the sifted mixture alternately with the milk. Add the oil and continue to blend until thoroughly smooth, scraping down any flour that clings to the sides of the blender jar.

If you are using tinned or blackened steel popover pans, oil each cup lightly and preheat the pan for a few minutes. Cut the margarine or butter into 6 equal pieces and add a piece to each cup. Return the pan to the oven briefly, until the margarine or butter is sizzling. Or grease and lightly dust 6 custard cups with flour and arrange them in a baking pan.

Fill the prepared pans about half full of batter and put them into the oven immediately. Bake 25 minutes—without opening the oven door!

Remove the popovers from the pan; they should have crusty tops and sides and lift out of the pan easily. Serve them right away.

OVEN PANCAKES

THESE LARGE, LIGHT, PUFFY PANCAKES ARE BAKED IN THE oven rather than on top of the stove. Use a preheated ovenproof skillet. If you customarily make more than

YIELD: 2 (10-inch) pancakes

PREPARATION TIME: 10 to 15 minutes to mix; 15 to 20 minutes to bake one pancake, it's helpful to have multiple skillets, but you can bake pancakes one after the other in the same pan too.

Batter for oven pancakes is rich in eggs, like that for popovers, but somewhat thicker. Pastry flour gives them a tender texture.

Serve these airy pancakes immediately, cut in wedges. Maple syrup, marmalade, fruit sauces, fruit butters, and fresh fruit are good toppings for breakfast or brunch; I like them with blackberries, raspberries, strawberries, or peaches. For a quick lunch or supper dish, try topping pancakes with seasoned sautéed spinach or mushrooms, or a savory sauce.

1 cup whole wheat pastry flour	4 eggs
¹/₄ teaspoon sea salt	1 cup milk or unsweetened soy milk
¹/₄ teaspoon freshly grated nutmeg	2 teaspoons sunflower or other vegetable oil
Grated zest from 1 lemon	

Preheat the oven to 425° and preheat two 10-inch ovenproof skillets on top of the stove over medium heat.

Sift together the flour, salt, and nutmeg.

In a medium-sized bowl, thoroughly whisk the lemon zest and eggs. Whisk in the milk. Add the dry mixture and whisk until smooth.

Coat the inside of the hot skillets with the oil and divide the batter between them. Bake the pancakes in the preheated oven 15 to 20 minutes, or until puffed and browned. Serve them immediately.

SPOONBREAD

SPOONBREAD IS A CORNMEAL SOUFFLÉ. EGG YOLKS ARE beaten into a smooth cornmeal porridge, which is then lightened by carefully folding in stiffly beaten egg whites. High oven heat encourages the foamy batter to

YIELD: 2 generous servings

PREPARATION TIME: About 20 minutes to prepare; 35 to 40 minutes to bake

Notes

• For 4 to 6 servings, double this recipe.

• Add minced fresh herbs: try about a tablespoon of dill, chives, or parsley, or about ¼ teaspoon thyme, rosemary, or sage. Ground cumin and coriander are other interesting additions.

• Stir ½ cup grated cheddar cheese into the cornmeal/egg yolk mixture.

climb the straight sides of a soufflé dish and form a crusty golden crown. Though spoonbread has a more substantial texture and doesn't rise quite as dramatically as featherweight soufflés, it's also less susceptible to falling. Like other soufflés, it's meant to be eaten with a fork—or spoon—rather than with fingers.

Serve this light custardy bread for breakfast or brunch with maple syrup or fruit butters. Spoonbread is also good for lunch or dinner; I like it with sautéed greens and baked sweet potatoes.

½ cup cornmeal, plus extra for dusting the pan	½ teaspoon sea salt
1½ cups milk or unsweetened soy milk	Freshly ground black pepper to taste (optional)
1 tablespoon unsalted soy margarine or butter	2 large eggs at room temperature
	Pinch of cream of tartar

Preheat the oven to 375°. Grease the bottom and sides of a small soufflé dish and dust it lightly with cornmeal.

Heat the milk in a saucepan over medium heat. Gradually whisk in the ½ cup cornmeal, and stir constantly with a wire whisk or wooden spoon until the mixture becomes thick and smooth. Reduce the heat and stir in the margarine or butter and seasonings. Cook, stirring, for several minutes. Remove from the heat and cool the mixture somewhat.

Separate the eggs. In a small deep bowl, beat the whites and cream of tartar until stiff but not dry.

Beat the yolks in a medium-sized bowl. Add the cornmeal mixture and combine thoroughly. Gently fold in the egg whites.

Spread the batter evenly in the prepared dish and smooth the top with a spatula. Bake 35 to 40 minutes, or until the spoonbread is puffed and browned. Serve immediately from the baking dish.

FIVE

Yeasted Breads

We HAD BEGUN TAKING BUSES WITHOUT DESTINATIONS, TO simultaneously rest our exhausted feet and explore new areas of Paris. But this particular morning our bus ride was purposeful and, despite the gray day, I was filled with anticipation. The drizzle escalated into a downpour as we stepped off the bus, and we strode up a steep street dodging rivulets. Suddenly, we were looking into Bernard Ganachoud's bakery at artistic arrangements of beautiful breads, wheat sheaves, and flowers.

Shortly before leaving for France, I had read an article describing Monsieur Ganachoud as one of the few Parisian master bakers still producing traditional loaves using top-quality ingredients, wood-fired brick ovens, and thoroughly fermented doughs. His breads were sold only at their freshest and exclusively from this shop. One wall and a long counter below it displayed an immense array of breads in many shapes and sizes. We stood almost mesmerized by the sight and by the wonderful aroma. Eating the breads turned out to be as pleasurable as looking at them.

I don't know how many times I've admired and bought a bakery loaf only to discover that, despite an impressive appearance, its taste and texture were less than admirable. The crumb might be too open or uneven, the flavor disappointingly bland or yeasty... Delightful experiences, such as the visit to Ganachoud's bakery, and frustrating ones alike inspire me to learn just what it takes to make an excellent bread.

Many people who bake yeasted breads regularly and proficiently have only a vague understanding of what actually happens to transform a mass of ingredients into a finished loaf. As often as not, they seem to regard the whole process as a bit of magic, and, because of this, their breads are often inconsistent— sometimes outstanding, other times just okay. Many factors affect the process and outcome of yeasted breads, including ingredient quality and proportions, mixing and baking techniques, temperature, and timing. Understanding these cause-and-effect relationships will help you bake the bread you want. I'm going to tell you what I do and why.

FERMENTATION

While practice is essential for mastering basic baking techniques, knowing a little chemistry is also important for consistently producing superlative yeasted breads. In short, when grain or flour is combined with liquid and live yeast organisms without oxygen, it undergoes fermentation, chemical changes which convert the grain's carbohydrates into simple sugars and produce carbon dioxide gas and alcohol. The gas leavens the dough, particularly when the grains composing it contain a large proportion of gluten proteins, since these can be developed into an elastic and expandable structure. The alcohol evaporates as the dough is handled; this is crucial, as the alcohol would ultimately do in the yeast. Finally, baking permanently fixes a loaf's gluten web, kills the yeast when it is no longer useful, and drives off any remaining alcohol.

Leavening may be the most dramatic outcome of dough fermentation, but fermentation also benefits bread in other more subtle but significant ways. During fermentation, the grain is broken down both physically and enzymatically, softening it and releasing its natural sweetness. Adequately fermented bread dough becomes slightly acidic, and this improves its flavor and digestibility. The gluten becomes stronger and stretchier, contributing to nicely shaped and even-textured loaves. Well-fermented bread ends up moister and keeps longer. Ample fermentation also enhances a bread's nutritional profile by releasing calcium, iron, zinc, and other minerals bound up in the grain.

The primary requirement for dough fermentation is time, and this is the very thing many bread recipes try to minimize. Yeast growth and leavening can be accelerated in various ways, but not without compromising the final product. Overly rapid dough rising results in poor texture, flat flavor, decreased digestibility, unavailable nutrients, and quick staling. Patience is truly the secret ingredient for exceptional yeasted breads.

It is necessary to rein in the yeast's development to allow for optimum fermentation. Since yeast multiplies readily in the right environment, start with a modest quantity in the dough and it will set a desirable pace for dough development. You'll be surprised at how effectively a small amount of yeast will leaven a sizable quantity of dough if given sufficient time and favorable conditions. Including a sponge stage and multiple dough risings at a moderate temperature (70° to 75°) gives the yeast a chance to develop gradually.

TIMING

The amount of hands-on work of yeasted bread making is about the same whether you make bread quickly or leisurely. The time added to achieve a well-developed dough is mostly waiting time, which you can mesh with other activities. Making a yeasted bread, unlike preparing a quick bread, isn't an uninterrupted start-to-finish project. You must keep attuned to the dough, but it does a lot of the work on its own.

You will become increasingly comfortable with the procedures and timing the more you bake. Gradually, besides developing finely tuned judgment and physical skills, you'll recognize improvisation and flexibility creeping into your baking routines. You'll begin substituting ingredients you have on hand rather than following recipes exactly and fit baking into your schedule rather than deferring all other activities. Eventually, your breads will become truly your own rather than simply replications of someone else's recipes.

One more thing. Probably the most familiar breads to most Westerners are yeasted breads, from simple wheat loaves to croissants, but few people realize that sourdough and natural-rise breads are also yeasted breads. Since these breads require some specialized techniques, we will cover them in later chapters. Still, much of the information in this chapter applies to them, too.

Making a Basic Yeasted Bread

THE BEST WAY TO LEARN ABOUT BREAD MAKING IS TO DO it, so let's get into the kitchen and start with a really basic yeasted bread. This detailed recipe is the prototype for the variations that follow: Stick to this basic recipe until you've mastered the techniques. The recipe yields about 3½ pounds of dough—enough for two good-sized loaves.

In both the basic bread and variations, I follow the

"sponge" method. This includes an initial step in which the yeast, some or all of the liquid, and part of the flour are combined and left to sit until the mixture becomes light and spongy, before finishing up the dough and kneading it.

The sponge method takes a little longer than the "straight-dough" method, but, given identical ingredients and conditions, bread made with a sponge has better flavor, texture, keeping qualities, and digestibility. During the sponge stage, the yeast multiplies and fermentation gets underway. The gluten begins to develop and strengthen as it is stretched by the activity of the yeast. This is especially important when making a bread containing some low-gluten flour: Prepare the sponge with high-gluten flour and incorporate the weaker flour into the dough later.

ASSEMBLING INGREDIENTS AND UTENSILS

Plan ahead. Inventory your bread-making supplies before baking day so you won't discover you're out of an ingredient you thought you had on hand. But remember, too, that shopping isn't the only way to cope. Many ingredients serve similar functions in bread and are possible substitutions. Use your imagination—and your leftovers—and you may come up with something extraordinary. Even little bits of things in the refrigerator or cupboard often inspire new recipes.

Home-scale baking proceeds more smoothly if the major ingredients are all at room temperature: cold liquids and flour inhibit leavening as effectively as a cool draft. Remove flour from cold storage early enough for it to warm to room temperature, or warm it briefly in an oven set on low heat. You don't want too much heat either, so if you scald milk, for instance, be sure it has cooled to lukewarm before adding it to the bread mix.

Okay, for this basic bread, you'll need the following ingredients and utensils.

INGREDIENTS

3 cups spring water	2½ teaspoons sea salt
¾ teaspoon active dry yeast	2 tablespoons oil
7½ to 8 cups whole wheat bread flour	

UTENSILS

Measuring spoons	Kneading surface
Liquid measuring cup	Metal dough scraper
Dry measuring cup	Unnapped kitchen towels
Large (ceramic) mixing bowl	2 loaf pans
Large wooden spoon	Razor blade
Rubber scraper or plastic dough scraper	

1. PROOFING THE YEAST

The first step is to "proof" the yeast—prove that it is lively. Heat ¼ cup of the water to lukewarm. It should be cool enough that you can comfortably rest your finger in it or drop it on your wrist. If you are uncertain, measure it with a thermometer; the water temperature should be between 100° and 115°.

Next, add the yeast. Honestly, ¾ teaspoon active dry yeast is enough and is better than more. Less is best for good bread. Remember that yeast is a live organism and it will multiply by feeding off the other ingredients. Just be sure to give the dough adequate time to develop.

Let's continue. I measure yeast directly out of a jar in the freezer and add it to the warm water. Sprinkle in about a teaspoon of flour to provide food for the yeast. Cover the cup and place it in a warm, draft-free spot. If you have a gas oven with a pilot light, that's a good place. In 5 to 10 minutes, the surface should appear slightly bubbly. Stir with your finger to be sure that the yeast has thoroughly dissolved. If you feel granules, return the cup to the warm spot for a few more minutes.

If bubbling does not occur within a reasonable time,

there may be something wrong with the yeast—it may be too old, or the water may have been too cold or too hot. Try stirring in a little more flour and give it another 5 to 10 minutes. If there is still no sign of life, throw out the mixture and begin again. Always keep extra yeast on hand.

2. Preparing the Sponge

Combine the yeast solution with the remaining $2^3/_4$ cups of water in the bowl. Gradually add about $3^1/_2$ cups of the flour to form a somewhat thick batter. If the flour is packed down, fluff it up as you measure it. With the wooden spoon, beat the batter in one direction about 100 strokes. Cover the bowl with a damp kitchen towel and large plate or other solid cover and set it in a draft-free spot for a couple of hours, or until the batter becomes active and bubbly.

A bread sponge does not require rigid time constraints: It can rise to its limit and fall back without unduly damaging the gluten. Though it is best to wait for a sponge to fully develop, the bread will benefit even if you move ahead before it reaches that point. The sponge gets the yeast and gluten off to a good start.

3. Mixing the Dough

Stir in $2^1/_2$ teaspoons of salt; sift it first if it's clumpy. Add the oil and beat well—about 100 times. Add 2 cups of flour, a cup at a time, stirring well after each. Before adding more flour, beat the batter energetically in one direction until it appears stringy, which is visible evidence that the gluten is developing. The beating will be easier if you anchor the bowl on a damp towel. Bend your knees slightly or put one foot up on a stool to put less strain on your back, and stir with your whole body rather than with just your arms or wrists.

Continue to add flour, a cup at a time, stirring well after each. The batter will soon become too stiff to stir

The Straight-Dough Method

This technique, an alternative to using the "sponge" method, gets bread off to a quicker start. (See page 79 regarding the advantages of including a sponge stage.)

Using the same ingredients, proceed as follows. Proof the yeast in 1/4 cup of the water. Stir together the proofed yeast, remaining water, salt, and oil. Add flour, a cup at a time, stirring after each addition, until the mixture reaches the consistency of a thick batter. Stir this energetically in one direction until it appears stringy, then gradually stir in more flour until a dough forms and pulls away from the sides of the bowl. Turn it out onto a floured surface, and let it relax, covered, before beginning to knead. Continue as with the sponge method, beginning with Kneading the Dough. For best results with this method, be sure to give the dough slow rises.

easily, but add part of another cup of flour and continue mixing. As the flour coats the dough, it will pull away from the sides of the bowl and ball up in the center. Clean off the spoon with the scraper. If the flour was readily absorbed and the dough is really sticky, add a bit more flour and mix again. The dough should be on the sticky rather than the dry side at this point, though.

Lightly sprinkle flour on the kneading surface and turn the dough out. Scrape any bits of dough or flour remaining in the bowl on top and cover the dough with a kitchen towel for 5 to 10 minutes to allow the gluten to relax. Meanwhile, wash and dry the bowl.

4. KNEADING THE DOUGH

Begin kneading the dough. Right-handed, I press down on the dough with the heel of my right hand, push down and out—away from myself—and simultaneously give it about a quarter turn counterclockwise. At the end of the push, my fingers pull the dough back over itself as it turns. My left hand serves as a guide in the pulling over and turning motion. For me, kneading is an integrated motion, during which the dough is pushed, pulled, and turned, as my entire body rocks forward and back. This dissected description sounds more complicated than kneading really is, and every individual must find his or her own way of doing it. Watching a skilled baker may help, but there is no single correct way to knead.

When the dough's surface seems somewhat sticky, sprinkle a bit of flour underneath and continue kneading. Be sure to add flour in small amounts; you don't want the dough sliding around or to add more flour than the dough requires. Whenever you pause during kneading, clean the surface with your dough scraper. If the dough sticks to the kneading surface, add more flour. The flour amount in a bread recipe is always a ballpark figure, because flour differs in moisture content from day to day.

Think of kneading as stretching exercises for the dough. Eventually, the gluten strands will interconnect in an organized structure that is elastic enough to expand under the pressure of the carbon dioxide gas produced by the yeast. As you knead, the dough will become increasingly smooth, tensile, and less sticky. Whole wheat flour will cause the dough to feel somewhat gritty, especially at first, compared to a dough made with refined flour.

Beginning bread bakers wonder how they will know when the gluten is adequately developed—when they have done enough kneading. Kneading time depends on the effectiveness of your technique, dough quantity, the flour's gluten content, and the length of the sponge stage. Fifteen to twenty minutes of steady kneading will probably do it, but you should learn to judge by the feel of the dough. It should be smooth, supple, and have a certain springy, bouncy quality. At this point, particularly with especially high-gluten doughs, you may see tiny blisters across the taut surface. Now scrape the work surface, sprinkle it lightly with flour, set down the dough and cover it with a damp towel for about 10 minutes.

5. FIRST BOWL RISE

Uncover the relaxed dough and quickly knead it 5 to 10 times to round it into a ball. The dough will feel great— smooth and elastic. Grease the bowl lightly, just enough to keep the dough from sticking. Put the dough into the bowl smooth side down and flip it to oil the other side. Cover the bowl with a damp towel and solid cover such as a large plate or tray to help keep the dough moist. After setting the dough to rise or "proof," clean off the kneading surface.

Professionals put dough to rise in a specially designed cabinet or *proof box* with temperature and humidity controls. Home bakers must improvise. The idea is to keep drafts out and some warmth in the dough but not heat

Fitting Yeasted Bread Making Into Your Schedule

Your bread-making routines must depend to some extent on your lifestyle and schedule. It's always pleasant to set aside most of a day for bread making, and this is probably a good way to start so that you get a clear sense of the sequence of events. Because the hands-on activities of bread making take so little time, you're really setting aside a day to accomplish some things at home besides a batch of fresh homemade bread. But, waiting for a free day every time you want to make bread may mean that you rarely do it.

Yeasted breads do require considered timing but are much more flexible than you might imagine, adaptable enough to fit around a wide variety of scheduling constraints. While carrying a bowl of dough around in the trunk of your car is one possibility, there are better alternatives. It comes down to your exerting control over the dough so that it rises optimally within a given time.

Remember that "optimal rising" means the dough rises to its utmost potential but does not go beyond that point. If dough doesn't rise enough, it will be underdeveloped and heavy; if it overrises and collapses, its gluten will be damaged and unable to stretch fully again. You have two timing options: to slow down the dough or speed it up, and there are various ways to do either.

Generally, stretching out bread making within reason results in bread with better flavor, texture, digestibility, nutrition, and keeping quality, and I would recommend this approach. Bread made in a hurry isn't likely to be a complete disaster on any front, though it probably will have a rather airy texture and undistinguished flavor. It won't have quite the nutritional worth of a longer fermented bread and will dry out rapidly. Still, you may prefer fast-rising bread to any that you can buy. Try out different timings and decide for yourself which results you like best.

What can you do to regulate rising so that you can fit yeasted bread making into your schedule? The two major variables are the amount of yeast you start with and the temperature of the dough as it rises. Even if you start with a small amount of yeast, you'll eventually end up with a lot of it in the dough if the conditions for its growth are favorable—mainly that it isn't so cold that it stays dormant. The warmer the dough is, the faster the yeast will multiply—up to about 130°; higher temperatures will kill it.

If you want reasonably well-developed bread in a short time—say, 3 hours or less, follow the straight dough technique and use a large amount of yeast (3 to 4 teaspoons for the basic whole wheat bread recipe) and keep the dough especially warm (85° to 90°). It's still best to give the dough two bowl rises as well as a shaped rise. Be sure it rises fully each time: Wait until it doesn't rebound when pressed before you deflate it after each rise. Plan to keep close tabs on the dough so that it doesn't overrise.

To move towards longer rising bread, decrease the yeast and/or the rising temperature. If you want particularly well-developed dough, start with as little as 1/4 teaspoon of yeast and keep the dough especially cool—at 50° or less. Find a spot that matches your desired rising pace: an unheated room, a porch, or the refrigerator. Always cover doughs and sponges tightly to keep them from drying out—and any critters from getting in! Experiment and figure out a timing routine that yields the bread you prefer and suits your schedule. The dough or sponge itself is your guide: If it isn't rising at a desirable rate, move it to a warmer or cooler spot and make a note to start with more or less yeast on your next try. This may take a while to work out just right.

There are several other factors to take into account and manipulate as necessary. Salt puts the brakes on rising, so don't add it to sponges that you want to rise rather quickly and vice versa. A moderate amount of sweetener accelerates rising, but an excess will have the opposite effect. Cold liquids will slow down rising and warm ones speed it up. But always use warm water for dissolving yeast unless indicated otherwise and don't add hot liquids to yeast once it has proofed. Dough or sponge consistency influences the pace of rising: A soft dough or thin sponge will rise faster than the same dough or sponge made stiffer by incorporating more flour.

Whatever your timetable, be sure to deflate dough and stir down sponges as necessary to remove the toxins that build up and to redistribute the yeast and reinvigorate the developing gluten. Do this at least every eight hours. If you make a sponge the consistency of dough, don't knead it thoroughly or you will have difficulty incorporating the remaining ingredients; it will get a thorough kneading later when you make the full dough. Also, don't include low-gluten flours in sponges, since a major purpose of a sponge is to build up gluten strength; add low-gluten flours at the final dough stage. Finally, when a dough rises in a cold spot, let it warm to room temperature throughout before you shape it.

You can work with the same variables when faced with unexpected interruptions. If you're called away just as you finish mixing or kneading the dough or after its first bowl rise, put it in a cool place or in the refrigerator. When you get back, let it warm to room temperature before resuming where you left off. An exception to this is shaped loaves. Enclose them in plastic bags, allowing space for rising, and, if they have risen fully when you return, put them right into a preheated oven; you may have to bake them a bit longer to compensate for their cold start. Chilling shaped loaves is a good way to stagger bakings if you can't fit all the loaves into the oven at the same time. Always remember, though, that chilling dough doesn't stop rising in its tracks; it takes a while for a warm dough to become cool through and through and its rising pace will diminish gradually. So even when you refrigerate dough, especially on short notice, keep in touch with it if possible to see that it doesn't overrise. Lastly, sponges and doughs can't go on indefinitely; try to move them toward finished bread within two to three days at the outside.

it. It should be surrounded by an even temperature rather than warmed from a single direction. This causes uneven rising, and if the heat is intense, hardening of a portion of the dough.

I find that cool room temperature is plenty warm. Wrap the covered bowl in a large beach towel or a blanket if the room is especially cool and drafty. Well-insulated dough will be 5° to 10° warmer than the room, especially since yeast produces heat as it works. On a hot day, place the covered bowl of dough in a cool spot, such as in the basement or in a sink full of cold water.

Several factors influence rising: the dough and room temperatures; the quantity of yeast and its viability; the type of flour; the amount of salt, oil, and sweetener; and how well you kneaded the dough. At high altitudes, dough rises more quickly, so plan on an extra rise or two to develop it fully.

At 70° to 75°, this dough's first bowl rise will take about 2 hours. Without a sponge stage, it may take longer. The dough will approximately double in size, but determine if it has risen sufficiently by pressing a finger against the surface. If the indentation remains, it has risen enough; if the dough springs back, it should rise longer. But take care not to let the dough overrise. It will become sour from the accumulation of fermentation by-products, and the yeast will exhaust its food source. The gluten will stretch to the breaking point, causing the dough to collapse in a heap with a permanently weakened structure.

6. Deflating the Dough

When the dough has risen enough, it is time to "punch it down" or "knock it back" in baking lingo. You can give it a literal punch to knock the air out, but a gentler touch is better for the dough. I turn it out onto the unfloured kneading surface and knead it gently a few times.

There are three reasons for doing this: to dispel the air, actually carbon dioxide gas and alcohol, which has accumulated in the dough during the fermentation process; to rearrange and re-energize the yeast organisms; and finally, to allow the gluten to retract and then stretch out again, furthering its development.

7. Second Bowl Rise

Form the dough back into a ball and return it to the bowl, covered, to rise again. This rise may take slightly less time than the first one. Test it as you did the first time.

8. Dividing the Dough

When the dough has risen adequately again, turn it out onto the work surface and cut it in half. Knead each piece briefly on an unfloured surface to expel gas and to round the dough into a ball. It should not feel at all sticky now, and you should not add flour at this point.

Cover the dough and leave it to rest for a few minutes. It is important to continue to keep the dough covered as much as possible to preserve its moistness. During this resting period, the developed gluten will relax, enabling you to work with the dough more easily and with less danger of tearing it. The more developed the dough, the more crucial this resting period, because the danger of overstretching and tearing the gluten strands is greater. While the dough rests, wash the bread bowl and grease the pans.

9. Shaping and Panning Loaves

Shaping is the beginning of the visual art phase of bread making. Loaves may be made in just about any shape and size, but some doughs are more suitable for particular manipulations than others. Smooth, strong wheat doughs like this one work for any loaf form. Doughs containing a large proportion of low-gluten flour are less tolerant of stretching than all-wheat doughs, and should always be formed into simple shapes.

To form a rectangular panned loaf, take a piece of the rounded, relaxed dough and gently press it out into a thick oval or slightly rectangular shape, about as long as the pan. Firmly roll the dough into a cylinder, then pinch a seam and each end closed. Place the rolled dough seam side down in the greased pan and press it evenly and firmly into the corners and against the sides. It should fill about two-thirds of the pan.

10. Shaped Dough Rise

Cover the shaped dough with a damp towel and set it in a draft-free spot at room temperature. The dough will continue to expand in the oven, so this rise shouldn't be as complete as those in the bowl. It will take about

Other Shapes for Bread

In this country, "loaf" is virtually synonymous with a rectangular form. Perhaps the notion of a loaf is as stereotyped in other regions of the world as it is here, but the associated shape is different, such as long thin baguettes in France. Certain kinds of bread are associated with particular shapes, for instance Jewish egg bread or challah is usually braided. Loaf shape may have symbolic meaning; this is often the case for special breads made for religious observances, festivals, or holidays.

Round and Oval Loaves

To form a round loaf, knead a piece of relaxed dough gently several times until it begins to round and the underside is smooth. Pinch the edges together in the middle to form a ball, then flip it over, smooth side up. With your hands gently cupping opposite sides of the ball, rotate it on the work surface in a clockwise direction several times until it is evenly rounded and the bottom is sealed. Now, forcefully drop the ball onto the kneading surface and then quickly repeat the rotating process; repeat this sequence once or twice more. Place the loaf on a parchment-lined, cornmeal-dusted, or lightly greased baking sheet or pie plate, or uniformly press it into a round metal, glass, or ceramic baking dish, filling about two-thirds of the pan's volume.

Oval loaves are elongated round loaves. Place both hands on the smooth top of a just-shaped round loaf and gently roll it back and forth until slightly elongated. Bake the loaf freestanding.

Braided Loaves

A strong, glutenous dough is best for braided loaves. They can consist of three or more strands. Divide the dough cut for a single loaf into smaller pieces of equal weight. Knead each one briefly to expel all air, and let the dough rest a few minutes to relax the gluten. Form each piece into a strand by placing your palms parallel on top and press down gently but firmly. Gradually move your hands apart while rolling the dough back and forth until the strand reaches the length and thickness you want. Be careful not to make strands too thin, or they may tear apart as they rise, before or during baking.

Press together one end of each strand and braid them loosely to allow for dough expansion, then pinch together the ends. Or, braid from the middle toward each end. Arrange the braid on a sheet or in a pan and tuck both ends under slightly.

Another way to form a three-strand braid begins with one long dough rope. Form a loop with two-thirds of the dough, overlapping the end slightly and pinching the point of overlap securely; leave the final third of the dough free. Turn the loop so the free end is at the top and drop it through the loop, pulling the end to the left. Twist the loop clockwise and drop the free end through it again. Repeat this pattern until the braid is complete.

A Woven Bread Basket

You can also weave dough strands. For a Christmas dinner, my husband and I baked a bread basket, lined it with a pretty cloth, and filled it with fresh rolls. It was on its second pass around the table before someone noticed that the basket itself was edible!

To weave a bread basket, grease the outside of an ovenproof bowl or pot and turn it upside-down on a baking sheet. Arrange an odd number, say 5 or 7, dough strands equidistant from one another across the bottom and down the sides of the pot like the spokes of a wheel. Press the ends together in the middle. These will be the basket's upright supports. Roll a long dough strand and pinch one end under one of the support strands close to the middle of the pot. Loosely weave it over and under the support strands, leaving ample slack to allow for dough expansion. When the first weaving strand is used up, pinch another one onto it and continue weaving. It's helpful to have one person rolling strands while another weaves. If you're working alone, roll several long strands before beginning to weave, so you can continue uninterrupted. Leave about an inch of the support strands to tuck into the woven portion to finish what will be the basket's top edge.

three-quarters of the time for a bowl rise, 1 to 1½ hours. Near the end of this final rise, preheat the oven to 400°.

When the dough rebounds slowly when pressed, it is ready to bake. The dough will be slightly rounded over the top of the pans. It will rise more in the oven, so don't overdo it. Don't rush the dough at this stage, but do watch that it doesn't overrise.

11. SURFACE TREATMENTS: CUTTING AND GLAZING

Slash the top of the loaves with a razor blade held almost parallel to the surface. Make one or more cuts ¼ to ½ inch deep. Make one long slash down the center, an S-shaped cut, two or more evenly spaced diagonal cuts, or a circular or crosshatch pattern on round loaves.

Besides adding a decorative touch this permits the interior dough to expand after the oven heat has already set the crust. Uncut loaves are likely to tear randomly on the top or sides. Docking, or piercing an unbaked loaf with a long-tined fork or a skewer, serves the same function for heavy textured, less glutenous doughs such as rye breads.

Next, you can apply a glaze or another substance to the dough surface to influence the character of the baked crust, as described at right.

12. BAKING THE BREAD

Arrange the prepared loaves in the preheated oven and bake them for 20 minutes. Now turn the oven to 350°. and bake 20 to 30 minutes longer. Starting out at a higher temperature gives the loaves "oven spring"—a final rising boost. Then they bake evenly throughout at the lower temperature without over-browning the exterior.

Be sure to leave space between pans and between pans and the oven walls so the heat can circulate freely and evenly around the loaves. Resist any urge to open the oven, especially in the early stages of baking. A win-

Surface Treatments for Bread and Rolls

- **Egg**—*either the whole egg or just the egg yolk or egg white—can be brushed on as a glaze; any of these mixed with a little water becomes an egg wash. A beaten whole egg or egg yolk gives bread a shiny, chewy crust and securely holds sesame, poppy, caraway, or other seeds. Egg white makes a crust shiny and hard, and it too acts as a glue for seeds. Apply egg glazes or washes just before baking or 5 to 10 minutes before taking the bread out of the oven.*
- **Water,** *brushed or sprayed onto the surface of the dough before and/or during baking, produces a hard, crisp crust. Incidentally, if you spray a loaf with an atomizer while it is in the oven, be careful not to hit the oven light, or you may end up with a glass-encrusted loaf. A little salt dissolved in the water, as well as an especially hot oven temperature, further enhance crustiness. Applying water to the dough surface simulates, to a degree anyway, the effect of steam injection in professional ovens.*
- *For a soft, tender crust, brush* **milk, oil, or melted butter** *on loaves before and/or after baking.*
- *For a shiny, chewy crust like that of commercial rye and pumpernickel breads, boil ½ teaspoon* **potato starch or cornstarch** *dissolved in about ¼ cup water for several minutes, until the solution is thick and clear. Brush this on the bread half to three-quarters of the way through baking and again just before it is done.*

dow in my oven door has solved the curiosity problem for me: I can check on the bread's progress without lowering the oven heat.

If you know your oven heats unevenly, creating hot spots, you may wish to shift pans around partway through baking. But wait until the loaves are at least half done and then rearrange them as quickly and efficiently as possible, because the oven temperature will drop rapidly with the door open and interfere with consistent baking.

Unlike old-fashioned brick ovens, most home ovens are constructed of thin sheet metal and cannot hold in the steam produced during baking that gives bread a moist interior and crisp crust. You may simulate brick oven baking on a small scale by using a baking cloche, described at left.

These loaves will take about 40 to 50 minutes to bake. For future reference, keep in mind that baking time is influenced by dough composition, loaf size, container shape and material, baking temperature and oven load. Denser, low-gluten breads take longer to bake than high-gluten ones, and they bake more thoroughly at a lower temperature for a longer time. Large loaves take longer to bake than small ones, given the same dough and oven temperature. The same amount of dough in a tall, narrow container will require longer baking than if it was spread out in a broad, shallow pan. Glass pans bake about 25° hotter than metal ones; therefore, for glass, turn down the thermostat by 25° or shorten the baking period. Cast-iron pans take longer to both heat and cool than steel or glass ones. Of course, bread bakes more quickly at a higher rather than a lower temperature, and a loaf baked in an oven filled with several other loaves will take slightly longer to bake than if it was the only thing in the oven. Consider all of these factors when you judge baking time.

Baking in a Cloche

Lightly dust the cloche base with cornmeal and set a round loaf in the center. Cover it with a damp towel and set it aside to rise. Meanwhile, soak the cloche top in water. When the loaf has risen, slash the top, spray it with water or brush it with a glaze and sprinkle on seeds if you wish. Remove the bell from the water and fit it on the base. Bake the bread at 450° for 15 minutes, then turn the oven to 400° and bake 30 minutes longer. Remove the cloche from the oven and lift off the bell. Carefully run a pancake turner or metal spatula under the loaf to loosen it from the base. The bottom of the bread should be well browned and sound distinctly hollow when tapped. If it doesn't seem done, replace the bell and return the cloche to the oven for 5 to 10 minutes or until the bread is ready.

Making Rolls and Other Small Breads

There are as many, if not more, roll shapes as loaves, and rolls may be formed from almost any bread dough. Rolls are usually somewhere between 2 and 4 ounces of dough, though they may be larger or smaller. I once made dozens of tiny "rollettes" to accompany dips at a friend's party. Coordinate roll size and baking time: Three-ounce yeasted rolls will bake in 20 to 25 minutes.

To prepare round rolls most effectively, cup one hand over a small, relaxed piece of dough. Exert gentle, downward pressure, simultaneously moving your palm rapidly in a circular motion until the dough is evenly rounded and bottom is sealed. For crusty rolls, bake them a couple of inches apart; baked up against one another, rolls will have soft sides. Bake three or four tiny balls together in a muffin cup for a cloverleaf roll.

Other rolls require rolling dough into a flat sheet, cutting out squares or triangles, and then rolling or folding these in various ways. For a crescent roll, roll an equilateral dough triangle from the base toward the point and arrange it on a sheet with the middle point lapped over in front just touching the sheet and the side points curled slightly inward. For a pinwheel roll, cut a dough square almost to the middle from each corner and then fold every other point into the center. For an envelope roll, fold each point of a dough square into the center.

A high-gluten dough that isn't too grainy works best for braided, spiraled or knotted rolls. Form compact dough strands from relaxed dough and twist them into single or double spirals, or knot or braid them.

Bread sticks are simply risen, baked dough strands, usually glazed and seeded or sprayed with water before and during baking for extra crunchiness. Bake them at 425° for about 20 minutes.

Pretzels are dough strands dipped into a baking soda or hot lye solution (add about 1 tablespoon baking soda or lye to a quart of cold water and then heat it to very hot but not boiling) before being knotted and left to rise on a baking sheet. Brush them with an egg wash and sprinkle on coarse salt before baking at 400° for about 15 minutes.

Form **bagels** by looping dough ropes about 7 inches long into rings and securely pinching the ends together; or, form balls and poke a hole through the center. Let these rest briefly and then boil them for a minute or two on each side in lightly salted water. Drain the bagels and place them on a parchment-lined or lightly greased baking sheet. Brush on an egg glaze, sprinkle on some seeds if you wish and bake them at 425° for about 25 minutes or until browned.

Like rolls, **English muffins** may be made from any yeasted bread dough. After it has risen in the bowl, roll the dough with a rolling pin into an even sheet about 1/2 inch thick. Cover the dough with a damp towel and let rest for a few minutes. Roll the dough gently again, because it probably will have contracted a bit. Cut adjacent rounds straight down without twisting with a biscuit or muffin cutter. For uniformity, weigh the rounds and adjust the dough thickness if necessary so that each round weighs 2 1/2 to 3 ounces. Place the rounds on a baking sheet sprinkled with cornmeal, cover them with a damp towel, and let them rise until they're light and puffy. Brush cornmeal on top and gently flip them over, a few at a time, onto a preheated, ungreased griddle or skillet set over low heat or into an electric frying pan preheated to 250°. Cook each muffin about 10 minutes, until the underside is lightly browned and the sides have firmed. Brush cornmeal on top and turn the muffins carefully. Cook 5 to 10 minutes more, until the second side is lightly browned and the muffins sound hollow when tapped. Knead the dough scraps together and let the dough rest, covered, for several minutes before rolling it and cutting more muffins. Or use the dough for a loaf or rolls.

13. TESTING THE BREAD

Bake the loaves until they have browned, all sides are firm, and they sound hollow when removed from the pans and tapped on the bottom. If the pans were adequately greased, the loaves should come out easily, usually by simply turning the pans over onto a rack. If the bread doesn't fall right out, thump the pan bottom in a couple of places and try again. A loaf that comes out of a pan easily is not necessarily done, though: Check the brownness of the bottom and tap it for a distinctly hollow sound. Conversely, the bread may be done and sticking because the pan was greased insufficiently or unevenly. Run a long metal spatula around the loaf to loosen it. If you know you greased the pan thoroughly and you haven't baked the bread overly long, put the loaf back in the oven for a few more minutes; it may slide out readily the next time you check it.

14. COOLING AND SLICING THE BREAD

When the bread has tested done, immediately transfer it to a wire rack to cool. The crust will soften somewhat upon cooling. Brushing oil or melted butter on it immediately after baking will accentuate this softening, as will covering the baked loaf with a towel or bowl as it cools. Be sure to allow the loaf some air circulation, though. Cool loaves completely, a several-hour process, before putting them away.

Cooled loaves slice much more evenly and thinly than hot ones, and the bread is more digestible because the cooking process is complete. Just-out-of-the-oven bread is almost irresistible, but the texture will be doughy because the bread is really still baking. Making a portion of a batch of dough into rolls or English muffins may provide a happy compromise for the cut-or-not-to-cut controversy which often ensues over freshly baked loaves. Small items cool much more quickly than large loaves and can be eaten sooner. See page 91 for directions for making rolls and other small breads.

A gentle back-and-forth sawing motion with a bread knife is the most effective way to slice bread.

15. STORING BREAD

Bread storage affects its continued good quality. The best method I've found for keeping yeasted breads is to put them in an earthenware bowl covered with a clean towel and an earthenware plate. Check the bread daily and if it seems too moist, slide the plate over to allow a little more air to enter.

I sometimes wrap a small loaf that will be eaten quite quickly in a clean dry towel or place it in a brown paper or waxed paper bag, but I avoid plastic for storage outside the refrigerator. Plastic bags, wraps, and containers prevent bread from breathing adequately and promote rapid molding. Plastic does keep bread from drying out when refrigerated and refrigerator storage does inhibit mold growth, but bread stored properly at room temperature retains its moistness and fresh flavor longer than refrigerated bread.

I rarely freeze loaves, because thawed bread's texture is often less satisfactory, more crumbly, than that of unfrozen bread. When I do freeze a whole or partial loaf, I slice it first, and take slices out of the freezer as I need them, generally to toast. Frozen slices thaw quickly and their flavor and texture remain relatively intact. Likewise, I often freeze baked rolls, English muffins, bagels, and such. These too thaw quite quickly and maintain good texture and flavor. Wrap them well before freezing and eat them within several months.

Depending on time, I defrost bread either in the refrigerator or at room temperature. It's best to let it thaw in the freezer wrappings, because the frost inside will be reabsorbed. If you're really in a hurry, put bread or rolls in a covered pan or wrap them in foil and heat them in a warm oven, but slower thawing produces a better texture.

I rarely freeze unbaked dough except for an occasional piece intended for a future pizza. After the first or second bowl rise, place the dough in a plastic container with a secure cover and large enough to allow for expansion. Defrost frozen dough in the refrigerator or at room temperature. It will take 6 to 8 hours in the refrigerator, about 3 hours at room temperature.

16. REVIVING BREAD

To reheat rolls, lightly spray them all over with water from an atomizer and place them directly on the rack of an oven preheated to 325° to 350°. This technique produces warm, crisp-crusted rolls in about 5 minutes. For soft-crusted rolls, heat them in a foil package or covered container. A brief steaming wondrously revitalizes somewhat dry breads.

Yeasted Bread Variations

ONCE YOU'VE MASTERED THE BASIC WHOLE WHEAT LOAF, you'll no doubt want to expand your bread-making horizons. Variety is the spice of life and there are many possible variations on this bread which can enhance yours.

SUBSTITUTE GRAINS

For subtle variation in flavor and texture, replace some whole wheat bread flour with another flour, such as rye or triticale. To maintain a strong dough, though, still use at least two-thirds whole wheat bread flour. Add some cornmeal, rye meal, or bran for a coarser crumb. Soaked cracked grains and cooked whole grains contribute moistness and their own unique nubbliness. Refer to chapter 1 for a description of different grains and their special contributions to breads.

Evaluating Yeasted Breads and Solving Problems

So, how should your bread have come out? Beyond an intoxicating fragrance, the quintessential yeasted loaf should have a pleasing form and be a uniform shade of brown. Picked up, the bread has a moderate heft indicating substance rather than either airiness or dead weight. Pressed lightly, the loaf is firm yet resilient. Cutting reveals a thin crust encasing an even-textured, compact interior that is moist and springy. A cooled loaf slices thinly without crumbling and its texture is somewhat chewy.

If your bread doesn't match this description, don't be discouraged. Even if it isn't picture perfect and problem-free, it probably still tastes good. Check the following chart to see if you can determine what went wrong, consider what to do about it, and then try again soon. Thoroughly mastering bread making takes a long time—perhaps a whole lifetime of doing it regularly—but that's what keeps it interesting!

Problem	Explanation	Solution
Bread is layered or streaked inside	Flour not absorbed by dough	Knead thoroughly and don't add a lot of flour at the end
Bread is heavy and dense	Too much flour in dough	Make dough less stiff
	Too much low-gluten flour	Use more high-gluten flour
	Dough didn't rise enough	Let dough rise longer or at higher temperature
	Too much salt, fat, or sweetener	Adjust balance of ingredients
Crumb coarse and crumbly	Too much low-gluten flour	Increase proportion of high gluten flour
	Dough not kneaded enough	Knead dough longer
	Dough rose too quickly	Use less yeast or more salt; rise in a cooler place
	Dough not properly developed	Dough probably hasn't had enough risings
	Dough overdeveloped—kneaded too much, risen too long, or not deflated well enough	Knead less and keep a closer eye on dough while rising
Crumb is uneven—compact in some areas and open in others	Dough overrose in pan	Bake loaf sooner next time
	Oven not hot enough	Increase baking temperature
	Not enough salt	Increase salt slightly
	Large difference between dough temperature and room temperature	Keep dough and room at a consistent temperature for final rise
Crust too hard and dry	Bread baked too long	Shorten baking time; for now, wrap loaf in towel as it cools or brush with melted margarine
	Oven temperature too high	Check oven
	Baked with too much steam	Spray less next time
Crust too soft	Bread underbaked	Bake another 10 to 15 minutes
	Loaf needs surface treatment	Spray with water at beginning of baking or brush with egg white glaze first
Crust browned unevenly	Temperature varies in different areas of oven	Move pans around as bread bakes—after it has "set"
Sides and bottom are pale	Baking in shiny (probably aluminum) pans	Use tinned or blackened steel pans; for now, remove loaves from pans and bake another 5 to 10 minutes
Loaf splits along sides	Shaped loaf didn't rise long enough before baking	Let loaf rise until it springs back slightly when pressed
Freestanding loaf spreads out too much	Dough didn't develop long enough	Let dough ferment longer, deflating it as necessary
	Not enough salt	Add salt
Bread tastes yeasty	Dough rose too quickly	Start with cooler ingredients; rise dough in cooler spot
	Too much yeast	Reduce yeast

SUBSTITUTE LIQUIDS

You can substitute milk, soy milk, nut or seed "milks," vegetable stock, or fruit juices for all or part of the water. Potato cooking water makes light loaves with a wonderful flavor and texture. Beer lends an intriguing flavor, particularly to rye breads. For extra richness, protein, and loft, substitute beaten eggs for part of the liquid. Puréed raw or cooked fruits or vegetables also count as liquid and often contribute a mellow sweetness. Apple or pear sauce and golden winter squashes and sweet potatoes are some of my favorites. Mashed cooked dried beans are a nourishing, flavorful, moisturizing addition to bread.

ADD SWEETENER

Honey, maple syrup, molasses, barley malt, rice syrup, or Sucanat are all options, but don't overdo it or you'll mask the natural sweetness of the grains themselves.

ADD DRIED FRUITS, GRATED VEGETABLES, NUTS, OR SEEDS

Raisins, currants, and other chopped dried fruits add chewy sweet spots. Seeds, chopped nuts, and sprouts provide a subtle crunch. Minced or grated vegetables or fruits also add textural and visual interest as well as flavor. The bright orange flecks in carrot bread are outstanding!

SUBSTITUTE FATS

Replace the oil with nut or seed butter. Imagine—peanut butter or almond butter bread! You can also increase the oil by a tablespoon or two to make the bread richer and more tender, but don't go overboard or it will be heavy and greasy tasting.

SPICE IT UP

Spices and herbs can inspire eyebrow-lifting appreciation. Caraway, dill, fennel, and anise are traditional accents in rye breads. Cumin, coriander, and oregano add an exotic touch to bean breads. Basil, rosemary, thyme, sage, and tarragon liven up a basic wheat loaf. Cinnamon, cloves, nutmeg, allspice, mace, and cardamom hint at festivity. Orange or lemon zest adds zing.

Modify the basic recipe, try out the recipes that follow, and tap your own improvisational spirit to devise more. Soon you'll be making your own signature yeasted breads.

TRITICALE-WHEAT BREAD

THOUGH SIMILAR TO WHOLE WHEAT BREAD, THE FLAVOR of this bread is subtly different, with an appealing ruggedness. Making an all-wheat sponge before adding the triticale flour strengthens the dough. This dough works well for encasing savory fillings, such as in **Piroshki** (page 332) and **Kasha Knishes** (page 333).

YIELD: 2 loaves

PREPARATION TIME: 2¹/₂ to 3 hours for sponge and dough; 5 hours for rising; 40 to 50 minutes to bake

3 cups spring water	2¹/₂ teaspoons sea salt
³/₄ teaspoon active dry yeast	2¹/₂ tablespoons corn or other vegetable oil
5 cups whole wheat bread flour	2¹/₂ cups triticale flour

Heat ¹/₄ cup of the water and cool it to lukewarm. Add the yeast and a teaspoon of wheat flour. Cover and set it in a warm spot to proof. Add the remaining water and stir in about 3¹/₂ cups of the wheat flour to form a thick batter. Cover and set it in a draft-free spot for about 2 hours, or until a sponge develops.

Stir in the salt, oil, and triticale flour. Gradually stir

Notes

• For a heftier loaf, use half triticale flour (3¾ cups), but still start off with the wheat flour in the sponge to strengthen the dough.

YIELD: 2 loaves

PREPARATION TIME: 2½ to 3 hours for sponge and dough; 5 hours for rising; 40 to 50 minutes to bake

in enough of the remaining wheat flour to form a dough.

Turn the dough out onto a lightly floured surface and cover it for several minutes. Knead the dough until smooth and elastic, adding wheat flour as necessary to keep it from sticking.

Form the dough into a ball and place it in a lightly greased bowl. Cover and set it aside for about 2 hours, or until the dough has risen and does not spring back when pressed. Turn the dough out and knead it briefly. Return it to the bowl for a second rise.

Shape and pan the dough. Cover the loaves and set them aside to rise for about an hour, or until the dough rebounds slowly when pressed.

Slash the tops of the loaves. Spray them with water or brush on an egg wash and sprinkle on some poppy seeds. Bake at 400° for about 20 minutes, then turn the oven to 350° and bake 20 to 30 minutes longer, until the loaves are brown, have firm sides, and sound distinctly hollow when removed from the pans and tapped on the bottom.

Cool the bread thoroughly before slicing or storing it.

(For more detailed instructions, refer to the directions for **Basic Yeasted Whole Wheat Bread,** beginning on page 78.)

ANADAMA BREAD

THERE IS AN OLD STORY ABOUT A NEW ENGLANDER, HIS wife Anna, and a cornmeal bread which somehow originated from a spat between them: something about him growing tired of the cornmeal mush she constantly served him or her growing weary of serving him. In any case, the mush somehow got turned into a bread called "anadama," apparently a contracted form of his exasperated cursing, "Anna, damn her!" This moist, fine-textured bread is usually sweetened with molasses, but you can substitute maple syrup or omit sweetener altogether and let the delicate corn flavor really shine. As always, use the freshest cornmeal you can find.

3 cups spring water	*2 teaspoons sea salt*
³/₄ teaspoon active dry	*2 tablespoons sesame or*
yeast	*other vegetable oil*
About 6 cups whole	*2 tablespoons unsulfured*
wheat bread flour	*molasses*
¹/₂ cup cornmeal	

Heat ¹/₄ cup of the water and cool it to lukewarm. Add the yeast and a teaspoon of flour. Cover and set it in a warm spot to proof. Stir in 1³/₄ cups of water and enough flour to form a thick batter. Cover and set it in a draft-free spot for about 2 hours, until a sponge develops.

Heat the remaining cup of water to boiling in a saucepan and gradually add the cornmeal, whisking constantly. The mixture will thicken immediately. Remove the pan from the heat and whisk in the salt, oil, and molasses. Cool the mixture to lukewarm, whisking often to prevent lumps, then stir it into the sponge. Gradually stir in enough of the remaining flour to form a dough.

Turn the dough out onto a lightly floured surface and cover it for several minutes, until it relaxes. Knead the dough until smooth and elastic, adding flour as necessary to keep it from sticking. Form the dough into a ball and place it in a lightly greased bowl. Cover and set it aside for about 2 hours, until the dough has risen and does not spring back when pressed. Turn the dough out and knead it briefly. Return it to the bowl for a second rise.

Shape and pan the dough. Cover the loaves and set them aside for about an hour or until the dough rebounds slowly when pressed.

Slash the tops of the loaves and spray them with water or brush on an egg wash. Bake at 400° for 20 minutes, then turn the oven down to 350° and bake 20 to

30 minutes longer, until the loaves are brown, have firm sides, and sound distinctly hollow when removed from the pans and tapped on the bottom.

Cool the bread thoroughly before slicing or storing it.

(For more detailed instructions, refer to the directions for **Basic Yeasted Whole Wheat Bread,** beginning on page 78.)

Finnish Rye

THIS MOIST, NATURALLY SWEET BREAD HAS A FINE, EVEN grain. It is traditionally shaped into round loaves. I often use part of the dough for the crust of a tart or for turnovers—see **Cabbage Kuchen** (page 326), **Kasha Knishes** (page 333), and **Piroshki** (page 332).

3 cups spring water	1 tablespoon sea salt
³/₄ teaspoon active dry yeast	3 tablespoons corn or other vegetable oil
4¹/₂ cups whole wheat bread flour	3 cups rye flour

Heat ¹/₄ cup of the water and cool it to lukewarm. Add the yeast and a teaspoon of wheat flour. Cover and set in a warm spot to proof. Add the remaining 2³/₄ cups water and gradually stir in about 3¹/₂ cups of wheat flour to form a thick batter. Cover and set it in a draft-free spot for about 2 hours, or until a sponge develops.

Stir the salt and oil into the sponge. Add the rye flour, a cup at a time. Gradually stir in as much additional wheat flour as necessary to form a dough.

Turn the dough out onto a lightly floured surface and cover it for several minutes. Knead the dough rather gently, since doughs containing rye flour are more fragile than all-wheat ones. Knead until the dough is smooth and resilient but stop as soon as it begins to feel sticky.

Form the dough into a ball and place it in a lightly

YIELD: 2 loaves

PREPARATION TIME: 2¹/₂ to 3 hours for sponge and dough; 5 hours for rising; 40 to 50 minutes to bake

Notes
• For a subtly sweet and tangy flavor, substitute dark beer for part of the water. Proof the yeast in ¹/₄ cup water, and use beer for part or all of the rest of the liquid.

greased bowl. Cover and set it aside for about 2 hours, or until the dough has risen and does not spring back when pressed. Turn the dough out and knead it briefly. Return it to the bowl for a second rise.

Shape and pan the dough. Cover the loaves and set them aside to rise for about an hour, or until the dough rebounds slowly when pressed.

Dock or slash the tops of the loaves. Bake at 400° for 20 minutes, then lower the heat to 350° and bake 20 to 30 minutes longer, until the loaves sound distinctly hollow when removed from the pan and tapped on the bottom.

Cool the bread thoroughly on a rack before slicing or storing it.

(For more detailed instructions, refer to the directions for **Basic Yeasted Whole Wheat Bread,** beginning on page 78.)

Sprouted Wheat Bread

When I taught preschool children, one of our projects was to sprout a variety of grains and beans. Surprisingly sweet wheat berry sprouts were always a favorite of even the most finicky three-year-olds. Wheat sprouts are extra nutritious—very high in B vitamins and vitamins A, C, and E plus protein. They sweeten and moisten this bread and may even enhance its rising. I like to use part of this dough for English muffins. Begin sprouting ¼ cup hard wheat berries about 3 days before you want to make the bread; the sprouts should be about the same length as the grains of wheat.

YIELD: 2 loaves

PREPARATION TIME: 2½ to 3 hours for sponge and dough; 5 hours for rising; 40 to 50 minutes to bake

2³/₄ cups spring water	*2¹/₄ teaspoons sea salt*
³/₄ teaspoon active dry yeast	*2 tablespoons corn or other vegetable oil*
6¹/₂ to 7 cups whole wheat bread flour	*1¹/₂ to 2 cups wheat sprouts (see page 11)*

Sprouts of grains, beans, and herb and vegetable seeds are highly nutritious foods, rich in protein and vitamins, and low in fat and calories. Sprouts are readily available commercially, but with little effort, you can obtain fresher, less expensive, and more varied sprouts by growing them yourself.

Be sure to use seeds which have not been treated with pesticides and herbicides. Pick over the seeds and remove any foreign matter. Place up to 1/4 cup in a quart jar and fill it with warm water. Cover the jar with cheesecloth or a nonmetallic screen and secure it with a rubber band or use a special plastic mesh screw-on cap made for this purpose. Soak the seeds for 8 to 12 hours, then drain off the water. Wrap the jar in a towel or set it on its side in a dark spot. Rinse and drain the seeds about every 12 hours until the sprouts are the length you desire; most take about 3 days to mature.

Notes
• Substitute milk or unsweetened soy milk for the 2½ cups of water; scald and cool it to lukewarm before adding it to the proofed yeast.

Heat ¼ cup of the water and cool it to lukewarm. Add the yeast and a teaspoon of flour. Cover and set it in a warm spot to proof. Add the remaining 2½ cups water. Stir in about 3 cups of the flour to form a thick batter. Cover and set it in a draft-free spot for about 2 hours, or until a sponge develops.

Stir the salt and oil into the sponge. Roll the sprouts in a towel to dry them, then coarsely chop and stir them in. Gradually stir in enough of the remaining flour to form a dough.

Turn the dough out onto a lightly floured surface and cover it for several minutes. Knead the dough until smooth and elastic, adding flour as necessary to keep it from sticking.

Form the dough into a ball and place it in a lightly greased bowl. Cover and set it aside for 1½ to 2 hours, or until the dough has risen and does not spring back when pressed. Turn the dough out and knead it briefly. Return it to the bowl for a second rise.

Shape and pan the dough. Cover the loaves and set them aside to rise for about an hour, or until the dough rebounds slowly when pressed.

Slash the tops of the loaves and spray them with water or brush on an egg wash. Bake at 400° for 20 minutes, then lower the heat to 350° and bake 20 to 30 minutes longer. The sprouts add moisture, so be sure you bake the bread long enough. The loaves should be well browned, have firm sides, and sound distinctly hollow when removed from the pans and tapped on the bottom.

Cool the bread thoroughly before slicing or storing it.

(For more detailed instructions, refer to the directions for **Basic Yeasted Whole Wheat Bread,** beginning on page 78.)

Very Berry Bread

COOKED WHOLE WHEAT BERRIES GIVE THIS BREAD A chewy, moist texture. Substitute cooked rye berries, rice, or millet for a different flavor. Use part of the dough to make excellent English muffins (see page 91).

3 cups spring water
3/4 teaspoon active dry yeast
7 1/2 cups whole wheat bread flour

2 1/4 teaspoons sea salt
2 tablespoons corn or other vegetable oil
2 cups cooked wheat berries (see page 19)

YIELD: 2 loaves

PREPARATION TIME: 2 1/2 to 3 hours for sponge and dough; 5 hours for rising; 40 to 50 minutes to bake

Heat 1/4 cup of the water and cool it to lukewarm. Add the yeast and a teaspoon of flour. Cover and set it in a warm spot to proof. Add the remaining 2 3/4 cups water. Gradually stir in 2 to 3 cups of the flour to form a thick batter. Cover and set it in a draft-free spot for about 2 hours, or until a sponge develops.

Stir the salt, oil, and wheat berries into the sponge. Gradually stir in enough of the remaining flour to form a dough.

Turn the dough out onto a lightly floured surface and cover it for several minutes. Knead the dough until smooth and elastic, adding flour as necessary to keep it from sticking.

Form the dough into a ball and place it in a lightly greased bowl. Cover and set it aside for 2 hours, or until the dough has risen and does not spring back when pressed. Turn the dough out and knead it briefly. Return it to the bowl for a second rise.

Shape and pan the dough. Cover the loaves and set them aside to rise for about an hour, or until the dough rebounds slowly when pressed.

Slash the tops of the loaves. Bake at 400° for about 20 minutes, then lower the heat to 350° and bake 20 to 30 minutes longer, until the loaves are brown, have firm sides, and sound distinctly hollow when removed from the pans and tapped on the bottom.

Cool the bread thoroughly before slicing or storing it.

(For more detailed instructions, refer to the directions for **Basic Yeasted Whole Wheat Bread,** beginning on page 78.)

SESAME BREAD

THE IRRESISTIBLE FLAVOR AND GENTLE CRUNCH OF roasted sesame seeds pervades this popular loaf.

YIELD: 2 loaves

PREPARATION TIME: 2$\frac{1}{2}$ to 3 hours for sponge and dough; 5 hours for rising; 40 to 50 minutes to bake

3 cups spring water
$^3/_4$ teaspoon active dry yeast
7$^1/_2$ cups whole wheat bread flour
$^3/_4$ cup sesame seeds, plus extra for garnishing loaves
2$^1/_4$ teaspoons sea salt
2 tablespoons sesame oil
Egg wash

Heat $^1/_4$ cup of the water and cool it to lukewarm. Add the yeast and a teaspoon of flour. Cover and set it in a warm spot to proof. Add the remaining 2$^3/_4$ cups water. Gradually stir in about 3$^1/_2$ cups of the flour to form a thick batter. Cover and set it in a draft-free spot for 2 hours, or until a sponge develops.

Meanwhile, roast the sesame seeds in a dry, heavy-bottomed skillet (cast iron works well) over medium heat; agitate the pan or stir often to prevent the seeds from burning. Grind the seeds coarsely with a mortar and pestle or food processor.

Stir the salt, oil, and sesame seeds into the sponge. Gradually stir in enough of the remaining flour to form a dough.

Turn the dough out onto a lightly floured surface and cover it for about 10 minutes. Knead the dough until smooth and elastic, adding flour as necessary to keep it from sticking.

Form the dough into a ball and place it in a lightly greased bowl. Cover and set it aside for about 2 hours, or until the dough has risen and does not spring back when pressed. Turn the dough out and knead it briefly. Return it to the bowl for a second rise.

Shape and pan the dough. Cover the loaves and set them aside to rise for about an hour, or until the dough rebounds slowly when pressed.

Slash the tops of the loaves, brush them with an egg wash and sprinkle on whole sesame seeds. Bake at 400° for about 20 minutes, then lower the heat to 350° and bake 20 to 30 minutes longer, until the loaves are brown, have firm sides, and sound distinctly hollow when removed from the pans and tapped on the bottom.

Cool the bread thoroughly before slicing or storing it.

(For more detailed instructions, refer to the directions for **Basic Yeasted Whole Wheat Bread,** beginning on page 78.)

Pecan Bread

Pecans are plentiful where I live in Texas and this bread is packed with them. You can substitute walnuts or other nuts.

$^1/_4$ cup spring water	$2^1/_2$ teaspoons sea salt
$^3/_4$ teaspoon active dry yeast	2 tablespoons walnut or other vegetable oil
$6^1/_2$ to 7 cups whole wheat bread flour	2 cups lightly toasted, coarsely chopped pecans
$2^3/_4$ cups milk or unsweetened soy milk, scalded and cooled to lukewarm	

Heat the water and cool it to lukewarm. Add the yeast and a tablespoon of flour, cover, and set it in a warm spot to proof. Add the milk and gradually stir in about $3^1/_2$ cups of the flour to form a thick batter. Cover and set it in a draft-free spot for about 2 hours, or until a sponge develops.

Notes
- Add the grated zest of a large lemon along with the salt, oil, and seeds.
- Substitute $^1/_4$ cup each of toasted poppy seeds and toasted sunflower seeds for $^1/_2$ cup of the sesame seeds.

Yield: 2 loaves

Preparation time: $2^1/_2$ to 3 hours for the sponge and dough; 5 hours for rising; 40 to 50 minutes to bake

Stir the salt and oil into the sponge. Gradually stir in enough of the remaining flour to form a dough.

Turn the dough out onto a lightly floured surface and cover it for several minutes. Knead the dough until smooth and elastic, adding flour as necessary to keep it from sticking.

Form the dough into a ball and place it in a lightly greased bowl. Cover and set it aside for about 2 hours, or until the dough has risen and does not spring back when pressed. Turn the dough out and knead it briefly. Return it to the bowl for a second rise.

Turn the dough out onto an ungreased surface and press it out into a flat circle. Sprinkle two-thirds of the chopped nuts over the dough and lightly press them into it. Fold the dough in half and press in the remaining nuts. Fold it in half again to enclose the nuts. Cover the dough for a few minutes, or until it has relaxed. Gently knead the dough. Initially, the nuts will tend to come to the surface but continue kneading until they seem to be evenly distributed. Cover the dough until it relaxes again.

Shape and pan the dough; I like to make round loaves. Cover the loaves and set them aside to rise for about an hour, or until the dough rebounds slowly when pressed.

Slash the tops of the loaves; spray them with water or brush on an egg wash. Bake at 400° for 20 minutes, then lower the heat to 350° and bake 20 to 30 minutes longer, until the loaves are brown, have firm sides, and sound distinctly hollow when removed from the pans and tapped on the bottom.

Cool the bread thoroughly before slicing or storing it.

(For more detailed instructions, refer to the directions for **Basic Yeasted Whole Wheat Bread,** beginning on page 78.)

Sweet Bread

THIS RICH, SWEETENED DOUGH MAKES AN EXCEEDINGLY tender-textured bread. I especially like to use this dough for **Sticky Buns** (page 341) or **Cinnamon Swirl** (page 340).

YIELD: 2 loaves

PREPARATION TIME: About 1 hour for sponge and dough; 5 hours for rising; 40 to 50 minutes to bake

¹/₂ cup spring water
³/₄ teaspoon active dry yeast
6 to 6¹/₂ cups whole wheat bread flour
1¹/₂ cups milk or unsweetened soy milk, scalded

¹/₄ cup maple syrup or mild-flavored honey
2 teaspoons sea salt
¹/₄ cup sunflower or other vegetable oil
2 eggs, beaten (about ¹/₂ cup)

Heat the water and cool it to lukewarm. Add the yeast and a teaspoon of flour, cover, and set it in a warm spot to proof. Stir in ¹/₂ cup of the flour, cover, and set it in a draft-free spot for about 30 minutes, or until a sponge develops.

Combine the hot milk, syrup, salt, and oil in a large bowl and set it aside until the mixture cools to lukewarm. Reserve 1 teaspoon of the beaten egg for a glaze and whisk the rest of it and the sponge into the milk mixture. Gradually stir in enough of the remaining flour to form a dough.

Turn the dough out onto a lightly floured surface and cover it for several minutes. Knead the dough until smooth and elastic, adding flour as necessary to keep it from sticking.

Form the dough into a ball and place it in a lightly greased bowl. Cover and set it aside for about 2 hours, or until the dough has risen and does not spring back when pressed. Turn the dough out and knead it briefly. Return it to the bowl for a second rise.

Shape and pan the dough. Cover the loaves and set

them aside to rise for about an hour, or until the dough rebounds slowly when pressed.

Slash the tops of the loaves. Whisk a little water with the reserved egg and brush it on the loaves. Bake at 400° for about 20 minutes, then lower the heat to 350° and bake 20 to 30 minutes longer, until the loaves are brown, have firm sides, and sound distinctly hollow when removed from the pans and tapped on the bottom.

Cool the bread thoroughly before slicing or storing it.

(For more detailed instructions, refer to the directions for **Basic Yeasted Whole Wheat Bread,** beginning on page 78.)

Spiced Honey Bread

THIS LIGHT, SPICY, FRAGRANT BREAD IS FESTIVE FOR HOL-idays but appealing all year round. For breakfast, try it toasted and spread with **Pear Butter** (page 255). This dough makes delicious English muffins (see page 91).

YIELD: 2 round loaves

PREPARATION TIME: 1 hour for sponge and dough; 5 hours for rising; 40 to 50 minutes to bake

$1/2$ cup spring water	1 tablespoon ground
$1/2$ teaspoon active dry yeast	coriander
	$1/2$ teaspoon cinnamon
$5^1/2$ to 6 cups whole wheat bread flour	$1/4$ teaspoon ground cloves
	2 teaspoons sea salt
$1/4$ cup sesame, walnut, or other oil	$1^1/2$ cups milk or unsweetened soy milk,
$1/4$ cup honey	scalded and cooled to
1 egg	lukewarm

Heat the water and cool it to lukewarm. Add the yeast and a teaspoon of flour, cover, and set it in a warm spot to proof. Stir in $1/2$ cup of the flour, cover, and set it in a draft-free spot for about 30 minutes, or until a sponge develops.

In a large bowl, whisk together the sponge, oil, honey, egg, spices, salt, and milk. Gradually stir in enough of the remaining flour to form a dough.

Turn the dough out onto a lightly floured surface and cover it for several minutes. Knead the dough until smooth and elastic, adding flour as necessary to keep it from sticking.

Form the dough into a ball and place it in a lightly greased bowl. Cover and set it aside for about 2 hours, or until the dough has risen and does not spring back when pressed. Turn the dough out and knead it briefly. Return it to the bowl for a second rise.

Shape two round loaves and put them in lightly greased pans or on a baking sheet lined with baking parchment. Cover the loaves and set them aside to rise for about an hour, or until the dough rebounds slowly when pressed.

Slash the tops of the loaves, and brush them with an egg wash if you wish. Bake at 400° for 20 minutes, then lower the heat to 350°, and bake 20 to 30 minutes longer, until the loaves are brown, have firm sides, and sound distinctly hollow when removed from the pans and tapped on the bottom.

Cool the bread thoroughly before slicing or storing it.

(For more detailed instructions, refer to the directions for **Basic Yeasted Whole Wheat Bread,** beginning on page 78.)

Golden Harvest Bread

MAKE THIS SUBTLY SWEET BREAD IN AUTUMN WHEN WINTER squashes are plentiful. Butternut squash is my favorite. Use a portion of the dough for a **Crisscross Coffee Cake** (page 344) or **Apple Butter Buns** (page 340).

YIELD: 2 loaves

PREPARATION TIME: 2¹/₂ to 3 hours for sponge and dough; 5 hours for rising; 40 to 50 minutes to bake

2 cups spring water	1¹/₂ cups mashed cooked
³/₄ teaspoon active dry	winter squash
yeast	2 teaspoons sea salt
6 to 7 cups whole wheat	2 tablespoons corn or
bread flour	other vegetable oil

Notes
• Substitute mashed cooked pumpkin, carrots, sweet potato, or yam for the squash.
• Substitute apple juice for the water.
• Add 2 tablespoons of maple syrup or a mild-flavored honey along with the squash, salt, and oil.

Heat $1/4$ cup of the water and cool it to lukewarm. Add the yeast and a teaspoon of flour, cover, and set it in a warm spot to proof. Add the remaining $1^3/4$ cups water and gradually stir in about $2^1/2$ cups of the flour to form a thick batter. Cover and set it in a draft-free spot for 2 hours, or until a sponge develops.

Stir the squash, salt, and oil into the sponge. Gradually stir in enough of the remaining flour to form a dough.

Turn the dough out onto a lightly floured surface and cover it for several minutes. Knead the dough until smooth and elastic, adding flour as necessary to keep it from sticking.

Form the dough into a ball and place it in a lightly greased bowl. Cover and set it aside for about 2 hours, or until the dough has risen and does not spring back when pressed. Turn the dough out and knead it briefly. Return it to the bowl for a second rise.

Shape and pan the dough. Cover the loaves and set them aside to rise for about an hour, or until the dough rebounds slowly when pressed.

Slash the tops of the loaves. Sometimes I brush these with an egg wash and sprinkle on sesame or poppy seeds. Bake at 400° for about 20 minutes, then lower the heat to 350° and bake 20 to 30 minutes longer, until the loaves are brown, have firm sides, and sound distinctly hollow when removed from the pans and tapped on the bottom.

Cool the bread thoroughly before slicing or storing it.

(For more detailed instructions, refer to the directions for **Basic Yeasted Whole Wheat Bread,** beginning on page 78.)

Spicy Bean Bread

This dough is smooth and satiny, and the baked bread is light and tender—perhaps not what you would expect from adding mashed cooked beans to bread. The beans add protein and give the bread a moist crumb. Ground roasted cumin seeds are a zesty complement to the subtly sweet flavor of the beans. You can substitute pinto beans, anasazi beans, or black turtle beans for the aduki beans.

YIELD: 2 loaves

PREPARATION TIME: About 1 hour for sponge and dough; 5 hours for rising; 40 to 50 minutes to bake

1 cup spring water	1¹/₂ cups bean stock (or
³/₄ teaspoon active dry	spring water)
yeast	2 teaspoons sea salt
7 cups whole wheat	2 tablespoons sesame, olive,
bread flour	or other vegetable oil
2 cups cooked aduki beans,	1 tablespoon roasted cumin
mashed (see page 360)	seeds, coarsely ground

Aduki beans, also known as *adzuki* or *azuki* beans, are small dark red beans native to Asia. They have a subtly sweet flavor and are low in fat and easy to digest. See page 360 for cooking directions.

Heat ¹/₄ cup of the water and cool it to lukewarm. Add the yeast and a teaspoon of flour, cover, and set it in a warm spot to proof. Stir in the remaining ³/₄ cup of water and 1 cup of flour, cover, and set it in a draft-free spot for about 30 minutes, or until a sponge develops.

Stir together the beans, stock, sponge, salt, oil, and ground seeds. Gradually stir in enough of the remaining flour to form a dough.

Turn the dough out onto a lightly floured surface, and cover it for several minutes until relaxed. Knead the dough until smooth and elastic, adding flour as necessary to keep it from sticking.

Form the dough into a ball and place it in a lightly greased bowl. Cover and set it aside for about 2 hours, or until the dough has risen and does not spring back when pressed. Turn the dough out and knead it briefly. Return it to the bowl for a second rise.

Shape and pan the dough. Cover the loaves and set

them aside to rise for about an hour, or until the dough rebounds slowly when pressed.

Slash the tops of the loaves. Bake at 400° for about 20 minutes, then lower the heat to 350° and bake 20 to 30 minutes longer, or until the loaves are brown, have firm sides, and sound distinctly hollow when removed from the pans and tapped on the bottom.

Cool the bread thoroughly before slicing or storing it.

(For more detailed instructions, refer to the directions for **Basic Yeasted Whole Wheat Bread,** beginning on page 78.)

CHALLAH

BRAIDED EGG BREAD IS TRADITIONAL FOR THE JEWISH Sabbath. With proper development, this dough will triple into a light, airy loaf. Shape one large braid or, for an especially fancy bread, set two or three three-strand braids in graduated sizes atop one another. Of course, this dough does not have to be braided; it makes beautifully browned bread in any shape or size. You can also use a portion of the dough to make bread-crusted vegetable tarts (see pages 324-329), as I often do for dinner parties. Leftover challah makes exceptional French toast (page 349).

YIELD: 1 large loaf

PREPARATION TIME: About 2 hours for sponge and dough; 5 hours for rising; 40 to 50 minutes to bake

1²/₃ cups spring water	2 teaspoons sea salt
¹/₂ teaspoon active dry yeast	3 tablespoons corn or other vegetable oil
5¹/₂ to 6 cups whole wheat bread flour	Poppy seeds for garnishing loaves (optional)
3 large eggs, beaten (³/₄ cup)	

Heat ¹/₄ cup of the water and cool it to lukewarm. Add the yeast and a teaspoon of flour, cover, and set it in a warm spot to proof. Stir in the remaining water and about 2 cups of the flour and set it in a draft-free spot for about an hour, or until a sponge develops.

Reserve 2 to 3 teaspoons of the egg to use for a glaze. Stir the remainder of the egg and the salt and oil into the sponge. Gradually stir in enough of the remaining flour to form a dough.

Turn the dough out onto a lightly floured surface and cover it for several minutes. Knead the dough until smooth and elastic, adding flour as necessary to keep it from sticking.

Form the dough into a ball and place it in a lightly greased bowl. Cover and set it aside for about 2 hours, or until the dough has risen and does not spring back when pressed. Turn the dough out and knead it briefly. Return it to the bowl for a second rise.

Shape the dough (see page 88 for braiding instructions). Set the bread on a lightly greased or parchment-lined baking sheet. (Small braids may also be baked in loaf pans rather than freestanding). Cover the loaf and set it aside to rise for about an hour, or until the dough rebounds slowly when pressed.

Brush the loaf with the reserved egg and sprinkle on poppy seeds if you wish. Bake at 400° for 20 minutes, then lower the heat to 350° and bake 20 to 30 minutes longer. The loaves should be well-browned, have firm sides, and sound distinctly hollow when removed from the pans and tapped on the bottom.

Cool the bread thoroughly before slicing or storing it.

(For more detailed instructions, refer to the directions for **Basic Yeasted Whole Wheat Bread,** beginning on page 78.)

GINGERY CARROT BREAD

YIELD: 2 loaves

PREPARATION TIME: 2½ to 3 hours for sponge and dough; 5 hours for rising; 40 to 50 minutes to bake

THE PLEASANTLY PUNGENT AROMA AND ZESTY FLAVOR OF fresh ginger contribute to the special character of this orange-speckled bread. Cashews provide fat, contributing moistness as well as their subtle flavor. Use some of the dough for English muffins (see page 91).

2½ cups spring water
¾ teaspoon active dry
   yeast
7 to 7½ cups whole
   wheat bread flour
⅓ cup lightly toasted
   cashews

2½ teaspoons finely grated
   fresh ginger
2½ teaspoons sea salt
2½ cups lightly packed
   grated carrots

Heat ¼ cup of the water and cool it to lukewarm. Add the yeast and a teaspoon of flour, cover, and set it in a warm spot to proof. Combine the proofed yeast with 1¾ cups of the water in a large bowl. Stir in about 2½ cups of the flour to form a thick batter. Cover and set it in a draft-free spot for about 2 hours, or until a sponge develops.

Thoroughly blend the cashews and remaining ½ cup water in a blender and stir it into the sponge, along with the ginger, salt, and carrots. Gradually stir in enough of the remaining flour to form a dough.

Turn the dough out onto a lightly floured surface and cover it for several minutes. Knead the dough until smooth and elastic, adding more flour as necessary to keep it from sticking.

Form the dough into a ball and place it in a lightly greased bowl. Cover and set it aside for about 2 hours, or until the dough has risen and does not spring back when pressed. Turn the dough out and knead it briefly. Return it to the bowl for a second rise.

Shape and pan the dough. Cover the loaves and set

them aside to rise for about an hour, or until the dough rebounds slowly when pressed.

Slash the tops of the loaves. Bake at 400° for 20 minutes, then lower the heat to 350° and bake 20 to 30 minutes longer, or until the loaves are brown, have firm sides, and sound distinctly hollow when removed from the pans and tapped on the bottom.

Cool the bread thoroughly before slicing or storing it.

(For more detailed instructions, refer to the directions for **Basic Yeasted Whole Wheat Bread,** beginning on page 78.)

*A*pple or *P*ear *S*auce *B*read

THIS BREAD IS FINE GRAINED AND SLIGHTLY SWEET. IN the pear-growing region of central France, bakers customarily add black pepper to pear bread dough. Follow their lead, or try allspice, nutmeg, freshly grated or ground ginger, lemon zest, or aniseed to accentuate the fruit flavor. Or let the fruit stand on its own as I have here. Refer to the recipe for **Pear Butter** (page 255); use the milled fruit sauce before it has been cooked down to fruit butter.

1¹/₄ cups spring water
³/₄ teaspoon dry yeast
7¹/₂ cups whole wheat
    bread flour
2¹/₂ cups unsweetened
    apple sauce or pear
    sauce, at room
    temperature

2¹/₂ teaspoons sea salt
2¹/₂ tablespoons walnut or
    other vegetable oil
Egg wash (optional)

Heat ¹/₄ cup of the water and cool it to lukewarm. Add the yeast and a teaspoon of flour, cover, and set it in a warm spot to proof. Combine the proofed yeast with the remaining cup of water in a large bowl. Stir in a cup or so of the flour to form a thick batter. Cover and set it in

Notes
• Omit the cashews and add 2 tablespoons sesame or other vegetable oil; incorporate the extra ¹/₂ cup water and another ¹/₂ to ³/₄ cup flour in the sponge stage.

YIELD: 2 loaves

PREPARATION TIME: 1¹/₂ to 2 hours for sponge and dough; 5 hours for rising; 40 to 50 minutes to bake a draft-free spot for about an hour, or until a sponge develops.

Stir the fruit sauce, salt, and oil into the sponge. Gradually stir in enough flour to form a dough.

Turn the dough out onto a lightly floured surface and cover it for a few minutes. Knead the dough until smooth and elastic, adding flour as necessary to keep it from sticking.

Form the dough into a ball and place it in a lightly greased bowl. Cover and set it aside for about 2 hours, or until the dough has risen and does not spring back when pressed. Turn the dough out and knead it briefly. Return it to the bowl for a second rise.

Shape and pan the dough. Cover the loaves and set them aside to rise for about an hour, or until the dough rebounds slowly when pressed.

Slash the tops of the loaves and brush on an egg wash. Bake at 400° for 20 minutes, then lower the heat to 350° and bake 20 to 30 minutes longer, or until the loaves are brown, have firm sides, and sound distinctly hollow when removed from the pans and tapped on the bottom.

Cool the bread thoroughly before slicing or storing it.

(For more detailed instructions, refer to the directions for **Basic Yeasted Whole Wheat Bread,** beginning on page 78.)

DATE-ORANGE BREAD

YIELD: 2 loaves

PREPARATION TIME: 1½ to 2 hours for sponge and dough; 5 to 6 hours for rising; 40 to 50 minutes to bake

DATE PURÉE SEASONED WITH FRESH ORANGE ZEST AND juice contributes sweetness to the flavor of this bread. Medjool dates are my favorite. I like to make round loaves and garnish them with poppy seeds. This dough is a good choice for making **Sticky Buns** (page 341) and other coffee cakes.

2 to 2¹/₄ cups spring
water
³/₄ teaspoon active dry
yeast
6 to 6¹/₂ cups whole
wheat bread flour
1 orange
1 heaping cup dates
(¹/₂ pound), pitted
and chopped

2 teaspoons sea salt
2 tablespoons sesame,
walnut, or other
vegetable oil
Egg wash (optional)
Poppy seeds, for garnishing
loaves (optional)

Heat ¹/₄ cup of the water and cool it to lukewarm. Add the yeast and a teaspoon of the flour, cover, and set it in a warm spot to proof. Combine the proofed yeast with ³/₄ cup of the water in a large bowl. Stir in 1 cup or so of the flour to form a batter. Cover and set it in a draft-free spot for about an hour, or until a sponge develops.

Meanwhile, finely grate the zest of the orange into a saucepan. Juice the orange, measure the juice, and add water to equal 1 cup. Add this and the dates to the saucepan. Simmer, covered, over low heat for about 30 minutes. Cool somewhat. Blend in a blender or food processor until smooth. Measure and add water to equal 2 cups.

Stir the date mixture into the sponge, along with the salt and oil. Gradually add enough of the remaining flour to form a dough.

Turn the dough out onto a lightly floured surface and cover it for several minutes. Knead the dough until smooth and elastic, adding flour as necessary to keep it from sticking. Handle the dough carefully, since it tends to be somewhat tacky.

Form the dough into a ball and place it in a lightly greased bowl. Cover and set it aside for about 2 hours, or until the dough has risen and does not spring back when pressed. Turn the dough out and knead it briefly. Return it to the bowl for a second rise.

Notes
• Substitute a lemon for the orange—of course you will need more water to make up the cup of liquid for cooking the dates.
• Substitute other dried fruits—apricots, figs, or prunes—for the dates.

YIELD: 2 loaves

PREPARATION TIME: About 1 hour for sponge and dough; 5 hours for rising; 40 to 50 minutes to bake

Shape and pan the dough. Cover the loaves and set them aside to rise for about an hour, or until the dough rebounds slowly when pressed.

Slash the tops of the loaves. Brush on an egg wash and sprinkle on poppy seeds if you wish. Bake at 400° for 20 minutes, then lower the heat to 350° and bake 20 to 30 minutes longer, or until the loaves are brown, have firm sides, and sound distinctly hollow when removed from the pans and tapped on the bottom.

Cool the bread thoroughly before slicing or storing it.

(For more detailed instructions, refer to the directions for **Basic Yeasted Whole Wheat Bread,** beginning on page 78.)

POPPY SEED BREAD

THIS FINE-GRAINED BREAD IS FILLED WITH THE SUBTLE flavor and crunch of poppy seeds. Use a half pound of the dough to make the crust for a **Cabbage Kuchen** (page 326).

½ cup spring water
½ teaspoon active dry
*   yeast*
7 to 7½ cups whole
*   wheat bread flour*
2 cups milk or
*   unsweetened soy milk*

½ cup poppy seeds, plus
*   extra for garnishing loaves*
¼ cup mild-flavored honey
2 teaspoons sea salt
¼ cup sesame or other
*   vegetable oil*
2 eggs

Heat the water and cool it to lukewarm. Add the yeast and a teaspoon of flour, cover, and set it in a warm spot to proof. Stir in ½ cup of the flour and set it in a draft-free spot for about 30 minutes, or until a sponge develops.

Scald the milk and pour it over the poppy seeds in a large bowl. Add the honey, salt, and oil and set this mixture aside until lukewarm. Beat the eggs and reserve a teaspoon or two for glazing. Beat the remaining egg and the sponge into the cooled mixture. Gradually stir in enough of the remaining flour to form a dough.

Turn the dough out onto a lightly floured surface and cover it for several minutes. Knead the dough until smooth and elastic, adding flour as necessary to keep it from sticking.

Form the dough into a ball and place it in a lightly greased bowl. Cover and set it aside for about 2 hours, or until the dough has risen and does not spring back when pressed. Turn the dough out and knead it briefly. Return it to the bowl for a second rise.

Shape and pan the dough. Cover the loaves and set them aside to rise for about an hour, or until the dough rebounds slowly when pressed.

Slash the tops of the loaves; brush on the reserved egg and sprinkle them lightly with poppy seeds. Bake at 400° for 20 minutes, then lower the heat to 350° and bake 20 to 30 minutes longer, or until the loaves are brown, have firm sides, and sound distinctly hollow when removed from the pans and tapped on the bottom.

Cool the bread thoroughly before slicing or storing it.

(For more detailed instructions, refer to the directions for **Basic Yeasted Whole Wheat Bread,** beginning on page 78.)

Nut Butter Bread

DEFINITELY NUTTY TASTING, THIS BREAD HAS A SMOOTH, even texture. You can use a nut butter made with any kind of roasted nuts, and it can be chunky or smooth, as you wish.

YIELD: 2 loaves

PREPARATION TIME: About 2 hours for sponge and dough; 5 hours for rising; 40 to 50 minutes to bake

1¹/₃ cups spring water	²/₃ cup unsalted nut butter
³/₄ teaspoon active dry yeast	2¹/₂ teaspoons sea salt
6 to 6³/₄ cups whole wheat bread flour	Egg wash (optional)
2 cups milk or unsweetened soy milk	Sesame seeds or chopped nuts, for garnishing loaves (optional)

Heat $^1/_3$ cup of the water and cool it to lukewarm. Add the yeast and a teaspoon of flour, cover, and set it in a warm spot to proof. Combine the proofed yeast with the remaining cup of water in a large bowl. Stir in $1^1/_2$ to $1^3/_4$ cups of the flour to form a thick batter. Cover and set it in a draft-free spot for about $1^1/_2$ hours, or until a sponge develops.

Meanwhile, scald the milk and gradually whisk it with the nut butter and salt. Cool to lukewarm.

Stir the milk mixture into the sponge. Gradually stir in enough of the remaining flour to form a dough.

Turn the dough out onto a lightly floured surface and cover it for several minutes. Knead the dough until smooth and elastic, adding flour as necessary to keep it from sticking.

Form the dough into a ball and place it in a lightly greased bowl. Cover and set it aside for about 2 hours, or until the dough has risen and does not spring back when pressed. Turn the dough out and knead it briefly. Return it to the bowl for a second rise.

Shape and pan the dough. Cover the loaves and set them aside to rise for about an hour, or until the dough rebounds slowly when pressed.

Slash the tops of the loaves; brush on an egg wash and sprinkle on sesame seeds or finely chopped nuts. Bake at 400° for 20 minutes, then lower the heat to 350° and bake 20 to 30 minutes longer, until the loaves are brown, have firm sides, and sound distinctly hollow when removed from the pans and tapped on the bottom.

Cool the bread thoroughly before slicing or storing it.

(For more detailed instructions, refer to the directions for **Basic Yeasted Whole Wheat Bread,** beginning on page 78.)

CRACKED WHEAT BREAD

CRACKED WHEAT ADDS A PLEASANT CRUNCHINESS TO THIS great bread. Coarse cracked wheat gives the best texture. You can substitute cracked rye, steel-cut oats, or toasted buckwheat groats. This dough makes wonderful rolls and English muffins (see page 91).

YIELD: 2 loaves

PREPARATION TIME: About 1¹/₂ hours for sponge and dough; 5 hours for rising; 40 to 50 minutes to bake

2¹/₂ cups spring water	³/₄ teaspoon active dry yeast
1 cup cracked wheat	6 to 6¹/₂ cups whole wheat
1 cup milk or	bread flour
unsweetened soy milk,	2 teaspoons sea salt
scalded and cooled	2 to 4 tablespoons corn
to lukewarm	or other vegetable oil
1 tablespoon lemon juice	Egg wash (optional)

Boil 2 cups of the water and pour it over the cracked wheat in a large bowl. Set it aside until lukewarm. Combine the milk and lemon juice and set this aside to curdle.

Meanwhile, heat the remaining ¹/₂ cup of water and cool it to lukewarm. Add the yeast and a teaspoon of flour, cover, and set it in a warm spot to proof. Stir in ¹/₂ cup of flour, cover, and set it in a draft-free spot for about 30 minutes, or until a sponge develops.

Mix the sponge, curdled milk, salt, and oil with the soaked wheat. Gradually stir in enough of the remaining flour to form a dough.

Turn the dough out onto a lightly floured surface and cover it for several minutes. Knead the dough until smooth and elastic, adding flour as necessary to keep it from sticking.

Form the dough into a ball and place it in a lightly greased bowl. Cover and set it aside for about 2 hours, or until the dough has risen and does not spring back when pressed. Turn the dough out and knead it briefly. Return it to the bowl for a second rise.

Notes
• Substitute a flavorful vegetable stock for the wheat-soaking water.
• Substitute 1 cup buttermilk or yogurt for the milk and lemon juice.

Shape and pan the dough. Cover the loaves and set them aside to rise for about an hour, or until the dough rebounds slowly when pressed.

Slash the tops of the loaves; brush on egg wash. Bake at 400° for 20 minutes, then lower the heat to 350° and bake 20 to 30 minutes longer, or until the loaves are brown, have firm sides, and sound distinctly hollow when removed from the pans and tapped on the bottom.

Cool the bread thoroughly before slicing or storing it.

(For more detailed instructions, refer to the directions for **Basic Yeasted Whole Wheat Bread,** beginning on page 78.)

STEEL-CUT OATS BREAD

NATURALLY SWEET, MOIST, AND CHEWY, THIS BREAD makes wonderful toast.

YIELD: 2 loaves

PREPARATION TIME: 1½ hours for sponge and dough; 5 hours for rising; 40 to 50 minutes to bake

3 cups spring water

1 cup steel-cut oats

½ teaspoon active dry yeast

6 to 7 cups whole wheat bread flour

2 tablespoons sesame or other vegetable oil

2 teaspoons sea salt

Egg wash (optional)

Poppy or sesame seeds, for garnishing loaves (optional)

Boil 2 cups of the water and pour it over the oats in a large bowl. Set it aside until lukewarm.

Meanwhile, heat ¼ cup of the remaining water and cool it to lukewarm. Add the yeast and a teaspoon of flour, cover, and set it in a warm spot to proof. Stir in the remaining ¾ cup water and a cup or so of the flour, cover, and set it in a draft-free spot for about an hour, or until a sponge develops.

Stir the sponge into the oats along with the oil and salt. Gradually stir in enough of the remaining flour to form a dough.

Turn the dough out onto a lightly floured surface and

cover it for several minutes. Knead the dough until smooth and elastic, adding flour as necessary to keep it from sticking.

Form the dough into a ball and place it in a lightly greased bowl. Cover and set it aside for about 2 hours, or until the dough has risen and does not spring back when pressed. Turn the dough out and knead it briefly. Return it to the bowl for a second rise.

Shape and pan the dough. Cover the loaves and set them aside to rise for about an hour, or until the dough rebounds slowly when pressed.

Slash the tops of the loaves. Brush them with an egg wash and sprinkle on sesame or poppy seeds. Bake at 400° for 20 minutes, then lower the heat to 350° and bake 20 to 30 minutes longer, or until the loaves are brown, have firm sides, and sound distinctly hollow when removed from the pans and tapped on the bottom.

Cool the bread thoroughly before slicing or storing it.

(For more detailed instructions, refer to the directions for **Basic Yeasted Whole Wheat Bread,** beginning on page 78.)

ℛOLLED OATS ℬREAD

THIS OAT BREAD HAS A FINER TEXTURE THAN THE PRE-ceding one. It's also great for toasting. For a delicious raisin bread, knead 2 cups of raisins into the dough before shaping it into loaves, or make one loaf with raisins and one loaf without.

3 cups spring water	3/4 teaspoon active dry yeast
1 cup rolled oats	6 cups whole wheat bread
2 teaspoons sea salt	flour
2 tablespoons sesame or other vegetable oil	

Boil 2 cups of the water and pour it over the oats in a large bowl. Add the salt and oil and set it aside until lukewarm.

Notes
• Add 2 tablespoons molasses, honey, or maple or brown rice syrup to the hot oat mixture.

YIELD: 2 loaves

PREPARATION TIME: About 1½ hours for sponge and dough; 5 hours for rising; 40 to 50 minutes to bake

Notes
•Add 2 tablespoons of maple syrup to the oats along with the salt and oil.

Heat ¼ cup of the water and cool it to lukewarm. Add the yeast and a teaspoon of flour, cover, and set it in a warm spot to proof. Add the remaining ¾ cup of water and stir in about 1 cup of the flour. Cover and set it in a draft-free spot for about an hour, or until a sponge develops.

Stir the sponge into the cooled oat mixture. Gradually stir in enough of the flour to form a dough.

Turn the dough out onto a lightly floured surface, and cover it for several minutes. Knead the dough until smooth and elastic, adding flour as necessary to keep it from sticking.

Form the dough into a ball and place it in a lightly greased bowl. Cover and set it aside for about 2 hours, or until the dough has risen and does not spring back when pressed. Turn the dough out and knead it briefly. Return it to the bowl for a second rise.

Shape and pan the dough. Cover the loaves and set them aside to rise for about an hour, or until the dough rebounds slowly when pressed.

Slash the tops of the loaves. Bake at 400° for 20 minutes, then lower the heat to 350° and bake for 20 to 30 minutes longer, or until the loaves are brown, have firm sides, and sound distinctly hollow when removed from the pans and tapped on the bottom.

Cool the bread thoroughly before slicing or storing it.

(For more detailed instructions, refer to the directions for **Basic Yeasted Whole Wheat Bread,** beginning on page 78.)

YIELD: 2 loaves

PREPARATION TIME: About 2½ hours to cook and cool the grits and prepare the sponge and dough; 5 hours to rise; 40 to 50 minutes to bake

TRUE GRITS BREAD

BOLSTER YOUR FORTITUDE WITH THIS SLIGHTLY SWEET and chewy bread. You may substitute another kind of grits—soy, rice, or barley—for corn grits.

3¼ cups spring water
½ cup corn grits
¾ teaspoon active dry
yeast
6 to 6½ cups whole
wheat bread flour

2 teaspoons sea salt
2 tablespoons corn
or other vegetable oil

In a medium-sized saucepan, bring 1½ cups of the water to a boil. Slowly sprinkle the grits into the boiling water, stirring constantly. Reduce the heat to low, cover tightly, and cook 5 minutes, until the grits have thickened. Turn off the heat and leave the pot covered until the grits have cooled to lukewarm.

Heat ¼ cup of the water and cool it to lukewarm. Add the yeast and a teaspoon of the flour, cover, and set it in a warm spot to proof. Combine the proofed yeast with the remaining 1½ cups water in a large bowl. Stir in 2 cups or so of the flour to form a thick batter. Cover and set it in a draft-free spot for about 2 hours, or until a sponge develops.

Stir the cooled grits, salt, and oil into the sponge. Gradually stir in enough of the remaining flour to form a dough.

Turn the dough out onto a lightly floured surface and cover it for several minutes. Knead the dough until smooth and elastic, adding more flour as necessary to keep it from sticking. This dough tends to be tacky and requires somewhat gentle kneading.

Form the dough into a ball and place it in a lightly greased bowl. Cover and set it aside for about 2 hours, or until the dough has risen and does not spring back when pressed. Turn the dough out and knead it briefly. Return it to the bowl for a second rise.

Shape and pan the dough. Cover the loaves and set them aside to rise for about an hour, or until the dough rebounds slowly when pressed.

Slash the tops of the loaves. Brush the tops lightly with oil. Bake at 400° for 20 minutes, then lower the heat to 350° and bake 20 to 30 minutes longer, or until the loaves are brown, have firm sides, and sound distinctly hollow when removed from the pans and tapped on the bottom.

Cool the bread thoroughly before slicing or storing it.

(For more detailed instructions, refer to the directions for **Basic Yeasted Whole Wheat Bread,** beginning on page 78.)

LIMPA RYE

FENNEL, CARAWAY, AND ORANGE FLAVOR THIS LIGHT, Swedish-style rye bread. You can substitute cracked wheat for the cracked rye.

YIELD: 2 round loaves

PREPARATION TIME: 2½ to 3 hours for sponge and dough; 5 hours for rising; 40 to 50 minutes to bake

2²/₃ cups spring water
½ cup cracked rye
2 teaspoons sea salt
³/₄ teaspoon active dry yeast
3½ to 4½ cups whole wheat bread flour
1½ teaspoons fennel seeds

1½ teaspoons caraway seeds
1 to 2 tablespoons freshly grated orange zest
Juice of 1 orange (about ⅓ cup)
2 tablespoons corn or other vegetable oil
2 cups rye flour

Heat 1 cup of the water to boiling and pour it over the cracked rye and salt in a large bowl; set aside until lukewarm.

Heat ⅓ cup of the water and cool it to lukewarm. Add the yeast and a teaspoon of wheat flour, cover, and set it in a warm spot to proof. Combine the proofed yeast with the remaining 1⅓ cups water in a large bowl. Gradually stir in about 3 cups of the wheat flour to form a thick batter. Cover and set it in a draft-free spot for about 2 hours, or until a sponge develops.

In a heavy-bottomed, ungreased skillet over medium

heat, roast the fennel and caraway seeds, stirring or agitating the pan often to prevent them from burning. Grind the seeds to a coarse consistency with a mortar and pestle or spice grinder.

Stir the soaked rye, ground seeds, orange zest, orange juice, and oil into the sponge. Gradually stir in the rye flour and then enough of the remaining wheat flour to form a dough.

Turn the dough out onto a lightly floured surface and cover it for several minutes. Knead the dough until smooth and elastic, adding more wheat flour as necessary to keep it from sticking. Knead carefully and expect the dough to remain a bit tacky.

Form the dough into a ball and place it in a lightly greased bowl. Cover and set it aside for about 2 hours, or until the dough has risen and does not spring back when pressed. Turn the dough out and knead it briefly. Return it to the bowl for a second rise.

Shape and pan 2 round loaves. Cover the loaves and set them aside to rise for about an hour, or until the dough rebounds slowly when pressed.

Dock or slash the tops of the loaves. Bake at 400° for 20 minutes, then lower the heat to 350° and bake 20 to 30 minutes longer, or until the loaves are brown, have firm sides, and sound distinctly hollow when removed from the pans and tapped on the bottom.

Cool the bread thoroughly before slicing or storing it.

(For more detailed instructions, refer to the directions for **Basic Yeasted Whole Wheat Bread,** beginning on page 78.)

Pumpernickel-Rye Bread

IRONICALLY, THE NEW YORK NIGHTCLUB FAT TUESDAY'S IS long and narrow, and a 14-piece jazz band was stretched out along practically the entire length of one wall of the club. The musicians were so close to us in the audience

YIELD: 2 large loaves

PREPARATION TIME: 2½ to 3 hours for sponge and dough; 5 hours for rising; 40 to 50 minutes to bake

that my knees were almost bumping those of the sax player. He had music on his stand, but as he played, his eyes were transfixed on the partially consumed loaf of pumpernickel just about under his nose at the end of our table. And he blew up a storm of improvisional licks. When I reached out to cut another slice of bread, he lowered his horn and, with a glint in his eyes, cautioned me, "You'd better leave that fine-looking bread right where it is—it's my inspiration." I hope this dark, rich pumpernickel bread will be your inspiration!

Carob powder is made from the dried ground pods of the locust tree, a Mediterranean evergreen. Sometimes called St. John's Bread because John the Baptist is thought to have eaten it when he lived in the wilderness, it is sold both raw and roasted. The longer carob is roasted, the darker it becomes and the richer its flavor. Carob is high in calcium and contains other minerals and vitamins. It is low in fat, easy to digest, and naturally sweet. Carob is often considered a chocolate substitute but deserves to be judged on its own merits. Substitute it equally for cocoa in beverages and baked goods but reduce the amount of sweetener. Store carob powder in a cool, dry spot and sift it through a strainer if it becomes caked.

3½ cups plus 2 tablespoons spring water
¼ cup soy grits
2 tablespoons Cafix or other instant grain beverage
¾ teaspoon active dry yeast
6 cups whole wheat bread flour
2 tablespoons roasted carob powder

2 tablespoons blackstrap molasses
Grated zest of 1 orange
2 teaspoons sea salt
4 tablespoons corn or other vegetable oil
1 cup rye flakes, ground to the consistency of coarse meal
1½ cups rye flour

Boil ½ cup of the water and pour it over the grits and Cafix. Set it aside until lukewarm.

Heat ¼ cup of the water and cool it to lukewarm. Add the yeast and a teaspoon of the wheat flour, cover, and set it in a warm place to proof. Add the proofed yeast to 2¾ cups of the water in a large bowl. Gradually stir in about 3½ cups of the wheat flour to form a thick batter. Cover and set it in a draft-free spot for about 2 hours, or until a sponge develops.

Mix the remaining 2 tablespoons of water and the carob powder to a smooth paste. Stir this, along with the soaked grits, molasses, orange zest, salt, and oil, into the sponge. Stir in the rye meal and rye flour and then gradually stir in enough of the remaining wheat flour to form a dough.

Turn the dough out onto a lightly floured surface and cover it for several minutes. Knead the dough until smooth and elastic, adding more wheat flour as necessary to keep it from sticking. Handle the dough carefully and expect it to remain somewhat tacky.

Form the dough into a ball and place it in a lightly greased bowl. Cover and set it aside for about 2 hours, or until the dough has risen and does not spring back when pressed. Turn the dough out and knead it briefly. Return it to the bowl for a second rise.

Shape the loaves; I make 2 round or oval freestanding loaves. Cover the loaves and set them aside to rise for about an hour, or until the dough rebounds slowly when pressed.

Slash or dock the tops of the loaves. Bake at 400° for 20 minutes, then lower the heat to 350° and bake 20 to 30 minutes longer, or until the loaves are brown, have firm sides, and sound distinctly hollow when removed from the pans and tapped on the bottom. For a shiny crust, brush a cornstarch wash (see page 89) onto the loaves halfway through baking and again about 5 minutes before they are done.

Cool the bread thoroughly before slicing or storing it.

(For more detailed instructions, refer to the directions for **Basic Yeasted Whole Wheat Bread,** beginning on page 78.)

$\mathcal{A}$LAN'S $\mathcal{F}$RENCH $\mathcal{B}$READ

THE FRENCH WOULD BE LOATHE TO LAY CLAIM TO MUCH of the "French" bread that is made in this country, since it lacks the well-developed flavor and crisp crust that characterize an exemplary French loaf. These signature traits depend on long, slow rises and a steamy, hot oven,

Notes
• Substitute oat flakes or bran for the rye flakes.
• Add 1 tablespoon caraway seeds and omit the orange zest if you prefer.
• For **Pumpernickel-Rye Raisin Bread,** knead 1 to 2 cups of soft raisins or currants into the dough before shaping.

YIELD: 2 small loaves or 1 large one

PREPARATION TIME: $2^{1}/_{3}$ to 3 hours for sponge and dough; 6 hours for rising; 20 to 50 minutes to bake

respectively. Years ago, Alan Harris, a friendly baker in Massachusetts, taught me his French bread secrets, including an especially effect way to shape the long, thin loaves called baguettes. This is a whole grain version of Alan's French bread recipe. Following tradition, this French bread is oil-free. For a head start on the bread, mix the sponge and let it rise in the refrigerator overnight.

$1^2/_3$ cups spring water	4 cups whole wheat
$1/_2$ teaspoon active	bread flour
dry yeast	$1^1/_2$ teaspoons sea salt

Heat $1/_3$ cup of the water and cool it to lukewarm. Add the yeast and a teaspoon of flour and set it in a warm spot to proof. Stir in the remaining $1^1/_3$ cups water and about 2 cups of the flour to form a thick batter. Set it in a draft-free spot for about 2 hours, or until a sponge develops.

Stir the salt into the sponge. Gradually stir in enough of the remaining flour to form a dough.

Turn the dough out onto a lightly floured surface and cover it for several minutes, or until it relaxes. Knead the dough until smooth and elastic, adding flour as necessary to keep it from sticking.

Form the dough into a ball and place it in a clean, ungreased bowl. Cover and set it aside at cool room temperature for about 2 hours, or until the dough has risen and does not spring back when pressed. Turn the dough out and knead it briefly. Return it to the bowl for a second rise.

Turn the dough out and cut it in two. Knead each piece briefly and round it into a ball. Set the balls on a lightly floured surface and cover them with a damp towel.

When the balls have risen into puffy dough balloons, shape the loaves. To form baguettes, press the air out of the dough until you have a flat circle, fold the circle in half, and pound the edges together with your fist. Turn the straight edge to face you, pull the curved edge over to meet the straight edge, and pound the two edges securely all along their length to form a narrow cylinder. Place your hands on top of and in the middle of the dough and, with a gentle but firm back-and-forth motion, roll the dough and move your hands toward the ends of the cylinder, expanding its length—just like making coils out of clay. Repeat until the dough is about 10 inches long (longer for a large baguette). For round loaves, shape as described on page 89.

Alan puts baguettes to rise, seam side up, between folds of heavy canvas dusted with flour. When they have risen, he carefully flips one at a time over onto a wooden paddle called a baker's peel, and transfers it to the floor of his oven to bake. If you have baking tiles or a baking stone, you can follow this technique. If you use long baguette pans or baking sheets, lightly sprinkle them with cornmeal before putting the loaves on them to rise seam side down. Let round loaves rise, seam side up, in baskets lined with flour-dusted cloth. Or, place them seam side down on cornmeal-dusted sheets, or in round containers greased and dusted with cornmeal.

Near the end of the rising period, which will take about 1 hour, preheat the oven to 450°. If you are baking on tiles or on a baking stone, preheat them as the oven heats. When the shaped loaves have risen and rebound slowly when pressed with a finger, slash the tops, spray them with cold water, and place them in the preheated oven. Spray the loaves every 5 minutes for the first 10 to 15 minutes of baking. Bake baguettes 20 to 25 minutes, or until the crust is brown and crisp. Bake a large round loaf at 450° for the first 15 minutes and then reduce the temperature to 350° and bake 20 to 30 minutes longer, or until it sounds distinctly hollow when tapped on the bottom.

Notes

- In addition to spraying the loaves to create steam in the oven, place a pan of boiling water on the bottom of the oven for the first 15 minutes of baking.
- For a crusty, whole grain **Italian Bread,** add 2 tablespoons olive oil to the sponge along with the salt.

BRIOCHE

YIELD: 6 (3½-inch) brioche or 12 muffin-sized ones

PREPARATION TIME: 3 to 3½ hours for sponge and dough; at least 30 minutes for chilling the dough; 1½ to 2 hours for shaping and rising; 15 to 25 minutes to bake

JAUNTY TOPKNOTS CHARACTERIZE THESE RICH FRENCH buns. Brioche are traditionally baked in special fluted tins that come in many sizes. If you don't have brioche pans, use Pyrex custard cups or muffin tins for smaller brioche or form the dough into a loaf—round with a topknot, braided, or some other shape. An egg wash gives brioche a deep brown crust; their crumb is soft and tender. Like other egg-rich breads, brioche tend to dry out quickly and they are best when freshly baked.

¼ cup spring water	1 tablespoon honey
2 teaspoons active dry yeast	½ teaspoon sea salt
1⅔ to 2 cups whole wheat bread flour	¼ pound (4 ounces or 1 stick) unsalted margarine or butter, melted and cooled to lukewarm
4 eggs, at room temperature	

Heat the water and cool it to lukewarm. Add the yeast and a teaspoon of flour, cover, and set it aside in a warm spot to proof. Whisk the proofed yeast with 1 egg in a medium-sized mixing bowl. Beat in ⅔ cup of the flour to form a batter. Cover and set it in a draft-free spot for 1½ to 2 hours, or until a sponge has developed.

Beat the honey, salt, 2 eggs, and ⅔ cup flour into the sponge. Beating vigorously, gradually add the melted margarine. Add flour, ⅓ cup at a time, stirring well after each addition, to form a dough. Turn the dough out onto a lightly floured surface and cover it for a few minutes. Wash the bowl and fill it with warm water.

Knead the dough, lightly sprinkling flour under it as necessary to keep it from sticking. When the dough is smooth and elastic, form it into a ball. Dry the bowl and put in the dough, cover, and set it in a draft-free spot for about an hour, or until well risen.

Turn the dough out onto a lightly floured surface and shape it into a long rectangle. From the short side, fold in $1/3$ of the dough and then fold in the opposite side. Sprinkle the dough lightly with flour and wrap it snugly in plastic wrap. Chill it in the refrigerator for at least 30 minutes. If you want to wait several hours or overnight to shape the dough, place the wrapped dough in a container and set a weight on top to restrict its rising; I put it in a loaf pan with a small breadboard on top and an old flatiron on top of that. Wrapped and weighted, the dough will keep for up to 3 days.

For traditional individual brioche tins, 3 inches in diameter at the top, cut the dough into 12 equal pieces; for $3^1/2$-inch Pyrex custard cups, cut it into 6 pieces. Cut a small piece off each piece to use for the topknot. Follow the regular roll-making technique described on page 91 to form balls. For each brioche, place the large ball into a well-greased pan. Form a point about $1/2$ inch long on the small ball. Dip a finger in flour and then poke a deep depression in the top of the large ball. Fit the small ball inside the hole. Arrange the brioche pans on a baking sheet, cover them lightly, and place them in a draft-free spot for 1 to 2 hours, or until the dough is well risen.

Preheat the oven to 425°. Beat the remaining egg with a bit of water. Brush the buns with this wash, then brush them a second time. Bake 5 minutes for small brioches or 10 minutes for larger ones. Turn the oven down to 375° and bake 10 to 15 minutes longer, or until the brioche are browned and a tester inserted into the center comes out clean. Remove them from the pans, cool briefly, and serve warm.

CROISSANTS

YIELD: 6 croissants

PREPARATION TIME: 2 hours to prepare and chill the dough; 30 to 40 minutes to layer the dough and several hours for chilling; 15 minutes to shape; 1½ to 2 hours for rising; about 15 minutes to bake

I VISITED PARIS FOR THE FIRST TIME WHEN I WAS NINE-teen, and this is where I tasted my first croissants. Each morning, I joined Parisians at a bustling café counter and washed down two light, flaky rolls with a large, handleless cup of steaming cafe au lait and felt very French. Now, a bite of the fresh crusty crescents can transport me back to my adventuresome youth. The expansive texture of these delicate pastries results from the many alternate layers of dough and fat that puff apart when exposed to high oven heat. Besides enhanced nutrition, whole wheat croissants have a fuller flavor than those made from refined flour. If I plan on croissants for a late breakfast, I do everything but the shaping the day before, chill the dough overnight, and take it out for shaping and rising about 2½ hours before serving.

³/₄ cup milk or unsweetened soy milk, scalded	¹/₄ cup whole wheat pastry flour
1½ teaspoons honey	1³/₄ cups whole wheat bread flour
¹/₂ teaspoon sea salt	¹/₄ pound (4 ounces or 1 stick) unsalted soy margarine
¹/₄ cup plus 1 teaspoon spring water	
1 teaspoon active dry yeast	1 egg

Combine the milk, honey, and salt in a medium-sized bowl and set it aside to cool to lukewarm.

Heat ¹/₄ cup of the water and cool it to lukewarm. Add the yeast and a teaspoon of flour, cover, and set it in a warm spot to proof.

Beat the proofed yeast and pastry flour into the milk mixture. Gradually stir in bread flour until a soft dough forms. Turn the dough out onto a lightly floured surface and knead it briefly—just a minute or two—until smooth. Developing the gluten too much will make the dough difficult to roll out later. Wash and dry the bowl and place the dough in it. Cover the bowl with plastic wrap or a plastic bag, and put it in the refrigerator for about $1\frac{1}{2}$ hours.

Cut the stick of margarine in half crosswise and then cut each piece in half lengthwise. Lay the pieces adjacent to one another on a piece of waxed paper. Draw a 4 x 6-inch rectangle on another piece of waxed paper and center it on top of the margarine. Using the drawing as a guide, roll the margarine into a 4 x 6-inch rectangle, and refrigerate it between the waxed paper.

On a lightly floured surface, roll the dough into a 6 x 11-inch rectangle. Peel the top piece of waxed paper off the margarine and position the margarine on one side of the dough, leaving a 1-inch border uncovered—the margarine will cover about two-thirds of the length of the dough. Remove the other piece of waxed paper and, with the back of a knife, score the margarine in half parallel to the short side of the rectangle. Fold the uncovered third of the dough over the center third and fold in the other side like a business letter. Place the short side of the folded dough parallel to the front edge of your work surface and carefully roll the dough into a 6 x 11 rectangle, and once again fold it in thirds. Wrap the dough tightly with lightly floured plastic wrap and then put it in a plastic bag. Refrigerate the wrapped dough, topped with a weight (I use an old flatiron). It's a good idea to put the wrapped dough in a loaf pan so that the weight will not topple off as the dough rises. Chill the dough for at least 1 hour, or up to several hours.

On a lightly floured surface, roll and fold the dough as before (but without adding more margarine) two more times. Wrap, refrigerate, and weight it. Chill it for at least 2 hours and as long as overnight.

On a lightly floured surface, roll the dough into a 6 x 18-inch rectangle. Cut it into three 6-inch squares. Cut each square into two triangles. With the wide side of a triangle facing you, roll the dough so that you expand the triangle to approximately 8 inches on each side. Roll up the triangle starting from the base, encouraging the two base points to curl inward and ending with the top point lapped over the front just to the bottom of the roll but not tucked underneath. Shape the other croissants in the same manner.

Arrange the croissants on a parchment-lined or ungreased baking sheet. Whisk the egg and 1 teaspoon water and brush a dab under each of the overlapping points. Brush the croissants with the egg wash. Set the sheet in a warm, draft-free spot for 1½ to 2 hours, or until the croissants are well risen.

Preheat the oven to 450°. Give the croissants a second coat of egg wash. Bake 15 minutes, or until they are deep brown and crusty. Serve them warm.

DANISH PASTRIES

YIELD: 8 individual pastries or 1 braid or coffee cake

PREPARATION TIME: 2 hours for the dough; 1 hour to layer the dough with 3½ hours of interspersed chilling; 1½ hours to shape and rise; 10 to 15 minutes to bake

DANISH DOUGH IS MADE BY A TECHNIQUE SIMILAR TO that for croissants, but these pastries are even richer and flakier. Danishes can be shaped in a number of ways and stuffed with a variety of fillings; here I fill them with a sweet and spicy ground almond mixture. Though these pastries take some time to make, they're fun to fuss with for a special occasion. You can do everything but shaping, rising, and baking the day before and chill the dough overnight; take the dough out 2 to 2½ hours before serving.

¼ cup whole wheat pastry flour plus extra for rolling the dough
1¼ cups whole wheat bread flour
6 tablespoons plus 1 teaspoon spring water

¼ teaspoon ground cardamom
3 tablespoons mild-flavored honey
¼ teaspoon sea salt
1 tablespoon active dry yeast

3 eggs

5 ounces (1¼ sticks)
   unsalted soy margarine
   or butter, chilled

Grated zest of 1 orange
   (about 1 teaspoon)

¼ teaspoon cinnamon

¼ cup lightly toasted
   almonds, finely chopped

Sift together the ¼ cup pastry flour and the bread flour and set it aside.

Heat 2 tablespoons of the water and whisk it with the cardamom, 1 tablespoon of the honey, and the salt in a medium-sized bowl; set this aside to cool.

Heat ¼ cup of the water and cool it to lukewarm. Add the yeast and a teaspoon of flour, cover, and set it in a warm spot to proof.

Add the proofed yeast to the bowl along with 1 egg and whisk well. Gradually beat in the flour to form a soft dough that pulls away from the sides of the bowl. Scrape down the bowl, cover it tightly with plastic wrap, and refrigerate for 1½ hours.

Roll the margarine between two pieces of waxed paper into a 4 x 6-inch rectangle. Refrigerate it until firm.

Turn the dough out onto a work surface lightly sprinkled with pastry flour. Adding flour as necessary to keep the dough from sticking, roll it into a 6 x 11-inch rectangle. Peel the waxed paper off one side of the margarine and position the margarine on one end of the dough, leaving a 1-inch border on three sides; it will cover about two-thirds of the length of the dough. Peel off the remaining waxed paper and lightly score the margarine down the middle, parallel to the short side of the rectangle. Fold the uncovered third of the dough over the center third. Fold the other side in to totally encase the margarine.

Flour the work surface and carefully roll the dough into a 6 x 11-inch rectangle. Fold it in thirds again. Wrap the folded dough in lightly floured plastic wrap and then

Notes
• Fruit butters and dried fruit purées are good alternative fillings; see **Pear Butter** (page 255). You can also used a cooked fruit filling, such as that for **Crisscross Coffee Cake** (page 344).

in a plastic bag. Refrigerate this package with a weight on top to prevent the gluten in the dough from stretching beyond its limits and breaking. Chill it for 1 hour.

Position the dough on a floured work surface with its short edge closer to you. Roll it into a 6 x 11-inch rectangle. Fold it in thirds and turn it so that the short side is again in front. Repeat. Wrap, refrigerate, and weight the dough. Chill it for 2 hours.

Roll and fold the dough 2 more times. Chill it, weighted, for 30 minutes.

To make the filling, whisk together the orange zest, 1 egg, the cinnamon, and the remaining 2 tablespoons honey in a small bowl. Thoroughly mix in the almonds. If the mixture is very stiff, juice the orange and add some of the orange juice; it should be moist but still hold its shape. Set this aside.

On a lightly flowered surface, roll the dough into an 8 x 16-inch rectangle. With a sharp knife, cut off a narrow strip of dough along each side and discard it. Cut the rectangle into 4-inch squares. You may shape and fill these in different ways:

ᴠ Place ⅛ of the filling in the center of each square. Fold one corner to the center and brush it with a bit of egg wash (the remaining egg beaten with the teaspoon of water). Fold the opposite corner to the center, and press it onto the first one to seal it.

ᴠ For envelopes, follow the procedure above but fold all four corners in, or fold the corners of the dough in and place the filling on top.

ᴠ For cockscombs, fill half of each square and brush the edges with egg wash. Fold the dough in half to enclose the filling. Make cuts almost to the filling at ¾- to 1-inch intervals along the long sealed side, and spread the pastry open along the cut side.

ᴠ For pinwheels, make a cut from each corner toward the center of the square (about an inch from the center).

Place filling in the center, and fold the edge to the right of each corner into the center, pressing the points together in the middle.

∾ To form a coffee cake, leave the 8 x 16-inch rectangle intact and spread the filling evenly over the surface. Roll up the dough from the long side and pinch the edges together. Form this filled log into a ring, joining the ends. Slash the top at equal intervals to allow for expansion.

∾ For spiral pastries, form a filled log and cut it crosswise into 1-inch slices. Lay each slice on its side to bake.

∾ For a crisscross coffee cake, follow directions on page 344.

Arrange pastries on a parchment-lined or lightly greased baking sheet. Cover them loosely with a towel or lightly floured plastic wrap or waxed paper. Let pastries rise for 45 minutes, or until they appear light and puffy.

Preheat the oven to 400°. Lightly brush the pastries with the remaining egg wash. Bake 10 to 15 minutes, or until they are well browned and crisp. Serve them warm.

KUGELHOPF

THERE ARE MANY VERSIONS OF THIS ALMOND-STUDDED bread and almost as many ways to spell its name, since several nations, including Austria and France, participated in its creation. Marie Antoinette may have been referring to kugelhopf when she declared, "Let them eat cake!" and ignited the French Revolution. The light, slightly sweet, raisin-and-nut-laced dough is often an unkneaded but vigorously beaten yeasted batter as it is here. For an elegant shaped bread, bake it in a traditional, decoratively fluted baking pan. Serve kugelhopf as a dessert with dry white wine or champagne or for breakfast plain, warmed, or toasted. **Pear Butter** (page 255) is a delicious topping.

YIELD: 1 large bread

PREPARATION TIME: About 1 hour to prepare; 3 hours for rising; 50 minutes to bake

$^1/_3$ cup dry white wine
(such as a chardonnay)

$^2/_3$ cup raisins

$^1/_2$ cup spring water

$^1/_2$ teaspoon active dry
yeast

3 cups whole wheat
bread flour

$^1/_4$ cup sunflower or
other vegetable oil

$^1/_4$ cup mild-flavored
honey

2 to 3 eggs—to equal
$^1/_2$ cup

1 cup milk or unsweetened
soy milk, scalded and
cooled to lukewarm

1 teaspoon sea salt

$^1/_3$ cup lightly toasted
chopped almonds

1 tablespoon unsalted
butter or soy margarine,
softened

2 tablespoons bran

16 whole lightly toasted
almonds

Pour the wine over the raisins in a deep bowl and marinate them for about an hour. Drain well and save the sweet wine—it's good served on the kugelhopf.

Heat the water and cool it to lukewarm. Add the yeast and a teaspoon of flour, cover, and set it in a warm spot to proof. Stir in $^1/_2$ cup of the flour. Cover and set it in a draft-free spot for about 30 minutes, or until a sponge develops.

In a large bowl, whisk together the oil and honey. Whisk in the eggs and then the milk, salt, and sponge. Add the remaining flour, $^1/_2$ cup at a time, beating well with a wooden spoon after each addition; the batter should become elastic as you develop the gluten in the flour. Stir in the raisins and chopped nuts. Scrape any dough on the sides of the bowl into the center, cover, and set it in a draft-free spot for about 2 hours, or until the batter has doubled.

Thoroughly grease a 9-inch, 10-cup kugelhopf tube pan (or a pan of comparable volume) with the softened butter or margarine. Dust the pan with the bran. Arrange the whole almonds in the bottom. Evenly distribute the batter in the pan; it will be about half full. Cover the pan with a damp towel for about an hour, until the batter has risen almost to the top.

Put the pan in a cold oven and set the temperature to 350°. Bake for 50 minutes, or until the bread is well browned and a tester inserted to the bottom of the pan comes out clean. Cool the kugelhopf in the pan briefly, then turn it out onto a rack to finish cooling.

CRUMPETS

CRUMPETS ARE MADE FROM A BEATEN RATHER THAN A kneaded yeasted dough and are cooked on a griddle. They are similar to English muffins (see page 91) but are somewhat more moist and porous.

(see page 91)

³/₄ cup spring water
¹/₂ teaspoon active dry yeast
1 cup whole wheat
 bread flour
¹/₂ cup milk or
 unsweetened soy milk,
 scalded and cooled to
 lukewarm

¹/₂ teaspoon sea salt
¹/₂ cup whole wheat pastry
 flour
¹/₄ teaspoon baking soda

Notes
• Add the finely grated zest of 1 lemon; whisk it into the liquid mixture before beating in the flour.

YIELD: 6 (4-inch) crumpets

PREPARATION TIME: 30 to 40 minutes to prepare; 2 to 4 hours for rising; about 20 minutes to cook each batch

Heat ¹/₂ cup of the water and cool it to lukewarm in a medium-sized bowl. Add the yeast and a teaspoon of flour, cover, and set it in a warm spot to proof. Stir in ¹/₂ cup of the bread flour, cover, and set it in a draft-free spot for about 30 minutes, until a sponge develops.

Stir in the milk, salt, pastry flour, and the remaining bread flour, beating well with a wooden spoon after each addition, to form a soft dough. Cover and set it aside for 1 to 2 hours, or until the dough has doubled.

Dissolve the baking soda in the remaining ¹/₄ cup water and thoroughly stir it into the dough to achieve a batterlike consistency. Cover the batter for 1 to 2 hours, or until it doubles.

Set a griddle over medium heat. Liberally grease the

Notes

• If you don't have crumpet rings (metal rings 4 inches in diameter and 3/4 inch high), remove the bottom from empty tuna or comparable cans; try to find cans without lead-soldered seams. Add batter to a depth of about 1/2 inch.

inside of the crumpet rings and lightly grease the surface of the hot griddle. Arrange crumpet rings on the griddle and spoon the dough into them, nudging it against the sides, to a depth of about 1/2 inch. Cook for 10 to 15 minutes, or until the top surface has bubbled and dried and the bottom has browned. Turn the crumpets and remove the rings. Cook 5 minutes or so, or until the second side browns. Cool the crumpets on a rack.

Carefully insert the tines of a fork around the edge of a crumpet and gently pull the halves apart. Serve them toasted, topped with margarine, butter, preserves, marmalade, or fruit butters.

YEASTED CORN BREAD

THIS YEASTED CORN BREAD HAS A DIFFERENT TEXTURE than its chemically leavened cousins and it keeps better. Serve it with chili or soups.

YIELD: 1 (8-inch) square or (9-inch) round pan

PREPARATION TIME: 15 to 20 minutes to prepare; 2 hours for rising; 30 minutes to bake

1/4 cup spring water	1/2 teaspoon sea salt
1 1/2 teaspoons active dry yeast	2 tablespoons sesame, corn, or other vegetable oil
1 cup whole wheat bread flour	1 egg
1 cup milk or unsweetened soy milk, scalded	1 cup cornmeal
2 tablespoons maple syrup	1/4 cup whole wheat pastry flour

Heat the water and cool it to lukewarm. Add the yeast and a teaspoon of the bread flour, cover, and set it in a warm spot to proof.

In a medium-sized bowl, combine the hot milk, syrup, salt, and oil; set it aside until lukewarm. Beat in the egg.

Sift together the cornmeal and bread and pastry flours.

Add the proofed yeast to the milk mixture and stir well. Vigorously stir in the dry mixture. Cover and set it in a draft-free spot for about an hour, or until a sponge develops.

Grease an 8-inch square or 9-inch round pan. Stir down the sponge and spread it evenly in the pan. Cover it for about 45 minutes, until the batter rises in the pan.

Preheat the oven to 350°. Bake the bread for 30 minutes, or until it has browned and a tester inserted in the center comes out clean. Serve the cornbread warm or at room temperature.

Notes
• Omit the bowl rise if you're short on time.
• The egg is optional; substitute 2 to 4 tablespoons of additional liquid.

Yeasted Biscuits

Exceptionally light and tender, these biscuits also make excellent burger buns when cut with a 4-inch cutter.

YIELD: 6 to 8 large biscuits

PREPARATION TIME: 50 to 60 minutes to prepare; 1 hour to rise; 15 minutes to bake

1¼ cups whole wheat pastry flour
1 cup whole wheat bread flour
½ cup spring water
1 teaspoon active dry yeast
½ cup milk or unsweetened soy milk, scalded

1 tablespoon honey or maple syrup
½ teaspoon sea salt
4 tablespoons cold unsalted soy margarine or butter, or vegetable oil

Sift together 1 cup of the pastry flour and the bread flour.

Heat the water and cool it to lukewarm. Add the yeast and a teaspoon of flour, cover, and set it in a warm spot to proof. Stir in ½ to ¾ cup of the sifted flour to form a batter. Cover and set the batter in a draft-free spot for about 30 minutes, or until a sponge develops.

Stir together the hot milk, honey, and salt; cool to lukewarm.

In a food processor fitted with the metal blade or in a

medium-sized bowl with a pastry blender, evenly cut the margarine, butter, or oil into the remaining sifted flour until it reaches the consistency of coarse meal. If you use a processor, transfer the mixture to a bowl. Make a well in the center of the dry mixture.

Whisk the cooled milk into the sponge. Pour this into the dry mixture and stir until a soft dough forms. Cover the bowl and set it aside for about 5 minutes.

Sprinkle a bit of pastry flour over the dough in the bowl and turn it out onto a floured surface. Knead the dough briefly, just until it comes together and is smooth. Roll or pat it ³/₄ to 1 inch thick. Cut out biscuits, dipping the cutter in flour each time and pressing straight down. Gently knead any scraps of dough together and resume cutting. Arrange the biscuits on an ungreased or parchment-lined baking sheet and cover them loosely with a damp towel. Set the sheet in a draft-free spot for about 1 hour, or until the biscuits are well risen.

Preheat the oven to 400°. Bake the biscuits for 15 minutes, or until they have browned and sound hollow when tapped on the bottom. Transfer them to a rack, cover loosely with a dry towel, and cool 10 to 15 minutes before serving.

FEATHERWEIGHTS

YIELD: 9 biscuits

PREPARATION TIME: 50 to 60 minutes to prepare; 1 hour to rise; 10 minutes to bake

AS THEIR NAME IMPLIES, THESE DUAL-LEAVENED BISCUITS are especially light. Their tender texture is a pleasant cross between a chemically leavened biscuit and a yeasted roll.

1 cup whole wheat pastry flour plus extra for the work surface

1 cup whole wheat bread flour

¹/₂ cup spring water

1 teaspoon active dry yeast

¹/₂ cup milk or unsweetened soy milk, scalded

1¹/₂ teaspoons lemon juice

1 tablespoon honey or maple syrup

¹/₂ teaspoon sea salt

¹/₂ teaspoon baking soda

1¹/₂ teaspoons baking powder
4 tablespoons cold unsalted soy
margarine or butter, or vegetable oil

Sift together the 1 cup pastry flour and the bread flour.

Heat the water and cool it to lukewarm. Add the yeast and a teaspoon of flour, and set it in a warm spot to proof. Stir in ¹/₂ cup of the sifted flour mixture. Cover and set it in a draft-free spot for 20 to 30 minutes, until a sponge develops.

Combine the milk, lemon juice, and honey; cool to lukewarm.

Sift the remaining sifted mixture with the salt, baking soda, and baking powder. In a food processor fitted with the metal blade or in a bowl with a pastry blender, cut the margarine, butter, or oil into this dry mixture until it reaches the consistency of a coarse meal. If you use a processor, transfer the mixture to a bowl. Make a well in the center of the dry mixture.

Whisk together the sponge and curdled milk and pour the mixture into the well. Stir gently until a soft dough forms. Cover and set it aside for 5 to 10 minutes.

Turn the dough out onto a surface sprinkled with pastry flour. Knead briefly, just until the dough is smooth. Roll or pat it about ³/₄ inch thick. Cut biscuits with a 2¹/₂-inch-diameter cutter—or a 4-inch cutter for bun-sized biscuits. Dip the cutter in flour before cutting each biscuit and press straight down without twisting. Knead dough scraps together and cut additional biscuits. Arrange the biscuits on an ungreased baking sheet. Cover and set it in a draft-free spot for about an hour, or until the biscuits are well risen.

Preheat the oven to 450°. Bake the biscuits for 10 minutes, or until a tester inserted in the center comes out clean. Transfer them to a cooling rack, and cover loosely with a towel for 10 to 15 minutes before serving.

YEASTED MUFFINS

WHEN YOU WANT ROLLS BUT DON'T HAVE THE TIME and/or inclination to knead a dough, follow this simple formula for wonderfully nutty-tasting, crusty, breadlike muffins.

$^{1}/_{4}$ cup spring water

$1^{1}/_{2}$ teaspoons active dry yeast

2 cups whole wheat bread flour

$1^{1}/_{4}$ cups milk or unsweetened soy milk, scalded and cooled to lukewarm

$^{1}/_{2}$ teaspoon sea salt

2 tablespoons vegetable oil

Heat the water and cool it to lukewarm. Add the yeast and a teaspoon of flour, cover, and set it in a warm spot to proof.

Add the proofed yeast to the milk in a medium-sized mixing bowl. Stir in the salt and oil. Stir in the flour, a cup at a time, to form a thick batter. Cover and set it in a draft-free spot for about an hour, until a sponge develops.

Stir the batter down and spoon it into 8 large, well-greased muffin cups. Cover the muffin tin for 30 minutes, or until the batter has risen.

Put the pan into a cold oven and set the temperature to 375°. Bake for 25 to 30 minutes, or until the muffins are brown and crusty and sound hollow when removed from the pan and tapped on the bottom. Cool them briefly and serve warm.

Notes

• Before baking, brush the tops lightly with water, milk, or beaten egg or egg white and sprinkle on sesame, poppy, or other seeds.

• There are endless possible variations on this basic recipe: for example, substitute another flour—whole wheat pastry, oat, rye, barley, buckwheat, corn, etc.—for $^{1}/_{2}$ to $^{2}/_{3}$ cup of the whole wheat bread flour; substitute water, apple juice, or vegetable stock for the milk; add $^{1}/_{2}$ cup soft raisins or other chopped dried fruits, the grated zest of a lemon or orange, or fresh or dried herbs or spices to the batter.

Yeasted Pancakes

THESE DELICIOUS GRIDDLECAKES HAVE A SLIGHTLY DIF-
ferent texture than those leavened with baking powder
and baking soda.

1 cup spring water
1½ teaspoons active dry
yeast
½ cup whole wheat
bread flour
1 cup whole wheat
pastry flour

½ cup milk or unsweetened
soy milk, scalded and
cooled to lukewarm
½ teaspoon sea salt
1 tablespoon corn or
other vegetable oil
1 tablespoon maple syrup

Heat the water and cool it to lukewarm in a medium-
sized mixing bowl. Add the yeast and a teaspoon of flour;
cover, and set it in a warm spot to proof. Stir in the bread
flour and ½ cup of the pastry flour. Cover and set it in
a draft-free spot for 20 to 30 minutes, until a sponge
develops.

Stir in the milk, salt, oil, syrup, and remaining ½ cup
pastry flour. Cover and set it aside for about an hour, or
until the batter rises again.

Heat a griddle until water dripped on it sizzles immediately; lightly grease the surface. Ladle on batter. Cook
the pancakes until bubbles form on top and the bottoms
are golden. Turn and cook several minutes, or until
browned. Serve the pancakes hot off the griddle, or keep
them in a warm oven until serving.

YIELD: About 1 dozen (3-inch)
pancakes

PREPARATION TIME: 1½ to 2
hours

Notes
- For **Yeasted Buckwheat
Cakes,** substitute buckwheat
flour for ¼ to ½ cup of the pastry flour added in the last stage
of the batter; ½ cup will give the
batter a pronounced rather than
a subtle buckwheat flavor and a
slightly heavier texture.
- Substitute cornmeal or other
flours, such as oat, rye, or barley, for the final ½ cup of whole
wheat pastry flour.
- For an even better flavor, and
to speed up breakfast preparation, start the night before. Stir
together the yeast (you may
reduce it to ½ teaspoon), water,
and ½ cup each whole wheat
bread and whole wheat pastry
flour; cover and set in a cool
spot. Proceed with the recipe in
the morning.

SIX

Bread Machine Baking

$\mathcal{B}$READ MACHINE BAKING IS THE NEWEST BREAD-MAKING TECH-nique of all. This no muss, no fuss method has become increasingly popular recently, mainly among those who rarely, if ever, make their own dough but are still enthralled with homemade loaves. Though handmade breads require little of your time and energy because the dough does most of the work on its own, an automatic bread maker demands even less in both respects. This microprocessor-controlled device kneads, proofs, shapes, and bakes bread dough all in one compact container; you simply add the ingredients and press the appropriate buttons. These appliances are a boon to many busy bread lovers: There are no doughy hands, strenuous mixing, or messy utensils and counters to contend with; yet you control what goes into your bread.

BREAD MACHINE BASICS

All bread makers on the market are rather similar, holding from 1 to 2 pounds of dough and producing square, rectangular, or round loaves, depending on motor capacity and pan size and shape. Many machines offer several timing cycles for different types of dough; I recommend models with a whole grain setting, indicating that they can accommodate heftier, longer-rising breads. A "delayed start" timer helps ensure that dough or baked bread is ready when you are, another useful feature. For safety's sake, don't use this timer for recipes that include eggs or milk products. Finally, a viewing window is fun and allows you to see what the dough's doing as it develops into bread.

Be sure to read the manufacturer's instruction booklet thoroughly, so you know the appropriate order for adding ingredients and understand the timing mechanisms of your particular machine. You may want to try some recipes that come with your machine to get a feel for its dough capacity. Get to know your machine in terms of dough consistency too. What's worked wonderfully for your best friend's machine may not be the same for yours.

WHAT'S MISSING IN MACHINE-MADE BREAD?

The main disadvantage of automatic bread makers is that they're machines; bread making is as much art as science. Unlike human bakers, machines can't adjust to variable conditions, such as air temperature and humidity or the moisture content of flour. Moreover, machine baking does away with the meditative moments and tactile pleasure many of us associate with working a dough by hand. Clearly, it's a trade-off, yet having an automatic bread maker doesn't necessarily prevent you from getting your hands into dough. Many machines include a special "dough" setting. Otherwise, you can always turn off the machine before baking begins, hand-shape the

finished dough into rolls, pizza, or whatever, and bake it in your regular oven.

The other major downside of bread machines is that even those with special settings don't really provide an ideal environment or sufficient time to develop a bread's best taste and texture. Breads leavened with less yeast under cooler conditions for a longer time will acquire more depth of flavor and a better texture. They'll also keep longer.

So, for all of its appealing advantages, automated bread making is no substitute for the art of handcrafting breads. It is best viewed as a practical compromise between convenience and quality for those who choose it. I consider it my challenge to help you make the most palatable whole-grain breads possible using an automatic bread machine.

MAKING THE BEST OF THE BREAD MACHINE SITUATION

As with any bread, always start with the best quality ingredients you can find. Especially finely ground high-gluten bread flour produces the lightest possible loaves. Use finely granulated active dry yeast unless your machine's manufacturer specifically recommends another type. If you doubt the yeast's viability, add a bit to lukewarm water and sprinkle a little flour on top. Placed in a warm spot, the mixture should start forming bubbles within a few minutes. Be sure any liquid has cooled to 80° and begin with other ingredients at room temperature.

Bread machine recipes require really precise measurements, making this kind of bread making more similar to quick breads than regular yeasted breads. Use a glass or clear plastic measuring cup for liquids and read them at eye level. Scoop flour, salt, yeast, and other dry ingredients with dry measuring cups and spoons and level them off with a straight-edged knife or metal spatula.

Substituting ingredients or altering amounts is just about the only way to make changes in machine-made breads. The process is almost totally out of your control—unlike the other techniques described in this book. But I've found that keeping a watchful eye and making small adjustments during the mixing cycle can make a significant difference in how breads turn out.

It's okay to have the top of the machine open as the dough is mixing and kneading, and I would recommend checking on it at this point. By the way, resist the urge to peek in during rising and baking cycles because heat will escape. If the flour isn't readily absorbed, add a bit more liquid. Dribble in about a teaspoon at a time, just until the flour is well incorporated. A dough that's too stiff and dry won't rise well and will have a dense texture. Conversely, sprinkle in extra flour if a dough seems excessively wet. Otherwise, it's likely to overrise and collapse before baking.

Heat and humidity are other variables that may necessitate adjusting dough consistency. On hot summer days in a home without air-conditioning, you might want to use cold water and perhaps decrease the yeast slightly to keep a dough from rising too quickly. In humid weather, a dough may need extra flour to prevent it from becoming too sticky. Always use your best judgment when evaluating machine doughs. There seems to be a delicate balance: A dough needs to be moist enough but not too moist. Despite exacting measurements, ingredient amounts remain somewhat approximate, just as with hand-kneaded doughs.

With practice, you'll get to know the best dough consistency for your particular machine. I've found that machine dough should be slightly stickier and moister than hand-worked ones. If you're planning to remove the dough from the pan and hand-shape it, you may want to make it slightly drier for easier handling.

Some automatic bread makers have a cool-down mode; otherwise, don't forget to remove the baked bread promptly to avoid a soggy loaf. The mixing and kneading blade will leave its impression in the bottom of each loaf and often stays lodged in a baked loaf when it's removed from the pan. This isn't a problem: Just remember to retrieve it before you give a loaf away or slice it, and be sure to pry the blade out carefully to preserve the nonstick coating on its surface. Fingers are probably the safest tool to use for this. Likewise, take care not to scratch the bread pan's nonstick surface when you wash it.

Making A Basic Bread Machine Loaf

MY MACHINE HAS A WHOLE GRAIN SETTING AND MAKES loaves weighing up to 2 pounds, containing a maximum of 5 cups of flour. The whole grain cycle takes $4^1/_2$ hours. It begins with a rest period, followed by mixing, kneading, three dough rises, and baking. The pan is a vertical rectangle, so smaller loaves come out approximately square. For a $1^1/_2$-pound whole wheat loaf, I load the following ingredients:

$1^1/_4$ cups water	$3^3/_4$ cups whole wheat bread
1 tablespoon maple syrup	flour
or honey	$1^1/_2$ teaspoons active dry
1 tablespoon vegetable oil	yeast
$1^3/_4$ teaspoons sea salt	

Follow the directions specified by the manufacturer of your particular bread machine.

GOLDEN SQUASH BREAD

THIS LOAF HAS A WONDERFULLY WARM COLOR AND SOFT, moist texture. Try substituting puréed pumpkin, sweet potato, or carrot for the squash. Moisture may vary,

YIELD: 1 ($1^1/_2$-pound) bread machine loaf

so you may have to adjust the amount of water or flour a bit.

³/₄ cup plus	*1 tablespoon vegetable oil*
2 tablespoons water	*1³/₄ teaspoons sea salt*
¹/₂ cup puréed cooked	*3¹/₂ cups whole wheat bread*
winter squash	*flour*
1 tablespoon maple syrup	*1¹/₂ teaspoons active dry*
or unsulfured molasses	*yeast*

Heat the water. Stir in the squash and cool the mixture to 80°. Add to the bread machine container along with the other ingredients in the order specified by the manufacturer.

APPLESAUCE BREAD

FOLLOW THE RECIPE FOR **GOLDEN SQUASH BREAD** (page 152), substituting applesauce (or pear sauce) for the squash purée.

YIELD: 1 (1¹/₂-pound) bread machine loaf

ANADAMA BREAD

THIS LOAF HAS A SUBTLE CORN FLAVOR AND SLIGHT crunch.

YIELD: 1 (1¹/₂-pound) bread machine loaf

1¹/₄ cups plus	*3¹/₂ cups whole wheat bread*
2 tablespoons water	*flour*
¹/₄ cup cornmeal	*1¹/₂ teaspoons active dry*
1³/₄ teaspoons sea salt	*yeast*
1 tablespoon vegetable oil	
1 tablespoon unsulfured	
molasses	

Heat the water to boiling and gradually add it to the cornmeal in a bowl, whisking constantly. Whisk in the salt, oil, and molasses and cool the mixture to 80°. Pour it into the bread machine container along with the other ingredients in the order specified by the manufacturer.

Cinnamon-Raisin Bread

YIELD: 1 (1½-pound) bread machine loaf

Toast this for a breakfast treat.

1¼ cups water
1 tablespoon honey
1 tablespoon vegetable oil
1¾ teaspoons sea salt
3½ cups whole wheat
  bread flour

½ cup raisins
¾ teaspoon ground
  cinnamon
1½ teaspoons active dry
  yeast

Add the ingredients to the bread machine container in the order specified by the manufacturer.

Egg Bread

YIELD: 1 (1½-pound) bread machine loaf

Eggs give extra oomph to this high-rising loaf.

2 medium eggs, beaten
  (⅓ cup plus 1
  tablespoon)
¾ cup plus 2
  tablespoons water
1 tablespoon honey
1 tablespoon vegetable oil

1¾ teaspoons sea salt
3¾ cups whole wheat
  bread flour
1½ teaspoons active dry
  yeast

Add the ingredients to the bread machine container in the order specified by the manufacturer.

Sesame Bread

YIELD: 1 (1½-pound) bread machine loaf

The fabulous flavor of sesame seeds pervades this loaf.

1⅓ cups water
1 tablespoon honey
1 tablespoon sesame oil
1¾ teaspoons sea salt
3⅔ cups whole wheat
  bread flour

2 tablespoons toasted
  sesame seeds
1½ teaspoons active dry
  yeast

Add the ingredients to the bread machine container in the order specified by the manufacturer.

Banana Bread

BANANAS GIVE THIS BREAD A SUBTLE TROPICAL TASTE twist.

YIELD: 1 (1½-pound) bread machine loaf

¾ *cup water*	1¾ *teaspoons sea salt*
⅔ *cup thoroughly mashed ripe banana*	3½ *cups whole wheat bread flour*
1 tablespoon honey	1½ *teaspoons active dry yeast*
1 tablespoon vegetable oil	

Add the ingredients to the bread machine container in the order specified by the manufacturer.

Oatmeal Bread

OATS ADD A SLIGHT CHEWINESS TO THIS ALL-PURPOSE loaf.

YIELD: 1 (1½-pound) bread machine loaf

1⅓ *cups plus 1 tablespoon water*	1¾ *teaspoons sea salt*
⅓ *cup rolled oats*	3⅓ *cups whole wheat bread flour*
1 tablespoon unsulfured molasses	1½ *teaspoons active dry yeast*
1 tablespoon vegetable oil	

Bring the water to a boil and pour it over the oats in a bowl. Cool this mixture to lukewarm (80°), then add it to the bread machine container along with the other ingredients in the order specified by the manufacturer.

Swedish Rye Bread

THIS LOAF HAS A SUBTLY SWEET FLAVOR AND COMPACT though soft texture.

YIELD: 1 (1½-pound) bread machine loaf

1¹/₄ cups plus 2
tablespoons orange
juice
1 tablespoon unsulfured
molasses
¹/₂ cup rye flour
1¹/₂ teaspoons ground
toasted fennel seeds

1 tablespoon vegetable oil
1³/₄ teaspoons sea salt
3¹/₄ cups whole wheat bread
flour
2 teaspoons active dry
yeast

Add the ingredients to the bread machine container in the order specified by the manufacturer.

SEVEN

Sourdough Breads

$\mathcal{T}$HE NEXT THING TO ARRIVE AT THE TABLE AFTER THE MENUS WAS a small round warm sourdough loaf. Its enticing aroma, satisfying flavor, and pleasing texture derived from the sourdough leaven and many slow risings. This crusty bread was a trademark of Le Papillon, a restaurant once located in an elegant turn-of-the-century neighborhood in Atlanta. The Victorian cottage that housed it was surrounded by fruit trees interspersed with picturesque flower and herb beds. Inside, tables in several spacious, high-ceilinged rooms were set with fresh linens, seasonal bouquets, and stoneware dishes. The restaurant was as welcoming as a gracious home. But the little sourdough loaves especially beckoned.

"Sourdough" describes any bread leavened with a starter, a fermented mixture that functions as a yeast culture in the dough. Some starter goes into the bread, and the rest is saved for the next batch. My sourdough starters are like part of the family, having resided with me for twenty-some years, and they boast a lineage because I obtained them from friends, who had obtained them from friends and so on. I like to imagine that each sourdough loaf I make contains a bit of history along with its unique subtly tangy flavor and chewy texture. I know I'm preserving a bread-making tradition by making this special sort of bread.

Sourdough Starters

SOURDOUGH STARTERS WERE ONCE SO VALUABLE THAT they were included in marriage dowries. They were taken to bed on cold nights and carried inside coats on winter treks. It's been said that early sourdough bakers found many other uses for starter too, from treating wounds, to chinking holes in cabins, to imbibing the "hooch," which separated on its top.

Saved starters were a step forward from bakers' dependence on wild yeasts and a new and spontaneous ferment for every bread batch. A viable starter along with a proven bread formula ensured consistently successful loaves. Early American pioneers and prospectors in remote areas depended so greatly on sourdough starters for reliable leavening that they, themselves, became known as "sourdoughs." Over time, commercial yeasts were developed, first fresh yeast cakes and later dried granules. Commercial yeasts simplified and standardized bread making, and the use of starters began to decline as these became widely available.

Nevertheless, breads leavened solely with commercial yeast can never really replace sourdough breads, since the two processes result in substantially different products. Sourdough breads tend to have a somewhat more compact, springy crumb and a chewier crust than yeasted breads, and their tangy aroma and taste are alluring to many bread lovers. The particular starter, specific recipe, dough development, and baking technique all contribute to a sourdough bread's uniqueness.

The most foolproof way to acquire a sound sourdough starter is to obtain some from a friend. Commercially available dried starter, which comes to life when mixed with liquid and placed in a warm environment, is another relatively reliable source. Look for dried starters in cookware shops and mail-order catalogs.

Although starters are easiest to get going in a bakery or a kitchen where bread is baked regularly, and are adversely affected by air pollution, you don't have to live in a rural bakery to create your own starter to pass on to future generations. Just stir together a cup of liquid and enough flour to make a medium-thick batter in a clean glass or ceramic container large enough to allow for expansion. Cover it with a clean unnapped towel or piece of muslin. Leave the mixture at room temperature for several days, stirring it occasionally. During this time, it will attract airborne wild yeasts, which feed on the grain starch and multiply, giving off carbon dioxide and alcohol. The starch mixture will also attract friendly bacteria, which participate in the grain fermentation and contribute to the starter's character. If a starter's aroma becomes offensive rather than pleasantly piquant, it has probably spoiled and you should try again.

Wheat or rye flours are typically used to prepare starters, although flour ground from any grain will ferment. The particular flour you use will influence the flavor the starter will contribute to bread and may also affect the starter's activity. Rye is particularly fermentable, and rye starters have long been popular with sourdough bakers. Whatever flour you choose to use, fresh whole grain flours ferment more readily than refined ones.

The liquid in a starter affects the flavor of baked goods too. I use spring water. A quality spring water is preferable for any bread that relies on natural fermentation for rising; distilled and purified waters lack the minerals that facilitate the process, and chemicals in tap water often interfere with it. Alternative liquids for starters are milk or vegetable, bean, and grain stocks.

In the early days, additional starchy substances such as hops, malt (barley or some other grain softened in water, sprouted, and kiln-dried), potatoes, or the cooking water of any of these were sometimes added to starters to enhance their leavening potential. My plain flour-and-water starters maintain plenty of leavening power, but you may want to experiment with extra ingredients. I would advise setting aside a portion of your proven starter, however, so all is not lost if an experiment fails.

Recipes for specialized starters appear in other sources, and you may want to try them after you've mastered the basic technique. Potatoes, onions, and yogurt are sometimes included. Many starter recipes call for some commercial yeast, but a starter begun this way usually has less character initially and may take longer to produce a characteristic sourdough flavor. All starters change over time, becoming increasingly complex in flavor so long as they are handled with care.

I have wheat and rye starters, and keep about a cup of each refrigerated in pint-sized canning jars, alternating their use. Always store a starter in a glass, ceramic, or wooden container, and stir it with a wooden spoon; metal and plastic can adversely affect its flavor. Allow enough room in any container for the starter to double in size; I have had an active starter blow the top off an inadequate jar. A starter can be stored at room temperature, but you must provide space for it to more than double. Also, you must use or refresh it daily to protect it from undesirable microbes. If you ever neglect your starter, wherever it's stored, and discover it's covered with a colorful mold, it is probably unsalvageable and you should toss it out.

RENEWING AND EXPANDING THE STARTER
Refrigerated starter needs renewing every week or so if it's not used for baking. A dark liquid consisting of

alcohol and water may separate on top; this is normal. Stir the starter in its container. Pour off about half the mixture and add fresh flour and water to replace what you discarded. For instance, if you keep a cup of starter on hand, throw out $1/2$ cup and stir in $1/3$ to $1/2$ cup of water and $1/2$ to $2/3$ cup of flour to make a batter with the original consistency. I do this in a bowl so I can wash out the storage jar as another preservative measure. Cover this refreshed starter and leave it at room temperature for several hours, until it is active and bubbly, then refrigerate it in a clean jar.

If I plan to be away from home for more than a couple of weeks or move long distance, I freeze my starters. Though they will keep for several months this way, I try to use them again soon. Thoroughly defrost a frozen starter before trying to bake with it, and expect it to take a while to regain its former vigor.

Bubbliness and a pungent aroma indicate you have an effective starter but don't absolutely guarantee good bread; sometimes unpleasant-tasting microorganisms overpower desirable ones. Using the starter in a batch of bread is the ultimate test. The first step is to expand the starter and create a surplus. This is similar to renewing the starter, except that you don't discard anything. Empty all the original starter into a bowl and stir in additional liquid and enough flour to maintain the same consistency. Use the kind of flour your starter contains. If you'll need 1 cup of starter for your bread recipe, add slightly less than a cup of water and a cup or so of flour to the original cup of starter. Cover the bowl with a plate and leave it in a draft-free spot at room temperature for several hours, or until it has risen in the bowl and is definitely active. I leave it overnight if I plan to bake the following morning. The warmer the spot and the longer the starter sits, the more pungent and lively it will become. Stir down the mixture and measure the cup you need for baking.

Pour the remainder into a clean jar and refrigerate it for future use; this is your new saved starter. Now you're ready to bake.

When my starters are in good shape, they leaven bread well on their own without giving it an overly sour flavor. Nevertheless, sometimes you may want to include a bit of commercial yeast, as I do in some cases. Added yeast will speed up the leavening process and does make a somewhat lighter bread, which may be desirable when you're adding heavy ingredients such as cooked or soaked grains; it depends on the effect you want. Yeasted sourdough breads don't keep as well as those without added yeast, and they usually have a less pronounced sourdough flavor. As you work with your sourdough starter, you'll become familiar with its behavior in baking and learn how to control it, with or without added yeast.

Instructions for making a basic sourdough whole wheat bread and a basic yeasted sourdough whole wheat bread follow. You may want to refer to these detailed accounts as you try out the recipes that come later. We'll finish the chapter with some small and specialty sourdough breads, such as muffins, biscuits, pancakes, and corn bread.

Making A Basic Sourdough Whole Wheat Bread

To MAKE THIS BASIC SOURDOUGH WHOLE WHEAT BREAD, follow the procedures for making yeasted breads (pages 78 to 95), but replace the proofed yeast with sourdough starter. You may use either a straight dough or a sponge method. I prefer the latter since it gives the yeast a chance to multiply and strengthens the gluten before the salt, oil, and remaining flour are added. If you use the sponge method, plan on about $2^1/_2$ to $3^1/_2$ hours for the sponge and preparation, 5 hours for rising, and 50 minutes to bake loaves. For the straight dough method, omit the sponge step. Stir together the starter, water,

salt, and oil, then add flour to form a dough and continue as described here; expect the dough to take longer
to rise, especially the first bowl rise.

Regardless of the method, you must first expand your
starter (see above). Do this several hours ahead of
time—the night before if you're starting your bread in
the morning—and remember to divide the mixture and
save a portion of it.

Next, assemble your equipment (see page 79) and the
ingredients. For 2 large loaves (about 4 pounds of
dough), you'll need

1 cup sourdough starter	*2 teaspoons sea salt*
2 cups spring water	*2 tablespoons oil (optional)*
7 cups whole wheat *bread flour*	

Now, follow these steps to make the basic bread; they
will also be referenced by many of this chapter's recipes:

⁓ 1. Combine the starter and water in a large bowl and
gradually stir in 2 to 3 cups of flour to form a thick batter. Cover the bowl and set it in a draft-free spot for 2 to
3 hours, or until the mixture has developed into a
sponge. You can leave the sponge longer, but the longer
it sits, the sourer it will become; stir it down periodically.
⁓ 2. Stir in the salt and oil. Add flour a cup at a time,
stirring well after each addition, until a dough forms.
The dough will pull away from the sides and ball up in
the center of the bowl.
⁓ 3. Turn out the dough onto a lightly floured surface,
and cover it for about 10 minutes, until it relaxes. Meanwhile, wash and dry the bowl. Thoroughly knead the
dough, adding flour as necessary to keep it from sticking. When it is smooth and elastic, form the dough into
a ball. Lightly grease the bowl and put the dough inside,
smooth side down. Now turn the dough over to grease
the top. Cover the bowl and set it aside for about 2

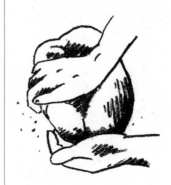

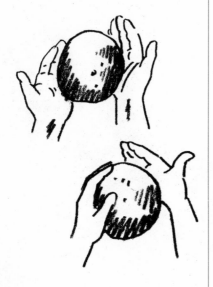

hours, or until a finger pressed into the dough leaves a depression.

ᵔ 4. Turn out the dough and knead it gently several times to deflate and round it. Return it to the bowl, cover, and set it aside for about 2 hours, until the dough has risen and does not rebound when pressed.

ᵔ 5. Divide the dough, then shape and pan the pieces. I often make freestanding round loaves. Cover the loaves and let them rise for about an hour, or until the dough springs back slowly when pressed.

ᵔ 6. Slash the tops of the loaves. Spray them with water or brush with an egg wash; sprinkle on seeds if you wish. Bake the loaves in a preheated 400° oven for 20 minutes, then lower the heat to 350° and bake for 20 to 30 minutes longer, until they are brown, firm-sided, and sound hollow when removed from the pans and tapped on the bottom.

ᵔ 7. Thoroughly cool the bread on a rack before slicing or storing it.

Making A Basic Yeasted Sourdough Whole Wheat Bread

THIS RECIPE FOR A BASIC YEAST-BOOSTED SOURDOUGH whole wheat bread also yields about 4 pounds of dough—enough for two large loaves. The flavor is slightly more complex than the basic yeasted whole wheat bread and a bit less tangy than the sourdough whole wheat bread without added yeast. Again, follow the procedures for making yeasted breads (pages 78 to 95), but this time you'll use both sourdough starter and proofed yeast.

As with the basic yeasted and basic sourdough breads, you may use either a straight dough or sponge technique for this bread. With the sponge technique, you'll have an additional choice: You can set a sourdough sponge to develop before adding the yeast or combine the sourdough starter and yeast in a sponge. I choose the first alternative, which gives the bread a more pronounced sourdough flavor. The second approach takes less time, if that is a consideration. Plan on between about 2 and 3½ hours for the sponge and dough preparation, about 4 hours for rising, and 40 to 50 minutes to bake loaves.

If you want to omit the sponge step altogether, proof the yeast in ¼ cup of the water and combine this mixture with the remaining water and starter. Then stir in the salt and oil, add enough flour to form a dough, and go on with kneading and subsequent steps.

Use all the same equipment (see page 79) for this bread as you would for a basic yeasted or sourdough bread, and remember to expand your starter ahead of time.

Assemble the following ingredients:

1 cup sourdough starter	¼ teaspoon active dry yeast
2 cups spring water	2 teaspoons sea salt
6½ to 7 cups whole wheat bread flour	2 tablespoons oil

Follow these steps to make the basic bread and refer to them as you make the other yeasted sourdough breads in this chapter:

∽ 1. Stir together the starter and 1¾ cups water in a large bowl. Gradually stir in 2 to 2½ cups flour to form a thick batter. Cover the bowl and set it in a draft-free spot for 2 to 3 hours, or until the mixture has developed into a sponge.

∽ 2. Heat the remaining ¼ cup water and cool it to lukewarm. Add the yeast and 1 teaspoon flour, cover and set it in a warm spot to proof.

∽ 3. Add the proofed yeast to the sourdough sponge along with the salt and oil. Add flour, stirring well after each addition, until a dough forms. It will pull away

Variations

You may think of sourdough bread as only the straightforward, unembellished loaves I've just described, but it's as wide open to variations as the yeasted breads in the previous chapter, and sourdough variations follow a similar pattern. In either plain sourdough or yeasted sourdough bread, you can substitute flours or liquids, or add ingredients, such as cooked whole grains or soaked cracked ones, seeds, nuts, dried fruits, raw fruits or vegetables, or sprouts, to vary the flavor and texture. Sourdough French bread is made from a simplified version of the basic recipe but relies upon a specialized baking technique for its unique personality. Try the simple variations that follow before you go on to the recipes in the next section. Once you've mastered those, you'll be ready to invent your own.

For **Multigrain Sourdough Bread,** substitute 1 cup of rye flour or rye meal (coarsely ground rye flakes)—or another flour, such as barley, rice, oat, or triticale—for 1 cup of wheat flour. For dough strength, always use wheat flour in the sponge and add low-gluten flours after the sponge has developed.

For **Sourdough Seed Bread,** knead ¼ cup toasted sesame seeds or flaxseeds into each loaf after the first bowl rise or just before the shaped rise. Toast the seeds in a dry heavy skillet over low to medium heat, agitating the pan often to keep the seeds from burning. Substitute other seeds or nuts.

(Continued on page 166)

Variations (cont.)

For **Sourdough Raisin Bread,** knead ³/₄ to 1 cup soft raisins for each loaf into the dough, after the first bowl rise or just before the shaped rise. The raisins will come to the surface of the dough as you knead, but continue kneading them back in until they are well distributed throughout the dough. Substitute other soft dried fruits for the raisins.

For **Italian Sourdough Bread,** use olive oil. For an especially crisp crust, place a shallow pan of boiling water on the lowest rack of the oven for the first 15 minutes of baking and spray the loaves with water every 5 minutes during that period. A baking cloche also gives this bread a superb crust. These techniques work to crisp the crust of any sourdough bread.

YIELD: 1 focaccia

PREPARATION TIME: About 20 minutes to prepare (not including dough preparation); 1 hour for rising; 20 minutes to bake

from the sides and ball up in the center of the bowl.

❧ 4. Turn out the dough onto a lightly floured surface and cover it for about 10 minutes, until it relaxes. Meanwhile, wash and dry the bowl. Thoroughly knead the dough, adding flour as necessary to keep it from sticking. When it is smooth and elastic, form the dough into a ball. Lightly grease the bowl and put the dough inside, smooth side down, then turn it over. Cover the bowl and set it aside for about 1¹/₂ hours, or until a finger pressed into the dough leaves a depression.

❧ 5. Turn out the dough and knead it gently several times to deflate and round it. Return the dough to the bowl, cover, and set it aside for 1 to 1¹/₂ hours, or until the dough has risen and does not rebound when pressed.

❧ 6. Divide the dough and shape loaves. As with basic sourdough bread, I often make freestanding round loaves. Cover the loaves and let them rise for about an hour, or until the dough springs back slowly when pressed.

❧ 7. Slash the tops of the loaves. Spray them with water or brush with an egg wash; sprinkle on seeds if you wish. Bake the loaves in a preheated 400° oven for 20 minutes, then lower the heat to 350° and bake for 20 to 30 minutes longer, until they are brown, firm-sided, and sound distinctly hollow when removed from the pans and tapped on the bottom.

❧ 8. Thoroughly cool the bread on a rack before slicing or storing it.

ROSEMARY FOCACCIA

YOU NEED ABOUT HALF A RECIPE OF **ITALIAN SOUR-dough Bread** to make this savory flat herb bread. (You can also use a whole recipe of regular **Italian Bread**— page 131.) Cut into strips, squares, or wedges, focaccia is a great addition to a buffet table, and it enhances a simple soup-and-salad meal.

About 2 pounds **Italian
Sourdough Bread**
dough
*1 teaspoon finely minced
fresh rosemary leaves,
or more to taste*

Cornmeal
3 to 4 teaspoons olive oil

After the second bowl rise, gently but thoroughly knead the rosemary into the dough on an unfloured surface. Form the dough into a ball and cover it for a few minutes. Dust a lightly greased pizza pan with cornmeal.

On a lightly greased surface, roll the dough out into a 12-inch circle about ¹/₂ inch thick. Transfer the dough to the pan. Cover and set it in a draft-free spot for about an hour, or until the dough is light and puffy.

Preheat the oven to 400°. Using your fingertips, make light indentations over the surface of the dough. Brush olive oil over the surface. Bake for 30 minutes, or until the focaccia is well browned and crusty. Cool it briefly on a rack, cut, and serve warm slices.

GOLDEN SOURDOUGH BREAD

SLIGHTLY SWEET, BARELY SOUR, THIS HARVEST BREAD HAS a somewhat compact, even texture. You can substitute pumpkin, carrots, sweet potatoes, yams, or other varieties of winter squash for the butternut squash. I like to use part of the dough to make **Cinnamon Swirl** or **Apple Butter Buns** (see page 340).

2¹/₄ cups spring water
1 cup sourdough starter
*8¹/₂ to 9 cups whole wheat
bread flour*
*1¹/₄ cups mashed cooked
butternut squash*

2 teaspoons sea salt
*2 tablespoons corn or other
vegetable oil*

Notes
• Substitute another herb, such as thyme or sage, for the rosemary, or use a compatible combination. If you use dried herbs, use half as much as the fresh.
• Bake the focaccia on a preheated pizza stone. Let it rise on a wooden peel generously dusted with cornmeal.

....

Olive oil varies considerably depending on how it is processed. "Extra virgin" on a label indicates the oil is from the initial pressing of olives and is unrefined. Extra virgin olive oils taste delectably fruity and there are subtle flavor differences, depending on the type of olives, region, growing conditions, and harvest season. Other "virgin" olive oils derive from later pressings and have more acidity and less pronounced flavor. "Pure" olive oil is extracted from the pulp and pits of pressed olives, and chemical solvents are sometimes used in this process. Pure olive oil is generally refined to remove unpleasant flavors. Olive oil is an especially nutritious oil because it is a monounsaturated fat, which appears to foster a healthy cholesterol balance in the body. It is high in vitamin E, making it somewhat less susceptible to rancidity than other oils.

....

YIELD: 2 loaves

PREPARATION TIME: 2¹/₂ to 3¹/₂ hours for sponge and dough; 5 hours for rising; 40 to 50 minutes to bake

Beat together 2 cups of the water, the starter, and 2½ cups flour in a large bowl. Cover and set it in a draft-free spot for 2 to 3 hours, until a sponge develops.

Thoroughly blend the squash and remaining ¼ cup water, and stir this into the sponge along with the salt and oil. Gradually stir in enough of the remaining flour to form a dough.

Follow steps 3 to 7 on pages 163–164. I often brush the loaves with an egg wash and sprinkle on sesame or poppy seeds before baking.

SOURDOUGH EGG BREAD

THIS IS A BASIC SOURDOUGH BREAD ENRICHED WITH egg—a sourdough challah! Like other egg-rich breads, this one has a fine texture. Make braided or unbraided loaves, freestanding or panned, or use a portion of the dough for sweet buns or a coffee cake.

2 cups spring water	3 eggs
1 cup sourdough starter	2 teaspoons sea salt
7 to 8 cups whole wheat bread flour	3 tablespoons sesame, corn, or other vegetable oil

Beat together the water, starter, and 2 to 2½ cups of flour to form a thick batter. Cover and set it in a draft-free spot for 2 to 3 hours, until it develops into a sponge.

Whisk the eggs and reserve about a tablespoon to use later for a glaze. Add the salt and oil to the rest of the beaten eggs and whisk well, then beat this mixture into the sponge. Gradually stir in enough of the remaining flour to form a dough.

Follow steps 3 to 7 on pages 163–164.

YIELD: 2 loaves

PREPARATION TIME: 2½ to 3½ hours for sponge and dough; 5 hours for rising; 40 to 50 minutes to bake

Notes
• Add 1 to 2 tablespoons of honey along with the salt, oil, and egg.

Sourdough Sprouted Lentil Bread

The sprouts contribute rising power to this dough and add flavor, moistness, and a nutty quality to the baked loaves. Begin sprouting $1/4$ cup green or brown lentils about 3 days before you plan to make the bread.

1 cup sourdough starter	*2 teaspoons sea salt*
2 cups spring water	*2 tablespoons sesame or*
7$1/2$ to 8 cups whole wheat	*other vegetable oil*
bread flour	
2 to 3 cups lentil sprouts	
(see page 102)	

Beat together the starter, water, and $2^1/2$ cups of the flour. Cover and set it in a draft-free spot for 2 to 3 hours, until a sponge develops.

Coarsely chop the sprouts and stir them into the sponge along with the salt and oil. Gradually stir in enough of the remaining flour to form a dough.

Follow steps 3 to 7 on page 163–164.

YIELD: 2 loaves

PREPARATION TIME: $2^1/2$ to 3 hours for sponge and dough; 5 hours for rising; 40 to 50 minutes to bake

Lentils look like small flattened spheres with convex surfaces. The two most familiar varieties in this country are greenish-tan or bright red-orange. Lentils require little or no soaking and cook relatively quickly. See page 360 for cooking directions.

Notes
• Substitute other kinds of sprouts for the lentil sprouts.

Sourdough Grits Bread

Corn and soy grits add a subtle crunch to the compact texture of this fine bread; it's one that I never tire of. The grits are interchangeable: use all soy, all corn, half of each, or another kind altogether, such as rice or barley grits.

2$1/2$ cups spring water	*2 teaspoons sea salt*
2 tablespoons soy grits	*2 tablespoons sesame or*
$1/4$ cup corn grits	*other vegetable oil*
1 cup sourdough starter	
7$1/2$ to 8 cups whole	
wheat bread flour	

YIELD: 2 loaves

PREPARATION TIME: 1 hour to soak the grits; $2^1/2$ to $3^1/2$ hours for sponge and dough; 5 hours for rising; 40 to 50 minutes to bake

Heat the water to boiling and pour it over the grits in a large bowl. Cover and set it aside until lukewarm. Stir in the starter and 2½ cups of the flour to form a thick batter. Cover and set it in a draft-free spot for 2 to 3 hours, until a sponge develops.

Stir the salt and oil into the sponge. Gradually stir in enough of the remaining flour to form a dough.

Follow steps 3 to 7 on page 163–164.

Hearty Sourdough Bread

SUBSTANTIALLY GOOD! MY FATHER-IN-LAW CALLS THIS stamina bread. Slice it thinly and savor its full flavor. Potato seems to enhance the rising of dough, giving breads a moist crumb and adding flavor and nutrients.

YIELD: 2 loaves

PREPARATION TIME: 1 hour to soak the grain; 2½ to 3½ hours for sponge and dough; 5 hours for rising; 40 to 50 minutes to bake

2½ cups spring water	7 to 8 cups whole wheat
1 medium-sized potato,	bread flour
cubed	2 teaspoons sea salt
1 cup cracked wheat or rye	2 tablespoons vegetable oil
1 cup sourdough starter	

Combine about ½ cup of the water and the potato in a blender and blend, gradually adding the remaining water, until the mixture is thoroughly smooth. Transfer it to a saucepan and heat to boiling. Pour it over the cracked grain in a large bowl. Cover and set it aside until lukewarm.

Stir in the starter and 2 cups of the flour to form a thick batter. Cover and set it in a draft-free spot for 2 to 3 hours, or until the batter develops into a sponge.

Stir the salt and oil into the sponge. Gradually stir in enough of the remaining flour to form a dough.

Follow steps 3 to 7 on page 163–164.

Sourdough Millet Bread

THIS AGREEABLE BREAD HAS A SUBTLE SWEET-AND-SOUR flavor and a somewhat compact, moist, nubbly texture.

Make extra millet for dinner and use it in this bread the next day. You can substitute cooked rice for the millet; my favorite is brown basmati rice. I like to use rice dough for **Indonesian Pizza** (page 315) or **Mexican Pizza** (page 314).

2 cups cooled cooked millet (see page 19)	7 cups whole wheat bread flour
2 cups spring water	2 teaspoons sea salt
1 cup sourdough starter	2 tablespoons sesame or other vegetable oil

Notes
• If the millet is on the dry side, add an extra ¼ to ½ cup water when you mix the batter.
• After the first bowl rise or just before shaping the dough, knead ¾ to 1 cup soft raisins into each loaf.

Stir together the millet, water, starter, and 2 cups of the flour in a large bowl. Cover and set it aside in a draft-free spot for 2 to 3 hours, until a sponge develops.

Stir the salt and oil into the sponge. Gradually stir in enough of the remaining flour to form a dough.

Follow steps 3 to 7 on page 163–164. I often brush the loaves with an egg wash and sprinkle on sesame seeds before baking.

SOURDOUGH FRENCH BREAD

THIS UNIQUE BREAD MADE SAN FRANCISCO FAMOUS—OR vice versa. With its hard crust, springy crumb, and well-developed flavor based on simple ingredients—flour, water, salt, and yeast—it meets the requirements of any fine French bread. But the chewiness of its crust, its especially fine-grained and moist texture, and its distinctive tangy taste set this sourdough-leavened French bread apart. Finely ground flour will give your loaves extra oomph.

YIELD: 1 large loaf

PREPARATION TIME: 2½ to 3 hours for sponge and dough; 5 to 6 hours for rising; 35 to 45 minutes to bake

1½ cups sourdough starter	1½ teaspoons sea salt
1½ cups spring water	Cornmeal, for dusting
4½ cups whole wheat bread flour	

Notes

- Steaming is what gives any French bread a wonderful crust; the steaming tactics I employ here simulate professional steam injection devices. Baking in a cloche will also give the bread a great crust.
- If you have baking tiles or a baking stone, let the shaped loaves rise upside-down on a lightly floured surface—French bakers use cloth-lined baskets for round loaves and canvas for long ones. Preheat your tiles or stone when you preheat the oven. Turn a risen loaf over, right side up, onto a baking peel—a flat wooden shovel-like implement—and then quickly transfer it to the hot tiles or stone by pushing the peel forward and immediately pulling the peel out from under the loaf. You can improvise a peel with a thin board or a piece of heavy cardboard.

YIELD: 2 large loaves

PREPARATION TIME: 2 to 3 hours for sponge and dough; 5 hours for rising; 40 to 50 minutes to bake

In a large bowl, stir together the starter, water, and 1½ cups of the flour. Cover and set it in a draft-free spot for 2 to 2½ hours, or until a sponge develops.

Stir in the salt. Gradually stir in additional flour to form a dough. Turn the dough out onto a lightly floured surface and cover it for several minutes. Knead the dough until smooth and elastic, adding flour as necessary to keep it from sticking.

Form the dough into a ball and place it in a lightly greased bowl. Cover and set it aside for about 2 hours, until the dough has risen and does not spring back when pressed. Turn the dough out and knead it briefly. Return it to the bowl for a second rise.

Form a round loaf or shape a baguette by the method described on page 130 and place it on a cornmeal-dusted pan. Cover the loaf for about an hour, or until the dough rebounds slowly when pressed.

Preheat the oven to 400°. Slash the top of the loaf and spray or brush it with cold water. Place a shallow pan of boiling water on the bottom rack of the oven and put the bread on the rack above it. After 5 minutes, open the oven door and quickly spray the loaf with cold water—remember to avoid spraying the oven light! Spray again after 5 minutes. After 5 more minutes (15 minutes into the baking), give the loaf one more spray and, before you close the oven door, remove the pan of water. Lower the heat to 350° and bake for 20 to 30 minutes longer, until the bread is well browned and crusty, and sounds hollow when tapped on the bottom.

YEASTED SOURDOUGH CRACKED WHEAT BREAD

THIS BREAD HAS A SUBTLER SOURDOUGH FLAVOR AND less heft than its cousin, **Hearty Sourdough Bread** (page 170).

3 cups spring water

1 cup cracked wheat or rye

1 cup sourdough starter

7$^1/_2$ cups whole wheat
   bread flour

$^1/_4$ teaspoon active dry yeast

2 teaspoons sea salt

2 tablespoons corn or other
   vegetable oil

Heat 2 cups of the water to boiling and pour it over the cracked wheat in a large bowl. Cover and set it aside until lukewarm. Stir in the starter and 2 cups of the flour to form a thick batter. Cover and set it in a draft-free spot for about 2 hours, until it develops into a sponge.

Meanwhile, heat $^1/_4$ cup of the water and cool it to lukewarm. Add the yeast and a teaspoon of flour, cover, and set it in a draft-free spot to proof. Stir in the remaining $^3/_4$ cup water and 1 cup or so of flour to form a thick batter. Cover and set it in a draft-free spot for 30 minutes to an hour, until it develops into a sponge.

Stir the yeast sponge into the sourdough sponge along with the salt and oil. Gradually stir in enough of the remaining flour to form a dough.

Follow steps 4 to 8 on page 166.

Yeasted Sourdough Oat Bread

Steel-cut oats contribute sweetness and a wonderfully chewy texture to this superb bread. It has an especially moist crumb and keeps particularly well. This dough makes delicious **English Muffins** (see page 91).

YIELD: 2 large loaves

PREPARATION TIME: 2 to 3 hours for sponge and dough; 5 hours for rising; 40 to 50 minutes to bake

3 cups spring water

1 cup steel-cut oats

1 cup sourdough starter

8 to 9 cups whole wheat
   bread flour

$^1/_4$ teaspoon active dry yeast

2 teaspoons sea salt

2 tablespoons sesame or
   other vegetable oil

Heat 2 cups of the water to boiling and pour it over the oats in a large bowl. Cover and set it aside until lukewarm. Stir in the starter and 2 cups of the flour to form

Notes
• For a sweeter dough, add 2 tablespoons maple syrup, honey, or rice syrup along with the salt and oil.

YIELD: 2 large loaves

PREPARATION TIME: 2 to 3 hours for sponge and dough; 5 hours for rising; 40 to 50 minutes to bake

a thick batter. Cover and set it in a draft-free spot for 2 to 3 hours, until it develops into a sponge.

Meanwhile, heat $1/4$ cup of the water and cool it to lukewarm. Add the yeast and a teaspoon of flour, cover, and set it in a draft-free spot to proof. Stir in the remaining $3/4$ cup water and 1 cup or so of the flour, cover, and set it in a draft-free spot for 30 minutes to an hour, until it develops into a sponge.

Stir the yeast sponge into the sourdough sponge along with the salt and oil. Gradually stir in enough of the remaining flour to form a dough.

Follow steps 4 to 8 on page 166.

Yeasted Sourdough Bran Bread

THIS BREAD IS DARK, DELECTABLE, AND PARTICULARLY high in healthy fiber. It's another good choice for making rolls and English muffins.

3 cups spring water
1 cup wheat bran
1 cup sourdough starter
7 to 8 cups whole wheat
    bread flour
$1/4$ teaspoon active dry
    yeast
2 teaspoons sea salt
$1/4$ cup corn or other
    vegetable oil

2 tablespoons blackstrap
    molasses
2 tablespoons honey or
    rice syrup
Egg wash (optional)
Poppy seeds, for garnishing
    the loaves (optional)

Heat 2 cups of the water to boiling and pour it over the bran in a large bowl. Cover and set it aside until lukewarm. Stir in the starter and 2 to $2^{1}/2$ cups of the flour to form a thick batter. Cover and set it in a draft-free spot for 2 to 3 hours, until it develops into a sponge.

Meanwhile, heat $1/4$ cup of the water and cool it to lukewarm. Add the yeast and a teaspoon of flour, cover, and set it in a draft-free spot to proof. Stir in the remaining ³/₄ cup water and 1 cup or more of the flour to form a thick batter. Cover and set it in a draft-free spot for 30 minutes to an hour, until a sponge develops.

Stir the yeast sponge into the sourdough sponge along with the salt, oil, molasses, and honey. Gradually stir in flour to form a dough.

Follow steps 4 to 8 on page 166. Brush the loaves with an egg wash and sprinkle on poppy seeds before baking.

Follow steps 4 to 8 on page 166.

Yeasted Sourdough Buckwheat Bread

THIS IS A BREAD FOR KASHA FANS! USE PART OF THE dough to make the crust for **Reuben's Pizza** (page 318).

Use part of the dough to make the crust for **Reuben's Pizza** (page 318).

2¹/₂ cups spring water
1 cup sourdough starter
7¹/₂ cups whole wheat
    bread flour
¹/₄ teaspoon active dry
    yeast
2 teaspoons sea salt
2 tablespoons vegetable oil

2 cups cooked toasted
    buckwheat groats (see
    page 19)
Egg wash (optional)
Poppy seeds, for garnishing
    the loaves (optional)

Stir together 2 cups of the water and the starter in a large bowl. Stir in 2¹/₂ cups of the flour to form a thick batter. Cover and set it in a draft-free spot for 2 to 3 hours, until it develops into a sponge.

Meanwhile, heat the remaining ¹/₂ cup of water and cool it to lukewarm. Add the yeast and a teaspoon of flour, cover, and set it in a draft-free spot to proof. Stir in abut ¹/₂ cup of the flour to form a thick batter, cover, and return it to the draft-free spot for 30 minutes to an hour, until it develops into a sponge.

Stir the yeast sponge into the sourdough sponge along with the salt, oil, and buckwheat groats. Gradually stir in enough of the remaining flour to form a dough.

Notes
• Soak the bran in unsweetened apple juice and omit the sweeteners.

YIELD: 2 loaves

PREPARATION TIME: 2 to 3 hours for sponge and dough; 5 hours for rising; 40 to 50 minutes to bake

Notes
• Substitute cooked brown rice or cooked millet (see page 19) for the buckwheat groats, or use a combination of cooked grains.

Follow steps 4 to 8 on page 166. Brush on an egg wash and sprinkle on poppy seeds before baking.

SOURDOUGH RYE BREAD

THIS BREAD IS PERMEATED WITH THE UNIQUE SWEETNESS of rye, and it has a compact texture that is perfect for thin slicing. For a truly all-rye bread, use a rye starter, though wheat starter will work just as well. For a lighter bread, substitute whole wheat bread flour for part of the rye flour, and, for best results, use the wheat flour in the sponge.

YIELD: 2 loaves

PREPARATION TIME: 3 to 3½ hours for sponge and dough; 5 hours for rising; 40 to 50 minutes to bake

1 cup sourdough starter	*2 teaspoons sea salt*
2 cups spring water	*2 tablespoons corn or*
7 to 7½ cups rye flour	*other vegetable oil*
¼ teaspoon active dry yeast	

Stir together the starter and 1½ cups of the water in a large bowl. Stir in about 2 cups of the flour to form a thick batter. Cover and set it in a draft-free spot for 2 to 3 hours, or until it develops into a sponge.

Meanwhile, heat the remaining ½ cup of the water and cool it to lukewarm. Stir in the yeast and a teaspoon of flour, cover, and set it in a draft-free spot to proof. Stir in about ½ cup of the flour to form a thick batter, cover, and set it aside for 30 minutes to an hour, until it develops into a sponge.

Stir the yeast sponge into the sourdough sponge along with the salt and oil. Gradually stir in flour to form a dough. Knead gently—rye doughs tend to be stickier than predominantly wheat doughs and require more careful handling. Moistening your hands and the kneading surface with water may help to prevent the dough from becoming overly sticky or tearing. Knead less than you would a wheat dough. If the dough becomes sticky, stop kneading. The dough will become resilient, but it will feel somewhat dense.

Form a ball and place it in a lightly greased bowl. Cover and set it aside at cool room temperature for about 2 hours, until the dough has risen and does not spring back when pressed; it won't rise as much as a dough containing wheat flour. Turn the dough out and knead it briefly. Return it to the bowl for a second rise.

Shape and pan the dough. I recommend a sided container, since freestanding loaves made with this dough tend to spread out rather than rise up. Cover the loaves and set them aside to rise for about an hour, or until the loaves have risen—these won't double in size.

Dock the loaves with a fork. Bake at 400° for 20 minutes, then lower the heat to 350° and bake for 20 to 30 minutes longer, until the loaves have firm sides and sound distinctly hollow when tapped on the bottom. For a shiny crust, brush on an egg glaze before baking or apply a cornstarch glaze (page 89) when the bread is about half baked, and then about 5 minutes before it is done.

Cool the bread thoroughly before slicing or storing it.

Pain pour Nicol!

ANY BREAD THAT CONTAINS COARSELY GROUND RYE IS generally called pumpernickel. My favorite story about the origin of this term is the one about Napoleon's horse Nicol. According to this tale, Nicol craved the dark rye bread customarily made by European peasants, and the imperial troops would scour the countryside seeking pain pour Nicol—"bread for Nicol." The appealing mix of flavors in this hearty bread satisfies human aficionados of pumpernickel, too. Try it with **Mushroom Pâté** (page 262). To prepare rye meal, grind or blend rye flakes to a coarse consistency.

YIELD: 2 large loaves

PREPARATION TIME: 2½ to 3 hours for sponge and dough; 5 hours for rising; 40 to 50 minutes to bake

Notes

• Substitute anise or caraway seeds for the fennel, and omit the orange zest if you prefer.

• Omit the yeast, ginger, and ¼ cup of both water and wheat flour; the dough might take slightly longer to rise, and the final product will be a bit heftier.

1 teaspoon freshly grated orange zest

1 medium-sized potato, cubed

3¼ cups spring water

½ cup cornmeal

1½ teaspoons fennel seed, coarsely ground

1 cup rye meal

1 cup sourdough starter

7 to 7½ cups whole wheat bread flour

¼ teaspoon active dry yeast

¼ teaspoon ground ginger

2 tablespoons blackstrap molasses

3 tablespoons corn or other vegetable oil

2½ teaspoons sea salt

1½ cups rye flour

Combine the zest, potato, and ½ cup of the water in a blender. Blend, gradually adding 1 cup of water, until smooth. Transfer this mixture to a saucepan and stir in the cornmeal. Add 1½ cups boiling water and cook over medium heat, stirring, until thick. Transfer it to a large bowl, stir in the fennel seed and rye meal, and cool to lukewarm. Stir in the starter and 3 cups of wheat flour to form a thick batter. Cover and set it in a draft-free spot for about 2 hours, until the batter develops into a sponge.

Meanwhile, heat the remaining ¼ cup of water and cool it to lukewarm. Add the yeast and about a teaspoon of wheat flour. Cover and set it in a draft-free spot to proof. Stir in the ginger and ¼ cup of wheat flour. Cover and return it to the draft-free spot for about 30 minutes, until it develops into a sponge.

Stir the yeast sponge into the sourdough sponge along with the molasses, oil, salt, and rye flour. Gradually stir in enough of the remaining wheat flour to form a dough.

Follow steps 4 to 8 on page 166. Spray the loaves with water or brush on an egg wash before baking, or brush on a cornstarch glaze (page 89) halfway though baking and again about 5 minutes before the bread is done.

SUPER SUNDAY SCONES

REMEMBER TO RENEW YOUR STARTER THE NIGHT BEFORE you want to make these scrumptious scones for a breakfast or brunch treat.

1¹/2 teaspoons lemon juice
¹/2 cup milk or
unsweetened soy milk,
scalded and cooled
to lukewarm
¹/2 cup sourdough starter
2 tablespoons vegetable oil
2 tablespoons maple syrup
¹/4 cup currants or other
chopped dried fruit
¹/2 cup rolled oats

1 cup whole wheat pastry
flour, plus extra for
shaping
¹/4 teaspoon sea salt
1 teaspoon baking powder
¹/2 teaspoon baking soda
¹/4 teaspoon ground
cinnamon
¹/4 teaspoon freshly grated
nutmeg

YIELD: 6 scones

PREPARATION TIME: Several hours or overnight to renew starter; 15 to 20 minutes to mix and shape; 10 to 15 minutes to bake

Add the lemon juice to the milk and set it aside until the milk curdles.

In a mixing bowl, stir together the starter, oil, syrup, and curdled milk. Stir in the currants. If time allows, cover the bowl and set this mixture aside for an hour or so.

Preheat the oven to 450°.

Grind the rolled oats to flour in a blender and sift it with the flour, salt, baking powder, baking soda, cinnamon, and nutmeg. Add this to the wet mixture and stir gently to form a soft dough. Turn the dough out onto a floured surface and knead it a few times, just until it comes together into a ball and is not sticky. Pat the dough into a round about 1 inch thick. Cut 6 wedges.

Arrange the wedges on a lightly greased or parchment-lined baking sheet and bake 10 to 15 minutes, until they have browned and a tester inserted in the center comes

Notes
• Substitute ¹/2 cup barley or rye flour for the rolled oats.
• Stir about ¹/3 cup peeled, finely diced apple into the wet mixture just before adding the dry ingredients.

out clean. Transfer the scones to a cooling rack and cover them loosely with a dry, unnapped towel, for 15 to 20 minutes. Serve them warm.

SOURDOUGH MUFFINS

THE SOURDOUGH STARTER CONTRIBUTES A SLIGHT TANG to the favor of these moist muffins. Baking soda leavens them, so they are quick to make. These are good keepers if there are ever any leftovers.

YIELD: 10 to 12 muffins

PREPARATION TIME: 20 minutes to prepare; 20 minutes to bake

1½ cups whole wheat
    pastry flour
½ cup rye flour
½ teaspoon sea salt
1 teaspoon baking soda
⅓ cup sunflower oil
⅓ cup maple syrup
1 egg
½ cup milk or
    unsweetened soy milk

Finely grated zest of
    1 orange
¼ cup orange juice
¾ cup sourdough starter
½ cup raisins or chopped
    dates or figs
½ cup lightly toasted,
    coarsely chopped pecans

Preheat the oven to 400°. Grease the muffin cups.

Sift together the flours, salt, and baking soda.

In a medium-sized mixing bowl, whisk together the oil and syrup. Thoroughly beat in the egg. Whisk in the milk, orange zest and juice, and the starter. Stir in the raisins. Add the dry mixture and nuts, and fold gently, mixing just enough to form a batter.

Fill the muffin cups. Bake for 20 minutes, or until a tester inserted in the center comes out clean. Cool the muffins for about 5 minutes in the pan, then loosen each one with a small metal spatula and turn them out onto a rack.

Notes

• Substitute more orange juice for part of the milk if the orange yields more than ¼ cup when squeezed.
• Substitute cornmeal or oat flour for the rye flour.
• Substitute ¼ cup of 1 part flaxseeds thoroughly blended with 3 parts water for the egg.

SOURDOUGH CORN BREAD

TENDER AND SLIGHTLY TANGY, THIS CORN BREAD IS AN excellent complement to bean dishes and soups.

1 cup sourdough starter

1 cup cornmeal

3/4 cup milk or unsweetened soy milk, scalded and cooled to lukewarm

2 tablespoons wheat germ, bran, or sesame or poppy seeds

1 cup whole wheat pastry flour

1/2 teaspoon sea salt

1/2 teaspoon baking soda

1/4 cup vegetable oil or melted unsalted butter or margarine

2 tablespoons maple syrup, honey, or rice syrup (optional)

1 egg

YIELD: 1 (8-inch) square or (9-inch) round bread

PREPARATION TIME: About 2 hours for sponge and batter; 20 to 25 minutes to bake

In a mixing bowl, stir together the starter, cornmeal, and milk. Cover and set it aside for about 2 hours, until the batter has developed into a sponge.

Preheat the oven to 400°. Grease an 8-inch square or 9-inch round baking pan. Add the wheat germ, bran, or seeds and tilt the pan to coat the bottom and sides.

Sift together the flour, salt, and baking soda.

Whisk together the oil, sweetener, and egg. Beat this mixture into the sponge. Gently fold in the dry mixture, mixing just enough to form a batter. Spread it in the prepared pan.

Bake in the preheated oven for 20 to 25 minutes, until the top is brown and a tester inserted in the center comes out clean. Cool the bread briefly and serve it warm.

Notes

• For an especially crusty corn bread, bake the batter in a preheated, greased 9-inch cast-iron frying pan.

• You may omit the baking soda; let the batter rise in the pan before baking.

• Substitute 1/4 cup of 1 part flaxseeds thoroughly blended with 3 parts water for the egg.

YIELD: 1 large loaf

PREPARATION TIME: 20 minutes to prepare; about 2 hours to rise; 1 hour to bake

Notes
• When this bread is a day or two old, I like to serve slices lightly toasted.

Sourdough Banana Bread

ONLY MILDLY SWEET, THIS IS DEFINITELY A BREAD RATHER than a dessert. Serve it with **Tahini-Miso Spread** (page 249).

¹/₄ cup sunflower oil or other light vegetable oil	1 cup sourdough starter
¹/₄ cup honey, maple syrup, or rice syrup	2 cups sifted whole wheat pastry flour
1 egg	¹/₂ teaspoon sea salt
1 cup mashed ripe banana	³/₄ cup lightly toasted, coarsely chopped walnuts
1 tablespoon lemon juice	2 tablespoons poppy seeds

In a large mixing bowl, whisk together the oil and sweetener. Beat in the egg. Whisk in the banana, lemon juice, and starter.

Sift together the flour and salt, and stir it into the liquid mixture to form a thick batter. Fold in the walnuts.

Grease a 9 x 5-inch glass or ceramic loaf pan and coat the bottom and sides with the poppy seeds. Evenly spread in the batter. Cover it with a damp towel and set it in a draft-free spot to rise for about 2 hours.

When the batter has risen almost to the top of the pan, place it in a cold oven and set the oven to 325°. Bake for 1 hour, or until a tester inserted in the center comes out clean. Cool the bread in the pan 15 to 20 minutes, then turn it out onto a rack. This bread slices best after it has thoroughly cooled.

Trail Biscuits

YIELD: 6 biscuits

PREPARATION TIME: 20 minutes to prepare; 30 to 60 minutes to rise; 30 minutes to bake

THESE NO-FRILLS, SLIGHTLY CHEWY SOURDOUGH BISCUITS are probably closest to those made by pioneer travelers and miners. My dad still has the gold scales his grandfather used when he prospected in California during the Gold Rush. Most likely, he attributed equal value to his sourdough.

1 cup whole wheat pastry
   flour, plus extra for
   shaping
1/2 teaspoon sea salt
1/4 teaspoon baking soda

1 tablespoon Sucanat
   (optional)
1 1/2 cups sourdough starter
Melted butter or margarine,
   or vegetable oil

Sift together the flour, salt, baking soda, and Sucanat. Add this mixture to the starter and stir to form a soft dough.

Turn the dough out on a floured surface and knead it gently a few times. Pat it out about 1/2 inch thick and cut it into wedges or other shapes. Arrange the wedges on an ungreased baking sheet, close together for soft-sided biscuits or further apart for crusty ones. Brush the tops with melted butter or margarine and set the biscuits in a warm, draft-free spot for 30 minutes, or until they are light and puffy.

Bake the biscuits in a preheated 375° oven for about 30 minutes, until they are browned and a tester inserted in the center comes out clean. Transfer them to a rack to cool, covered with a cloth towel, for about 15 minutes. Serve them warm.

Sourdough Waffles

Serve these waffles with maple syrup, fruit butters, and fresh berries in season.

2/3 cup sourdough starter
2/3 cup spring water
1 1/2 cups whole wheat
   pastry flour
1/4 teaspoon sea salt
1 tablespoon maple syrup

1 tablespoon sesame or
   other vegetable oil
1/2 cup milk or unsweetened
   soy milk, scalded and
   cooled to lukewarm

Yield: 4 to 6 waffles, depending on the waffle iron

Preparation time: Several hours or overnight for the sponge; about 1 hour for the batter; 3 to 5 minutes to cook each batch

Stir together the starter, water, and 1 cup of the flour in a glass or ceramic bowl. Cover and let it sit at room temperature for several hours or overnight, until the batter develops into a sponge.

Notes
- Substitute cornmeal or rye, oat, barley, or buckwheat flour for the ½ cup of whole wheat pastry flour added to the sponge.
- Add ½ cup of puréed baked winter squash or sweet potato to the batter, along with the salt, syrup, oil, and milk, and substitute cornmeal for the ½ cup of whole wheat pastry flour added to the sponge. Thin the batter with more milk as needed.

Beat in the salt, syrup, oil, milk, and remaining ½ cup flour. Cover the mixture and set it aside for about 1 hour, until it appears "spongy" again.

Preheat your waffle iron if necessary and lightly grease the grids. Ladle on the batter and bake, following directions for your particular waffle iron. Serve the waffles immediately or keep them warm and crisp by placing them directly on a rack in the oven set on low heat.

EIGHT

Natural-Rise Breads

THE ITHACA SEED COMPANY WAS A BOOKSTORE/RESTAURANT located in an old cinder block garage down an alleyway just off the Cornell University campus in the late 1960s. I was drawn to the bookstore first. There were floor-to-ceiling shelves of counterculture titles to peruse, comfortable overstuffed chairs and sofas, and no pressure to buy. But the kitchen clatter and aromas quickly diverted my attention. The restaurant served a fixed-price dinner each evening, and these simple meals introduced me to a whole grain- and bean-based cuisine, including naturally leavened bread. Actually, "unleavened" might describe those hearty loaves more accurately. Yet, despite their density, there was something about those breads that intrigued me: Though heavy and compact, the thick slices were chewy and flavorful.

For many of you, "naturally leavened" may connote the leaden loaves that appeared in early natural foods establishments like the Seed Company. Indeed, some so-called natural-rise breads really are lifeless lumps that plunge to the depths of your stomach as soon as you swallow. It's understandable that experiencing a few such indigestible disasters would make anyone wary of the term.

But not all natural-rise breads deserve such a bad reputation. Given the opportunity, doughs prepared without commercial yeast or sourdough starters will rise into some of the most outstanding breads imaginable. When I first tasted a fine natural-rise bread, I felt I had reached the end of a journey, a long unconscious search for the ultimate in flavor and texture. No two batches ever emerge from the oven just alike, but there is something about skillfully made natural-rise bread that is extraordinarily satisfying. I have witnessed its broad appeal—even to whole grain skeptics who dared to try it.

Well-made naturally leavened breads have an especially moist and flavorful fine-grained crumb. This is because thoroughly fermented dough absorbs liquid particularly well and produces a subtle, complex flavor mix that highlights grains' natural sweetness. Natural-rise loaves' chewy crusts seal in both moisture and flavor, preserving freshness. Stored at room temperature, a natural-rise loaf reaches its peak in flavor and texture several days after baking as its crust softens and crumb mellows. You will be amazed at how easy it is to slice natural-rise breads thinly, and you'll find that a little of their hearty goodness goes a long way.

Natural-rise bread making is based on the principle that, given time and temperate moist conditions, a fresh whole grain dough without commercial yeast or sourdough starter will undergo fermentation and rise. Left long enough in a slightly cool, draft-free spot, an unyeasted dough will attract ambient yeast and go through chemical changes analogous to those that take place in yeasted doughs or sourdoughs, though fermentation and rising will occur at a slower pace. As the carbohydrates are broken down during dough fermentation, other changes take place, developing flavor and making nutrients more absorbable. The grains in natural-rise doughs are partially digested during the long fermentation process, and, therefore, natural-rise breads are particularly nutritious and easy for the body to process.

In doughs leavened with commercial yeast, the yeast typically proliferates at such a rapid rate that the dough reaches its peak of elasticity well before it is fully developed in other ways. In natural-rise dough, however, the yeast multiplies at a pace more compatible with full development. A basic natural-rise bread's rising process might take up to 40 hours but is more often about 24 hours. "Two or three days to make bread!" I can hear you shouting out loud. But trust me. Patience may be out of vogue, but this bread is truly worth the wait.

Natural-rise breads' long proofing period can even be advantageous, because most of the time the dough is developing without any help from you. Lengthy intervals between dough-working tasks make this bread process ideal for a busy schedule. You might prepare the dough one evening and bake it the following morning, evening, or the morning after that, depending on dough development. Only a few quick kneading sessions intervene between the initial mixing and kneading and baking. Also, natural-rise bread making is particularly appealing in hot weather, because you can both work the dough and bake the bread in the cool of the evening or early morning. A low oven temperature is a further warm weather plus.

Creating natural-rise breads is more suspenseful and magical than any other type of bread making. Though mysterious, commercial yeast and sourdough starters are at least perceptible. Natural-rise doughs seem to expand by faith alone, and working with them challenges a baker's confidence and patience. You'll probably find it helpful to become well versed in yeasted baking techniques before tackling natural-rise breads.

Except for commercial yeast, a natural-rise bread requires the same ingredients as a basic yeasted bread. There are, however, important considerations to bear in mind. Fresh whole grain flour and pure spring water are especially crucial for success. Whole grains contain all the necessary elements for thorough fermentation to occur, so the less refined a flour, the better for naturally leavened breads. Minerals in spring water facilitate fermentation, while chemicals typically found in tap water may impede it. Quality sea salt regulates fermentation and enhances flavor, while also fending off undesirable microorganisms. Include about $1/4$ teaspoon salt for each cup of flour. A small amount of good-quality oil will make the crumb a bit more rich and tender.

I sometimes add a booster of some kind to speed up natural-rise breads' fermentation and rising. Unlike a sourdough starter, some of which is always saved for future bakings, a natural-rise booster only serves for a single batch of dough. It may be a fermented—or fermentable—liquid, such as preservative-free, unpasteurized apple cider or grape juice, or even, as I once discovered, leftover onion soup! Slightly soured cooked whole grains or porridge also provides a stimulus for rising. Amasake, a traditional Oriental fermented grain preparation, is another particularly effective and appealing booster for natural-rise breads, contributing sweetness as well as leavening power. Adding sprouted grains or beans and substituting dissolved miso for salt seem to accelerate dough development too. All of these boosters contribute to natural-rise breads' flavor and texture, as well as abetting leavening. You'll see later in the chapter that techniques for boosted natural-rise breads vary somewhat from the following basic natural-rise bread recipe.

NATURAL-RISE BREADS ARE MADE BY THE SAME GENERAL methods used for making yeasted breads, so you might want to review the instructions in Chapter 5. The biggest difference is that rising periods for natural-rise breads are considerably longer than those for yeasted or sourdough breads. Natural-rise breads can be made with either a sponge or a straight-dough method, but most develop thoroughly without a sponge stage. Breads which include a leavening booster such as cider or amasake do require an initial sponge.

Assemble the same utensils you use for yeasted or sourdough breads (see page 80). The ingredients required to make one large loaf of a basic natural-rise whole wheat bread are

2^1/$_2$ *cups lukewarm spring water*	6 *cups whole wheat bread flour*
1^1/$_2$ *teaspoons sea salt*	
2 *tablespoons corn or sesame oil*	

Proceed with the following steps:

❧ 1. Stir together the liquid, salt, and oil in a large bowl. Gradually add flour, a cup at a time, beating well after each addition, until the dough is too stiff to stir. (Another way preferred by some bakers to mix this type of dough is to start with the flour in the bowl. Mix in the oil with your fingers until it is evenly distributed throughout the flour, then dissolve the salt in the liquid and add it to the flour until a workable dough forms. You may have to adjust the flour or liquid slightly to achieve the correct dough consistency.)

❧ 2. Turn the dough out on a lightly floured surface, cover, and let it rest for several minutes.

❧ 3. Knead the dough until it is smooth and resilient. Natural-rise doughs tend to be a bit more difficult to

Making a Basic Natural-Rise Whole Wheat Bread

Variations

It's easy to vary this bread's flavor and texture. Try substituting another flour for a small proportion (10 to 20 percent) of the whole wheat. Maintain at least 80 percent whole wheat bread flour, though, to ensure the dough strength necessary for rising. As you'll see in some of the following recipes, cooked whole grains and soaked cracked grains provide textural interest as well as flavor. Chopped raw or cooked vegetables such as onions or carrots, fruit chunks or purées, dried fruits, minced fresh or crushed dried herbs, spices, sprouts, seeds, and nuts also contribute to a bread's personality. Explore the possibilities and devise your own recipes.

work with than yeasted doughs or sourdoughs, so thorough kneading may take a little extra time and effort. I knead on a lightly floured surface, though some people find it easier to knead on a slightly wet surface. You might want to experiment with both alternatives.

❧ 4. When the dough is ready, form it into a ball. Wash the bowl, grease it lightly, and place the dough inside, turning it to grease the top. Cover the bowl with a damp towel and solid cover and set it in a draft-free spot.

❧ 5. Depending upon temperature and the specific dough, the rising period may take anywhere from 8 to as much as 40 hours. Warm temperatures (over about 70°) promote more rapid fermentation but also may increase sourness in the bread, since bacteria that produce a sour flavor thrive in warmer doughs. So it's better to keep it on the cool side. Cool room temperature is generally fine. Even if it hasn't risen, turn the dough out and knead it briefly every 6 to 8 hours; at the same time, redampen the towel covering the bowl. The fragrance and feel of the dough will gradually alter: It will acquire a sweet-and-slightly-sour smell and will spread out and begin to rise, though probably not as dramatically and evenly as a commercially yeasted or sourdough dough.

❧ 6. When the dough has risen, turn it out and knead it briefly. Cover it for a few minutes, until it relaxes again. Then shape a loaf and press it into a greased pan; the dough should fill about two-thirds of the pan. You could make a freestanding loaf, but this is a soft dough and the support provided by a sided container results in better shaped bread.

❧ 7. Lightly grease the top of the loaf and cover it with a damp towel, or put the pan into a large plastic bag and trap air inside when you twist it closed, forming a big bubble around the pan. Set it aside until the dough rises to the top of the pan. This may take from 2 to 6 hours at room temperature. To speed up rising, set the panned dough in a warmer location, such as inside a gas oven with a pilot light. Be sure the temperature isn't hot enough to kill the yeast, that is, over about 120°. In a warm spot, the dough will probably rise in 30 minutes to an hour.

∿ 8. Once the dough has risen, slash the top and place it in a cold oven. Set the oven to 300°. By heating the oven with the loaf already in it, you'll give the bread an extra boost. Bake the bread for 1½ hours, or until it is well browned and slips out of the pan readily. The loaf should sound distinctly hollow when removed from the pan and thumped on the bottom.

∿ 9. Set the bread on a rack and cool it thoroughly before slicing or storing. Keep the loaf in a covered container or wrapped in clean, dry towels in a cool, dry location. If it begins to dry out, steam slices briefly.

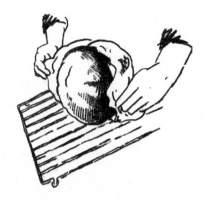

ℳiso 𝐵read

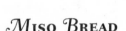

MISO TAKES THE PLACE OF SALT IN THIS NATURAL-RISE bread and gives it a special, unique flavor. Different kinds of miso will subtly alter the taste of the bread. Be sure to use unpasteurized miso: it has active enzymes that assist the fermentation and rising of the dough. This loaf is superbly moist and slices thinly.

YIELD: 1 large loaf

PREPARATION TIME: 30 to 40 minutes for the dough; 8 or more hours for rising; 1½ hours to bake

2 tablespoons unpasteurized miso	6 to 6½ cups whole wheat bread flour
2½ cups warm spring water	
2 tablespoons sesame or other vegetable oil	

In a large bowl, whisk the miso and ¼ cup of the warm water to a smooth paste. Whisk in the remaining water and the oil. Gradually stir in enough of the flour to form a dough.

Follow steps 2 to 9 on page 189–191.

ℳiso is fermented soybean paste, consisting of cooked soybeans, salt, water, a grain culture (see **Koji** on page 200), and often cooked rice, barley, or another grain. Different types of miso vary in color, flavor, saltiness, and texture. Light-colored misos, such as mellow barley or mellow rice miso, contain proportionately fewer soybeans, more grain, and less salt than dark misos and are aged for a shorter time. I use miso as a seasoning in many dishes instead of salt. Miso is high in protein and its enzymes promote digestion. To preserve these beneficial enzymes, do not boil a mixture after adding miso. Like other salty substances, miso enhances the flavor of foods, but it also adds a special depth and richness.

BARLEYCORN BREAD

YIELD: 1 large loaf

PREPARATION TIME: About 1 hour for the dough; 8 hours or more for rising; 1½ hours to bake

JOHN BARLEYCORN IS ONLY PRESENT IN THIS BREAD AS A by-product of dough fermentation, but the wonderfully nutty flavor of roasted barley flour and cornmeal pervades the finished loaf. This is a light, even-textured bread.

2 tablespoons sesame or other vegetable oil	3 cups spring water
½ cup barley flour	2 teaspoons sea salt
½ cup cornmeal	5½ to 6 cups whole wheat bread flour

Heat 1 tablespoon of the oil in a heavy-bottomed skillet over low heat. Stir in the barley flour and cornmeal, and cook, stirring often, until the grains are lightly roasted and fragrant; transfer to a large bowl.

Heat the water to boiling, add the salt, and gradually whisk with the roasted flours to form a smooth batter. Whisk in the remaining tablespoon of oil. Gradually stir in enough of the wheat flour to form a dough.

Follow steps 2 to 9 on page 189–191.

NATURAL-RISE GRITS BREAD

YIELD: 1 large loaf

PREPARATION TIME: 30 to 60 minutes for the dough; 12 or more hours for rising; 1½ hours to bake

THIS FINE LOAF HAS THE WONDERFUL DEPTH OF FLAVOR that only its key ingredient—time—can bestow. Grits add a subtle crunch.

3 cups spring water	6 to 7 cups whole wheat bread flour
2 teaspoons sea salt	
¼ cup soy grits	
2 tablespoons corn or other vegetable oil	

Notes
• Substitute corn, barley, or rice grits, cracked wheat or rye, or steel-cut oats for soy grits.
• Brush the loaf with an egg wash and sprinkle on sesame seeds just before baking.

Heat the water to boiling, add the salt, and pour over the grits in a large bowl. Cover and cool to lukewarm.

Stir in the oil and gradually add enough of the flour to form a dough.

Follow steps 2 to 9 on page 189–191.

Natural-Rise Oat Bread

Oats give this bread an especially sweet, rich taste and a pleasantly chewy texture.

3 cups spring water	2 tablespoons sesame or
1 cup rolled oats	other vegetable oil
2 teaspoons sea salt	5 to 6 cups wheat bread flour

Yield: 1 large loaf

Preparation time: 1 hour for the dough; 8 or more hours for rising; 1½ to 2 hours to bake

Heat the water to boiling and pour it over the oats and salt in a large bowl. Cover and set aside until lukewarm.

Stir the oil into the oats. Gradually stir in enough of the flour to form a dough.

Follow steps 2 to 9 on page 189–191.

Notes
- Substitute rolled wheat, rye, or barley for the oats.

Natural-Rise Sprout Bread

Sprouts may accelerate the rising of this moist, flavorful bread. Begin sprouting ¼ cup of wheat berries about three days ahead of time; the sprouts should be about the same length as the wheat berries when you make the dough.

2½ cups spring water	2 cups wheat sprouts,
1½ teaspoons sea salt	coarsely chopped (see
2 tablespoons sesame or	page 102)
other vegetable oil	
6 cups whole wheat	
bread flour	

Yield: 1 large loaf

Preparation time: 30 to 40 minutes for the dough; 8 or more hours for rising; 1½ hours to bake

Heat the water and cool it to lukewarm.

In a large bowl, stir together the water, salt, and oil. Gradually stir in 2½ cups of the flour to form a thick batter. Stir in the sprouts. Gradually stir in enough of the remaining flour to form a dough.

Follow steps 2 to 9 on page 189–191.

STEAMED BROWN BREAD

YIELD: 1 loaf

PREPARATION TIME: 30 to 40 minutes for the dough; 8 or more hours for rising; 3 hours to steam (or 1 hour to pressure-steam)

BOSTON BROWN BREAD IS A STEAMED BREAD TRADITIONally made with a mixture of cornmeal and rye and wheat flours. It is customarily sweetened with molasses, and leavened with baking soda and/or baking powder. In the Northeastern grocery stores of my childhood, cans of brown bread were stacked on the same shelf as the baked beans, with which it was commonly served. Steamed breads are especially moist and digestible, and this compact, even-textured, raisin-studded variation-on-a-classic is no exception. Slice it razor thin and serve it warmed, toasted, plain, with a spread, or with beans! For the steaming arrangement, you'll need a fairly deep, straight-sided container for the bread that will fit inside a large pot or a canning kettle. I use a deep, ovenproof ceramic bowl. You can also use a couple of smaller containers, such as wide-mouthed, pint-sized canning jars or cans (without lead-soldered seams).

1 cup cornmeal	*1 teaspoon sea salt*
1 cup rye flour	*1½ cups spring water*
1½ to 1¾ cups whole wheat bread flour	*½ cup raisins (optional)*

Sift the cornmeal, rye flour, 1 cup of the wheat flour, and salt into a medium-sized bowl and make a well in the center. Warm the water and pour it into the dry mixture. Stir until a dough forms.

Follow steps 2 to 5 on page 189–190.

When the dough has risen, knead in the raisins. Cover the dough for several minutes.

Shape and pan the dough; the container should be about two-thirds full. Cover and set it aside to rise.

Cover the container with a lid or with waxed paper, baking parchment, or heavy muslin tied on with a string. Set it on a rack in a deep pot and add boiling water

halfway up the sides of the container. Cover the pot and steam the bread for 3 hours, adding more water if necessary, or steam it in a pressure cooker for 1 hour. For small containers, steam 1¹/₂ hours or pressure-steam for 30 minutes.

Cool the bread in the container on a rack briefly; remove it from the pan to finish cooking.

CIDER-RICE BREAD

APPLE CIDER WORKS WONDERS AS A BOOSTER IN THIS subtly sweet and chewy natural-rise bread, which strikes an excellent balance between hearty and light. Be sure to get unpasteurized cider without preservatives so that it will ferment rather than spoil. Once the cider-rice sponge is ready, the bread-making process is similar to methods and time requirements for making a basic yeasted whole wheat bread using the sponge technique.

YIELD: 2 loaves

PREPARATION TIME: 8 to 12 hours for the rice; 2¹/₂ hours for sponge and dough; 5 to 6 hours for rising; 1¹/₂ hours to bake

1 cup short- or medium-grain brown rice	*7 to 8 cups whole wheat bread flour*
2 cups spring water	*2 teaspoons sea salt*
2 cups apple cider (unpasteurized, with no preservatives)	*2 tablespoons corn or other vegetable oil*

Combine the rice and water in a medium-sized saucepan and bring to a boil. Stir once, cover tightly, turn the heat to very low, and cook 40 minutes. Turn off the heat and leave the pot covered for an hour or more, until the rice has cooled to lukewarm. Transfer the rice to a large bowl. Add the cider and cover for several hours or overnight, until the mixture is obviously bubbly and active.

Beat in 2 cups of the flour to form a thick batter. Cover and set it aside for about 2 hours, or until a sponge develops.

Stir the salt and oil into the sponge. Gradually stir in enough of the remaining flour to form a dough.

• Small wineries sometimes sell unpasteurized grape juice that doesn't contain any preservatives; substitute this for the apple cider.
• This dough is great for rolls; bake 3- to 4-ounce rolls for about 45 minutes.

Turn the dough out onto a lightly floured surface and cover it for several minutes, until it relaxes. Knead the dough until it is smooth and elastic, adding more flour as necessary to keep it from sticking.

Form the dough into a ball and place it in a lightly greased bowl. Cover and set it in a draft-free spot for about 2 hours, or until the dough has risen and a finger pressed into it leaves a depression. Turn the dough out and knead it briefly. Return it to the bowl and set it aside for about 2 hours, until the dough has risen again.

Shape and pan the dough. Cover the pans and set them aside until the dough has risen to the top. Slash the tops of the loaves. Bake at 300° for about $1^{1}/_{2}$ hours, until the loaves are well browned, firm, and sound distinctly hollow when removed from the pans and tapped on the bottom.

Cool the bread thoroughly before slicing or storing it.

Natural-Rise Rye Berry Bread

Like **Cider-Rice Bread,** this bread relies on fermented apple cider to boost its rising, and the methods and time requirements for making it resemble those for a basic yeasted whole wheat bread—once the cider-rye sponge has developed. Rye berries contribute their unique rugged flavor. Use part of the dough to make rolls or terrific bagels!

Yield: 3 loaves

Preparation time: 12 to 24 hours for the rye berries; 2 to 12 hours for sponge and dough; 5 to 6 hours for rising; $1^{1}/_{2}$ hours to bake

4 cups spring water
$1^{1}/_{2}$ cups rye berries
3 cups apple cider (unpasteurized, no preservatives)
8 to 9 cups whole wheat bread flour

$^{1}/_{4}$ cup blackstrap molasses
$^{1}/_{4}$ cup corn or other vegetable oil
1 tablespoon sea salt
1 tablespoon fennel seeds
1 tablespoon caraway seeds

Heat the water to boiling and pour it over the rye berries in a saucepan. Cover and soak for at least an hour. Uncover and bring to a boil. Cover, turn the heat to very low, and cook for about an hour, until the rye is tender and the water absorbed. Cool the grain in the pot.

Transfer the rye berries to a large bowl and add the cider. Cover and soak for 12 to 24 hours, until the mixture is bubbly and active—the length of this period depends on the sweetness/hardness of the cider.

Stir in enough of the flour to form a thick batter. Cover and set in a draft-free spot for several hours, until the batter develops into a sponge.

Stir the molasses, oil, salt, and fennel and caraway seeds into the sponge. Gradually stir in enough of the remaining flour to form a dough.

Turn the dough out onto a lightly floured surface and cover it for several minutes. Knead the dough thoroughly, adding flour as necessary to keep it from sticking.

Form the dough into a ball and place it in a lightly greased bowl. Cover and set it in a draft-free spot for about 2 hours, or until the dough has risen and does not spring back when pressed. Turn the dough out and knead it briefly, then return it to the bowl for about 2 hours, until it has risen again.

Shape and pan the dough. Cover the loaves and set them aside until the dough rises to the top of the pans.

Slash the tops of the loaves. Bake at 300° for 1½ hours, or until the loaves are well browned, firm, and sound hollow when removed from the pans and tapped on the bottom.

Cool the bread thoroughly before slicing or storing it.

Rice Kayu Bread

KAYU IS A JAPANESE GRAIN PORRIDGE THAT IS TRADITIONally cooked to a soft, creamy consistency. I prefer the

Notes
• Substitute wheat berries or whole oats for the rye berries, and omit the molasses, fennel, and caraway.

YIELD: 1 large loaf

PREPARATION TIME: 24 hours or so for the rice; 30 to 40 minutes for the dough; 6 to 12 hours for rising; 1½ hours to bake

Notes

- For **Millet Kayu Bread,** substitute 1 cup millet for the rice.
- Substitute 3 to 4 cups leftover rice or millet, or a combination of cooked grains, and omit the cooking water. You can also add leftover vegetables and even salad; blend these with a bit of liquid (or leftover soup) and mix with the grain(s).
- For **Barley Kayu Bread:** Heat 2¼ cups water to boiling and pour it over ¾ cup whole barley in a medium-sized saucepan. Soak for 1 hour or longer. Bring to a boil, reduce the heat, cover loosely, and cook until the barley is tender. Add more water if necessary. Cool the barley to lukewarm, then transfer it to a large bowl. Cover and let sit at room temperature for about 24 hours, until the barley smells slightly sour. Proceed as for **Rice Kayu Bread.**

texture of relatively firm grains of rice in this bread, but adjust the amount of liquid to suit your own taste. Slice this loaf thinly and savor its complex flavors.

1 cup short- or medium-grain brown rice	*2 tablespoons sesame or other vegetable oil*
2½ to 3 cups spring water	*5 to 6 cups whole wheat bread flour*
1½ teaspoons sea salt	

Combine the rice and 2 cups of the water in a medium-sized saucepan and bring it to a boil. Turn the heat to low, cover the pot tightly, and cook 40 minutes. Leave the lid in place and cool the rice. Transfer the rice to a large bowl, cover, and leave it at room temperature for about 24 hours, or until it smells slightly sour.

Warm the remaining ½ to 1 cup water and add enough of it to the rice to achieve a thick, porridge-like consistency. Stir in the salt and oil. Gradually stir in enough of the flour to form a dough.

Turn the dough out onto a lightly floured surface and cover it for several minutes. Knead the dough thoroughly, adding flour as necessary to keep it from sticking. Cover the dough until it relaxes.

Shape and pan the dough—this doesn't rise in the bowl before shaping. Slash the top of the loaf and enclose it in a large plastic bag tied to form a big bubble. Set it aside for 6 to 12 hours, until the dough has risen in the pan.

Place the loaf in a cold oven and set it to 300°. Bake for 1½ hours, or until the bread is well browned, firm, and sounds distinctly hollow when removed from the pan and tapped on the bottom.

Cool the bread thoroughly before slicing or storing it.

Basic Amasake Bread

This bread is sweet-tasting and fine-grained. The technique for making it is similar to that for **Rice Kayu Bread** (page 197) except that this one starts off with a sponge. This recipe is a prototype for the next several breads.

1 cup **Amasake**
2 cups spring water
7 cups whole wheat
  bread flour

2 teaspoons sea salt
2 tablespoons sesame or
  other vegetable oil

∼ 1. In a large bowl, stir together the amasake and water. Stir in 3 cups of the flour to form a batter. Cover and set it aside for 2 or more hours, until a sponge develops.

∼ 2. Stir in the salt and oil. Gradually stir in enough of the remaining flour to form a dough.

∼ 3. Turn the dough out onto a lightly floured surface and cover it for a few minutes. Knead the dough thoroughly, adding flour as necessary to keep it from sticking; it will stay a bit tacky. Cover the dough for several minutes, until it relaxes.

∼ 4. Shape and pan the dough. Slash the top of the loaf. Cover the pan with a large pot or put it into a large plastic bag, gathered and tied to form a big bubble—you want to keep the dough from drying out but prevent anything from sticking to its surface. Leave it for several hours or overnight, until the dough has risen to the top of the pan.

∼ 5. Place the pan in a cold oven. Set the oven to 300° and bake the bread for 1½ hours, or until it is well browned, the sides are firm, and the loaf sounds distinctly hollow when removed from the pan and tapped on the bottom.

∼ 6. Cool the bread thoroughly before slicing or storing it.

YIELD: 1 large loaf

PREPARATION TIME: 2 to 3 hours for sponge and dough; several hours or overnight for rising; 1½ hours to bake

Notes
• For **Amasake-Raisin Bread,** knead a cup of raisins into the dough before shaping.

Amasake

Amasake, which means "sweet sake" in Japanese, is prepared by combining freshly cooked rice, or another grain, with a cultured rice called koji and setting it in a warm spot for 12 or so hours. During this time, enzymes in the koji break down the complex carbohydrates in the grain into simple sugars, rendering them sweet-tasting and easily digestible. This rice puddinglike mixture can be blended with water or fruit to make smoothie-type beverages; it is also an ingredient in some nondairy ice creams. I use amasake in a number of recipes that follow; it boosts rising and adds sweetness to these breads.

(continued on page 200)

YIELD: 1 large loaf

PREPARATION TIME: 12 to 24 hours for the rice and dough; 6 to 12 hours for rising; 1¹/₂ hours to bake

Koji is grain, usually rice or barley, that has been cultured with an aromatic mold called *Aspergillus Oryzae*. It is used to prepare miso, sake, rice vinegar, shoyu, tamari, certain pickles, and amasake (see page 199). You can find koji in natural foods stores, or order it from mail-order sources.

Amasake (cont.)

You may find ready-made amasake in natural foods markets and mail-order catalogs; look for koji there too. If you do purchase amasake, be sure that it has active enzymes for effective leavening.

1 cup short-grain brown rice
2³/₄ cups water
1 cup rice koji

Combine the rice and water in a large saucepan and bring to a boil. Cover tightly, reduce the heat to very low, and cook 1 hour. Leave the lid in place and cool the rice to lukewarm. Thoroughly stir in the koji. Transfer the mixture to a glass or ceramic container and compact it with a wooden spoon or spatula. Place it, covered with a lid or plate, in a warm spot for about 12 hours, until obviously active and bubbly when stirred.

Store amasake in a clean, tightly covered quart jar in the refrigerator; it will keep 3 to 4 weeks.

AMASAKE-RICE BREAD

THIS BREAD TASTES SIMILAR TO **BASIC AMASAKE BREAD** (page 199), but cooked rice adds texture.

1 cup short- or medium-grain brown rice	1¹/₂ teaspoons sea salt
2 cups spring water	2 tablespoons sesame or other vegetable oil
1 cup **Amasake** (page 199)	5 cups whole wheat bread flour

Rinse the rice, combine it with the water in a saucepan, and bring to a boil. Give a quick stir, cover tightly, reduce the heat to very low, and cook 40 minutes. Leave the lid in place and cool the rice to lukewarm.

In a large bowl, thoroughly stir together the rice and amasake. Cover and set it in a draft-free spot for 12 to 24 hours, until the mixture is active and bubbly, particularly when stirred.

Stir in the salt and oil. Gradually stir in enough of the flour to form a dough.

Follow steps 3 to 6 in **Basic Amasake Bread** on page 199.

$\mathcal{A}$MASAKE-$\mathcal{M}$ILLET $\mathcal{B}$READ

THIS BREAD AMAZED ME THE FIRST TIME I BAKED IT. IT IS subtly sweet and light, somehow summery.

1 cup millet
2 cups spring water
1 cup **Amasake**
  (page 199)
1½ teaspoons sea salt

2 tablespoons sesame, corn,
  or other vegetable oil
5 to 5½ cups whole wheat
  bread flour

YIELD: 1 large loaf

PREPARATION TIME: 12 to 24 hours for the millet and dough; 6 to 12 hours to rise; 1½ hours to bake

Rinse the millet. Heat the water to boiling and pour it over the millet in a medium-sized saucepan. Return it to a boil, stir once, and cover tightly. Turn the heat to very low and cook for 30 minutes. Leave the pot lid in place and cool to lukewarm.

Transfer the millet to a large bowl and thoroughly mix in the amasake. Cover and set it in a draft-free spot for 12 to 24 hours, until it is sweet-smelling and bubbly when stirred.

Stir in the salt and oil. Gradually stir in enough of the flour to form a dough.

Follow steps 3 to 6 in **Basic Amasake Bread** on page 199.

AMASAKE-BARLEY BREAD

THIS IS A GREAT BREAD—FULL OF CHEWY NUBS OF BARLEY and wonderfully complex flavors. Hull-less barley has an incomparable flavor and texture; if you can't find a hull-less variety, look for barley that has been minimally pearled.

²/₃ cup whole barley
2²/₃ cups spring water
1 cup **Amasake**
  (page 199)
2 teaspoons sea salt

2 tablespoons sesame, corn,
  or other vegetable oil
5 cups whole wheat bread
  flour

YIELD: 1 large loaf

PREPARATION TIME: Several hours or overnight to soak and cook the barley; 12 to 24 hours for ferment and dough; 6 to 12 hours to rise; 1½ hours to bake

Rinse the barley and place it in a medium-sized saucepan. Heat the spring water to boiling and pour it over the barley. Cover and soak it for several hours or overnight. Bring it just to a boil, reduce the heat to very low, cover loosely, and cook for 50 to 60 minutes, until the barley is tender and the water has been absorbed. Cover and cool to lukewarm.

Transfer the barley to a large bowl and thoroughly stir in the amasake. Cover and leave it at room temperature for 12 to 24 hours, until the mixture is bubbly, particularly when stirred.

Stir in the salt and oil. Gradually stir in enough of the flour to form a dough.

Follow steps 3 to 6 in the recipe for **Basic Amasake Bread** on page 199.

AMASAKE-OAT BREAD

THE CHEWY SWEETNESS DERIVED FROM WHOLE OATS paired with amasake makes this bread superb.

YIELD: 1 large loaf

PREPARATION TIME: Several hours or overnight for oats; 12 to 24 hours for ferment and dough; 6 to 12 hours to rise; 1¹/₂ hours to bake

³/₄ cup whole oats
2¹/₄ cups spring water
1 cup **Amasake**
   (page 199)
1¹/₂ teaspoons sea salt

2 tablespoons sesame or
   other vegetable oil
5 cups whole wheat bread
   flour

Rinse the oats. Heat the water to boiling and pour it over the oats in a medium-sized saucepan. Cover and soak for several hours or overnight. Bring it to a boil, then cover and reduce the heat to very low. Cook for 40 to 60 minutes, until the oats are tender and the water has been absorbed. Leave the pan covered and cool the oats to lukewarm.

Transfer the oats to a large bowl and stir in the amasake. Cover and leave it at room temperature for 12 to 24 hours, until the mixture is bubbly, particularly when stirred.

Stir in the salt and oil. Gradually stir in enough of the flour to form a dough.

Follow steps 3 to 6 in **Basic Amasake Bread** on page 199.

AMASAKE-CORN BREAD

THIS NATURAL-RISE CORN BREAD REQUIRES SOME TIME but little of your energy or attention. It is a sweet, moist companion to beans and soups, and is good sliced and toasted for breakfast, too.

YIELD: 1 (8-inch) square or (9-inch) round bread

PREPARATION TIME: About 1 hour to prepare; several hours or overnight to ferment; $1\frac{1}{2}$ to 2 hours to bake

2 cups spring water
2 cups cornmeal
*$\frac{2}{3}$ cup **Amasake***
   (page 199)
1 cup whole wheat
   pastry flour

1 teaspoon sea salt
1 tablespoon corn or other
   vegetable oil

Heat the water to boiling and stir with the cornmeal in a medium-sized bowl to form a smooth batter; cool to lukewarm. Stir in the amasake and flour. Cover and set it in a draft-free spot for several hours or overnight, until the mixture is bubbly.

Beat in the salt and oil. Spread the batter evenly in a well-greased 8-inch square or 9-inch round pan. Put the pan into a cold oven and set the oven to 300°. Bake for $1\frac{1}{2}$ hours, or until a tester inserted in the center comes out clean. The bread will brown and shrink slightly from the sides of the pan. Turn the bread onto a rack to cool.

AMASAKE MUFFINS

AMASAKE BOTH SWEETENS AND LEAVENS THESE MOIST, chewy muffins. This recipe provides basic ingredient proportions and describes a technique for making natural-rise muffins; vary the grains and/or include additional sweetener, dried fruits, or lightly toasted seeds or

YIELD: 6 muffins

PREPARATION TIME: Several hours to prepare and ferment the batter; 80 to 90 minutes to bake

Notes
• If you substitute flour (for instance, a cup of oat flour) for the rolled oats, omit the grain-soaking step. Simply mix the amasake, a cup of warm water, and the 2 cups of flour together to form the batter.

chopped nuts to modify the flavor and texture. This particular version is good with both sweet and savory spreads.

1 cup spring water	1/2 teaspoon sea salt
1 cup rolled oats	2 tablespoons sesame or
1 cup **Amasake**	other vegetable oil
(page 199)	
1 cup whole wheat	
pastry flour	

Boil the water and pour it over the oats in a medium-sized bowl. Set it aside for about an hour, until the mixture cools to lukewarm. Stir in the amasake. Thoroughly stir in the flour to form a batter. Cover and leave the mixture several hours or overnight, until it becomes somewhat bubbly and rises in the bowl.

Beat in the salt and oil. Distribute the batter among well-greased muffin tins; fill each cup just about to the top for muffins that will rise well above the top of the pan. Place the muffin tin in a cold oven and set the oven to 300°. Bake 80 to 90 minutes. Test by inserting a tester in the center of a muffin. Cool the muffins about 30 minutes before serving.

MIXED GRAIN WAFFLES

THE FLAVORS MINGLE AND MELLOW, AND THE GRAINS soften as this batter rests. In the morning, it becomes light, crisp waffles. Serve them with maple syrup or **Pear Butter** (page 255).

YIELD: 4 waffles—2 to 4 servings

PREPARATION TIME: 10 minutes to mix; several hours or overnight to ferment; 4 to 5 minutes to bake each batch

1/3 cup whole wheat	1/2 teaspoon sea salt
pastry flour	1 2/3 cups unsweetened soy
1/3 cup rye flour	milk, scalded
1/3 cup barley flour	1 tablespoon sesame or
1/3 cup oat flour	other vegetable oil
1/3 cup cornmeal	

In a medium-sized mixing bowl, sift together the flours and salt. Gradually whisk in the milk to form a batter. Cover and set it aside for several hours or overnight. Add the oil and whisk well.

Lightly grease the waffle iron grids—remember, a mixture of two parts vegetable oil to one part liquid soy lecithin works especially well to prevent sticking. Ladle on batter and bake following the directions for your waffle iron—about 2 minutes per side for a stove-top cast-iron one.

Serve the waffles immediately or place them directly on the rack in a low oven to keep warm and crisp.

NINE

Flat Breads

As we stepped into the small Mexican restaurant, the irresistible aroma of fresh corn tortillas engulfed us. In the same instant, a loud voice bellowed: "What do you think you're doing here?!" The unexpected outcry immediately aroused simultaneous sensations of bewilderment, free-floating guilt, and amusement, though something in the stern tone discouraged all six of us from laughing. We focused on an imposing, aproned woman in an open kitchen across the room. At once, we knew that this must be the illustrious "Señora," whose reputation for eccentricity was apparently well-founded. Somehow, we persuaded her to let us stay and eat, even though we hadn't called ahead. Before the meal was finished, she had offered to sell us the restaurant, including recipes for dishes she had cooked for the president of Mexico. To this day, I associate corn tortillas with this singular personality.

Most cuisines feature a flat bread of some sort, tortillas being the predominant bread in Mexico. Some of the French make crêpes, while others make socca, a crêpe-like chickpea flour bread. Dosas, chapatis, and parathas prevail in different parts of India. Mandarin pancakes and scallion bread are Chinese. The Japanese call their thick, meal-sized griddlecakes okonomiyaki. Pita is now almost as popular in the United States as in its original home, the Middle East. Lavosh is a traditional Lebanese flat bread. Johnnycakes are probably more American than apple pie, and they vary from thick patties to lacy rounds. Crackers of various types are found throughout the world.

Although they all end up flat, a few of these breads do some rising or puffing along the way. Pita and lavosh are made from yeasted doughs and rise in the early stages of their development, which makes the dough stronger and enhances its flavor. Pita puffs up in the oven as a result of steam inside the dough, not from the yeast, and falls flat as it cools. Some crackers use leavenings but end up flat because they are rolled thinly and baked quickly.

Most flat breads, however, are unleavened, made from either kneaded doughs or beaten batters and usually cooked on the stovetop. Though unleavened flat breads may be cooked immediately after mixing, they benefit in flavor, texture, and nutrition from a rest period between mixing and baking. The extra time allows the grains to absorb the liquid, which tenderizes them and releases their full flavors. Some fermentation may also take place, making the grains easier to digest and assimilate.

Flat breads don't rely much on gluten development to achieve their shape, so they provide creative bakers with opportunities to use other flours besides wheat. Kneaded flat breads require some high-gluten flour for adhesiveness, but up to about half of the flour in these doughs can be low in gluten. Batter-based flat breads, such as crêpes, don't require wheat gluten at all.

Crêpes

CLASSIC FRENCH CRÊPES ARE PAPER-THIN PANCAKES prepared from a batter consisting of wheat or buckwheat flour, liquid, salt, egg, and sometimes a little oil. Vigorously blend the ingredients by hand or machine and then leave the batter for 30 minutes, preferably longer. This rest period before cooking allows the flour particles to soak up liquid and become soft and spongy, resulting in light, tender crêpes. I make crêpe batter in the evening to cook the following morning or mix it in the morning for dinner crêpes.

Every crêpe maker has a favorite pan. Traditional French crêpe pans are made from relatively thin carbon steel and are flat bottomed with low, sloping sides. Be sure to season this type of pan well. Using a lightweight pan enables you to manipulate the pan with one hand as you spread the batter evenly with the other. For especially efficient crêpe making, work with two pans at once: Cook the first side in your crêpe pan, then flip the crêpe over into a heavy skillet or griddle to finish cooking as you start the next crêpe in your crêpe pan.

The following recipes produce fine, delicate crêpes that go easy on eggs, call for a variety of whole grain flours, and sometimes substitute other liquids for milk. See the **Sandwiches and Filled Flat Breads** chapter for crêpe fillings or invent your own.

WHEAT CRÊPES

YIELD: 12 (6-inch) crêpes

PREPARATION TIME: About 1 hour, plus a minimum of 30 minutes to rest the batter

USE THE DIRECTIONS FOR THESE DELICIOUS FRENCH PANcakes as a prototype for the crêpe recipes that follow.

1 cup whole wheat pastry flour	1 1/2 cups milk or unsweetened soy milk
Pinch of sea salt (optional)	1 tablespoon vegetable oil
1 egg	

To prepare the batter by hand, sift the flour and salt into a bowl; whisk the egg, liquid, and oil in another bowl, then vigorously whisk everything together. To make the batter in a blender, blend the egg and, with the machine still running, add the salt and then gradually add flour for as long as it is absorbed. Add some of the liquid and continue to add the remaining flour and liquid alternately. Finally, add the oil and blend until thoroughly smooth. Strain the batter if any lumps remain, pour it into a deep bowl or pitcher, and cover. Rest the batter for 30 minutes to several hours—in the refrigerator if for more than a brief period.

Set your crêpe pan over medium-high heat. Be sure the pan is hot before you begin cooking. Test it by sprinkling a few drops of water on the surface; they should sizzle and evaporate immediately. Grease the pan lightly.

Give the batter a stir, then, with one hand, pour some batter into the center of the pan from a ladle, pitcher, or large spoon. With the other hand, immediately lift, tilt, and rotate the pan to spread the batter. Quickly return any excess to the batter container and place the pan back on the burner. The amount of batter needed for each crêpe will depend on the size of your pan, but it will probably be about 2 to 4 tablespoons. The batter should spread out readily to less than 1/8 inch thick. If the batter seems too thick, thin with additional liquid, whisking in a small amount at a time. Sometimes it takes a little while to achieve the right batter consistency, amount of batter per crêpe, and pan heat. You'll probably want to make a couple of test crêpes initially.

Crêpes cook quickly and are ready to turn in as little as 30 seconds, when the edges begin to curl and the underside has browned. Slide a slim spatula under the crêpe to loosen it from the pan and flip it over. Cook the second side briefly; this side will be speckled rather than evenly browned when it is done. Lightly grease the pan again if the crêpes seem to be sticking at all. To keep crêpes soft for easy rolling, stack them on a plate covered with an inverted bowl.

Notes
- Substitute oat, rye, or barley flour for part of the wheat flour.

Crêpes store quite well. Separate them with waxed paper to keep them from sticking together. They will keep for a day or two in the refrigerator, longer in the freezer. Wrap them well for freezing, perhaps in meal-sized packages. Thaw crêpes in a covered container in a 300° oven for about 10 minutes.

BUCKWHEAT CRÊPES

YIELD: 12 (6-inch) crêpes

PREPARATION TIME: About 1 hour, plus a minimum of 30 minutes to rest the batter

THESE CRÊPES ARE AS THIN AND DELICATE AS WHEAT ones, but hearty buckwheat flour gives them a different character. If you want to tone down the buckwheat flavor, use part whole wheat pastry flour.

1 cup buckwheat flour
¼ teaspoon sea salt
1 egg

1½ cups water
1 tablespoon vegetable oil

Whisk or blend the ingredients together to form a smooth batter. Cover and set it aside for 30 minutes to several hours, or overnight.

Set a crêpe pan over medium-high heat and grease it lightly. Add batter and lift and rotate the pan immediately to spread it out evenly, about ⅛ inch thick. Turn the crêpe when the bottom is golden and the edges begin to curl. Cook it briefly on the second side. Stack and cover crêpes to keep them warm.

(For detailed instructions, refer to the directions for **Wheat Crêpes** on page 208.)

CORN CRÊPES

YIELD: 12 (6-inch) crêpes

PREPARATION TIME: About 1 hour, plus a minimum of 30 minutes to rest the batter

THESE CRÊPES ARE MEXICAN IN MOOD YET MORE DELIcate than tortillas. Wrap them around **Refritos** (page 256) or **Guacamole** (page 255) and top them with a salsa (page 270–271).

²/₃ cup cornmeal

¹/₃ cup whole wheat
   pastry flour

¹/₄ teaspoon sea salt

1 egg

1¹/₄ cups water or vegetable
   stock

1 tablespoon corn or other
   vegetable oil

Sift together the cornmeal, flour, and salt, then whisk or blend this mixture with the other ingredients to form a smooth batter. Cover and set it aside for 30 minutes to several hours, or overnight.

Set a crêpe pan over medium-high heat and grease it lightly. Add batter and lift and rotate the pan immediately to spread it out evenly, about ¹/₈ inch thick. Turn the crêpe when the bottom is golden and the edges begin to curl. Cook it briefly on the second side. Stack and cover crêpes to keep them warm.

(For detailed instructions, refer to the directions for **Wheat Crêpes** on page 208.)

Lemon Crêpes

FOR A REFRESHING DESSERT, FOLD THESE INTO QUARTERS and spoon **Lemon Sauce** (page 213) on top, or roll them around sorbet or a fruit filling, such as that for **Crisscross Coffee Cake** (page 344).

YIELD: 12 (6-inch) crêpes

PREPARATION TIME: About 1 hour, plus a minimum of 30 minutes to rest the batter

1 cup whole wheat
   pastry flour

Pinch of sea salt

Grated zest of 1 lemon

1 egg

1 tablespoon Sucanat,
   mild-flavored honey, or
   maple syrup

1¹/₂ cups milk or
   unsweetened soy milk

1 tablespoon light
   vegetable oil

Whisk or blend the ingredients together to form a smooth batter. Cover and set it aside for 30 minutes to several hours, or overnight.

Set a crêpe pan over medium-high heat and grease it lightly. Add batter and lift and rotate the pan immediately to spread it out evenly, about ⅛ inch thick. Turn the crêpe when the bottom is golden and the edges begin to curl. Cook it briefly on the second side. Stack and cover crêpes to keep them warm.

(For detailed instructions, refer to the directions for **Wheat Crêpes** on page 208.)

CAROB CRÊPES

YIELD: 12 (6-inch) crêpes

PREPARATION TIME: About 1 hour, plus a minimum of 30 minutes to rest the batter

CAROB CRÊPES ARE DEFINITELY FOR DESSERT. DRIZZLE A little carob syrup or maple syrup over them, or roll them around ice cream, dairyless frozen desserts, or fresh fruit—peaches are good.

¼ cup roasted carob powder
¾ cup whole wheat pastry flour
Pinch of sea salt
1 egg
1½ cups milk or unsweetened soy milk

1 tablespoon mild-flavored honey, maple syrup, or Sucanat
1 tablespoon walnut or other light vegetable oil

Whisk or blend the ingredients together to form a smooth batter. Cover and set it aside for 30 minutes to several hours, or overnight.

Set a crêpe pan over medium-high heat and grease it lightly. Add batter and lift and rotate the pan immediately to spread it out evenly, about ⅛ inch thick. Turn the crêpe when the bottom is golden and the edges begin to curl. Cook it briefly on the second side. Stack and cover crêpes to keep them warm.

(For detailed instructions, refer to the directions for **Wheat Crêpes** on page 208.)

ORANGE CRÊPES

SERVE THESE FOR DESSERT WITH **ORANGE SAUCE** (at right) or rolled around fresh berries or other fillings.

1 orange	*2 eggs*
About 1 cup unsweetened apple juice	*1 tablespoon orange-flavored liqueur, such as Grand Marnier or Cointreau*
1 cup whole wheat pastry flour	*1 tablespoon light vegetable oil*
Pinch of sea salt	

Grate the zest of the orange. Juice the orange and add apple juice to equal 1¼ cups.

Whisk or blend the zest and juice with the other ingredients to form a smooth batter. Cover and set it aside for 30 minutes to several hours, or overnight.

Set a crêpe pan over medium-high heat and grease it lightly. Add batter and lift and rotate the pan immediately to spread it out evenly, about ⅛ inch thick. Turn the crêpe when the bottom is golden and the edges begin to curl. Cook it briefly on the second side. Stack and cover crêpes to keep them warm.

(For detailed instructions, refer to the directions for **Wheat Crêpes** on page 208.)

YIELD: 12 (6-inch) crêpes

PREPARATION TIME: About 1 hour, plus a minimum of 30 minutes to rest the batter

Lemon Sauce

1½ teaspoons kuzu powder
2 teaspoons cold water or unsweetened apple juice
½ cup unsweetened apple juice
2 tablespoons maple syrup
½ teaspoon finely grated lemon zest
1 tablespoon fresh lemon juice
Pinch of salt

Combine the kuzu and cold water or apple juice in a small bowl; set it aside until the kuzu is completely dissolved.

Whisk together the ½ cup of apple juice, maple syrup, lemon zest, lemon juice, and salt in a small saucepan. Whisk in the dissolved kuzu. Bring the mixture to a simmer over low heat, whisking constantly, until it thickens. Serve the sauce warm or at room temperature. Makes about ⅔ cup sauce.

Notes

• For **Orange Sauce,** substitute orange zest for the lemon zest and orange juice for all or part of the apple juice; adjust the amount of maple syrup to taste.

Tortillas

TORTILLAS ARE COMPOSED OF CORN OR WHEAT FLOUR. IN northern Mexico, tortillas are typically prepared solely from wheat flour. All-corn tortillas are prevalent elsewhere. I sometimes make tortillas with a combination of cornmeal and wheat flour.

You might ask, why make tortillas at all when they are now so easy to buy ready-made? The answer is simple: Freshly made tortillas really do taste better than prepared ones. Also, with the right ingredients and equipment, tortilla making isn't much of a chore, particularly when a team is working at it—one person flattening the tortillas and another cooking them. If you are working alone, prepare all the tortillas before beginning to cook. Stack them between pieces of waxed paper to prevent them from sticking together or drying out.

Traditional corn tortillas are made with masa, a special corn dough prepared by soaking or simmering dried corn kernels in a lime solution to soften their hard hulls and then grinding them to a smooth consistency; increased availability of the B vitamin niacin is an added benefit. For centuries in Mexico, masa was deftly patted by hand into thin rounds and toasted on griddles called comales. Now it is more often rolled and cut mechanically and baked on conveyor belts in large factories.

Making homemade masa is more of a production than most of us would want to undertake on a regular basis— or maybe even ever. If you're intrigued by the challenge, you can purchase whole corn and lime from some mail-order sources and natural food stores. If tortillas are produced commercially in your community and you'd like to try working with masa, you might inquire about buying some fresh masa. Use it up the same day though, because it doesn't keep well in a raw form even when refrigerated or frozen, and tortillas made with old masa will be heavy.

Masa harina, dried masa in a flour form, is the best alternative to fresh masa for an adhesive tortilla dough, and you can keep this product on hand. Mixed with warm water and seasoned with a bit of salt, masa harina almost instantly becomes a manageable dough. When I lived in Tennessee, I was delighted to find organic blue corn masa harina, which I used to make lavender tortillas. They created quite a color display served with black or brown beans, chartreuse guacamole, and bright red salsa! Blue cornmeal is now readily available in most areas, but blue masa harina is rare, even in the Southwest. However, yellow corn masa harina is on almost every grocery store shelf.

I've made my share of corn tortillas from cornmeal. If the cornmeal is finely ground, it's possible to achieve a workable dough. But the uncooked tortillas are quite fragile compared to those made with masa or masa harina doughs, and the finished product is coarser and less flexible, though flavorful. A more workable option is to use a combination of cornmeal and wheat flour.

A tortilla press is a great asset in making corn tortillas. This handy, inexpensive device consists of two hinged cast-aluminum or wooden disks with a handle for applying pressure. Lay a piece of waxed paper or sheet of heavy-mil plastic long enough to double over on the bottom disk, position a dough ball about the size of a walnut in the center, and fold the waxed paper or plastic over the ball. Lower the top disk, pull the handle over it, and push down. The dough will instantly spread out into a thin 6-inch round. Lift up the dough and carefully pull the paper or plastic off one side; with this exposed side resting on your palm, peel the paper or plastic off the other side and cook the tortilla.

If you don't have a press, you can still make corn tortillas. Position the dough ball in the center of a waxed paper or plastic square and place another square on top. Press down on the dough with a pie plate, then use a rolling pin to flatten it further into a thin 6-inch circle. This method is more tedious and time-consuming than using a press, but effective nonetheless.

Tortilla doughs composed of all or mostly wheat flour are too glutenous to flatten with a press. Roll them thinly with a rolling pin on a lightly floured surface. You may rest these doughs as little as 30 minutes before rolling, but leaving them longer improves their handling, flavor, and digestibility.

Cook tortillas on a hot, well-seasoned griddle or heavy skillet just until they are barely toasted, turning them once. As they are done, stack them in a bowl or basket lined with an unnapped towel or large cloth napkin and tuck another over the top to retain their warmth.

All tortillas are at their best as soon as they are cooked, though you may reheat them. Lay individual tortillas on a hot griddle for a few moments on each side, steam them briefly, or wrap and heat them in a low to moderate oven for a few minutes until warm. You can keep cooked tortillas in the refrigerator for several days, and they also freeze well.

Tortillas of all kinds are used in combination with other foods in numerous ways, from crisp chips for dipping to rolled or folded stuffed packages. Refer to **Sandwiches and Filled Flat Breads** for filling ideas.

CORN TORTILLAS

YIELD: 8 (6-inch) tortillas

PREPARATION TIME: About 15 minutes, plus 30 minutes to rest the dough

THOUGH YOU MAY NOT WANT TO TACKLE THEM ON A daily basis, homemade corn tortillas aren't really much of a production if you use a masa harina dough and a tortilla press. This activity can even be part of a party. You can make the dough and keep it at room temperature for several hours. Along with wheat tortillas, these are the basic breads of Mexico, and they are used in various ways in Mexican cuisine—see Chapter 11 for some of them.

1 1/2 cups masa harina
1/2 teaspoon sea salt (optional)
2/3 to 3/4 cup water

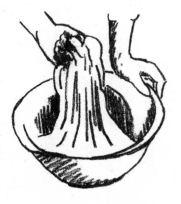

In a medium-sized bowl, add water to the masa harina and salt to form a soft dough. It should be moist but not sticky. Knead until smooth, adjusting the consistency with more water or masa if necessary until it is puttylike. When you flatten a small ball of dough into a thin round with your fingers, it shouldn't crack around the edge; if it does, knead in a little more water. Place the dough in a covered bowl and let it rest at least 30 minutes.

Divide the dough into 8 equal balls and cover them. Press or roll out the tortillas as described on pages 215–216. If you prepare them all before you begin to cook, don't peel off the waxed paper or plastic until just before you cook each tortilla.

Heat an ungreased griddle until water dripped on it sizzles. Cook a tortilla for about 30 seconds on one side, turn, and cook 30 seconds. Turn it twice more, again cooking 30 seconds on each side. The tortilla may puff up during cooking, especially if you press down on the center with your fingers or a towel; it will deflate when removed from the heat. Immediately wrap the cooked tortilla in a towel. Cook the remaining tortillas, stacking and wrapping them as they are done. Serve them warm.

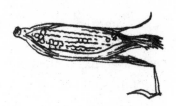

WHOLE WHEAT TORTILLAS

IN MEXICO, WHEAT FLOUR TORTILLAS ARE GENERALLY made with white flour and lard. Whole wheat flour gives these a delicious, nutty flavor and, along with the vegetable oil, contributes to a better nutritional profile. Use them for Mexican dishes such as **Burritos** (page 305) and **Fajitas** (page 306).

¹/₂ cup whole wheat bread flour	¹/₄ teaspoon sea salt
¹/₂ cup whole wheat pastry flour	1¹/₂ teaspoons sesame, corn, or other vegetable oil
	¹/₂ cup hot spring water

In a small bowl, stir together the flours and salt. Drizzle in the oil and, using a fork or your fingers, evenly distribute it throughout the flour. Add the water and stir to form a dough. Turn the dough out onto a lightly floured surface and cover it with a towel. Wash the bowl and lightly grease it.

Thoroughly knead the dough, lightly sprinkling either bread or pastry flour on the kneading surface only as necessary to keep the dough from sticking. When the dough is smooth and resilient, form it into a ball and return it to the bowl. Cover with a damp towel and plate, and set it aside for at least 30 minutes, but preferably several hours or overnight. It will keep for several days refrigerated, tightly covered with plastic wrap.

Divide the dough into 6 equal pieces, form balls, and cover them with a damp towel. Using flour as necessary to keep the dough from sticking, roll each ball as thin as possible into a circle about 10 inches across. Stack the tortillas between waxed paper and cover.

Heat a griddle until water dripped on it sizzles immediately. Lay a tortilla on the griddle and cook 20 seconds, until the bottom is slightly browned and bubbles appear on the surface. Turn it and cook 15 to 20 seconds more.

Notes
• For **Sesame-Wheat Tortillas,** omit the oil and add 2 tablespoons of ground roasted sesame seeds to the dough. These have an irresistible aroma and flavor.

It should still be soft and pliable. Immediately wrap the tortilla in a towel. Cook and wrap the remaining tortillas in the same manner. Serve them warm.

Corn-Wheat Tortillas

THESE COMBINATION TORTILLAS HAVE A SUBTLE CORN flavor and the flexibility and larger size of wheat tortillas. This dough, too, can be made ahead of time.

YIELD: 6 (10-inch) tortillas

PREPARATION TIME: About an hour, plus a minimum of 30 minutes to rest the dough

1/2 cup cornmeal (yellow or blue)
1 tablespoon sesame, corn, or other vegetable oil

1/2 cup spring water
1/4 teaspoon sea salt
1/2 cup whole wheat bread flour

In a small bowl, thoroughly mix the cornmeal and oil. Heat the water to boiling; add the salt and pour over the cornmeal. Wait a few minutes, until the cornmeal has absorbed the water and has cooled to lukewarm.

Stir in the flour to form a dough. Turn the dough out onto a lightly floured board. Wash the bowl and lightly grease it. Thoroughly knead the dough, lightly sprinkling flour under it only as necessary to keep it from sticking. When it is smooth and resilient, form a ball and place it in the bowl. Cover with a damp towel and plate, and set it aside for at least 30 minutes, but preferably for several hours or overnight.

Divide the dough into 6 equal pieces, form balls, and cover them. On a lightly floured surface, roll each ball into a 10-inch circle. Stack the tortillas between waxed paper and cover.

Cook tortillas on a hot griddle for about 20 seconds on each side, until lightly browned but still soft and pliable. Wrap them in a towel and serve warm.

Chapatis and Parathas

WHEAT IS GROWN IN NORTHERN INDIA, AND MUCH OF IT is eaten as bread. Chapatis are unleavened Indian flat breads made from a kneaded dough and cooked on a griddle. They are usually made with finely ground wheat flour, but you may mix in small amounts of other flours or ground seeds to vary the taste and texture. Freshly ground flour noticeably enhances these breads' flavor. Resting the dough before rolling and cooking also improves its flavor, handling, and nutritive value.

Unless you are working with someone else, roll out all the chapatis before beginning to cook, because cooking will demand your undivided attention. Alternatively, you may finger-press chapatis. These will probably be somewhat thicker and take longer to cook than rolled ones. During cold upstate–New York winters, my friend Jonathan cooks exceptional hand-shaped chapatis on his wood stove.

Bubbles often form in chapatis when they contact a hot griddle and, like pita, the steam often causes these breads to temporarily puff up. The steam promotes thorough cooking and lightness and, as you'll see in the recipe for chapatis, certain cooking techniques encourage this ballooning effect.

Parathas are a chapati variation, prepared by rolling layers of oil or *ghee* (clarified butter) into the dough before it is rolled the final time. The layers separate somewhat upon cooking, producing a light though still flat bread. You can stuff parathas with various fillings.

Chapatis and parathas are traditionally served with meals, often torn into pieces and used to scoop up vegetable and meat preparations. I sometimes roll whole chapatis or parathas around fillings too.

CHAPATIS

IN INDIA, CHAPATIS ARE COMMONLY SERVED WITH SPICY curries, dals, and vegetable dishes. They are excellent vehicles for all kinds of spreads and fillings, but they're also delicious "nekked," as we say in Texas.

³/₄ cup whole wheat bread flour
³/₄ cup whole wheat pastry flour

³/₈ teaspoon sea salt
³/₄ cup warm spring water

YIELD: 12 (7-inch) chapatis

PREPARATION TIME: About 1 hour, plus a minimum of 30 minutes to rest the dough

Sift the flours and salt into a small mixing bowl and make a well in the center. Pour in the water and stir until a dough forms. Turn the dough out and cover it with a towel. While the dough rests briefly, wash the bowl and grease it lightly.

Thoroughly knead the dough, lightly sprinkling flour under it only if necessary to keep it from sticking. After 10 to 15 minutes, when the dough is smooth and springy, form it into a ball. Place it in the bowl, covered with a damp towel and a plate, and set it aside for at least 30 minutes, but preferably several hours or overnight. Refrigerated, it will keep for several days.

Divide the dough into 12 equal pieces, form balls, and cover them. Using flour as necessary to prevent sticking, roll each ball into a thin circle about 7 inches in diameter. Stack the chapatis between pieces of waxed paper and cover.

Heat a griddle until water sizzles immediately when dripped on the surface. Lay a chapati on the griddle and cook 30 to 40 seconds, until the edges begin to curl up and the bottom is slightly browned. Turn it over. With a towel, pot holder, or oven mitt, lightly press down on the surface of the chapati as it is cooking to encourage air pockets to form; it may puff up completely. If it doesn't

Notes

• Store chapatis in the refrigerator for several days, or freeze them, separated by waxed paper and well wrapped, for longer storage. To reheat the breads, briefly place them on a hot griddle, or wrap and heat them in the oven.

• Substitute oat, rye, millet, barley, or rice flour for all or part of the whole wheat pastry flour. For dough strength, always use about half whole wheat bread flour.

• Substitute lightly toasted ground sunflower seeds for about 2 tablespoons pastry flour. Sesame seeds or poppy seeds are also good.

puff, hold it over a gas flame briefly with tongs or, if you have an electric stove, set the chapati on a wire rack over the burner coil. This should all be done quickly so that the chapati stays soft and flexible rather than becoming brittle and crisp. Don't worry if the chapatis never puff—they'll still taste good.

Immediately wrap cooked chapatis in a towel. Serve them warm.

PARATHAS

LIKE CHAPATIS, PARATHAS ARE GRIDDLE BREADS THAT double as eating utensils for the delicious, spicy dishes featured in northern India cuisine. Paratha dough often contains ghee or oil, and layers of ghee or oil are also rolled into it, making parathas richer and lighter than chapatis. Parathas are sometimes filled before they are cooked (see **Cauliflower-Stuffed Parathas,** page 223).

YIELD: 12 (7-inch) parathas

PREPARATION TIME: 50 to 60 minutes, plus a minimum of 30 minutes to rest the dough

Ghee is the Indian term for clarified butter, the fat that is left when milk solids and water are removed from butter. To prepare ghee, melt unsalted butter over low heat, then carefully skim off the foam on the surface and throw it away. Strain the remaining golden oil through a fine mesh or muslin, taking care not to separate any sediment on the bottom of the pan. Clarified butter does not burn at high temperatures and keeps indefinitely. In recipes, you can substitute an oil with a high smoking point for ghee.

³⁄₄ cup whole wheat bread flour	*1 tablespoon ghee or vegetable oil, plus extra for rolling into the dough*
³⁄₄ cup whole wheat pastry flour	*³⁄₄ cup warm spring water*
³⁄₈ teaspoon sea salt	

Sift the flours and salt into a small mixing bowl. Drizzle in the 1 tablespoon of ghee or oil and thoroughly mix it in with a fork or your fingers. Make a well in the center. Pour in the water and stir until a dough forms. Turn the dough out and cover with a towel. While the dough rests briefly, wash the bowl and grease it lightly.

Thoroughly knead the dough, lightly sprinkling flour under it only if necessary to keep it from sticking. After 10 to 15 minutes, when the dough is smooth and springy, form it into a ball. Place it in the bowl, covered with a damp towel and a plate, and set it aside for at

Cauliflower-Stuffed Parathas

To make this recipe, begin by preparing the dough for parathas, in advance if possible. The filling may also be made ahead of time, though the flavor is best when it's fresh. Unlike regular parathas, the dough for stuffed ones is not layered; it is simply rolled, filled, and rolled out again, thicker than regular parathas. Since stuffed parathas end up relatively flat, they too are often used to scoop up dals and other savory mixtures. They are also good accompaniments for soups and salads. Use the spicy potato filling for **Dosas** (page 233) as an alternative stuffing.

 1 tablespoon ghee or vegetable oil, plus extra
    for brushing the parathas
 2 green onions, finely chopped
 1 clove garlic. minced
 1 teaspoon finely grated fresh ginger
 Freshly ground black pepper to taste
 ¹/₂ teaspoon ground cumin
 ¹/₈ teaspoone each ground coriander, cardamom,
    cloves, cinnamon, turmeric, and cayenne
 1 cup finely chopped cauliflower
 2 tablesppons vegetable stock or water
 Sea salt to taste
 Parathas dough (page 222)

To make the filling, add the 1 tablespoon ghee or oil to a skillet over medium heat and sauté the onions, garlic, and ginger briefly. Stir in the spices and cook, stirring, for a minute or two. Add the cauliflower and sauté for a few minutes. Add the stock, cover, and steam for about 5 minutes, stirring occasionally, until the cauliflower is tender. Remove the lid and cook away any extra liquid. Add salt to taste and set aside to cool.

Divide the dough into 6 equal pieces and roll each one into a ball. On a lightly floured surface, roll or press each ball into a 4-inch circle. Brush the center with a bit of ghee or oil, and spoon about 1¹/₂ tablespoons of filling on top. Draw the edges of the dough around the filling and pinch them firmly together to enclose it. Cover with a damp towel.

On a lightly floured surface, gently roll the stuffed parathas into 6-inch circles; a bit of filling may ooze out here and there but try to minimize this. Stack them, separated by waxed paper, on a lightly floured baking sheet and cover.

Set a griddle over medium-high heat and grease it lightly. Cook each paratha for 2 to 3 minutes; its surface will heave and perhaps puff a bit. Pressing the surface lightly with a spatula encourages puffing. When the bread has lightly browned, turn it and cook for another minute. Lightly brush the surface with ghee or oil, turn it again, and cook for about 15 seconds. Brush with ghee or oil, turn it once again, and cook briefly. Cover the parathas to keep them warm until serving.

Notes
• Reheat stuffed parathas, loosely covered, in a moderate oven for several minutes.

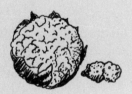

least 30 minutes, but preferably several hours or overnight. Refrigerated, it will keep for several days.

Divide the dough into 12 equal pieces, form balls, and cover them. Using flour as necessary to prevent sticking, roll each ball into a thin circle about 7 inches in diameter. Lightly brush it with ghee or oil. Fold it in half, brush with ghee or oil, then fold in half again. Roll this wedge back into a circle of the original size. Repeat this process two or three times more. Stack the dough discs between pieces of waxed paper and cover them with a damp towel.

Heat a griddle until water sizzles immediately when dripped on it. Cook a paratha for about a minute, until the bottom begins to brown. Brush a little ghee or oil on the top. Turn and cook the second side. Brush the top of the paratha lightly with ghee or oil, and turn it again if it doesn't seem quite done; parathas take slightly longer to cook than chapatis. The breads will probably puff up to some degree as they cook.

Stack cooked parathas on a plate, covered with a towel or an inverted bowl. Serve them warm.

Pita

MIDDLE-EASTERN POCKET BREAD CAUGHT THE AMERICAN fancy over a decade ago and continues to occupy a firm niche in our casual cuisine. There's something appealing about a hollow, stuffable bread. Stuffed pita is less messy to handle than many sliced bread sandwiches, and there are seemingly endless potential fillings. Slice open one edge of a whole pita, cut it in half to make two symmetrical pockets, slice it horizontally into two disks to roll around a filling or use as a base for toppings, or cut it into wedges to go with dips.

You need a strong, well-developed dough for pita. Use the recipes that follow or any plain yeasted or sourdough dough from Chapters 5 and 7. Next time you're making a basic bread, use part of the dough for pita. Just prepare the dough up to the point of shaping. As with any other yeasted bread, the bowl rises for pita stretch and strengthen the gluten in the dough. This prepares pita dough well for when it puffs during baking as steam expands inside it.

Roll pita dough gently and evenly. Place the dough disks on baking sheets dusted with cornmeal, cover, and let them rest for 30 minutes. I put two breads on each baking sheet and bake one sheet at a time. Set a timer for 30 minutes after you roll the first two breads, and they'll be ready to bake by the time you've finished rolling the other breads.

Preheat the oven so that it'll be hot when the first breads are ready to bake. Gently shake the sheet to be sure the dough isn't sticking. If the dough disks don't slide freely, lift them carefully and sprinkle more cornmeal underneath so they won't tear as they puff up or not puff up at all.

Baking pita makes me happy to have the window in my oven door: I sit in front of it and cheer them on. Make sure the oven heats back to 500° before you put in each tray of breads, and use the lowest rack. An immediate blast of bottom heat is important for producing steam in the dough. Pita actually cooks from the inside out. It should be thoroughly baked, yet still soft, rather than crisp.

Look for filling ideas in Chapter 11, **Sandwiches and Filled Flat Breads.**

$\mathcal{A}$MALTHEA'S $\mathcal{P}$ITA

WHEN WE WERE NAMING OUR BAKING BUSINESS, THE cornucopia kept coming to mind as a positive, bounteous symbol. Though this term and its image had been overworked commercially to the point of banality, it still held an appeal to us. So we researched its origins and learned that, according to Greek legend, the cornucopia, or horn of plenty, had belonged to Amalthea, a goat—or nymph—who had nurtured the infant god Zeus when he was hidden in a cave on the isle of Crete. Zeus's father, Cronus, the king of the Titans, had received a prophecy that one of his children would wrest his power and had swallowed each of Zeus's older brothers and sisters immediately after birth. When Zeus was born, his

YIELD: 6 (8-inch) breads

PREPARATION TIME: 45 minutes to prepare; 4 to 5 hours for rising; 5 minutes to bake each tray of breads

• To reheat pitas, wrap them in foil or place them in a covered baking dish and warm them at 350° for just a few minutes, so that they heat through but don't become dry and crisp.
• Pita freezes well; place waxed paper between breads so they will not stick together (then you can take them out one at a time) and wrap them well.

mother presented Cronus with a swaddled stone and whisked the baby away to Crete, where Amalthea broke off one of her horns and used its inexhaustible, over-flowing riches to nourish his growth. We chose Amalthea as the name for our business as a symbol of nurturance.

This is the recipe we used for the pita we sold with the Amalthea label. We hand-rolled so many breads on a baking day that we often suffered from "pita elbow," but the wonderful breads were worth the discomfort. These are strong, flavorful, and dependable.

½ teaspoon active dry yeast	1 teaspoon sea salt
1 cup lukewarm spring water	1 tablespoon olive or other vegetable oil
2½ cups whole wheat bread flour	1 tablespoon soy flour (optional)
	Cornmeal, for dusting

In a medium-sized bowl, sprinkle the yeast over the water and add a teaspoon of wheat flour. Cover and set it in a warm spot for 5 to 10 minutes to proof. Stir in 1 cup of the wheat flour to form a batter. Cover and set it aside for 30 minutes, or until a sponge develops.

Stir the salt, oil, and soy flour into the sponge. Add the wheat flour, ½ cup at a time, stirring well after each addition, until the dough pulls away from the sides of the bowl and balls up in the center. Turn the dough out onto a lightly floured surface and cover it for a few minutes.

Thoroughly knead the dough, adding flour only as necessary to keep it from sticking. When the dough is smooth and elastic, form it into a ball and place it in a lightly greased bowl. Cover and set it in a draft-free spot for 1 to 2 hours, or until the dough has risen and does not rebound when pressed with a finger.

Turn the dough out and knead it briefly. Put the dough back in the bowl, cover, and set it aside to rise for another 1 to 2 hours, until it does not spring back when pressed.

Divide the dough into 6 equal balls. Cover them for 30 minutes. On a lightly floured surface, use a rolling pin to roll each ball into an 8-inch circle slightly less than $^1/_4$ inch thick. Arrange these on baking sheets lightly dusted with cornmeal and cover them for 30 minutes.

Move a rack to the lowest position (leaving lots of space above it) and preheat the oven to 500°. Before baking, make sure that the dough circles are not sticking to the baking sheet; if they are, sprinkle more cornmeal underneath. Cross your fingers and bake the bread for 5 minutes. The breads should puff up like balloons and be lightly browned. Do not open the oven door to peek before the 5 minutes is up, and be sure the oven has reheated to 500° before putting in another sheet. If a bread doesn't puff, it will still taste good but won't have a pocket to fill.

Wrap baked breads with a dry towel as soon as you remove them from the oven. Serve them warm. Thoroughly cool breads before storing them.

Sourdough Pita

THIS IS A SOURDOUGH VERSION OF PITA WITH A SIMILAR texture but a slightly tangy taste. Use this just as you do regular yeasted pita for dips and fillings. I think it goes particularly well with Indian dishes, such as **Lentil Dal** (page 257) and **Indian Eggplant** (page 254).

YIELD: 6 (8-inch) breads

PREPARATION TIME: $2^1/_2$ to $3^1/_2$ hours for sponge and dough; 4 to 5 hours for rising; 5 minutes to bake each tray of breads

1 cup spring water	1 tablespoon olive or other
$^1/_2$ cup sourdough starter	vegetable oil
3 cups whole wheat	Cornmeal or rice flour,
bread flour	for dusting
1 teaspoon sea salt	

In a medium-sized bowl, stir together the water, starter, and 1¹/₂ cups of the flour to form a batter. Cover and set it aside for 2 to 3 hours, until a sponge develops.

Stir in the salt and oil. Add enough of the remaining flour, ¹/₂ cup at a time, stirring well after each addition, to form a dough. Turn it out onto a lightly floured surface and cover it while you wash the bowl.

Thoroughly knead the dough until it is smooth and elastic, adding flour only as necessary to keep it from sticking. Form the dough into a ball and place it in a lightly greased bowl. Cover and set it aside for about 2 hours, or until the dough has risen and does not rebound when pressed. Turn the dough out and knead it briefly. Put it back in the bowl for a second rise.

Divide the dough into 6 equal balls and cover them for 30 minutes. On a lightly floured surface, roll each ball into an 8-inch circle with a rolling pin. Arrange these on baking sheets lightly dusted with cornmeal or rice flour. Cover them for 30 minutes.

Move a rack to the lowest position (leaving lots of space above it) and preheat the oven to 500°. Before baking, check to be sure that the breads are not sticking to the sheet; if they are, sprinkle more cornmeal or rice flour underneath. Bake one sheet at a time, for 5 minutes each. Be sure the temperature has returned to 500° before putting in another sheet. Do not open the door during baking. The breads should puff up completely and be lightly browned.

Wrap the baked breads in a towel as you take them out of the oven. Serve them warm. Cool breads thoroughly before storing them.

LEBANESE WRAPPER BREAD

THIS IS LAVOSH—LARGE, THIN, FLEXIBLE MIDDLE EAST-ern flat breads, made from a strong, yeasted wheat dough. They're used for scooping or wrapping up veg-etable or bean dips, salads, or kebabs. You can bake them either on a sheet in a hot oven or on top of the stove, draped over an inverted wok or on a griddle if the breads are small enough to fit. As with pita, the yeast in this dough contributes to its flavor and texture; the bread doesn't rise when baked.

¹/₄ teaspoon active dry yeast	*1¹/₄ to 1¹/₂ cups whole wheat bread flour*
¹/₂ cup lukewarm spring water	*¹/₂ teaspoon sea salt*

In a medium-sized mixing bowl, sprinkle the yeast over the warm water. Sprinkle in a teaspoon of flour, cover, and set in a draft-free spot for a few minutes to proof the yeast. Stir in ¹/₂ cup of the flour to form a batter. Cover and set it aside for about 30 minutes, until a sponge develops.

Stir in the salt. Add flour, ¹/₄ cup at a time, stirring after each addition, until a dough forms. Turn it out onto a lightly floured surface and cover it for several minutes.

Thoroughly knead the dough, lightly sprinkling flour under it only as necessary to keep it from sticking. When the dough is smooth and resilient, form it into a ball. Place it in a lightly greased bowl, cover, and set it aside for 1 to 2 hours, until the dough has risen and does not rebound when pressed with a finger.

Turn the dough out and knead it a few times. Return it to the bowl, covered, to rise a second time.

Cut the dough into 6 equal pieces and roll each one into a ball. Set the balls on a lightly floured surface and cover them for 30 minutes.

Other Flat Breads

YIELD: 6 (12-inch) breads

PREPARATION TIME: About 1¹/₂ hours to prepare and roll out the dough; 2¹/₂ to 4¹/₂ hours for rising; 30 to 40 seconds to bake each bread

Tempeh Shish Kebabs in Lebanese Wrapper Bread

These shish kebabs are especially for warm weather, when fresh herbs and summery vegetables are plentiful, and you can cook outdoors. When it's inclement, grill the kebabs in the broiler in the kitchen, roll them up in the warm flat breads, and just pretend you're on a picnic.

8 large mushrooms
1 large bell pepper, cut into 1-inch squares
1½ teaspoons olive oil, plus extra for
　　brushing basil leaves the eggplant
1 (4-ounce) cake tempeh
1 small eggplant
2 cloves garlic, minced
2 tablespoons mellow barley miso
¼ cup lemon juice
6 tablespoons tahini
Freshly ground black pepper to taste
2 tablespoons minced fresh basil leaves
2 tablespoons minced flat-leaf parsley
8 cherry tomatoes
4 **Lebanese Wrapper Breads** (page 229)
2 green onions, finely
　　chopped

Steam the mushrooms and bell pepper, and reserve 1 cup of the steaming water.

Add the 1½ teaspoons oil to a small skillet over medium heat. Add the tempeh and brown both sides. Add ¼ cup of the reserved steaming water and cover tightly. Steam until the liquid has cooked away. Cut the tempeh into 8 squares.

Cut the eggplant crosswise into 1-inch slices; salt them lightly and layer in a colander; place a plate and a weight of some kind on top. Press at least 30 minutes, then rinse and pat dry. Lightly brush both sides of the slices with olive oil and

arrange them on a baking sheet. Broil, turning once, until they are just tender, or bake them at 350° for 10 to 15 minutes, until tender. Cut the slices into 1-inch cubes.

In a medium-sized bowl, whisk together the garlic, miso, lemon juice, and tahini. Whisk in ⅔ cup of the steaming water to form a smooth sauce. Grind in black pepper and whisk in the basil and parsley. Fold in the mushrooms and the bell pepper, tempeh, and eggplant pieces. Marinate 20 to 30 minutes or longer.

Arrange the marinated items and cherry tomatoes on skewers. Grill or broil, turning and basting the kebabs with marinade several times, until they are browned. Simmer extra marinade briefly, until it thickens somewhat.

Wrap the breads in foil and warm them briefly over the grill or in a moderate oven. Fill them with the cooked kebab components, garnished with some of the thickened marinade and green onions. Roll or fold them, and serve immediately.

Notes

• If you use Oriental eggplant, it isn't necessary to salt and press; simply slice, brush with oil, and broil or bake.

• Substitute 1-inch chunks of lightly steamed zucchini or another summer squash, or boiled or steamed small new potatoes or peeled whole onions for the eggplant.

• Substitute 8 ounces of well-pressed, steamed or blanched tofu for the tempeh and omit the 1½ teaspoons of olive oil. Cut it into 8 cubes before adding it to the marinade.

• Substitute other fresh herbs, such as dill or tarragon, for the basil and/or parsley.

On a lightly floured surface, with a rolling pin, roll each ball into a 12-inch circle. Stack them, separated by waxed paper and covered with a damp towel.

Preheat the oven to 500°. Bake bread on an

ungreased pan for 15 to 20 seconds on each side. Alternatively, use a hot griddle or inverted wok on top of the stove. In any case, work quickly so that the breads stay soft and flexible.

As each bread is done, fold it in quarters, and wrap it in a dry towel. Serve the breads warm.

JOHNNYCAKES

AS IT HITS THE HOT GRIDDLE, THIS THIN BATTER IMMEDIately spreads out into delicate, lacy rounds, which are crisp, lightly browned, and decidedly corn-flavored when they're done. The fresher the cornmeal, the better the flavor. Serve these for breakfast, drizzled with maple syrup, or top them with **Refritos** (page 256), **Tofu Sour Cream** (page 281), **Salsa** (page 270 or 271), and chopped cilantro for lunch or dinner.

1²/₃ cup spring water	2 teaspoons corn or other
¹/₄ teaspoon sea salt	vegetable oil
1 cup cornmeal	

Heat 1 cup of the water to boiling, add the salt, and pour it over the cornmeal in a medium-sized bowl. Whisk vigorously until the mixture is smooth, then whisk in the remaining ²/₃ cup water to form a loose batter. Cover and set it aside for 30 minutes to several hours, or overnight.

Heat a griddle until water sprinkled on it sizzles immediately, then grease it lightly. Whisk the oil into the batter. Ladle out about a tablespoon of batter for each pancake. Cook until the top surface appears dry. Carefully run a metal spatula under the pancakes, flip them over, and cook several minutes more, until they are quite crisp.

Serve johnnycakes hot off the griddle or cover them with an inverted bowl to keep them warm.

Notes
• Refrigerate or freeze the breads when they have cooled thoroughly. Wrap and reheat at 350° for several minutes.

YIELD: About 2 dozen 3-inch pancakes

PREPARATION TIME: 30 to 40 minutes, plus a minimum of 30 minutes to rest the batter

Yɪᴇʟᴅ: 1 (12-inch) socca—2 to 4 servings

Pʀᴇᴘᴀʀᴀᴛɪᴏɴ ᴛɪᴍᴇ: 40 to 45 minutes

....

Garbanzo beans, also known as *chickpeas,* are lumpy beige beans about ¹/₂ inch in diameter. Rich in iron, calcium, and protein, they have a somewhat nutty flavor and round out and hold their shape when cooked. Garbanzo beans are used extensively in Middle-Eastern, Mediterranean, and Indian cuisines. See page 360 for cooking directions.

....

Notes
• You can also prepare the batter in a blender or food processor.

Socca

Sᴏᴄᴄᴀ, ᴀ ᴄʀᴇ̂ᴘᴇ-ʟɪᴋᴇ ꜰʟᴀᴛ ʙʀᴇᴀᴅ ᴍᴀᴅᴇ ꜰʀᴏᴍ ɢᴀʀʙᴀɴᴢᴏ bean flour, is a specialty of Nice, in southern France, where it is sold as a snack in the marketplace and by vendors on the street. Traditionally, socca is baked in large, shallow copper pans in wood-fired ovens; lacking both of those, I improvise with my blackened steel pizza pan and home oven. Garbanzo bean flour and olive oil give socca a wonderfully robust flavor. I grind garbanzo beans in my grain mill; the flour is also sometimes available in ethnic markets and natural food stores. Serve socca as an hors d'oeuvre or with a hearty Provençal-style soup or vegetable stew and a fine red wine.

²/₃ cup garbanzo bean flour	1 tablespoon olive oil, plus extra for the pan
¹/₄ teaspoon sea salt	Freshly ground black pepper to taste
²/₃ cup spring water	

Sift the flour and salt into a medium-sized bowl. Gradually whisk in the water to form a batter. Whisk in the 1 tablespoon oil and some pepper. Cover and set the batter aside for 30 minutes or so; it will thicken somewhat upon standing as the flour absorbs the water.

Preheat the oven to 450°. Liberally grease a large pizza pan with olive oil. Give the batter a stir and pour it onto the pan; it should spread out to about ¹/₈ inch thickness. Bake for 5 minutes, until the top is well set and beginning to brown; it will have a crêpe-like consistency. Brush the top lightly with olive oil and bake a minute or two longer, watching it closely.

Serve the socca hot from the oven cut into wedges or strips and with extra pepper ground on top.

Dosas

DOSAS ARE SOUTH INDIAN PANCAKES MADE FROM A grain or grain and legume batter, which is usually fermented. The most traditional recipes call for soaking uncooked whole grains and beans for several hours or overnight, then blending them with sufficient water to form a thin batter. You can also make dosa batter with flour and water or another liquid, as I have here. Like crêpes, dosas are cooked on a hot, lightly oiled griddle on top of the stove. They are slightly thicker, moister, and more porous than crêpes, and they take longer to cook. Though usually served for breakfast in India, dosas are delicious for brunch, lunch, or dinner, too. They are often folded over a spicy vegetable filling, in which case they are called masala dosas, "masala" meaning spicy (see **Marsala Dosas**, page 234). Dals and chutneys are other good accompaniments.

> *1 cup rice flour*
> *1¹/₂ to 1³/₄ cups unsweetened soy milk*
> *¹/₄ teaspoon sea salt*

In a medium-sized bowl, whisk the flour with 1¹/₂ cups of the soy milk. Whisk in the salt. Cover and set the batter aside for several hours or overnight, until it has fermented; it should smell slightly tangy and appear bubbly when you stir it. If it is not readily pourable, thin the batter with additional soy milk.

Heat a griddle until water dances on the surface and grease it lightly. Stir the batter and ladle or pour about ¹/₄ cup on the griddle. Immediately spread it out as thin as you can with the back of a wooden spoon. The batter will bubble as soon as it hits the griddle, but wait until the underside is golden brown and the surface appears dry before carefully turning it over with a thin-bladed spatula. Cook the second side for a shorter time.

YIELD: 8 (6-inch) dosas

PREPARATION TIME: Several hours or overnight to ferment the batter; 30 minutes to cook

Notes
• Substitute other flours, such as whole wheat pastry, barley, or oat flour, for the rice flour.
• Substitute water for the soy milk.

Masala Dosas

A piquant potato mixture such as this one is traditional for filling dosas in southern India. Prepare the dosa batter ahead of time and then have the filling ready before you cook the dosas. Serve the dosas immediately after you fill them.

> 2 medium-sized potatoes, diced
> 1 tablespoon sesame oil or ghee
> 1 teaspoon black mustard seeds
> 1 1/2 cups finely chopped onion
> 1 small chile, finely chopped
> 1/2 teaspoon ground cumin
> 1/2 teaspoon ground turmeric
> 1 1/2 teaspoons finely grated fresh ginger
> 1 tablespoon grated coconut
> 1/2 teaspoon sea salt
> 1 1/2 teaspoons lemon juice
> 8 **Dosas** (page 233)

Boil the potatoes in water to cover until they are just tender. Drain, reserving the cooking water.

Add the oil to a skillet over medium heat. Add the mustard seeds and cook, stirring, until it begins to pop. Add the onion and continue to cook, stirring often, until it is just tender. Stir in the minced chile and sauté for several minutes. Add the cumin, turmeric, ginger, and coconut, and sauté briefly. Stir in the potatoes, 1/2 cup of the reserved potato water, and salt. Cover the pan and cook, stirring frequently, for several minutes, until the liquid is absorbed. Mash the potatoes somewhat with a fork. Stir in the lemon juice.

Prepare the dosas, then spoon on the filling and fold them over. Serve immediately.

Notes

- This filling is also good with chapatis, parathas, and other flat breads.

Black mustard seeds are used in Indian dishes, especially in curries. Their flavor is somewhat milder than yellow mustard seeds. Add them to heated oil in a pan and stir until they pop before adding onion and other ingredients.

Serve dosas immediately or keep them in a warm oven until you are ready. Although dosas are best when freshly made, leftovers may be refrigerated and reheated in a low to moderate oven or in a steamer. You can also keep extra batter in the refrigerator or freezer.

Mandarin Pancakes

YIELD: 12 (6-inch) pancakes

PREPARATION TIME: About an hour, plus a minimum of 30 minutes to rest the dough

THESE THIN, TORTILLA-LIKE PANCAKES ORIGINATED IN northern China, where wheat is an important crop. A mandarin was a high-ranking official in imperial China, and the application of the term to these pancakes identifies them as aristocratic fare. My use of whole wheat flour might seem to undermine their refined image, but these pancakes are still exceedingly thin, and they are more flavorful than their white flour counterparts. Though the pancakes are almost translucent, their delicate appearance is deceptive, since they are sturdy enough to securely hold a stir-fried filling. They are usually associated with Peking duck and mu-shu pork, but they are excellent with stir-fried vegetables too (see page 236).

¹/₃ cup whole wheat pastry flour	¹/₂ cup spring water, boiling
²/₃ cup whole wheat bread flour	Sesame oil

Mix the flours in a small bowl and make a well in the center. Pour in the boiling water and stir to form a soft dough. Turn the dough out onto a lightly floured surface and cover it for a few minutes.

Thoroughly knead the dough, adding flour only as necessary to keep it from sticking. After 10 to 15 minutes, when the dough is smooth and springy, form it into a ball and place it in a lightly greased bowl. Set it aside, covered, for at least 30 minutes, but preferably several hours or overnight.

On an unfloured surface, roll the dough with your palms into a 12-inch log. Cut it into 12 (1-inch) pieces and press each piece into a 2-inch circle. Brush one side of each round lightly with sesame oil. Press the oiled sides of two rounds together. Pair the remaining rounds in the same way, and let them rest briefly, covered.

On a lightly floured surface, roll each pair of rounds with a rolling pin into a 6- to 7-inch circle. Stack them, separated by pieces of waxed paper to keep them from sticking together, and cover.

Heat a griddle until water dripped on it sizzles immediately. Place one double pancake on the griddle and cook it briefly, just until the underside begins to brown. Turn it and cook the second side briefly—the pancake should still be soft and flexible. Remove and carefully pull the two thin pancakes apart. Place them on a plate with another plate inverted on top. Cook the remaining pancakes in the same manner. Serve them warm.

Daikon is a long white Japanese radish with a sweet yet pungent flavor. Cooking daikon, such as in stir-fries or stews, tones down its hotness. Daikon may also be pickled. It's said that this radish aids digestion.

Hot sherry is sherry flavored with chile peppers. This is a lively addition to stir-fries and other dishes. Add about a dozen ripe serrano peppers to a fifth of dry sherry and let them steep for a week or two, until the sherry is sufficiently flavored.

Notes
• To reheat, steam the pancakes for a few minutes.
• These pancakes freeze well. Insert waxed paper between them before freezing.

Filled Mandarin Pancakes

Vary the vegetables in this filling to suit your taste and what you have on hand; bean sprouts, snowpeas, julienned green beans, turnips, and other kinds of mushrooms are all possible substitutions. If you plan on serving this dish in the evening, soak the dried mushrooms earlier in the day. You can also substitute fresh shiitake mushrooms for the dried ones; use a mild vegetable stock in the recipe in place of the mushroom-soaking water. Make the pancakes ahead of time and steam them briefly as you're cooking the filling just before serving. Since mandarin pancakes are eaten out of hand, make the stir-fry rather dry.

1 cup water
6 small dried shiitake mushrooms
$^{1}/_{2}$ teaspoon roasted sesame oil
2 tablespoons tamari
1 tablespoon **Hot Sherry** (page 235)
8 ounces tofu, well pressed and cut into
    small strips
1 teaspoon kuzu powder
2 tablespoons sesame oil
2 eggs, beaten
$^{2}/_{3}$ cup carrot, cut into
    1-inch julienne
$^{2}/_{3}$ cup daikon, cut into 1-inch julienne
$^{1}/_{4}$ cup finely chopped green onions
1 teaspoon minced garlic
1 teaspoon finely grated fresh ginger
2 cups finely sliced Chinese cabbage or
    bok choy
12 **Mandarin Pancakes** (page 234)

Heat the water to boiling and pour it over the mushrooms in a small bowl. Soak the mushrooms for 30 minutes, or until the caps are completely softened; the stems will stay hard. Drain, reserving the soaking water. Discard the tough stems and slice the caps into thin slivers—you should have about $^{1}/_{4}$ cup.

Whisk together the roasted sesame oil, 1 tablespoon of the tamari, and the hot sherry in a small bowl. Add the tofu pieces and stir gently. Marinate for 30 minutes or so, stirring occasionally.

Combine the kuzu, 1 teaspoon of the mushroom soaking water, and the remaining tamari; set aside until the kuzu has thoroughly dissolved.

Set a wok over medium-high heat and add 1 tablespoon of the sesame oil. Pour in the beaten egg and cook it, lifting the edge with a spatula as necessary to allow the uncooked portion to run underneath. As soon as the egg has set, fold it into thirds and transfer it to a cutting board. Cut it into thin strips.

Heat the wok and add the remaining oil. Sauté the carrot and daikon strips, stirring constantly, until they are almost tender. Toss in the green onions, garlic, ginger, and slivered mushrooms, and continue to cook, stirring, for several minutes. Add the cabbage and sauté briefly. Add $^{3}/_{8}$ cup of the shiitake soaking water and the tofu in its marinade. Cover and steam briefly, until the tofu is hot and soft. Add the egg strips and the kuzu mixture, and cook, stirring, until the liquid thickens.

Wrap the pancakes in a damp towel and steam for a few minutes to reheat them. Serve immediately alongside the filling, having people fill and roll up their own and eat them out of hand.

Japanese Vegetable Pancakes

Thick griddlecakes, called *okonomiyaki*, are a flavorful fast food in Japan. Try these all-vegetable ones, brushed with a spicy sauce and sprinkled with various garnishes, for a quick, nourishing meal at home.

1 cup whole wheat flour
1/2 teaspoon sea salt
1 teaspoon baking powder (optional)
1 cup unsweetened soy milk, vegetable stock, or water
2 eggs
4 shiitake mushrooms, thinly sliced
2 green onions, finely chopped
1 small carrot, grated
1 small turnip or daikon, grated
1 cup thinly sliced Chinese cabbage or bok choy

1 cup finely chopped spinach or other greens
1 tablespoon dark miso
2 tablespoons tahini
2 tablespoons vegetable stock or water
1/4 teaspoon roasted sesame oil
1/4 teaspoon umeboshi vinegar
Pickled ginger
Nori, toasted and torn or cut into thin strips
Cilantro leaves, coarsely chopped

Sift the flour, salt, and baking powder into a medium-sized mixing bowl. Whisk in the soy milk and eggs. Fold in the mushrooms, onions, carrot, turnip or daikon, cabbage, and spinach.

Preheat a griddle until water dripped on the surface sizzles immediately and lightly grease the surface. Stir the batter, ladle it onto the griddle, and spread it evenly; okonomiyaki are usually made quite large and about 1/2 inch thick. Cook for 4 to 5 minutes, until the underside has browned. Turn and cook several minutes more;

Yield: 2 to 4 servings

Preparation time: About 30 minutes to prepare; about 10 minutes to cook

Pickled ginger is prepared by briefly salt pressing very thinly sliced fresh ginger and then marinating it in rice vinegar along with leaves of the herb *shiso*, which give it a pink cast. Look for pickled ginger without additives and preservatives in Asian markets and natural foods stores. It is a zippy-tasting, refreshing accompaniment to many Asian-style dishes and a digestive aid.

Nori, also called *laver,* is a dried dark purple seaweed pressed into paper-thin sheets, which turn olive green when toasted. Nori's form makes it an ideal wrapper for grains and vegetables, as in sushi rolls. An enzyme that breaks down cholesterol is prevalent in nori.

Shiitake mushrooms are valued for their nutritional content and strengthening qualities as well as their rich, full flavor. These light grayish-brown, large-capped mushrooms, originally from Japan, are available both fresh and dried. Just a small amount of fresh or dried shiitakes adds a special touch to soups, stews, sauces, and grain and noodle dishes. Pour boiling water over dried shiitakes and soak them for about 30 minutes, then discard their tough stems and save the soaking water for stock. Store fresh shiitakes in a paper bag in the vegetable drawer of your refrigerator. Dried ones keep almost indefinitely wrapped tightly in a dark, cool, dry cabinet.

Notes

• Substitute dried shiitake mushrooms. Pour boiling water over them to cover and soak for about 30 minutes, until they are fully reconstituted. Drain and use the soaking water as part of the liquid in the batter. Discard the tough stems and thinly slice the caps.

• Small cubes of tofu (pressed and marinated or not) or strips of cooked tempeh are good additions to the batter; fold them in with the vegetables.

YIELD: 2 (10-inch) breads

PREPARATION TIME: About 45 minutes, plus a minimum of 30 minutes to rest the dough

Roasted sesame oil, extracted from roasted sesame seeds, is darker than regular sesame oil and has a particularly enticing fragrance and rich nutty flavor. It is typically used as a seasoning rather than as a cooking oil.

these pancakes take longer to cook through than thinner ones.

Meanwhile, whisk together the miso, tahini, the 2 tablespoons stock or water, roasted sesame oil, and vinegar. Turn the pancakes back to the first side and spread on the sauce. Serve them immediately, garnished with the ginger, nori, and cilantro.

CHINESE SCALLION BREAD

CHOPPED SCALLIONS ARE ROLLED RIGHT INTO THESE delicious flat breads, which are sold by street vendors in China, where they are a popular snack food. Serve them as appetizers or as tasty companions to soup.

²/₃ cup whole wheat bread flour	1 teaspoon roasted sesame oil
²/₃ cup whole wheat pastry flour	¹/₂ teaspoon sea salt
²/₃ cup spring water	¹/₂ cup finely chopped green onions
5 teaspoons sesame oil	

Sift the bread and pastry flours into a medium-sized mixing bowl and make a well in the center. Heat the water to boiling, pour it into the well, and stir to form a dough. Turn the dough out onto a lightly floured surface and cover it for several minutes.

Thoroughly knead the dough, dusting the surface with flour only as necessary to keep it from sticking. When it is smooth and springy, place the dough in a lightly greased bowl, cover, and set it aside for at least 30 minutes, but preferably for several hours or even overnight.

Divide the dough in half and form each piece into a ball. With a rolling pin on a lightly floured surface, roll one of the balls into a 12-inch circle. Brush 1 teaspoon regular sesame oil and ¹/₂ teaspoon roasted sesame oil over the surface. Evenly sprinkle on $^1/_4$ tea-spoon salt, then half the green onions. Tightly roll the dough into a long cylinder and pinch the ends closed. Firmly coil it, snail-like, into a circle, tucking the outer end underneath.

On a lightly floured surface, gently roll the coil into a 10-inch circle, periodically turning the dough to keep it from sticking. Place the round on a baking sheet lightly dusted with flour and loosely cover it with a towel.

Prepare the second ball of dough in the same manner.

Heat a griddle or large skillet until water sizzles when dripped on the surface. Add $1^1/_2$ teaspoons regular sesame oil and tilt the pan to evenly coat the surface. Cook one of the breads 1 to 2 minutes on each side, until lightly browned in spots. Add the remaining $1^1/_2$ teaspoons oil and cook the other bread.

Cut the breads into wedges and serve them hot.

Notes
• Refrigerate or freeze left-overs. Reheat them at 450° for several minutes.

Crackers

LIKE FINE HOMEMADE BREAD, ONE TASTE OF FRESH homemade crackers may spoil your appetite for the commercial product for good! Oh, no—another requisite baking project, you might think. But even if you add cracker making to your regular baking routines, you won't be in for much additional work. Crackers are simple, rather unexacting flat breads. Matzos, for instance, are nothing more than flour and water. Homemade crackers are fresher and less expensive than store-bought ones, even when you take the preparation time into account.

Many crackers are made without leavens, and even those that are leavened with baking powder, baking soda, or yeast remain fundamentally flat, so you don't have to be particularly concerned about rising. Crispness rather than rise is a cracker's signature characteristic.

You may make specific cracker doughs, but an easier approach is to treat cracker making as an extension of bread making. When you make a yeasted, sourdough, or natural-rise bread dough, or tortilla or chapati dough, set a portion aside. Just a small piece of dough goes a long way when you're making crackers. I like to use grainy doughs for crackers, such as those for yeasted or sourdough cracked wheat or steel-cut oat breads. Natural-rise cider-rice, rye berry, and grits bread doughs all make good crackers, as do yeasted sprouted wheat and rye doughs. Sesame-wheat crackers are outstanding!

A pasta machine doubles as an excellent cracker roller, or use a rolling pin and roll the dough $1/8$ inch thick or less, as evenly as possible. Roll it on a lightly greased surface or directly on a greased baking sheet. Roll seeds on top for an extra special crunch. Cut out crackers with a sharp knife or use biscuit or cookie cutters for fancier shapes. Prick the surface with a fork to prevent air bubbles.

Bake crackers immediately at 350°. Most take 10 to 15 minutes to become lightly browned and crisp. Doughs containing cooked grains might take slightly longer, and these bake through better at a slightly lower temperature. Keep a close eye on baking crackers because they burn easily.

Cool crackers thoroughly before storing them. They should stay fresh for a couple of weeks in a tightly closed tin or other well-sealed container. To recrisp crackers, place them on a baking sheet in a low oven for a few minutes.

GRAHAM CRACKERS

YIELD: About 2 dozen crackers

PREPARATION TIME: 40 minutes to prepare; 10 to 15 minutes to bake

THESE SLIGHTLY SWEET WHOLE WHEAT CRACKERS ARE A classic American "comfort food." They assuaged our anxieties in kindergarten and still help us get through sleepless nights. Homemade grahams are especially fresh and crisp, and they don't have to be square.

¹/₄ *cup milk or unsweetened soy milk*

1 *teaspoon lemon juice or vinegar*

¹/₄ *cup sunflower or other vegetable oil*

¹/₄ *cup honey or maple syrup*

2 *cups sifted whole wheat pastry flour*

¹/₂ *teaspoon baking soda*

¹/₂ *teaspoon baking powder*

¹/₄ *teaspoon sea salt*

Notes
• Substitute ¹/₄ cup buttermilk or beaten yogurt for the milk or soy milk, and omit the lemon juice.

Combine the milk and lemon juice, and set the mixture aside for a few minutes to curdle. In a small bowl, whisk the oil and honey. Whisk in the curdled milk.

In a medium-sized bowl, sift the sifted flour, baking soda, baking powder, and salt. Make a well in the center and pour in the liquid mixture. Stir gently until the dough pulls away from the sides of the bowl and balls up in the center.

Preheat the oven to 350°. Lightly grease baking sheets or line them with baking parchment.

Using a rolling pin on a lightly greased or lightly floured surface, roll the dough out about ¹/₈ inch thick. Cut out traditional squares or other shapes; I like to use cookie cutters. Arrange them on the prepared sheets and prick the dough with a fork. Bake in the preheated oven for 10 to 15 minutes, until lightly browned.

Transfer the crackers to racks and cool them thoroughly before storing in a tightly closed tin. They will keep well for several weeks.

PART THREE

Getting into Bread: Making Breads into Meals

*T*HE DISHES ARE DONE AND KITCHEN CLEANED UP. FRESHLY BAKED bread rests on racks on the table, cool but still enticingly fragrant. I cut off and munch a piece with undivided attention, savoring every nuance in flavor and texture. What greater pleasure, I think, than fresh bread?

Yet, as good as fresh bread is on its own, I customarily think of it as a foundation for meals. When planning a meal, I start with a grain, often bread, and go from there. So, when I make bread, I'm usually already considering how it will fit into a meal plan.

There are a number of ways to build meals upon breads. You can start with baked breads and serve slices topped with spreads or made into sandwiches. Pita pockets beg for stuffings, and flat breads are natural wrappers for something or other. Bread dough is the basis for pizzas, bread-crusted tarts, main dish turnovers, and sweet or savory spiral-filled loaves or buns. Even dry leftover bread odds and ends are recyclable.

Besides challenging one's ingenuity, basing meals on breads is extremely efficient. Bread making is no longer a separate task but a key part of meal preparation and a healthy daily meal plan. Although all the breads in this book are highly nutritious, combining them with other foods often enhances their nutritional worth. Equally important, these combinations taste great!

Leftover cooked grains, extra baked sweet potatoes or squash, excess carrots or applesauce, a sourdough starter that needs exercising, or simply a craving for a certain grain may dictate the particular bread I decide to make at a given time. Maybe I have the makings for a spread that goes well with rye bread and want to make a cabbage kuchen for dinner with part of the dough. When cilantro abounds in my garden, I know I'll be whipping up some tortillas or chapatis to go with Mexican or Indian dishes. Pita is a particular favorite in the summer for impromptu picnics; I serve it with Middle Eastern salads and dips. On leisurely weekend mornings, I may make popovers, muffins, pancakes, or scones, or finish up a loaf as French toast. I can assure you that this integrative planning becomes habitual and requires little forethought after awhile.

Since we're shifting gears now from baking to cooking, we'll be working with some new ingredients. First, when I specify "a large clove of garlic" in recipes, I mean a large clove—one that will fill a teaspoon when minced. Several recipes call for peeled fresh tomatoes. Slip tomatoes into boiling water very briefly and then transfer them immediately to cold water; the skins will slip off readily. Roasted sweet and hot peppers also appear here and there in coming chapters. Roast a pepper by rotating it on a fork over a gas flame, or put it under the broiler and turn it several times until evenly charred. Cool the pepper in a covered bowl, then peel off the skin and remove the seeds and membranes if desired. Some recipes call for pressed tofu. Sandwich tofu between folded unnapped cloth or paper towels on a tray or plate and place a moderately heavy object on top. I have a square stone paperweight that is just right for one block of tofu, and I find that putting the tofu and weight inside a small plastic berry or cherry tomato basket keeps the arrangement stable. Lots of things work as weights, including a container of water, but whatever you use should gradually compress the tofu, not squash it. If you're pressing several blocks of tofu at once, place them on a baking sheet with another sheet on top and weight on top of that, or arrange the tofu in a colander and cover it with a towel, plate, and weight.

Moving on to cooking will require some other tools too. Besides various pots and pans, you'll need a cutting board and some good-quality knives in assorted sizes. Keep your knives well sharpened, because dull blades are both frustratingly ineffective and accidents waiting to happen. A toaster oven is a versatile appliance that not only toasts or warms breads but also toasts nuts and bakes and broils vegetables and sandwiches using minimal energy. A flame tamer is a hollow round metal plate that buffers burner heat and spreads it evenly over the bottom of a pan. It's great for minding simmering sauces or anything else prone to burning. But if I had to single out the most useful kitchen tool to appear on the scene in recent years, it would undoubtedly be the salad spinner. By quickly and effectively drying fresh herbs and greens, this simple apparatus saves much time and many paper towels.

Spreads and sauces, the focus of the next chapter, are good vehicles for integrating baking and cooking. These are toppings and fillings for breads and doughs in the chapters that follow. All kinds of leftovers insufficient to constitute a significant part of a meal on their own have new potential when viewed as ingredients for combination items. We'll finish up with some ideas for using a baker's ultimate leftover—bread.

TEN

Spreads and Sauces and Such

$\mathcal{T}$HERE'S OFTEN A FINE LINE BETWEEN SPREADS AND SAUCES, AND they frequently stand in for one another with the greatest of ease. Sometimes the only difference between a spread and a sauce is consistency. For instance, tahini-miso spread thinned with a bit of orange juice readily becomes tahini-miso sauce. Spreads and sauces alike play multiple culinary roles: organizing flavors, harmonizing textures, and adding accents in taste and appearance to specific dishes and to meals as a whole. I like to think of them as "accessories" for food in the same way scarves, belts, jewelry, shoes, handbags, and hats coordinate garments and transform them into stylish outfits.

A repertoire of spreads, sauces, and condiments is an asset for cooking in general but is especially important for the collaborative dishes we're about to undertake. Aside from breads, these toppings and fillings are some of the basic raw materials you'll need to create a broad variety of bread-based dishes, whether a simple sandwich or a flamboyant pizza. No doubt, like me, you'll find yourself coming back to these versatile recipes repeatedly for both old and new applications.

There's a lot of variety here, even though these tasty, nutritious combinations are all vegetarian and nondairy. They are based on beans, tofu, nuts, seeds, vegetables, and fruits. Herbs, spices, citrus zest, garlic, ginger root, and hot peppers add extra pizzazz. Some of the recipes—hummus, baba, refritos, guacamole, salsas, pesto, and dal—are borrowed from other cultures and adapted to my own particular taste and ingredient preferences. Others, such as tofu spreads and sauces, pesto variations, and bean and vegetable pâtés, derive more from sheer invention, though they too often reflect cultural influences. A few basics, including fruit and nut butters, baked garlic, tomato sauces, and hollandaise, round out the selection.

Though many spreads and sauces have a particular ethnic bent or are customarily linked with particular breads or bread-based dishes in some other way, there are no fixed rules for combining. Let your senses be your guide, and trust your instincts. Add your own favorite spreads and sauces to this collection, and update it as you discover new ones.

When I was very young, my favorite sandwich was made with peanut butter, jelly, and Marshmallow Fluff. During my kindergarten year, I ate that particular trio every day. Now that I'm an advocate of a balanced diet and, moreover, now that I know about the tremendous variety of smooth, chunky, sweet, savory, spicy, and herby spreads and sauces that can be experienced in one short lifetime, it seems a shame that I devoted an entire year to such a boring combination. Yet, I'm sure I have more than made up for lost time in the years since.

Tahini-Miso Spread

THIS RICH-TASTING, CREAMY SESAME SPREAD IS GOOD ON all kinds of breads, from quick to flat. It goes well with a variety of flavors, both sweet and savory. I like it on muffins for breakfast or combined with vegetables or fruits in sandwiches for lunch (see **Blondie's Dagwood,** page 287). This spread is quick to make as needed. It also keeps well tightly covered in the refrigerator.

¹/₄ cup unsalted raw or roasted tahini	*Freshly grated orange zest to taste*
1 to 2 teaspoons mellow barley miso to taste	

In a small bowl, thoroughly whisk together the tahini and miso. Add zest to taste. Thin the spread, if desired, by mixing in fruit juice, stock, or water.

YIELD: About ¹/₃ cup

PREPARATION TIME: 10 minutes

Notes
- Roasted tahini gives the spread a richer flavor. Buy it roasted, or stir raw tahini in a pan over low heat for several minutes, until it becomes a bit darker in color and wonderfully fragrant; cool before mixing in the miso.
- Substitute lemon zest or minced fresh herbs, such as dill, basil, tarragon, chives, or parsley, for the orange zest.

Peanut Butter–Banana Spread

I'M STILL A PEANUT BUTTER FAN, THOUGH NOW I CAN DO without the Fluff and even the jelly. Mashed banana moistens this spread and gives it a natural sweetness. Substitute other fruits in season; try strawberries, raspberries, peaches, nectarines, or apple or pear sauce. Miso seasons the mixture and makes it more digestible. This spread is good with many kinds of breads. I often spread it on toast for a quick breakfast or lunch.

1 tablespoon unsalted peanut butter	*¹/₂ to 1 teaspoon mellow barley miso*
¹/₄ cup mashed banana	

In a small bowl, thoroughly mash together the peanut butter and banana; mix in the miso to taste.

YIELD: 1 or 2 servings

PREPARATION TIME: 10 minutes

CURRIED-TOFU SPREAD

YIELD: Enough for 2 to 4 sandwiches

PREPARATION TIME: 30 minutes

Tofu, or *bean curd,* is a white, cheeselike substance, prepared by curdling soy milk, draining off the whey, and pressing the curds to mold them into solid cakes that vary in consistency from soft and custardy to extra firm. Particularly soft, smooth, and sweet-tasting *silken tofu,* often featured in Japanese dishes, is prepared slightly differently: a rich soy milk mixed with coagulant is transformed into tofu inside sterile, sealed aseptic packages immersed in a hot water bath.

Economical, easy to digest, and cholesterol-free, tofu contains high-quality protein, plus iron, B vitamins, and other nutrients. It is rich in calcium if a calcium-containing compound, such as calcium chloride or calcium sulfate, is used as a coagulant. Store tofu refrigerated, under water in a covered container, and change the water daily; it will keep for a week or so. Rather bland on its own, this Asian staple readily sops up seasonings of all sorts. Extraordinarily versatile, tofu can be mashed, blended, marinated, simmered, steamed, baked, broiled, deep-fried, sautéed, or stir-fried. Use very soft silken tofu for sauces and desserts, firmer tofu for soups, stews, stir-fries, and kebabs.

To press tofu, place it in a colander or strainer or sandwich it between paper or cloth towels on a tray and set a flat-bottomed pan and a weight of some kind on top. To blanch tofu, immerse it in boiling water and simmer it for a few minutes, then drain it well. Freezing tofu (in a plastic freezer bag or tightly closed container) turns it an off-white color and renders it spongy, chewy, and especially absorbent once it has thawed.

TOFU HAS A FANTASTIC CAPACITY TO ABSORB FLAVORS. Here, seasoned with curry spices, it assumes an Indian character. You can make this spicy spread a bit ahead of time so that the flavors have a chance to mingle. It goes well with lots of breads, especially grainy ones, such as cracked wheat, oat, or rice breads. Combine it with thinly sliced tomatoes or apples and crisp lettuce for a terrific sandwich, or stuff it into a pita.

$1/4$ teaspoon each ground turmeric, cumin, coriander, and chili powder	8 ounces tofu, pressed and blanched
$1/8$ teaspoon each ground cloves, cardamom, cinnamon, and cayenne	2 green onions, finely chopped
1 tablespoon sesame, peanut, or canola oil	$1/4$ cup loosely packed parsley, finely chopped
1 clove garlic, minced	3 tablespoons lightly toasted, finely chopped almonds, or roasted peanuts
1 teaspoon finely grated fresh ginger	1 teaspoon lemon juice
1 small carrot, finely chopped or grated	3 to 4 tablespoons **Tofu Mayonnaise** (page 267) or other mayonnaise
	Sea salt to taste

Combine the turmeric, cumin, coriander, chili powder, cloves, cardamom, cinnamon, and cayenne with a mortar and pestle or spice grinder.

Heat the oil in a small skillet. Briefly sauté the garlic and ginger. Stir in the spice mixture and carrot and continue to cook, stirring, for 1 to 2 minutes. Remove from the heat.

In a bowl, mash the tofu well with a large fork. Add the sauté, green onions, parsley, almonds, lemon juice, and 3 tablespoons of the mayonnaise, and mix thoroughly. Add more mayonnaise as needed to achieve the desired consistency. Season with salt to taste.

Serve the spread at room temperature or chilled.

HERBED TOFU–ALMOND SPREAD

MUSTARD GREENS GIVE THIS SPREAD A PLEASANT SPICI-ness. Substitute other greens or vegetables, such as finely chopped watercress, arugula, celery, bell pepper, or radish, for all or part of them. Refrigerated, this spread will keep well for a couple of days; the flavor may even improve. Serve it on thinly sliced bread, rolled up in flat breads, or stuffed into pita. Garnish with sprouts or fresh tomatoes in season.

YIELD: Enough for 4 to 6 sandwiches

PREPARATION TIME: About 30 minutes

1 pound tofu, pressed and blanched
2 cloves garlic, minced
2 to 3 teaspoons each minced fresh basil, tarragon, and dill weed
1 teaspoon prepared mustard
1/4 teaspoon celery seed
2 large green onions, finely chopped
1 small carrot, grated
1/4 cup finely chopped parsley
1/2 cup finely chopped tender mustard greens
1/2 cup lightly toasted almonds, finely chopped
*1/3 to 1/2 cup **Tofu Mayonnaise** (page 267) or other mayonnaise*
1 teaspoon mellow rice or mellow barley miso
Sea salt to taste

In a bowl, mash the tofu well. Add the garlic, minced herbs, mustard, celery seed, green onions, carrot, parsley, greens, and almonds, and mix thoroughly.

In a small bowl, whisk together 1/3 cup of the mayonnaise and the miso. Add this to the tofu mixture and stir thoroughly. Add more mayonnaise as needed to achieve the desired consistency. Season the spread with sea salt to taste.

YIELD: Enough for 4 sandwiches

PREPARATION TIME: 25 minutes

....

Umeboshi, small unripe Japanese plums pickled with sea salt and purple shiso leaves, are a remarkably versatile seasoning applicable to any cuisine—and an amazingly effective digestive aid. Umeboshi paste is simply puréed pickled plums. Umeboshi "vinegar" is the pickling brine. Try small amounts of the paste or vinegar in salad dressings, sauces, spreads, and grain, bean, and vegetable dishes. Umeboshi plums, paste, and vinegar are available in natural foods stores and Oriental markets.

....

Notes
• Substitute finely chopped chives or Chinese chives for the green onions.
• Substitute lightly toasted, finely chopped sunflower seeds or walnuts for the sesame seeds.

YIELD: 4 to 8 servings

PREPARATION TIME: About 1 hour

TOFU-SESAME SPREAD

SESAME SEEDS ARE PRESENT IN THREE DIFFERENT FORMS in this tasty, nourishing blend. Spread it on thin slices of bread or in pita, and layer thin tomato and crisp radish slices, lettuce or other dark greens, and sprouts on top. Or serve it as a dip for crunchy raw vegetables or bread sticks.

12 ounces tofu, pressed and blanched	*1 large clove garlic, minced*
1 tablespoon lemon juice, plus extra to taste	*1 tablespoon dark miso*
1/2 teaspoon roasted sesame oil	*3 green onions, finely chopped*
1 teaspoon umeboshi paste, or to taste	*1/4 cup finely chopped parsley*
1/4 cup tahini	*2 to 4 tablespoons toasted sesame seeds*

In a medium-sized bowl or in a food processor, mash or blend the tofu well. Add the lemon juice, roasted sesame oil, umeboshi paste, tahini, garlic, and miso. Combine thoroughly. Mix in the green onions and parsley. Add sesame seeds to taste. Thin the spread, if desired, with vegetable stock or water.

ROASTED GARLIC

THE FIRST TIME I TASTED A WHOLE ROASTED ONION, I WAS surprised by the sweet succulence I discovered beneath the charred outer layers. The mellowness of roasted garlic is similarly amazing. Enjoy this rich, nutty-tasting spread on a crusty bread.

4 large, whole heads firm, fresh garlic	*Water*
1/4 teaspoon sea salt	*2 tablespoons olive oil*

Peel the parchment-like skin of the garlic down to the layer adjacent to the cloves. Place the peeled garlic in a small pot and add the salt and water to cover. Bring to a boil and simmer for about 1 minute. Remove the garlic, reserving the water.

Arrange the garlic in an oiled baking dish and drizzle the oil over it. Bake at 350° for about an hour, basting the bulb several times with the reserved liquid, until the cloves are exceedingly soft when pierced.

Spoon the liquid in the pan over the bulbs and serve them whole, instructing diners to separate the cloves and squeeze them to extract the creamy spread inside.

Baba

Baba Ganouj, Baba Ghanoush, Baba Ghanoosh.... I just call this scrumptious Middle Eastern eggplant purée "Baba." Serve it as a dip for raw vegetables and pita (page 225–228), or use it in a sandwich. Baba will keep for a couple of days refrigerated.

1 medium-sized eggplant	2 teaspoons dark miso, or
1 large clove garlic,	to taste
minced	¼ cup parsley, finely
5 teaspoons lemon juice	chopped
5 tablespoons tahini	

Pierce the eggplant in several places with a fork. Place it on a baking sheet and bake at 450° for 30 to 50 minutes, until the eggplant appears wrinkled and is very soft.

In a medium-sized bowl, whisk together the garlic, lemon juice, tahini, and miso to form a smooth paste. (Or use a blender or food processor fitted with the metal blade.)

When the eggplant is cool enough to handle, cut it in half and scoop out the pulp. Add these eggplant

Notes

• Grind a bit of fresh pepper or sprinkle a bit of minced fresh or crushed dried herbs, such as thyme or rosemary, over the garlic bulbs before baking.

• Substitute elephant garlic for the smaller varieties; leave the bulbs intact or separate them into cloves. Allow extra baking time.

Yield: About 1½ cups

Preparation time: 30 to 50 minutes to bake the eggplant; 20 minutes thereafter

Garlic is a member of the *allium* family, along with onions, scallions, leeks, shallots, and chives. Its outstanding flavor ranges from strong and pungent when raw to mild and mellow when braised or baked. Garlic's natural immune-boosting properties are widely recognized. Keep unpeeled garlic in a well-ventilated container, such as a basket, in a cool, dry place. To preserve it longer, separate the cloves, cover them with oil, and refrigerate, or freeze the cloves and remove and peel them while frozen as needed. Press the side of a garlic clove with a cleaver to make peeling much easier.

Elephant garlic, a giant cousin of regular garlic, is a bit sweeter and milder.

"innards" to the garlic-tahini mixture and thoroughly mash or blend the two together. Stir in the parsley.

Serve baba at room temperature or chilled, spread in a smooth layer on the bottom and around the sides of a shallow bowl and drizzled with a bit of olive oil if you wish.

INDIAN EGGPLANT

GREEN TOMATOES ADD A HINT OF TARTNESS TO THIS DELIcious eggplant dish. It can be a spread, dip, or filling for flat breads. Serve it for lunch or dinner along with some fresh, warm **Chapatis** (page 221) or **Parathas** (page 222) and perhaps a **Dal** (page 257). Refrigerated, this will keep for a couple of days.

YIELD: About 4 cups

PREPARATION TIME: About 1 hour

1¹/₂ pounds eggplant	1 large onion, finely chopped
³/₄ teaspoon fennel seeds	2 medium-sized green tomatoes, finely chopped
1 teaspoon ground coriander	³/₄ teaspoon sea salt, or to taste
¹/₂ teaspoon each chili powder, ground turmeric, and ground cumin	1 tablespoon chopped cilantro
1 tablespoon sesame or canola oil or ghee	

Pierce the eggplant with a fork, place it on a baking sheet, and bake at 450° for 30 to 50 minutes, until it appears wrinkled and is very soft. Set the eggplant aside until it is cool enough to handle, then scrape the pulp into a bowl and mash it thoroughly.

Toast the fennel seeds in a dry skillet. Grind them to a coarse consistency in a mortar or spice grinder. Add the coriander, chili powder, turmeric, and cumin, and grind again.

Add the oil or ghee to a skillet over medium heat and sauté the onion for a few minutes. Add the tomatoes and continue sautéing until the vegetables are tender. Stir in the spice mixture and cook, stirring, for a couple of min-

Notes
• Substitute ripe tomatoes and add a teaspoon of lemon juice at the end of the cooking.
• If you like things hot, add all or part of a small chile, minced, along with the eggplant.

utes. Stir in ³/₄ teaspoon salt and the eggplant, reduce the heat, and cook for several minutes, stirring occasionally, until the excess liquid has cooked away. Garnish with the cilantro.

GUACAMOLE

WELL-RIPENED AVOCADOS HAVE A SMOOTH, CREAMY TEXture and a full, rich, nutty flavor. Many recipes for this traditional Mexican purée call for tomato, onion, garlic, chiles, or other spices, but I think guacamole is best at its simplest—with just a touch of lime, black pepper, and salt, and a light sprinkling of chopped fresh cilantro leaves. Serve it with soft or crisp tortillas or raw vegetable chunks, or use it as a sandwich spread or salad topping. The flavor, texture, and color of guacamole are best when it is fresh; if you must wait to serve it, keep it tightly covered.

YIELD: About 1 cup

PREPARATION TIME: 10 minutes

1 medium-sized ripe avocado, peeled and pitted	Freshly ground black pepper to taste
1 to 1¹/₂ teaspoons lime juice	Sea salt to taste
	2 tablespoons coarsely chopped cilantro

In a small, shallow bowl, mash the avocado pulp with a fork to the consistency of a coarse paste. Stir in lime juice to taste. Season to taste with pepper and salt. Garnish the guacamole with the cilantro and serve it immediately.

Notes
• The two most commonly available avocados are the dark, bumpy-skinned Haas from California, and the brighter green, smooth-skinned Fuerte from Florida. I usually prefer the Haas because they tend to be richer-tasting than the sometimes watery Florida ones, although I've had some Florida avocados that were excellent, too.

PEAR BUTTER

WHEN I MOVED TO TEXAS, I DISCOVERED KIEFFER PEARS, which are crisp yet juicy when they are ripe. They make wonderful pear sauce and pear butter, projects I look forward to every autumn. You can substitute other kinds of pears, though you may need to adjust the cooking time, because most kinds take less time to soften.

YIELD: 2¹/₂ to 3 pints, depending on consistency

PREPARATION TIME: 30 minutes to prepare; several hours to cook

Notes

- Add ground allspice, cinnamon, and nutmeg to taste.
- For **Lemon-Ginger Pear Butter,** stir 1 teaspoon lemon zest and 1 teaspoon finely grated ginger root or 1 teaspoon ground ginger into the sauce after you have milled it.
- For **Pear Sauce,** do not cook the milled fruit to a thick consistency.
- Make plain or spiced **Apple Sauce** or **Apple Butter** by the same method. Firm-fleshed, tart apples, such as Pippins, Northern Spies, Crispins, and Granny Smiths, make especially flavorful apple sauce and apple butter. Use one variety or a combination.
- For **Peach Butter,** remove the skins before pitting and dicing the fruit by dipping the peaches briefly in boiling water and then plunging them into cold water. The skin should slip off readily. Proceed with the recipe. This fruit butter, too, is good plain or spiced.

YIELD: About 6 cups

PREPARATION TIME: 35 minutes

5 pounds of pears (Kieffer, Comice, Bartlett, Seckel, Anjou, Bosc, etc.)

Quarter the pears lengthwise, core, dice, and place the chunks in a 6-quart heavy-bottomed pot. Cover and set it on a flame tamer over medium heat. Cook, stirring occasionally, until the fruit is soft, 2 to 3 hours for Kieffer pears. Put the fruit through a food mill or force it through a strainer to remove the skins. Return the sauce to the pot, partially cover, and cook until it reaches the consistency you desire.

Pour the hot mixture into sterilized canning jars, leaving about ½ inch of head space; screw on sterilized lids and process in a boiling water bath for 20 minutes. Store the sealed jars in a cool, dry cupboard or pantry.

Or, store the sauce in the refrigerator or freezer after it has cooled.

REFRITOS

REFRIED BEANS ARE A STAPLE IN LATIN AMERICA—AND IN my house. Serve them simply with greens, rice, and **Corn or Wheat Tortillas** (page 216–219), or use them as a key component of other dishes, such as **Mexican Pizza** (page 314), **Bean Burritos** (page 305), and **Towering Tostadas** (page 302). Refried beans are traditionally cooked in lard; using olive oil lowers the cholesterol in these, and they are tremendously tasty. They will keep several days refrigerated, or you can freeze them.

1 to 2 tablespoons olive oil
2 medium-sized onions, finely chopped
2 medium-sized bell peppers, finely chopped

4 to 8 large cloves garlic, minced
Freshly ground black pepper to taste
2 teaspoons ground cumin
½ teaspoon ground coriander

5 cups cooked red beans— pinto, kidney, anasazi, aduki— or black turtle beans (see page 292)	$^1/_2$ to 1 cup bean stock 2 tablespoons dark miso, or to taste 1 tablespoon lemon juice

Add the oil to a large skillet over medium heat. Sauté the onions until they are translucent. Add the bell pepper, garlic, black pepper, cumin, and coriander, and continue sautéing until the vegetables are tender. Stir in two-thirds of the cooked beans and reduce the heat to low.

Add a few tablespoons of bean stock to the remaining beans and mash them to a paste. Stir the mashed beans into the sautéed mixture. Cover and cook over low heat, stirring occasionally, for 15 to 20 minutes.

Thoroughly mix the miso with 2 tablespoons of bean stock and stir into the hot beans. Mix in the lemon juice. If the bean mixture is too thick, stir in additional stock.

LENTIL DAL

THESE ARE DELICATELY SPICE REFRIED BEANS, INDIAN style. Serve them with basmati rice and flat breads, such as **Chapatis** (page 221), **Parathas** (page 222), and **Yeasted** or **Sourdough Pita** (pages 225 and 227). This is also a delicious topping or filling for **Dosas** (page 233).

1 cup red lentils 1 (2-inch) piece kombu (optional) 3 cups water 1 teaspoon ground turmeric 1$^1/_2$ teaspoons cumin seeds 1 teaspoon ground coriander $^1/_4$ teaspoon ground cardamom $^1/_8$ teaspoon each ground cinnamon, cloves, and cayenne	1 tablespoon vegetable oil or ghee 1 small onion, finely chopped Freshly ground black pepper to taste 1$^1/_2$ tablespoons lemon juice 1$^1/_2$ tablespoons mellow barley miso, or to taste Vegetable stock, water, or coconut milk $^1/_2$ cup cilantro, coarsely chopped

Pinto beans belong to the kidney bean family. A common ingredient in Southwestern cuisine, they are a speckled pinkish tan and have a sweet, mild flavor. See page 360 for cooking directions.

YIELD: About 3 cups

PREPARATION TIME: 1 to 1$^1/_2$ hours

Coconut milk is a creamy, rich liquid prepared by blending either fresh or soaked dried coconut with hot water and then straining the purée. Use equal parts of fresh coconut and water or 1 part dried unsweetened coconut to 1$^1/_2$ parts water; in either case, 1 cup of coconut will yield about 1 cup of coconut milk. Canned commercial milk without additives or preservatives is readily available in most Asian and natural foods stores. Freeze coconut milk to keep it longer than a couple of days.

Notes
• Substitute a bit of finely minced chile for the cayenne; sauté it with the onion briefly before you add the spices.
• If fresh cilantro is not available, garnish the dal with 1 to 2 tablespoons of chopped fresh mint leaves.

Sort through the lentils and pick out any foreign matter. Rinse the lentils under cool water. Place them and the kombu in a 1½- to 2-quart saucepan. Add the water and bring it to a boil over medium heat. Skim off the foam, reduce the heat to low, and stir in the turmeric. Loosely cover the pot and cook, stirring occasionally, for 45 to 60 minutes, until the lentils are tender: they will separate into a thick layer on the bottom and a soupy layer on top. Turn off the heat and cover the pot tightly.

Heat a heavy-bottomed skillet over low to medium heat and roast the cumin seeds for several minutes, stirring or agitating the pan often to prevent them from burning. Grind the seeds to a coarse consistency in a mortar or spice grinder; add the coriander, cardamom, cinnamon, cloves, and cayenne, and grind again.

Add the oil to a skillet over medium heat. Sauté the onion until it is tender. Add black pepper and the spice mixture and cook briefly, stirring constantly to keep the spices from burning. Stir in the cooked lentils. Turn the heat to low and cover the pan. Cook for several minutes, until the mixture is hot and the flavors are blended.

Whisk the lemon juice and miso to a thick paste. Stir this into the lentil mixture. If it is too thick, thin with several tablespoons of water, vegetable stock, or coconut milk. Garnish servings with the cilantro.

CURRIED GARBANZOS

SERVE THIS SPICY BEAN DISH AS A DIP OR FILLING FOR flat breads, such as **Chapatis** (page 221), **Parathas** (page 222), or **Dosas** (page 233). It will keep for several days refrigerated.

YIELD: About 3 cups

PREPARATION TIME: 30 to 40 minutes

½ teaspoon cumin seeds
½ teaspoon ground turmeric
1 teaspoon ground coriander

⅛ teaspoon each ground cloves, cardamom, cinnamon, and cayenne
1 tablespoon vegetable oil or ghee

1 medium-sized onion,
 finely chopped
1 large clove garlic,
 minced
1 teaspoon finely grated
 fresh ginger
Freshly ground black
 pepper to taste
1 medium-sized ripe
 tomato, chopped

2 cups cooked garbanzo
 beans (see page 360)
1/4 cup bean or vegetable
 stock
1 tablespoon lemon juice
1 tablespoon dark miso
1/2 cup cilantro, coarsely
 chopped

Notes

• Substitute a minced small chile for the cayenne. Add it to the sauté along with the garlic and ginger.

Set a heavy-bottomed skillet over medium heat and roast the cumin seeds for several minutes, stirring or agitating the pan often to prevent them from burning. Grind them to a coarse powder in a mortar or spice grinder. Add the turmeric, coriander, cloves, cardamom, cinnamon, and cayenne, and grind again.

Add the oil to a skillet over medium heat and sauté the onion for several minutes. Stir in the garlic and ginger, and continue sautéing until the onion is just tender. Grind in black pepper, add the spice mixture, and cook briefly, stirring constantly. Stir in the tomato, garbanzo beans, and stock, and bring the mixture just to a simmer. Cover and turn the heat to low. Cook for 10 to 15 minutes, until the tomato is soft and the flavors have blended. Whisk together the lemon juice and miso, and stir it into the skillet mixture.

Serve warm, garnished with the cilantro.

Hummus

Hardly "ho-hummus," a term coined by my friend Darcee to describe uninspired versions of the Lebanese garbanzo bean spread or dip, this one is a pert and lively blend. Serve it with warm **Pita** (page 225) or other flat breads, or with crisp raw vegetables. Hummus will keep for several days refrigerated.

Yield: About 1 1/2 cups

Preparation time: 15 minutes

Tahini is a creamy paste made by blending hulled raw or roasted sesame seeds. It is high in protein, vitamins, and minerals, including calcium, and adds a wonderfully smooth texture and nutty flavor to spreads, sauces, and dressings. Try to find tahini made from organically grown, mechanically hulled seeds to avoid chemical residues from pesticides or processing solvents. It is available in natural foods stores, ethnic markets, and many supermarkets. Refrigerated after opening, tahini will keep for several months.

YIELD: About 1½ cups

PREPARATION TIME: 15 minutes

Navy beans are small oval white beans with a mild flavor. They are a variety of kidney beans and were once a staple in the United States Navy diet. Great northern beans are larger versions of navy beans. See page 360 for cooking directions.

¼ cup tahini
2 tablespoons lemon juice
2 cloves garlic, minced
2 teaspoons dark miso
3 tablespoons bean or
  vegetable stock, plus
  extra as needed
1 cup cooked, drained
  garbanzo beans (see
  page 360)
¼ cup parsley

In a blender or a food processor fitted with the metal blade, thoroughly blend the tahini, lemon juice, garlic, miso, and stock to a smooth paste. Add the garbanzo beans and blend well. Blend in the parsley. If necessary, blend in additional stock, a tablespoon at a time, until it is the consistency you desire. Add a touch more miso and/or lemon juice if needed.

WHITE BEAN SPREAD

SERVE THIS LIGHT, REFRESHING DIP OR SPREAD WITH **Pita** (page 225) or other flat breads, or with crisp raw vegetables and briny black olives.

2 cloves garlic, minced
3 tablespoons bean or
  vegetable stock, plus
  extra as needed
2 tablespoons lemon juice
2½ teaspoons mellow
  barley miso
¼ cup tahini
¼ cup mint leaves
1 cup cooked navy beans
  (see page 360)
Minced mint leaves or
  parsley, for garnish

In a blender or food processor fitted with the metal blade, combine the garlic, stock, lemon juice, miso, and tahini, and blend until thoroughly smooth. Blend in the mint and beans. To thin, blend in an additional tablespoon or two of bean stock. Garnish the spread with minced mint leaves or parsley, if desired.

This will keep for several days refrigerated.

Mediterranean Bean Spread

I used to stop at a Middle Eastern restaurant on the road between Northampton and Amherst, Massachusetts, and often ordered an unusual red bean purée, along with more familiar hummus and baba. This is my version of that wonderful concoction. I usually serve this dip or spread with large folded circles of **Lebanese Wrapper Bread** (page 229), as the restaurant did, but it goes well with other flat breads and raw vegetables, too.

1 tablespoon olive oil	1 tablespoon dark miso
1 small onion, chopped	2 tablespoons tahini
1 large clove garlic, minced	3 tablespoons bean or vegetable stock, plus extra as needed
Freshly ground black pepper to taste	
1/4 teaspoon fresh thyme leaves, minced	1 cup cooked red beans— anasazi, pinto, aduki, kidney, etc. (see page 360)
Pinch of cinnamon	
2 teaspoons lemon juice	2 tablespoons minced parsley

Add the oil to a small skillet over medium heat and sauté the onion for several minutes. Add the garlic and continue sautéing until the onion appears tender. Add the pepper, thyme, and cinnamon, and cook briefly.

Transfer to a blender or food processor fitted with the metal blade. Add the lemon juice, miso, tahini, and stock, and blend until smooth. Add the beans and blend thoroughly. Thin with additional bean stock if desired.

Serve at room temperature or chilled, garnished with the parsley.

This will keep refrigerated for several days.

Yield: About 1 1/2 cups

Preparation time: 25 minutes

Anasazi beans are the unhybridized ancestors of pinto beans. They resemble pinto beans in size and shape but are maroon with white patches. Anasazi beans taste much like pinto beans, but their flavor is fuller and sweeter. They hold their shape better when cooked and are also more digestible.

Kidney beans are small reddish-brown kidney-shaped beans. They have a rather sweet flavor and hold their shape well when cooked. See page 360 for cooking directions.

ANASAZI BEAN SPREAD

YIELD: About 1½ cups

PREPARATION TIME: 20 to 30 minutes

ANASAZI MEANS "ANCIENT ONES" IN THE NAVAJO INDIAN language, and anasazi beans are in fact the ancestors of pinto beans. This spread or dip combines the special sweetness of these beans, the mild heat of a poblano pepper, and the delightful poignancy of cilantro in a rich, appealing blend. You can substitute other red beans, such as pinto beans or kidney beans, for the anasazi beans.

1 small poblano pepper	3 tablespoons bean or
1 tablespoon olive oil	vegetable stock, plus
1 small onion, chopped	extra to taste
1 clove garlic, minced	1 cup cooked anasazi beans
1 teaspoon ground cumin	(see page 360)
2½ teaspoons dark miso	½ cup cilantro
2 teaspoons lemon juice	

Roast and peel the pepper as described on page 244.

Add the olive oil to a small skillet over medium heat. Sauté the onion for several minutes. Add the garlic and continue sautéing until the onion is tender. Stir in the cumin and cook briefly. Transfer to a blender or food processor fitted with the metal blade. Add the miso, lemon juice, and bean stock, and blend. Add the beans, ¼ of the pepper, and the cilantro, and blend again. Taste and blend in more of the pepper as needed. If the mixture seems too thick, add more stock.

Notes
• Substitute another chile variety for the poblano. Follow the roasting procedure or mince the pepper and add part or all of it to the sauté. Peppers, even of the same variety, vary in hotness, and I prefer to control the hotness of the spread by the roast-and-add-it-gradually method above.

MUSHROOM PÂTÉ

YIELD: 6 or more servings

PREPARATION TIME: 30 minutes to prepare; 1½ hours to bake

SERVE THIS DELECTABLE SPREAD AS AN APPETIZER OR AS part of a light meal. I especially relish it with rye or pumpernickel bread.

1 teaspoon kuzu powder

1¹/₂ tablespoons Marsala

2 tablespoons vegetable oil
   or unsalted butter or
   soy margarine

1 small onion, chopped

¹/₄ cup chopped celery

8 ounces mushrooms,
   sliced

¹/₄ to ¹/₂ teaspoon each
   minced fresh basil,
   oregano, and rosemary
   (or ¹/₈ teaspoon dried)

Freshly ground black pepper
   or cayenne to taste

¹/₄ cup chopped parsley

8 ounces tofu

1 tablespoon mellow rice or
   mellow barley miso

1 tablespoon lemon juice, or
   to taste

¹/₂ cup lightly toasted
   walnuts

¹/₂ cup bread crumbs

Marsala is a rather sweet dessert wine which originated in Marsala, Sicily. It is an interesting addition to tomato sauces and other savory dishes.

Combine the kuzu and Marsala, and set it aside until the kuzu has thoroughly dissolved.

Add the oil to a skillet over medium heat. Sauté the onion until it appears translucent. Stir in the celery, mushrooms, herbs, and pepper and continue sautéing until the celery is just tender. Stir in the parsley and remove the pan from the heat.

In a blender or a food processor fitted with the metal blade, blend the tofu. Add the miso and lemon juice, and blend well. Add the walnuts, bread crumbs, dissolved kuzu, and the sauté. Blend thoroughly. Taste and adjust seasonings.

Grease a small loaf pan. Line it with waxed paper and grease the paper. Pour the mixture into the pan and spread it evenly. Bake in a preheated 325° oven for 1¹/₂ hours. Cool it on a rack for 30 minutes or so. Carefully invert the pâté onto a plate and gently peel off the paper.

Serve the pâté warm or chilled.

LENTIL PÂTÉ

THIS RICH-TASTING PÂTÉ IS GOOD WARM OR CHILLED, spread on thin slices of bread or toast. Serve it as an appetizer or with a salad for a light but luxurious meal.

YIELD: A lot!—a full 8-inch springform pan

PREPARATION TIME: 30 minutes to prepare; 1 hour to bake

1 tablespoon olive oil
1 medium-sized onion,
  finely chopped
2 cloves garlic, minced
1 medium-sized bell
  pepper, finely chopped
Freshly ground black
  pepper to taste
1 teaspoon ground cumin
Pinch of cinnamon
1/2 teaspoon minced fresh
  thyme leaves, or
  1/4 teaspoon dried
1 tablespoon minced fresh
  basil leaves, or
  1 1/2 teaspoons dried

1 teaspoon minced fresh
  oregano leaves, or
  1/2 teaspoon dried
4 ounces tofu, mashed
3 cups cooked green or
  brown lentils (see
  page 360)
2 tablespoons lemon juice
2 tablespoons mellow
  barley miso
1/2 cup parsley, finely
  chopped
1/2 cup toasted fine bread
  crumbs
1/4 cup lightly toasted
  pine nuts

Add the oil to a skillet over medium heat. Sauté the onion until it appears translucent. Stir in the garlic and bell pepper, and continue sautéing until the pepper is just tender. Add the black pepper, cumin, cinnamon, thyme, basil, and oregano, and sauté briefly. Stir in the tofu and remove the skillet from the heat.

Put the lentils and sauté into a food processor fitted with the metal blade. Mix together the lemon juice and miso to form a smooth paste, and add it to the processor; blend well. Add the parsley, bread crumbs, and pine nuts, and blend briefly.

Grease the bottom and sides of an 8-inch springform pan. Trace around the bottom of the pan on a double-thickness of waxed paper. Cut out the two circles and grease one side of each; fit one paper circle, greased side up, in the bottom of the pan; spread the lentil mixture evenly in the pan; place the second circle of paper, greased side down, on top, and cover the pan with an ovenproof plate.

Bake the pâté in a preheated 375° oven for 1 hour.

Remove the plate and place the pan on a cooling rack for at least 30 minutes.

Peel off the waxed paper, invert the pâté onto a plate, and peel off the other paper.

Serve the pâté warm or chilled. It will keep in the refrigerator for several days.

Neapolitan Pâté

When I was a child, we sometimes had Neapolitan ice cream for special occasions. It was in brick form sliced vertically so that every serving had some of each of the chocolate, vanilla, and strawberry layers. This triple-decker, tricolor spread looks something like that memorable ice cream, but it is composed of individually seasoned carrot, spinach, and cauliflower layers. Though a bit of a production to assemble, it is a triumph in flavor and appearance. Serve it with thin slices of bread or toast.

YIELD: 4 generous portions or more smaller servings

PREPARATION TIME: An hour or so to prepare; 45 minutes to bake

Vermouth is a white wine that contains aromatic herbs and spices. Its flavor ranges from sweet to dry.

1¹/₂ teaspoons kuzu powder
1¹/₂ teaspoons dry vermouth
12 ounces tofu
1 teaspoon sea salt, or to taste
3 tablespoons lemon juice
3 tablespoons vegetable oil
2 tablespoons tahini
1 large onion, finely chopped
3 large cloves garlic, minced
Freshly ground black pepper to taste

1¹/₂ cups thinly sliced carrot
1 teaspoon minced fresh tarragon (or pericon), or ¹/₂ teaspoon dried
²/₃ cup vegetable stock or water
8 ounces (8 cups, loosely packed) fresh spinach leaves, finely chopped
¹/₄ teaspoon freshly grated nutmeg
1¹/₂ cups thinly sliced cauliflower
1 teaspoon minced fresh dill weed, or ¹/₂ teaspoon dried

Combine the kuzu and vermouth, and set it aside for several minutes, until the kuzu is thoroughly dissolved.

Grease the bottom and sides of a 1-quart soufflé dish. Fit a circle of waxed paper into the bottom and a strip around the inside, and grease them.

Blend the tofu in a food processor fitted with the metal blade. While the machine is running, add $3/4$ teaspoon of the salt, the lemon juice, 5 teaspoons of the oil, and the tahini. Blend until the mixture is thoroughly smooth. Blend in the dissolved kuzu. Transfer the mixture to a 2-cup measure and set the unwashed processor aside.

Add 1 teaspoon of oil to a skillet over medium heat. Sauté the onion and garlic until the onion is just tender. Grind in pepper and continue to cook, stirring, for a minute or two. Transfer two-thirds of the sauté to a bowl.

Add 1 teaspoon of oil, the carrot, and the tarragon to the onions in the skillet. Sauté briefly over medium heat. Add $1/4$ cup of stock, tightly cover the pan, and reduce the heat to low. Steam for several minutes, until the carrot is tender. Transfer the sauté to the processor and blend. Add one-third of the tofu mixture and blend well. Add salt to taste. Evenly spread the carrot purée in the bottom of the prepared dish.

Add half the remaining sautéed onions, 1 teaspoon of oil, and the spinach and nutmeg to the skillet. Sauté briefly over medium heat. Add 2 tablespoons of stock, cover, reduce the heat, and steam briefly, until the spinach is tender but still bright green. Transfer to the processor (well scraped of the carrot purée) and blend. Add another third of the tofu mixture and blend well. Season with salt to taste. Carefully spread the spinach purée evenly over the carrot layer.

Add the cauliflower, 1 teaspoon of oil, the remaining onions, and the dill to the skillet and sauté briefly. Add $1/4$ cup of stock, cover, and steam until the cauliflower is tender. Blend in the processor. Add the remaining tofu mixture and blend well. Add salt to taste. Spread on top of the spinach layer.

Bake the pâté in a preheated 300° oven for 45 to 50 minutes, until a knife inserted in the center comes out clean. Cool the pâté thoroughly before inverting it onto a plate and peeling off the waxed paper. Serve pâté at room temperature or chilled.

Tofu Mayonnaise

THIS MAYONNAISE IS LIGHTER AND LESS CALORIC THAN conventional ones, but you can use it in the same way: as a sandwich spread or as an ingredient in other spreads, as a dressing for potato and egg salads, and so on. It makes an ideal dip for artichokes.

YIELD: About ¹/₂ cup

PREPARATION TIME: 10 minutes

4 ounces (extra-firm) silken tofu
1 tablespoon lemon juice
1 tablespoon cider vinegar
1 tablespoon olive oil
1 tablespoon canola or other light vegetable oil

Freshly ground black pepper to taste
¹/₄ teaspoon prepared Dijon or stoneground mustard
¹/₄ teaspoon sea salt, plus extra to taste

Combine all the ingredients in a blender or a food processor fitted with the metal blade and blend until thoroughly smooth.

This will keep for several days in a covered container in the refrigerator.

Notes
• Blend in a small amount of a minced fresh herb, such as dill, tarragon, or basil. Fresh parsley is another good addition.

Presto—Pesto!

PESTO HAS BECOME ALMOST AS COMMON AS TOMATO sauce and is an easy way to make an elegant meal in almost minutes. It might coat pasta one evening and top **Pesto Pizza** (page 313) the next. It is a crowning touch to beans, new potatoes, and summer squash tossed with a bit of olive oil and seasoned with freshly ground black

YIELD: About 1¹/₂ cups

PREPARATION TIME: 20 minutes

Notes

• Fresh tarragon is a good addition: Substitute it for about ½ cup of the basil.

pepper. Try pesto on baked potatoes or use it as a sandwich spread or a sauce for stuffed pita (see **Poco Pesto Pockets,** page 294).

The pleasantly piquant aroma of fresh basil is synonymous with summer for me, and that's when I crave this sauce and prepare it often. You can freeze it for use throughout the year, though I think freshly made is much better. There are many varieties of basil; experiment with lemon, anise, Thai, cinnamon, and others, in addition to the familiar Italian variety. This is a nondairy version of pesto, but few would guess it: dark barley miso provides the rich saltiness of aged hard cheese. Use a salad spinner to most effectively dry the herbs.

2 to 4 cloves garlic, sliced	¼ cup olive oil
7 to 8 cups loosely packed fresh basil leaves	2 to 3 teaspoons dark barley miso, or to taste
½ cup loosely packed flat-leaf parsley	¼ cup lightly toasted pine nuts or walnuts
1 tablespoon lemon juice, plus extra to taste	2 to 4 tablespoons vegetable stock, as needed

Combine half of the garlic, the basil, parsley, lemon juice, oil, and 2 teaspoons of miso in a food processor fitted with the metal blade and blend thoroughly. Add the nuts and pulse to a slightly coarse texture. Blend in more garlic and miso as desired. If the sauce requires thinning, gradually add stock until it reaches the desired consistency and reseason if necessary.

WATERCRESS PESTO

IN TENNESSEE, I HAD A FRIEND WHO WOULD BRING ME A large bucket of beautiful fresh watercress every time he came to visit in the spring. This splendid pesto resulted from those gifts.

YIELD: About 1½ cups

PREPARATION TIME: 15 minutes

2 to 4 large cloves garlic,
   sliced
8 cups loosely packed
   watercress, leaves and
   fine stems
1 to 2 cups loosely packed
   parsley
1 to 2 tablespoons
   lemon juice

¹/₄ cup walnut, hazelnut,
   or olive oil
¹/₂ cup lightly toasted,
   coarsely chopped walnuts
Sea salt to taste
2 tablespoons vegetable
   stock, as needed

Notes
• Add fresh dill weed to taste.

Combine half of the garlic with the watercress, parsley, 1 tablespoon of the lemon juice, the oil, and ¹/₄ cup of the nuts in a food processor fitted with the metal blade. Blend until the mixture is smooth. Add salt and the remaining nuts and pulse several times to a slightly coarse texture. Taste and add more garlic, lemon juice, and salt as needed. If the sauce is too thick, gradually blend in stock, then taste and reseason if needed.

Tex-Mex Pesto

THIS IS A REGIONAL VARIATION ON EVER-POPULAR PESTO sauce. Try it on pasta or pizza and in sandwiches.

1 teaspoon minced garlic
1 tablespoon olive oil
2 generous cups cilantro
¹/₄ cup chopped green onion
¹/₄ cup lightly toasted
   pecans or pepitas
   (pumpkin seeds)

1 tablespoon lime juice,
   or more to taste
Sea salt to taste

YIELD: About ³/₄ cup

PREPARATION TIME: 25 minutes

Add the garlic, oil, cilantro, onion, pecans or pepitas, and 1 tablespoon lime juice to a food processor fitted with the metal blade and pulse several times to combine the ingredients. Or, chop everything fine and mix it together in a bowl. Add salt and more lime juice to taste.

YIELD: About 2 cups

PREPARATION TIME: About 30 minutes

....

Tomatillos are small, firm, tomatolike fruits that vary from chartreuse to purple and are enclosed in papery husks. Often featured in Mexican and Southwestern sauces, tomatillos have a tart, lemony flavor and gelatinous texture that functions as a thickener. They are high in vitamins A and C. Look for tomatillos in the produce section of supermarkets and in farmers markets in season. Buy them in their wrappers; they'll keep several weeks refrigerated. Remove the husks before cooking the tomatillos.

....

EMILIO'S SALSA VERDE

THIS ISN'T EMILIO'S RECIPE, BUT HE GAVE ME THE IDEA of combining green tomatoes and tomatillos in salsa verde. Serve it as a dip or sauce. This will keep for several days refrigerated.

2 small poblano peppers	1/2 pound tomatillos,
1 tablespoon olive oil	chopped
1 small onion, minced	1/4 teaspoon sea salt, or
1 clove garlic, minced	to taste
1/2 pound green tomatoes,	1/4 cup cilantro
chopped	

Roast and peel the peppers as described on page 244 and set them aside.

Add the oil to a skillet over medium heat. Sauté the onion and garlic for several minutes, until the onion appears translucent and is almost tender. Stir in the tomatoes and tomatillos, and continue to cook, stirring occasionally, for several minutes, until they are just tender. Stir in 1/4 teaspoon of salt.

Combine the sauté, 1 roasted pepper, and the cilantro in a blender or a food processor fitted with the metal blade. Pulse briefly to a chunky texture. Taste the salsa and add more salt and roasted pepper as needed.

AVOCADO SALSA CRUDA

THIS UNCOOKED SAUCE IS A PERKY MIXTURE OF FLAVORS and textures. It is rather fragile, so serve it as soon as possible. Scoop it up with any kind of tortillas (pages 214–219), or try it with **Mexican Bean Burgers** (page 292), **Bean Burritos** (page 305), or **Towering Tostadas** (page 302).

YIELD: 2 to 3 cups

PREPARATION TIME: About 15 minutes

2 teaspoons minced green onions	2 tablespoons lime juice
1 small chile, minced	1 large tomato, cubed
1 large ripe avocado, peeled and cubed	1/4 cup coarsely chopped cilantro
	Sea salt to taste

Stir the ingredients together and serve immediately.

Pico de Gallo

A PICO DE GALLO—LITERALLY TRANSLATED "ROOSTER'S beak"—is a Mexican salad or relish of raw vegetables or fruits chopped to a chunky consistency, probably named for the traditional way of eating it by picking up pieces with the fingers as a rooster pecks kernels of grain. This one, redolent of fresh cilantro, is the customary sauce for **Fajitas** (page 306), but is a suitable condiment for other Mexican-style dishes as well. It tastes best freshly made.

YIELD: 2 to 2½ cups

PREPARATION TIME: 25 minutes

1 clove garlic, minced	1 generous cup loosely packed cilantro, finely chopped
1 medium-sized mild onion, finely chopped	Sea salt to taste
1 medium-sized tomato, finely chopped	
½ to 1 small serrano pepper, minced	

Combine all of the ingredients in a medium bowl, adjusting the amount of chile and salt to taste.

Serve immediately.

Roasted Red Pepper Sauce

THIS IS A DELIGHTFUL, VIBRANT REDDISH-ORANGE TOP-ping for pasta or pizza, or a spread for sandwiches. Any sweet red pepper will work, but especially look for dark red, thick-skinned, fleshy pimientos in your market at

YIELD: 1½ to 2 cups

PREPARATION TIME: 40 minutes

Pimientos, also called *pimentos,* are perhaps best known as the stuffings for green olives. These medium-sized, smooth-sided, dark red peppers are plump at the stem end and taper to a point at the other end. Their flesh and skin are both relatively thick, making these peppers ideal for roasting.

the end of summer; these are the sweetest and are increasingly available fresh. Heat-tolerant pericon is a Texas substitute for tarragon; these two herbs' flavors are similar, though pericon tends to be somewhat stronger.

8 medium-sized red
    peppers
1 tablespoon olive oil
1 tablespoon lemon juice
1 to 2 cloves raw or
    roasted garlic

1 tablespoon minced fresh
    basil leaves
1 tablespoon minced fresh
    tarragon leaves (or
    pericon), or to taste
Sea salt to taste

Roast and peel the peppers as described on page 244. Place them in a blender or a food processor fitted with the metal blade; add the remaining ingredients and blend the mixture to a coarse purée.

This sauce will keep for several days refrigerated.

ITALIAN GREEN SAUCE

OUTSTANDING IN COLOR AND FLAVOR, THIS BRIGHT green sauce makes an excellent topping for pasta and pizza (page 312) and can also serve as a sandwich spread or a dip. This is at its best and brightest when freshly made. Cover any leftover sauce tightly and refrigerate it; it will keep for several days.

YIELD: 1 to 1½ cups

PREPARATION TIME: 25 minutes

1 tablespoon olive oil
1 small onion, finely
    chopped
1 large clove garlic,
    minced
Freshly ground black
    pepper to taste
¼ teaspoon freshly
    grated nutmeg

¼ cup fresh basil leaves,
    minced, or
    ¾ teaspoon dried
1 tablespoon fresh tarragon
    leaves, minced, or
    ½ teaspoon dried
4 to 5 cups loosely packed
    fresh spinach leaves
½ cup loosely packed parsley

4 ounces tofu, preferably
   silken
1 tablespoon lemon juice
1 tablespoon mellow
   rice miso (optional)

Vegetable stock, as needed
Sea salt to taste

Sauté the onion and garlic in the oil until tender. Add the pepper, nutmeg, basil, and tarragon, and continue sautéing briefly. Remove from the heat.

Blend the sauté with the spinach, parsley, tofu, lemon juice, and miso in a blender or a food processor fitted with the metal blade. Gradually blend in stock until the desired consistency is achieved. Season with salt to taste.

Hearty Tomato Sauce

This is a basic sauce with many uses. I usually make extra to freeze. Miso contributes to its rich flavor and digestibility; don't boil the sauce after you've added it.

Yield: About 2 quarts

Preparation time: 45 minutes to assemble; several hours to cook

2 quarts fresh or canned
   chopped tomatoes
   (about 4 pounds)
2 tablespoons olive oil
1 large onion, finely
   chopped
3 to 6 cloves garlic, minced
1 medium-sized carrot,
   finely chopped
1 medium-sized parsnip,
   finely chopped
1 medium-sized turnip,
   finely chopped
1 large bell pepper,
   finely chopped
1/2 pound mushrooms,
sliced

Freshly ground black pepper
   to taste
4 to 6 teaspoons minced
   fresh basil, or 2 teaspoons
   dried
1 1/2 teaspoons minced
   fresh oregano, or
   3/4 teaspoon dried
1/2 teaspoon minced fresh
   thyme, or 1/4 teaspoon
   dried
1/4 cup dry red wine
2 tablespoons finely
   chopped parsley
2 tablespoons dark miso

Peel fresh tomatoes as described on page 244.

In a large (5- to 6-quart), heavy-bottomed pot, heat the oil; add the onion, garlic, carrot, parsnip, and turnip, and sauté for several minutes. Add the bell pepper, mushrooms, black pepper, and dried herbs, and continue to sauté for several minutes. Stir in the tomatoes and wine. Cover the pot and bring the sauce just to a simmer. Partially uncover the pot and allow the sauce to cook at a low simmer, stirring occasionally, until it reaches a desirable consistency. Add fresh herbs near the end of cooking. Tomato sauce burns easily, so it's a good idea to place the pot on a flame tamer.

Stir in the parsley. Whisk the miso with several tablespoons of the thickened sauce to form a smooth paste. Thoroughly stir it into the tomato sauce.

Expeditious Tomato Sauce

KEEP THIS QUICKLY PREPARED TOMATO SAUCE ON HAND for impromptu pizzas. It will keep well for several days refrigerated; freeze for longer storage.

YIELD: 1 cup—enough for 2 pizzas

PREPARATION TIME: 35 minutes

1 tablespoon olive oil
1 medium-sized onion, finely chopped
1 large clove garlic, minced
Freshly ground black pepper to taste
1 teaspoon minced fresh basil, or 1/2 teaspoon dried

1 teaspoon minced fresh oregano, or 1/2 teaspoon dried
1 1/2 cups chopped fresh tomatoes
1 teaspoon dark miso
1 teaspoon vegetable stock or dry red wine

Add the olive oil to a skillet over medium heat. Sauté the onion for several minutes, until it appears translucent. Stir in the garlic and continue sautéing until the onion is just tender. Add the pepper and herbs and cook briefly, stirring often. Stir in the tomatoes, cover the pan, and reduce the heat to low; simmer until the tomatoes have juiced and the skins are soft. Remove the pan from the heat.

In a blender or a food processor fitted with the metal blade, blend the mixture to a coarse purée. Return the purée to the skillet and cook it over low heat for several minutes, until thick. Whisk together the miso and stock and stir it into the sauce.

LISA'S TOMATO KETCHUP

USE SOME OF THE SUMMER'S TOMATO BOUNTY TO PRE-pare this thick, smooth, spicy condiment; you'll never be satisfied with the commercial stuff again.

YIELD: About 3 pints

PREPARATION TIME: 2 to 3 hours

6 pounds (about 24 large) tomatoes	1 teaspoon whole allspice
1 cup chopped onion	1 stick cinnamon
1/2 cup chopped bell pepper, preferably red	1 tablespoon sea salt
1 1/2 teaspoons celery seed	1 1/2 cups apple cider vinegar
1 teaspoon mustard seed	1 tablespoon paprika
	Honey to taste

Peel the tomatoes as described on page 244, then chop them. Combine with the onion and pepper in a large pot and cook until soft. Put the mixture through a food mill and return it to the pot. Simmer for about an hour, until the volume is reduced by about one-half.

Put the celery seed, mustard seed, allspice, and cin-namon into a cheesecloth bag, and add it and the salt to the tomato mixture; cook gently about 25 minutes, stir-ring frequently. Stir in the vinegar and paprika, and cook until thick. Add honey to taste near the end of cooking.

Remove the cheesecloth bag. Process the ketchup in a boiling water bath or refrigerate it when cool.

YIELD: About 2 cups

PREPARATION TIME: 15 minutes to prep; about 1 hour to cook

....

Chile peppers contain a substance called *capsaicin* which creates a burning sensation upon contact with skin. I always wear rubber gloves when I handle chiles to avoid irritation. To tone down chile peppers' fire, remove their seeds and membranes, since these are the areas where capsaicin is concentrated. There are many species of hot peppers. Following is a brief description of some of the most common ones.

Poblanos are mildly hot, dark green peppers, usually 3 to 5 inches long. They are shaped something like bell peppers, though a bit more triangular: wide at the stem end and narrowing to somewhat of a point. Their skin is relatively thick, and I usually roast and peel these peppers before adding them to a dish.

Anchos are ripe dried poblanos, deep reddish-brown in color. They are the major ingredient in commercially prepared chile powder.

Serranos are 1 to 2 inches long, narrow, and smooth sided. They vary from green to bright red-orange but are all sizzling hot.

Jalapeños resemble serranos but are larger, up to about 3 inches long. They are flavorful and relatively hot.

Anaheims are 6 to 8 inches long and about 2 inches wide. These mildly hot peppers turn from green to red as they mature and can be used at either stage.

....

Notes
• For a spicier sauce, add ³/₄ teaspoon ground cumin and ¹/₄ teaspoon ground coriander.

BLENDER HOT SAUCE

THIS IS A SIMPLY PREPARED, COOKED TOMATO SALSA WITH many uses. Use it for **Mexican Pizza** (page 314), **Empanadas de Picadillo** (page 335), **Bean Burritos** (page 305), or **Tofu Enchiladas** (page 302). Serve it as a topping on **Towering Tostadas** (page 302) or **Mexican Bean Burgers** (page 292), or simply as a dip for soft or crisp **Tortillas** (page 214). This sauce will keep for a couple of weeks in the refrigerator; it also freezes well.

1 large onion, diced
4 large cloves garlic, sliced
1 jalapeño (approximately 1¹/₂ inches long) or other chile, seeds and membranes removed if desired

6 or 7 peeled, medium-sized ripe tomatoes or 1 (1-pound) can
1¹/₂ teaspoons dark miso, or sea salt to taste

Combine the onion, garlic, and pepper in a blender; add half the fresh tomatoes, or half of the canned tomatoes plus the juice. Blend well and transfer the mixture to a saucepan. Briefly pulse the remaining tomatoes and add this coarse purée to the saucepan.

Over medium heat, bring the sauce to a simmer. Turn the heat to low and cook, stirring occasionally, until the sauce reduces and thickens, about 1 hour. Cook the sauce on a flame tamer to prevent it from burning.

Season with miso or salt. If you use miso for seasoning, mix it with a small amount of the hot, thickened sauce before adding it to the saucepan.

Enchiladas de Mole

In these enchiladas, the corn tortillas are coated with subtly spiced mole sauce and rolled around juicy tempeh strips and thinly sliced sweet onions.

2 teaspoons sesame or olive oil
1 (8-ounce) cake tempeh
¹/₂ cup vegetable stock or water
1 teaspoon tamari
6 **Corn Tortillas** (page 216)
1¹/₃ cups **Mole Sauce**
1 medium-sized sweet onion, thinly sliced

Add the oil to a skillet over medium heat. Brown the tempeh on both sides. Add the stock and tamari, tightly cover the pan, and cook until the pan is almost dry. Remove the tempeh from the pan and cut it into thin strips.

If the tortillas are not freshly made and still warm and pliable, wrap them in a towel, steam briefly, and then leave them in the covered steamer off the heat for several minutes. Or wrap and heat them in a moderate oven for several minutes.

Spread a thin layer of the sauce on the tortillas, lay tempeh strips and onion slices down the middle, and roll them up. Arrange on plates, top with the remaining sauce, and serve immediately.

Mole Sauce

IN ONE CENTRAL AMERICAN INDIAN LANGUAGE, A STEW or its sauce is a *molli*, meaning concoction. The Spaniards altered the word to *mole*, perhaps an association with the Spanish verb *moler*, to grind. Moles are rich, smooth, subtly seasoned Mexican sauces that typically include ground chiles, herbs, spices, nuts or seeds, tomatoes, and a touch of chocolate. They are usually served with poultry or meats in stewlike preparations, often for festive occasions. This nontraditional version substitutes carob for chocolate. I like it as a sauce for tempeh-filled enchiladas (see box) and I often make extra sauce to freeze for another meal. This sauce is also good on pasta and as a topping for a pita sandwich stuffed with chopped greens, finely sliced onions, tempeh strips, and sliced jicama and avocado tossed with lime juice. Mexican oregano refers to a piquant variety of this many-specied herb that thrives in Mexico and the southwestern United States; substitute another oregano if you can't find it.

YIELD: About 1¹/₃ cups

PREPARATION TIME: 45 minutes

Notes

• If you prefer a hotter sauce, add an additional roasted pepper or two.

• Substitute fresh Anaheim peppers for poblanos. Or use anchos, dried red poblanos; stirring often, roast them in a hot pan, then soak them in hot water to cover for 15 to 20 minutes, and drain before blending.

1 (3-inch) poblano pepper
2 medium-sized ripe tomatoes
1 large clove garlic, peeled
$1/8$ teaspoon ground cinnamon
$1/8$ teaspoon ground cloves
$1/4$ teaspoon fresh Mexican oregano
$3/4$ cup vegetable stock or water
1 tablespoon lightly roasted almonds
$1 1/2$ teaspoons roasted carob powder
1 tablespoon hot water
$1/2$ teaspoon sea salt, or to taste

Roast and peel the pepper as described on page 244. Set it aside.

In a small ovenproof pan (with sides, to catch the juice) broil the tomatoes and garlic for 20 to 30 minutes, turning them occasionally, until they are evenly charred. (I do this in the enamel tray of my toaster oven.) The garlic will be tender and the tomatoes will be soft and juicy and somewhat blackened.

Combine the prepared pepper and garlic, cinnamon, cloves, and oregano in a blender or a food processor fitted with the metal blade. Blend, gradually adding $1/2$ cup of the stock, until the mixture is thoroughly smooth. Pour it into a skillet and cook over medium heat, stirring often, for several minutes.

Meanwhile, put the tomatoes and their juice and the almonds in the blender or processor and blend until thoroughly smooth. Stir this into the mixture in the skillet.

In a small bowl, whisk the carob and 1 tablespoon hot water until the carob is thoroughly dissolved. Stir this, the remaining stock, and the $1/2$ teaspoon salt into the pepper-tomato mixture. Cook over very low heat, stirring occasionally, for about 20 minutes, until the sauce has thickened somewhat and the flavors have melded. The sauce should be rather thin; if it is too thick, add more stock, then taste and add more salt if needed.

Spicy Peanut Sauce

This zesty, rich sauce has myriad applications. Use it as a dip for raw vegetables, a dressing for cooked vegetables and grains, or a topping for **Indonesian Pizza** (page 315) or a pita sandwich. Covered tightly and refrigerated, this sauce will keep well for several days; freeze it for longer storage.

1 tablespoon peanut or
 sesame oil
1 large sweet onion,
 finely chopped
2 cloves garlic, minced
1 teaspoon finely grated
 fresh ginger
Pinch of cayenne, or to
 taste

1 cup unsalted peanut
 butter
2 tablespoons tamari
3 cups vegetable stock,
 water, or coconut milk
Lemon juice to taste
Sea salt to taste

YIELD: About 3 cups

PREPARATION TIME: 30 to 40 minutes

Notes
• Substitute a minced fresh chile for the cayenne.
• Substitute tahini for up to half of the peanut butter.
• Substitute a mellow miso for the salt: make a paste with the miso and a few tablespoons of sauce, then stir the mixture into the cooked sauce.

Heat the oil in a heavy-bottomed saucepan. Sauté the onion until it is browned. Add the garlic, ginger, and cayenne, and continue cooking, stirring frequently. Remove the pan from the heat and add the peanut butter and tamari. Stir in 1 cup of the stock. Place the pan over low heat and add the remaining stock. Cook, stirring often, until the sauce is thickened, about 30 minutes. Season with lemon juice and salt.

Sesame Sauce

This smooth, light sauce has a touch of tartness. It's a perfect topping for **Nouvelle Falafel** (page 295) and other vegetable-stuffed pitas.

1 tablespoon lemon juice
1 1/2 teaspoons dark miso,
 or more to taste
1/2 teaspoon umeboshi
 paste

1 teaspoon roasted sesame
 oil
2 tablespoons tahini
1/4 to 1/2 cup vegetable stock

YIELD: 1/2 cup

PREPARATION TIME: 15 minutes

Notes
• Add minced garlic to taste.

Yield: About 1¼ cups

Preparation time: 15 minutes

In a small bowl, whisk the lemon juice, miso, and ume-boshi paste until smooth. Thoroughly whisk in the oil and tahini. Gradually add stock until the mixture reaches the consistency you desire.

Mellow Mustard Sauce

This sauce is a natural with tempeh, sauerkraut, kasha, or rye bread. Use it to make **Reuben's Pizza** (page 318) or **Reuben's Pockets** (page 294).

2 teaspoons kuzu powder
2 teaspoons cold vegetable
    stock or water
2 tablespoons mustard,
    preferably stoneground
1½ teaspoons lemon juice

1 tablespoon mellow barley
    miso
¾ cup vegetable stock or
    water
2 tablespoons sauerkraut
    juice

Combine the kuzu and 2 teaspoons cold liquid and set it aside for a few minutes, until the kuzu is thoroughly dissolved. Whisk in the remaining ingredients. Transfer the mixture to a small saucepan and cook over low heat, stirring often, just until it thickens.

Ginger Aioli

Yield: About ⅔ cup

Preparation Time: 15 minutes

I have to credit Café Sport, a wonderful restaurant in Seattle, with inspiring this recipe. This sauce is excellent on fish or as a dip or a sandwich spread. For best results, have the ingredients at room temperature. This will keep for up to a week refrigerated; the taste will mellow as the flavors meld. (*Recipes containing uncooked eggs are not recommended for immuno-compromised individuals or small children.*)

1 clove garlic, minced
2 teaspoons finely grated
    fresh ginger
1 small egg

½ cup vegetable oil
¼ teaspoon sea salt, or
    to taste
2 teaspoons lemon juice

In a blender or in a food processor fitted with the metal blade, blend the garlic, ginger, and egg. While the machine is running, very slowly dribble in the oil as the mixture emulsifies. Blend in half of the salt and half of the lemon juice. Taste and add more as needed.

Tofu Sour Cream

This sauce is a very convincing impostor, and it is much lower in fat and cholesterol than the real thing. It tends to thicken somewhat upon standing.

YIELD: About 1 cup

PREPARATION TIME: 15 minutes

8 ounces silken tofu
$^1/_2$ teaspoon sea salt
2 tablespoons lemon juice

1 tablespoon canola or other mild-flavored vegetable oil
1 tablespoon tahini

In a blender or a food processor fitted with a metal blade, blend the tofu thoroughly. Add the remaining ingredients and blend until the mixture is thoroughly smooth. Blend in a little water if it is too thick.

Hollandaise à l'Arberti

Hollandaise sauce is a traditional topping for steamed vegetables, such as broccoli and asparagus, and for poached eggs. It's good on sandwiches, too: Serve it over open-faced arrangements or vegetable-stuffed pitas. This adaptation, named for the friend who developed it, uses whole eggs rather than egg yolks and less fat than the classic sauce does, but it still tastes quite rich. It is also practically foolproof to make—just be sure to use gentle heat, whisk constantly, and remove the sauce from the heat as soon as it thickens. This sauce is best served fresh, though it will keep in the refrigerator for several hours.

YIELD: $^3/_4$ to 1 cup

PREPARATION TIME: 15 minutes

Notes

- Substitute dill for the tarragon.

2 eggs
$^1/_4$ cup milk or
    unsweetened soy milk
2 tablespoons lemon juice
$^1/_8$ teaspoon sea salt
Freshly ground black
    pepper to taste

$^1/_4$ teaspoon minced fresh
    tarragon leaves, or
    $^1/_8$ teaspoon crushed dried
3 tablespoons unsalted
    butter or soy margarine

Beat together the eggs, milk, lemon juice, salt, pepper, and tarragon in the top of a small double boiler. Heat the mixture over barely boiling water, whisking constantly, until it begins to thicken. Add the butter and continue whisking until the sauce has almost reached the desired consistency. Remove the sauce from the heat and transfer it to another container to stop the cooking process.

Serve the sauce warm, at room temperature, or chilled.

ELEVEN

Sandwiches and Filled Flat Breads

ONCE UPON A TIME IN THE EIGHTEENTH CENTURY, AS THE STORY
is told, the Fourth Earl of Sandwich was such a compulsive gam-
bler that he demanded his food be brought to him at the gambling
table to allow his perpetual attendance. Normal meals proved
extremely messy and inconvenient, which didn't please him. Someone cleverly solved the problem by putting two slices of bread
together with something in between. With this compact arrangement in one hand and the other free to tend his game, the Earl
munched away happily, ensuring his place in history.

The "sandwich" may have represented a novel leap for European
cuisine, but other cultures around the world had paired breads with
fillings and eaten them out of hand for eons before Westerners
caught on to the idea. Traditional flat breads of all types are natural
holders of other foods. People in southern India typically fold rice
pancakes called dosas over spicy vegetable and bean mixtures.
Northern Chinese roll their mandarin pancakes around stir-fries,

and Latin Americans have devised numerous ways to combine corn and wheat tortillas with fillings. The French usually serve their crêpes with savory or sweet stuffings, and Middle Easterners wrap shish kebabs in large, thin flat breads called lavosh and pack small croquettes known as falafel into pita.

Even when served plain, flat breads are usually intended as edible "plates" for toppings or consumable "utensils" for dips and sauces. Northern Indians dispense with silverware and use chapatis and parathas to pick up morsels of other foods. Mexicans layer toppings on crisp corn tortillas and shovel up bites of salsa and guacamole with soft tortillas or tortilla chips. Middle Easterners use wedges of pita or torn pieces of lavosh to scoop up hummus, baba, and other dips and salads.

These days, we Westerners hardly make a distinction between sandwiches and filled flat breads. They're so close in concept that it's often difficult to identify where one category ends and the other begins. A sandwich can be as plain as one piece of bread topped with a single item or simple spread or as elaborate as the extravagant structures Dagwood Bumstead builds to devour in the middle of the night. It may be open-faced, closed, or a gaping pita pocket. Though usually handheld, a sandwich is occasionally knife-and-fork fare. Sandwiches may be fancy and fussed over but are more often, true to their namesake's spirit, casual meals assembled on short notice and frequently consumed on the go. The international rosters of filled flat breads fulfill the same criteria.

By combining the broad repertoire of breads and the selection of toppings and fillings presented earlier, countless appealing combinations are possible. Stuffed pitas have become one of the most sought-after sandwiches in recent years, and "wraps," large tortillas folded around some sort of filling, are hot on their heels in popularity. The burger, an all-American sandwich mainstay, remains as ubiquitous as ever. I've included several vegetarian versions prepared with grains and beans or soybean products, which make them high-protein yet low-cholesterol alternatives. They can be assembled ahead of time and cooked just before you're ready to eat.

Culinary traditions link most flat breads with particular fillings, but I see no reason why flat breads and fillings can't be mixed and matched in our more cosmopolitan setting. Fill wheat tortillas with hummus or Mediterranean bean spread, crêpes with curried potatoes, chapatis with refritos and salsa, or mandarin pancakes with almond butter and sliced bananas. Pita already gets stuffed with anything and everything. The filled flat breads and sandwiches that follow provide examples of various formats, some quite traditional, others more innovative, but all within my own basic guidelines—light on fats and dairy products.

By the way, sandwiches and filled flat breads are great user-uppers of the dibs and dabs that accumulate in every kitchen. A tablespoon or two of pesto or another sauce makes a splendid sandwich spread; small amounts of cooked grains, beans, vegetables, and nuts merge in delicious meatless burgers; the leavings in a salad bowl stuff a pita. A blend of flavors created in this way almost always ends up greater than the sum of its parts.

GRILLED PEANUT BUTTER AND PEAR

WHEN I TRAVELED IN EUROPE FOR SEVERAL MONTHS, I was surprised to find that I missed—actually, craved—peanut butter. One of my companions took pity on me and obtained a small jar from the PX in Istanbul. Peanut butter never tasted so good! Cut and arrange the fruit carefully, and these simple open-faced sandwiches will be works of art.

YIELD: 2 open-faced sandwiches

PREPARATION TIME: 15 minutes

Notes
- Substitute an apple or peach for the pear.

YIELD: 2 open-faced sandwiches

PREPARATION TIME: 15 minutes

| 2 tablespoons unsalted peanut butter | 2 slices bread |
| 1 teaspoon mellow barley miso, or to taste | 1 medium-large ripe pear |

Put the peanut butter in a small bowl and place the bowl in a warm oven briefly to soften the peanut butter. Thoroughly mix in the miso. Lightly toast the bread. Spread the seasoned nut butter on both slices. Quarter and core the pear, and peel it if the skin is thick or tough. Cut thin lengthwise slices and arrange them over the nut butter. Broil the sandwiches several minutes, until the fruit is very tender. Serve them immediately.

ALMOND BUTTER STRATAWICH

IF I HAD TO CHOOSE BETWEEN ALMOND BUTTER AND peanut butter, I'd be in a fix. As much as I like the old familiar flavor of peanut butter and rely on its great versatility, it would still have a tough time measuring up to sweet, crunchy almond butter. This is a truly classy spread! Now, go out to the garden and pluck a ripe tomato, pick a cucumber, and pinch a few sprigs of dill, and you're halfway to an easygoing summertime lunch. I especially like to use thin slices of rice or millet bread for these open-faced sandwiches.

2 tablespoons unsalted crunchy almond butter	2 slices bread
1 teaspoon mellow barley miso, or to taste	Thinly sliced cucumber and tomato
	Minced fresh dill weed

Put the almond butter in a small bowl in a warm oven for a few minutes to soften it. Thoroughly stir in the miso and spread the mixture on the bread. Arrange cucumber and tomato slices on top and sprinkle minced dill over all. Serve the sandwiches open-faced.

Blondie's Dagwood

Blondie always looks so trim and seems so sensible that I can't imagine her indulging in junk food. I picture her making a sandwich such as this one if she ever joins Dagwood in a nocturnal kitchen foray. I'm partial to thinly sliced natural-rise bread for this sandwich.

Yield: 1 sandwich

Preparation time: 15 minutes

2 slices bread	Thinly sliced carrot,
Tahini-Miso Spread	cucumber, tomato, and
(page 249)	radish
Mustard	Alfalfa or other sprouts
Tofu Mayonnaise	Lettuce, spinach, or
(page 267) or **Ginger**	other greens
Aioli (page 280)	
Sliced mild cheese or	
baked seasoned tofu	

Spread one slice of the bread with Tahini-Miso Spread and the other slice with mustard and Tofu Mayonnaise or Ginger Aioli. Arrange the cheese or tofu slices on top of the Tahini-Miso Spread. Add layers of sliced vegetables. Top with sprouts and greens. Perch the second piece of bread on the peak.

Now try to get your mouth around this monster.

T.L.T. for Two

Tempeh is a traditional Indonesian soy food that is rapidly becoming popular in the United States, especially among vegetarians. Made from whole soybeans, sometimes combined with grain, tempeh is high in protein and free of cholesterol. Because tempeh is a fermented product, it is easy to digest and is rich in B vitamins. Like tofu, tempeh is exceedingly versatile in terms of seasoning and preparation techniques, but its texture is chewier. Tempeh is generally available as flat cakes, sold fresh or frozen in natural foods stores. Here,

Yield: 2 sandwiches

Preparation time: About 30 minutes to prepare the tempeh; 10 minutes to assemble

Notes

• For even quicker T.L.T.s, look for commercially prepared tempeh "bacon" in the refrigerator or freezer case of natural food stores.

....

Tamari, originally the liquid that rose to the surface of all-soybean miso as it aged, now refers to naturally fermented wheat-free soy sauce, containing only soybeans, salt, and water. This seasoning's flavor is stronger than that of shoyu and is best added early in cooking. Look for tamari in natural foods stores and Asian markets.

Tempeh, a traditional staple in Indonesia, is a highly nutritious and digestible fermented soyfood made from hulled, split, and cooked soybeans that are formed into cakes about 1/2 inch thick and inoculated with a starter. Grains or other beans are sometimes added to vary tempeh's flavor. Tempeh has a hearty, meatlike texture and neutral flavor but readily absorbs seasonings in cooking or marinating. Fry, sauté, bake, deep-fry, simmer, broil, or stir-fry it. Tempeh is high in protein and B vitamins, contains no cholesterol, and is easy to digest. It will keep about 6 months frozen and about 1 week fresh or thawed in the refrigerator.

....

Various Veggie Burgers

YIELD: 6 burgers

PREPARATION TIME: 25 minutes to prepare; 25 minutes to cook

tempeh replaces bacon in an American institution: bacon, lettuce, and tomato sandwiches.

1/2 teaspoon fennel seed	Olive or sesame oil
1/2 teaspoon cumin seed	4 slices bread
2 cloves garlic, minced	**Tofu Mayonnaise** (page
Freshly ground black	267) or other mayonnaise
pepper to taste	Thinly sliced tomato
1 tablespoon tamari	Lettuce
1/2 cup water	
1 (4-ounce) cake tempeh,	
sliced into 1/4-inch strips	

Roast the fennel and cumin in a dry heavy skillet over medium heat for several minutes, agitating the pan or stirring the seeds frequently to prevent them from burning. When they are fragrant and crunchy, transfer the seeds to a mortar and pestle or spice grinder, and pulverize them to a coarse consistency.

Combine the ground seeds, garlic, pepper, tamari, and water in a medium-sized skillet or saucepan; add the tempeh strips and bring just to a boil. Cover and simmer gently about 15 minutes.

Remove the tempeh from the marinade and arrange it on a greased baking sheet. Broil the tempeh for about 15 minutes, turning it at least once, until it is brown and somewhat crisp.

Toast the bread, if desired, and make the sandwiches.

TOFU BURGERS

THESE LIGHT BURGERS ARE SEASONED WITH HERBS AND finely chopped vegetables; walnuts and bread crumbs add a subtle crunch. Powdered kuzu, a tasteless, healthy substance prepared by grinding the roots of the kuzu (or kudzu) plant, helps to hold the burgers together. You can substitute egg for the dissolved kuzu if you prefer. Serve the burgers with crisp lettuce leaves or sprouts, fresh tomato slices, and your other favorite fixings.

1 tablespoon kuzu powder

1 tablespoon cold vegetable
  stock or water

1 tablespoon olive oil

1 small red onion,
  finely chopped

2 large cloves garlic,
  minced

1 small bell pepper,
  finely chopped

1 small carrot, grated

Freshly ground black
  pepper to taste

2 teaspoons minced fresh
  basil leaves

2 tablespoons finely
  chopped parsley

1 1/2 pounds tofu, pressed
  well

1 tablespoon mellow barley
  or mellow rice miso

1/4 cup fine bread crumbs

1/4 cup lightly toasted,
  finely chopped walnuts

Sea salt to taste

6 whole grain buns

Notes

• Add other minced fresh herbs, such as oregano, thyme, tarragon, or dill, to the burger mixture, or sauté crushed dried herbs (about half the amount of the fresh ones) along with the vegetables.

• Substitute 1 beaten egg for the dissolved kuzu.

• The burgers may be baked rather than broiled. Arrange them on an oiled baking sheet and bake at 400° for 20 to 40 minutes, until browned and firm.

Combine the kuzu and cold liquid; set it aside until the kuzu is thoroughly dissolved.

Add the oil to a skillet over medium heat. Briefly sauté the onion, garlic, bell pepper, carrot, black pepper, and herbs, until the vegetables are just tender.

Thoroughly mash together the tofu and miso. Mix in the sauté, crumbs, walnuts, and dissolved kuzu, and add salt to taste.

Shape the mixture into 6 patties and arrange them on an oiled baking sheet. Brush them lightly with oil and broil until the tops are well browned. Carefully turn the patties over and broil until they are firm and browned.

Serve the burgers immediately in the buns.

Kuzu, a vine native to Japan, is now prevalent in the southeastern United States, where it is called *kudzu* and is generally viewed as an undesirable weed. The powdered root, also called kuzu, is used as a thickening agent in cooking; it is a white, tasteless starch that becomes transparent when cooked. Dissolve kuzu in a cold liquid before adding it to a hot liquid you wish to thicken. Though more expensive than arrowroot and cornstarch, kuzu is more effective and has medicinal properties. Kuzu is often lumpy; grind chunks with a mortar and pestle before measuring and dissolving it.

Moroccan Burgers

A traditional North African grain, couscous is cracked durum wheat that has usually been refined. It is generally precooked and requires only soaking to prepare. You might want to plan ahead next time you're making garbanzo beans and couscous so that you have leftovers for these rather exotic-tasting burgers. You can substitute cooked rice or cracked wheat or bulgur for the couscous, or 8 ounces of tofu for the garbanzo beans. Serve the

Yield: 4 burgers

Preparation time: 30 minutes to prepare; 20 to 30 minutes to bake

Couscous

Couscous is light and fluffy, and quick to prepare. I mix it with a little oil before soaking to keep the individual grains more separate; olive oil imparts a subtle, rich flavor.

- 1 cup couscous
- 1 teaspoon oil
- 1 1/2 cups water or vegetable stock
- 1/2 teaspoon sea salt

In a medium-sized bowl, thoroughly mix together the couscous and oil with a fork or your fingers.

Heat the water or stock to boiling, add the salt, and pour it over the couscous. Cover it with a plate for 10 to 15 minutes, until the grain has absorbed the liquid.

Fluff with a fork before serving.

Notes

- For eggless burgers, omit the egg and beat an extra tablespoon of stock and 1 tablespoon tahini with the miso and lemon juice.

---

burgers with lettuce, tomatoes, cucumber, and chopped green onions. **Sesame Sauce** (page 279) makes a great topping.

- 1 tablespoon olive oil
- 1 medium-sized onion, finely chopped
- 1 large clove garlic, minced
- Pinch of cayenne
- 1/2 teaspoon ground coriander
- 1/2 teaspoon turmeric
- 1 1/2 teaspoons ground cumin
- 1/4 cup currants or chopped raisins
- 2 tablespoons bean or vegetable stock
- 1 egg
- 1 tablespoon dark miso
- 1 tablespoon lemon juice
- 1 cup cooked garbanzo beans (see page 360)
- 1 cup cooked couscous (see box)
- 1/4 cup lightly toasted, finely chopped almonds
- 1/4 cup parsley, finely chopped
- 1/3 cup fine bread crumbs
- 4 whole grain buns or pita

Add the oil to a skillet over medium heat. Add the onion and garlic, and sauté until the onion is almost tender. Add the cayenne, coriander, turmeric, and cumin, and sauté briefly, stirring constantly. Stir in the currants and stock; cover and cook briefly. Remove the pan from the heat.

Beat the egg in a mixing bowl. Add the miso and lemon juice, and beat until smooth. Add the garbanzo beans and mash well. Use a food processor to blend the mixture if you prefer. Thoroughly mix in the sauté, couscous, almonds, and parsley.

Shape the mixture into 4 balls. Roll them in bread crumbs and form 1/2-inch-thick patties. Arrange them on a lightly greased baking sheet and bake at 400° for 20 to 30 minutes, until firm and lightly browned. Or broil them.

Serve the burgers immediately in the buns or pita.

TEMPEH BURGERS

HERE, JUICY SEASONED TEMPEH BECOMES VEGETARIAN "hamburger." Even meat-eaters may crave these quarter-pounders after just one taste. If time allows, marinate the tempeh for several hours before cooking.

YIELD: 2 burgers

PREPARATION TIME: Several hours to marinate tempeh; 20 to 30 minutes to prepare sandwiches

¼ cup tamari
4 teaspoons brown rice
*   vinegar*
1 cup vegetable stock
*   or water*

1 (8-ounce) cake of tempeh,
*   cut in half*
1 tablespoon sesame oil
2 whole grain buns

Combine the tamari, vinegar, and stock or water in a shallow bowl or small pie plate. Marinate the tempeh in this mixture, refrigerated, preferably for several hours or overnight. If the tempeh isn't covered by the marinade, turn it periodically.

Remove the tempeh from the marinade and drain it, reserving the marinade.

Add the oil to a skillet over medium heat. Brown the tempeh on both sides. Add the remaining marinade and tightly cover the pan. Cook until the pan is dry.

Serve the tempeh on the buns with your favorite condiments and garnishes.

MEXICAN BEAN BURGERS

YIELD: 4 burgers

PREPARATION TIME: 40 minutes

Black turtle beans, often known simply as black beans, are a member of the kidney bean family and are native to Mexico. They have an oval or very slight kidney shape and a matte black surface. Black beans' flavor is sweet but hearty. They tend to foam considerably at the beginning of cooking. See page 360 for cooking directions.

BEANS AND RICE ARE A CLASSIC LATIN AMERICAN COMBInation; prepared in this north-of-the-border format, they provide a quick, highly nutritious meal. Serve these burgers warm on whole grain buns (corn or rice breads are especially compatible) topped with a salsa (pages 270–271) and/or **Guacamole** (page 255).

1 tablespoon olive oil	1 tablespoon dark miso
1 small onion, finely chopped	1/4 teaspoon sea salt, or to taste
1 clove garlic, minced	1 1/2 cups cooked pinto,
1 small poblano pepper (or other mild pepper), finely chopped	anasazi, or black beans (see page 360)
1 small carrot, grated	1 1/2 cups cooked brown rice (see page 19)
1 small turnip, grated	1/4 cup lightly toasted,
1 teaspoon ground cumin	finely chopped almonds
1/2 teaspoon ground coriander	1/4 to 1/2 cup toasted fine bread crumbs
1 egg	4 buns

Add the oil to a skillet over medium heat. Add the onion and garlic, and sauté until the onion appears translucent. Stir in the pepper, carrot, and turnip, and sauté until these vegetables are just tender. Add the cumin and coriander, and cook briefly, stirring.

In a medium-sized bowl, whisk the egg, miso, and salt. Mash in the beans. Mix in the rice, almonds, and the sauté to form a moist but firm mixture.

Shape the mixture into 4 balls and roll them in the crumbs. Flatten the balls into thick patties and arrange them on an oiled baking sheet. Bake at 400° for 20 to 30 minutes, until they are browned and crisp on the outside. Or broil the burgers, turning them once.

Serve the burgers immediately on the buns.

CURRIED-LENTIL BURGERS

I OFTEN USE LEFTOVERS FROM AN INDIAN DINNER AS THE basis for these burgers. Basmati rice is particularly good in them. Spread some *GingerAioli* (page 280) on the buns.

YIELD: 4 burgers

PREPARATION TIME: 25 minutes to prepare; 20 to 30 minutes to bake

1½ teaspoons sesame or other vegetable oil

2 green onions, finely chopped

1 clove garlic, minced

1 teaspoon finely grated fresh ginger

¼ cup finely chopped carrot

Freshly ground black pepper to taste

½ teaspoon ground cumin

1½ teaspoons mellow barley miso

1½ teaspoons lemon juice

1 cup **Lentil Dal** (page 257)

2 tablespoons raisins

1½ cups cooked rice (see page 19)

¼ cup lightly toasted cashew pieces, finely chopped

⅓ to ½ cup toasted fine bread crumbs

4 whole grain buns

Add the oil to a small skillet over medium heat. Add the onion, garlic, ginger, and carrot, and sauté for several minutes, until the carrot is just tender. Add pepper and the cumin, and cook, stirring, for a minute or two.

In a medium-sized bowl, whisk the miso and lemon juice to a smooth paste. Stir in the dal, raisins, rice, cashews, and the sauté to form a thick yet moist mixture. If it seems too moist—probably due to the consistency of the dal—add more rice or stir in some bread crumbs; taste and adjust the seasonings, if necessary, by adding a bit more miso and lemon juice.

Shape the mixture into 4 balls. Roll them in the crumbs until they are thoroughly coated. Flatten the balls into thick patties and place them on an oiled baking sheet. Bake at 400° for 20 to 30 minutes, until they are browned and crisp on the outside; they will still be moist inside. Or broil the burgers, turning them once.

Serve the burgers immediately on the buns.

Stuffed Pitas

YIELD: 2 sandwiches

PREPARATION TIME: About 30 minutes

Notes
• Try different kinds of stock to vary the flavor. Mushroom stock and beet stock are both delicious!
• For out-of-pocket Reubens, top slices of a rye or pumpernickel bread with lettuce leaves, sauced tempeh, minced green onions, and sauerkraut; serve the sandwiches open faced or closed.

YIELD: 1 sandwich

PREPARATION TIME: 25 minutes

REUBEN'S POCKETS

SOMEHOW TEMPEH, MUSTARD, AND SAUERKRAUT JUST seem to belong together. Serve these overstuffed pockets with dill pickles.

2 teaspoons vegetable oil	Lettuce leaves or other
1 (8-ounce) cake tempeh	tender greens
½ cup vegetable stock	4 green onions, finely
or water	chopped
½ recipe **Mellow**	2 cups well-drained
Mustard Sauce	sauerkraut
(page 280), uncooked	
2 **Pita** (page 225 or 227)	

Add the oil to a skillet over medium heat. Brown the tempeh on both sides. Add the stock and cover the pan tightly. Cook until the liquid has been absorbed, turning the tempeh once or twice. Remove the pan from the heat and cut the tempeh into short thin strips. Add the mustard sauce ingredients to the skillet and cook over low heat, stirring often, until the sauce thickens.

Wrap the pitas in foil and warm them in a 300° oven. Cut each one in half to form two pockets. Line them with greens and spoon in the sauced tempeh. Sprinkle in some onions and tuck in sauerkraut. Serve the sandwiches immediately.

Poco Pesto Pockets

FOR ITS FANS, THERE ARE NEVER TOO MANY WAYS TO CONsume pesto; here it enhances pita stuffed with a combination of raw and cooked summer vegetables. Pungent arugula is an especially effective foil for the sweetness of the basil. This sandwich provides a good way to use up small amounts of leftover pesto sauce and vegetables.

*1 **Pita** (pages 225 or 227)*	*¹/₄ cup lightly blanched or*
*¹/₄ cup **Pesto** (page 267)*	*steamed sugar snap peas*
1 to 2 cups torn spinach	*or green beans*
leaves or chopped	*¹/₄ cup cooked, sliced*
arugula	*potatoes*
¹/₄ cup sliced, lightly	*1 medium tomato, diced*
steamed zucchini or	*2 tablespoons minced parsley*
other summer squash	

Wrap the pita in foil and warm it in a 300° oven. Cut it in half to form 2 pockets. Spread half the pesto in each pocket, add the greens and vegetables, and sprinkle parsley on top.

Nouvelle Falafel

TRADITIONAL FALAFEL, MIDDLE EASTERN GARBANZO BEAN croquettes, contain eggs and are deep-fried. In this baked version, tofu replaces the egg. Tuck these crisp, spicy little balls into pita with chopped tomatoes and cucumbers; drizzle **Sesame Sauce** (page 279) on top.

1¹/₂ teaspoons olive oil	*2 tablespoons lightly toasted*
1 small onion, finely	*sesame seeds*
chopped	*1 tablespoon dark miso*
2 large cloves garlic,	*1 tablespoon lemon juice*
minced	*¹/₂ cup parsley*
Pinch of cayenne, or to	*2 **Pita** (page 225 or 227)*
taste	*1 medium-sized tomato,*
1¹/₂ teaspoons ground	*chopped*
cumin	*1 medium-sized cucumber,*
¹/₂ teaspoon ground	*chopped*
coriander	***Sesame Sauce** (page 279)*
2 ounces tofu	
1¹/₂ cups cooked garbanzo	
beans (see page 360)	

Notes
• Substitute **Watercress Pesto** (page 268) for the basil pesto.
• Substitute **Tex-Mex Pesto** (page 269) for the pesto and fill the pita with torn greens, steamed or blanched peas and beans, and diced tomatoes and avocado.

Arugula, sometimes called *rocket* or *roquette*, has a peppery flavor that adds character to salads. Native to the Mediterranean and western Asia, it is increasingly popular in the West. Its flavor blends particularly well with tomatoes, eggplant, and basil. Arugula's pungency increases as the plant matures but is tamed by cooking.

YIELD: 2 sandwiches

PREPARATION TIME: 40 minutes

Notes

• For crunchier falafel, roll the balls in fine bread crumbs before baking.

Add the oil to a small skillet over medium heat. Add the onion and garlic, and sauté until the onion is tender. Stir in the cayenne, cumin, and coriander and cook briefly, stirring.

Blend the sauté, tofu, garbanzo beans, and sesame seeds in a food processor fitted with the metal blade. Blend in the miso and lemon juice. Add the parsley and blend briefly.

Shape the mixture into 8 balls and arrange them on a lightly greased baking sheet. Bake them at 375° for 20 to 30 minutes, until lightly browned.

Wrap the pitas in foil and warm them in a 300° oven for a few minutes. Cut each pita in half to form 2 pockets. Divide the falafel among the pita, add the chopped raw vegetables, and top with the sauce.

Filled Crêpes

PROVINCETOWN WAS JUST WAKING UP FOR THE SEASON when we arrived in early June. One of the new merchants there to try her hand at a frenetic and hopefully lucrative summer was Genevieve, a Frenchwoman. She was setting up a small crêpe cafe, and her primary piece of equipment was a large, freestanding griddle imported from France. She poured on the thin batter, distributed it quickly and evenly with a wooden spreader and peeled off large, perfect pancakes. She arranged cheeses, vegetables, or whatever a patron requested from her daily selection of fillings, in the center of a crêpe and folded it into a neat golden brown package. I admired Genevieve's deft crêpe-making skills and sense of adventure. Her dream, she confided, was to open a wild foods restaurant, supplied with the edible treasures of her foraging. I've often wondered if she ever managed to fulfill this passion. If she has, I'm sure the menu includes an ever-changing choice of unusual filled crêpes.

Filled crêpes are fine light fare for any time of the day or night. A seasoned tomato-and-egg-filled crêpe makes a light yet satisfying breakfast, and crêpes stuffed with sautéed mushrooms, herbed spinach, or a vegetable stew like ratatouille are just right for lunch or dinner. Crêpes with sweet fillings are great for dessert or late night snacks—doused with brandy or liqueurs, they become fabulous flaming wonders.

In France, buckwheat crêpes usually enclose savory main dish fillings and wheat ones contain sweet dessert mixtures. Neighborhood crêperies are appealing, lively establishments, offering numerous delectable choices in both categories, served with several kinds of *cidre* (apple cider), the traditional French beverage with crêpes. Even in their native land, crêpe fillings are almost any imaginable combination of meat, fish, poultry, cheese, vegetables, fruits, or sauces. Filled crêpes provide a great opportunity to use up leftovers in an organized, "classy" way. You can ignore French custom and fill wheat crêpes with main dish fillings and buckwheat crêpes with compatible sweet ones.

Always serve crêpes with the evenly browned first-cooked side on the outside. Though they're usually rolled around the filling, crêpes can also be simply folded over it or folded into a package around it. For an impressive dessert or main dish, stack crêpes flat, layer-cake style, with a sweet or savory filling spread between them. Serve this "crêpe cake" cut into wedges.

Crêpe dishes are ideal for entertaining, because you can prepare crêpes and most fillings ahead of time, then quickly assemble and heat them just before serving. Keep crêpes on hand in the freezer, and you'll have the makings of an elegant meal even on short notice. A few of my favorite recipes for filled crêpes follow.

Herbed-Spinach Crêpes

Here, crêpes are rolled around a creamy herbed spinach stuffing. You can make the filling ahead of time.

Yield: 6 filled crêpes

Preparation time: 30 minutes

Serve these plain or garnish them with a drizzle of **Tomato Sauce** (page 274) or **Roasted Red Pepper Sauce** (page 271).

8 ounces tofu	¹/₄ teaspoon freshly grated
¹/₂ teaspoon sea salt	nutmeg
2 tablespoons lemon juice	2 teaspoons minced fresh
1 tablespoon canola or	tarragon, or 1 teaspoon
other light vegetable oil	dried
1 tablespoon tahini	2 teaspoons minced fresh
1¹/₂ teaspoons mellow	dill weed, or 1 teaspoon
rice miso	dried
1 tablespoon olive oil	8 cups fresh spinach leaves
1 medium-sized onion,	(8 ounces), chopped
finely chopped	¹/₄ cup parsley, finely
1 large clove garlic,	chopped
minced	6 **Buckwheat Crêpes**
Freshly ground black	(page 210) or **Wheat**
pepper to taste	**Crêpes** (page 208)

Blend the tofu in a food processor fitted with the metal blade. Add the salt, lemon juice, vegetable oil, tahini, and miso. Blend until thoroughly smooth and set the processor aside.

Add the olive oil to a skillet over medium heat. Sauté the onion and garlic until the onion is tender. Add the pepper, nutmeg, tarragon, dill, spinach, and parsley, and sauté briefly.

Add the sauté to the tofu mixture. Blend briefly to combine the ingredients, but maintain some texture.

Fill the crêpes and roll them up. Serve them warm.

MUSHROOM-STUFFED CRÊPES

BUCKWHEAT CRÊPES ESPECIALLY COMPLEMENT THIS FILLing. If you make the filling ahead of time, be sure to warm it over low heat so as not to destroy beneficial enzymes in the miso in the sauce.

YIELD: 6 filled crêpes

PREPARATION TIME: 30 to 40 minutes

3 tablespoons unsalted
butter or margarine or
vegetable oil
1 medium-sized onion,
finely chopped
2 cloves garlic, minced
1 pound fresh
mushrooms, sliced
Freshly ground black
pepper to taste
1 tablespoon minced
fresh basil

3 tablespoons whole
wheat pastry flour
³/₄ cup milk or
unsweetened soy milk
1 tablespoon mellow rice or
mellow barley miso
¹/₄ cup parsley, minced
6 **Buckwheat Crêpes**
(page 210) or **Wheat
Crêpes** (page 208)

Add 1 tablespoon of the butter to a skillet over medium heat and sauté the onion and garlic until the onion is translucent. Gradually add the mushrooms and continue sautéing for several minutes. Add some pepper and the basil.

In a small skillet, melt the remaining 2 tablespoons butter over low heat. Whisking constantly, sprinkle in the flour to make a smooth roux and cook for several minutes to brown the flour. Whisking constantly, slowly pour in the milk or soy milk. Cook, whisking, until the mixture thickens. Remove from the heat and thoroughly whisk in the miso.

Stir the sauce and parsley into the sauté.

Fill the crêpes, roll or fold them, and serve warm.

Sweet Potato and Apple Crêpes

DELICATE SPICING ENHANCES THE NATURAL SWEETNESS of the sweet potato, apple, and onion in this filling. Garnish the crêpes with chopped toasted almonds or pecans and a dollop of sour cream, yogurt, or **Tofu Sour Cream** (page 281). You can make the filling ahead of time. It's also good in omelets; this is enough for 2 large ones.

YIELD: 6 filled crêpes

PREPARATION TIME: About 30 minutes

1 tablespoon sesame or
   other vegetable oil
1 medium-sized sweet
   onion, finely chopped
1 large apple, peeled,
   cored, and finely diced
1 large sweet potato,
   peeled and finely diced
Freshly ground black
   pepper to taste
$^1/_4$ teaspoon ground
   allspice
$^1/_4$ teaspoon freshly
   grated nutmeg

$^1/_8$ teaspoon ground
   cinnamon
$^1/_8$ teaspoon ground cloves
6 tablespoons unsweetened
   apple juice or vegetable
   stock
$^1/_2$ teaspoon sea salt, or
   to taste
6 **Wheat Crêpes** (page
   208) or **Buckwheat
   Crêpes** (page 210)

Add the oil to a skillet over medium heat and sauté the onion for several minutes. Stir in the apple and sweet potato and sauté briefly. Add pepper and the spices and cook briefly, stirring constantly. Add the apple juice or stock, cover, reduce the heat to low, and cook until the sweet potato is tender. Season with salt and mash slightly.

Fill the crêpes and serve them immediately.

Filled Tortillas

WHEN I MOVED TO TEXAS, I QUICKLY LEARNED THAT TOR-tillas and salsa are to Texans what bread and butter are to other Americans. Upon being seated in a Texan restaurant, a basket of crisp corn tortilla chips and spunky red or green sauce always seems to arrive with the menus. Though far from the only cuisine in this immense, extraordinarily diverse state, Tex-Mex, north-of-the-border makeovers of traditional Mexican dishes, is pervasive.

While Tex-Mex has become popular throughout the United States, its heritage predates the mid-1800s, before Texas statehood. Legend has it that Tex-Mex was created by Mexican laundresses in San Antonio who moonlighted by cooking for the armies of Mexico and the Republic of Texas and the Texas Rangers. They took tough cuts of beef and chile peppers and concocted laundry-tubfuls of what became known as chili con carne, a variation on centuries-old Mexican Indian stews. Eventually, they offered other Mexican-derived dishes at their chili stands, forerunners of modern-day Tex-Mex restaurants.

Mexican and Tex-Mex cuisines feature both corn and wheat tortillas extensively, and adaptations of some traditional preparations have become fixtures on the American fast-food scene. For instance, most Americans think of tacos as crisp fried corn tortillas, folded into a "U" shape and stuffed with ground beef, beans, shredded lettuce, chopped tomatoes, and grated cheese. In Mexico, a taco is any type of tortilla folded or rolled around any type of filling, and the tortillas can be soft, slightly fried, or fried crisp, though soft ones are most common. Enchiladas consist of soft corn tortillas coated with a sauce, rolled around a filling, and usually heated in the oven. Tostadas are flat, crisp corn tortillas piled with an assortment of toppings. Burritos are made with soft flour tortillas; one end is tucked up inside between the folded sides to permit eating out of one's hand without leakage. Tex-Mex fajitas ("sashes" in Spanish) are a burrito variation. Their name comes from their traditional filling—thin strips of grilled skirt steak resembling sashes; now, sashlike strips of anything qualify as fajita fillings.

Except for enchiladas, filled tortillas are generally handheld and fall into the category of antojitos, snack foods sold and eaten on the street in Mexico. Miniature versions make great appetizers, and they are also perfectly acceptable main dishes if served in sufficient quantity. Use Mexican-style fillings or substitute less conventional ones, as I have in some cases here.

YIELD: 2 to 4 servings

PREPARATION TIME: 20 to 30 minutes

Notes
• Substitute **Avocado Salsa Cruda** (page 270) for the guacamole and salsa.

TOWERING TOSTADAS

SEVERAL LAYERS OF CLASSIC MEXICAN INGREDIENTS TOP the crisp corn tortilla of this tostada, but possibilities for toppings are practically endless; exercise your imagination and use your leftovers to come up with new combinations.

4 **Corn Tortillas**
    (page 216)
Corn or sesame oil
2 cups warmed **Refritos**
    (page 256)
¹/₄ cup finely chopped
    green onions
2 cups finely chopped
    lettuce or other tender
    greens
1 cup **Guacamole**
    (page 255)

¹/₂ cup **Blender Hot
    Sauce** (page 276) or
    Emilio's Salsa Verde
    (page 270), plus extra
    for passing
Coarsely chopped cilantro
    leaves
Lightly toasted, chopped
    almonds
Sour cream or **Tofu
    Sour Cream**
    (page 281)

Brush both sides of each tortilla lightly with oil. Place them on a baking sheet and bake for several minutes at 350° until crisp—watch that they don't burn!

For each tostada, spread ¹/₂ cup of the beans on a tortilla and then evenly distribute the green onions, lettuce, guacamole, salsa, cilantro, and almonds, in that order. Top with the sour cream.

Serve the tostadas immediately, with additional salsa for those who want more.

TOFU ENCHILADAS

THESE SAUCED, SEASONED, TOFU-FILLED CORN TORTILLAS are a light alternative to cheese-laden enchiladas. Soften the tortillas by wrapping them in an unnnapped towel, steaming for about a minute, and then leaving them in the covered steamer off the heat for about 15 minutes.

YIELD: 6 enchiladas

PREPARATION TIME: About 40 minutes

Or wrap and heat them in a moderate oven for several minutes—just until they are soft and pliable. Serve the enchiladas with an avocado salad or sautéed greens.

Notes
• Mexican oregano is one of the many species of oregano throughout the world; if you don't have it, substitute another zesty-flavored variety.
• Substitute a red salsa, such as **Blender Hot Sauce** (page 276), for the salsa verde.

1 tablespoon sesame or other vegetable oil	1 teaspoon minced fresh Mexican oregano, or ¹/₂ teaspoon dried
1 medium-sized onion, finely chopped	12 ounces tofu, well mashed
2 cloves garlic, minced	1¹/₂ tablespoons lemon juice
¹/₄ cup finely chopped or grated carrot	1¹/₂ tablespoons mellow barley miso
¹/₄ cup finely chopped or grated turnip	6 **Corn Tortillas** (page 216)
¹/₂ teaspoon ground coriander	**Emilio's Salsa Verde** (page 270)
1¹/₂ teaspoons ground cumin	¹/₄ to ¹/₂ cup fresh cilantro leaves, coarsely chopped
1 teaspoon chili powder	

Add the oil to a skillet over medium heat and sauté the onion, garlic, carrot, and turnip until tender. Grind together the coriander, cumin, and chili powder, and stir this mixture along with the oregano into the sauté. Stir in the tofu, cover the pan, turn the heat to low, and cook for several minutes, until the mixture is heated through and the flavors are well blended. Whisk the lemon juice and miso to a smooth paste, and stir it in. Remove the pan from the heat.

Soften the tortillas and lightly spread them with salsa. Spoon in the filling and roll them up. Arrange the enchiladas on plates and top with more salsa and the cilantro. Serve them immediately. If you must wait to serve the filled enchiladas, hold them in a covered casserole in a warm oven; garnish with the cilantro just before serving.

YIELD: 2 servings

PREPARATION TIME: About 45 minutes

Notes
• Omit the tofu and scramble in 2 beaten eggs after you have added the potato and seasonings.

SCRAMBLED POTATO TACOS

WARM, SOFT TORTILLAS FOLDED OVER A SPICY POTATO filling are a favorite breakfast item in central Texas. They are usually made with wheat tortillas, but corn tortillas are good, too. Tofu reduces the cholesterol in this version, but you can substitute eggs. Serve the tacos with **Refritos** (page 256) and a salsa (pages 270–271)—if you can take the heat!

1 poblano pepper
1 large potato (^{1}/$_2$ pound), cut into small cubes
1 tablespoon sesame oil
1 medium-sized onion, finely chopped
2 large cloves garlic, minced
^{1}/$_2$ teaspoon ground coriander

1^1/$_2$ teaspoons ground cumin
4 ounces tofu, cut into small cubes
1 tablespoon lemon juice
^{1}/$_2$ teaspoon sea salt, or to taste
*2 **Wheat Tortillas** (page 218) or 4 **Corn Tortillas** (page 216)*

Roast and peel the pepper as described on page 244. Chop and set it aside.

Simmer the potato cubes in water until they are just tender; drain and save the water for bread, soup stock, and other uses.

Over medium heat, sauté the onion and garlic in the oil until the onion is just tender. Stir in the coriander and cumin, and cook briefly, stirring constantly. Add 1 tablespoon of the chopped pepper and the tofu, and cook, stirring, for several minutes, until the tofu is hot and soft. Stir in the cooked potato, lemon juice, and ^{1}/$_2$ teaspoon salt. Lower the heat, cover, and heat the mixture for several minutes, stirring occasionally. Taste and add more chopped poblano pepper or salt if necessary.

Wrap the tortillas in foil and warm them in the oven or steam them briefly, then fill and fold or roll them. Serve the tacos immediately.

BEAN BURRITOS

SOME OF THE BEST BEAN BURRITOS I EVER TASTED WERE from a pushcart on the main street in Amherst, Massachusetts. The cart had some kind of warming device for large flour tortillas and refried beans and a cooler for crisp greens, guacamole, and shredded cheese, and the vendor assembled fresh, custom-made burritos right on the spot. You can quickly put together your own burritos at home if you have some basic ingredients on hand—perhaps the leftovers from a Mexican dinner.

YIELD: 2 servings

PREPARATION TIME: 15 to 20 minutes

2 **Whole Wheat Tortillas** (page 218)
2 cups **Refritos** (page 256)
2 cups finely shredded greens
¹/₂ cup **Guacamole** (page 255)

¹/₂ cup **Emilio's Salsa Verde** (page 270) or **Blender Hot Sauce** (page 276)
¹/₄ cup cilantro, coarsely chopped

Wrap the tortillas with foil and warm them in the oven or steam them briefly. Reheat the refried beans.

Spread half the beans down the middle of the upper two-thirds of each tortilla; then evenly distribute the greens, guacamole, salsa, and cilantro, in that order.

Fold up the bottom third of the tortilla and fold in the sides, leaving the top open. Serve the burritos, to be eaten out of hand, immediately.

Notes
• Substitute **Corn-Wheat Tortillas** (page 219) for the all-wheat tortillas.
• Substitute 1 cup **Avocado Salsa Cruda** (page 270) for the guacamole and salsa.
• Add 2 or more tablespoons of grated cheese, such as Monterey jack or mild cheddar, to each burrito.
• Chopped roasted almonds and finely chopped green onions are other tasty additions.

STUFFED CHAPATIS

USE CHAPATIS AS WRAPPERS RATHER THAN AS PINCERS for this Indian version of Mexican burritos.

YIELD: 2 servings

PREPARATION TIME: 15 to 20 minutes

2 **Chapatis** (page 221)
1 cup **Lentil Dal**
  (page 257)
2 green onions, finely
  chopped
2 tablespoons raisins
  (Monukka raisins are
  particularly good)

1 banana, sliced
¼ cup chopped, lightly
  toasted cashews or
  almonds
2 tablespoons finely
  chopped cilantro or
  mint leaves

Wrap the chapatis in foil and warm them in the oven or steam them briefly. Warm the dal.

Spread half the dal down the center of the upper two-thirds of each chapati. Evenly distribute the onions, raisins, banana slices, and nuts on top. Sprinkle the cilantro or mint over all. Fold the unfilled end of each chapati up, then fold the sides in, leaving the top open.

Serve the filled chapatis immediately—to be eaten out of hand.

Tempeh Fajitas

THIN STRIPS OF COOKED MARINATED TEMPEH ARE EXCEL-lent vegetarian stand-ins for the traditional skirt steak "sashes" in this popular Mexican dish.

2 garlic cloves, minced
⅓ cup lime juice
1 (8-ounce) cake tempeh
1 tablespoon olive oil
½ cup vegetable stock
  or water

1 teaspoon tamari
2 to 4 **Whole Wheat**
  Tortillas (page 218)
Pico de Gallo (page 271)

Whisk together the garlic and lime juice, and pour it over the tempeh in a flat dish. Cover and marinate in the refrigerator, preferably for several hours, occasionally turning the tempeh.

Add the oil to a skillet over medium heat. Remove the

tempeh from the marinade and brown it on both sides. Add the stock and tamari and cover the pan tightly. Steam, turning the tempeh several times, until the pan is almost dry. Cut the tempeh into thin strips.

Wrap the tortillas with foil and warm them in the oven or steam them briefly. Arrange the tempeh strips down the middle, spoon some pico de gallo on top, and fold or roll up the tortillas.

Serve immediately with additional pico de gallo.

Notes

• Substitute **Corn-Wheat Tortillas** (page 219) for the all-wheat ones.

TWELVE

Filled Doughs:
Pizzas, Tarts, Turnovers, Filled Buns

MY GRANDFATHER, A TRAVELING SALESMAN WHOSE TERRITORY covered three Midwestern states, loved to tell about his first experience with pizza. One evening, tired and hungry, Grandpop pulled into a small town in Iowa. The motel proprietor recommended a nearby Italian restaurant. The menu included "pizza," a dish Grandpop had never heard of, and he ordered the largest size in spite of the waitress's warnings; he was a big man and he was famished. The huge bread-crusted "pie" she brought out was large enough to feed several hungry husky men, and he always remembered to order smaller pizzas on subsequent visits.

It seems almost every culture has at least one traditional filled dough, and pizza is undoubtedly the most familiar example in the United States. But Italians have turnovers and spiral-filled doughs too, as do many other cuisines. Steamed buns from China are another variation on the theme. In each case, the filling is either spread on top of the dough before cooking, or the dough is folded over or rolled around the filling, sealing it inside.

I've borrowed these basic formats for my own dough and filling combinations: pizzas, savory bread-crusted tarts, turnovers, spiral-filled loaves or rolls, coffee cakes, and steamed buns. I think about preparing them when I am making bread. My fillings are often reinterpretations of traditional ethnic fillings. Besides being convenient to make when you're making bread, most filled doughs are even more suitable than sandwiches for munching out of hand without a mess, so they're excellent for parties, picnics, or lunchboxes.

This chapter's recipes document some of my explorations with doughs, toppings, and fillings. Hopefully, these will encourage you to use what you especially like or have on hand when you bake. A turnover filling may be as easy as a simple stir-fry or combination of grated cheese or nut butter and sliced vegetables or fruits. Surprisingly small quantities of sauce and toppings suffice for a pizza. Filled doughs often provide a solution for the little bits of leftovers you're tempted to throw out. Think before you toss: Today's potential trash might be a key element of tomorrow's delightful, innovative dinner. Some filled doughs require rather extensive planning and effort, but many don't take much forethought or prep work at all.

Preparation times shown for recipes assume you have bread dough and certain sauces on hand. For my small family, I usually use part of a regular bread recipe for a filled item and make the rest into a loaf or rolls. Doughs for filling should have at least one bowl rise, but I recommend two full rises for best flavor and strength. If the dough is ready before the filling, cover and refrigerate it.

Pizzas

THE PIZZA MY GRANDFATHER WAS INTRODUCED TO FIFTY-some years ago was the classic Neapolitan form of the

dish that endured, pretty much unchanged until quite recently in America: a white wheat crust spread with tomato sauce and topped with melted mozzarella cheese plus a choice of sliced onions, mushrooms, bell pepper strips, anchovies, pepperoni, or sausage. Occasionally, someone got creative and included something a little different, such as olives, broccoli, sliced eggplant, or zucchini. But, basically, pizza was pizza.

Today's innovative cooks are busy inventing pizzas to please every taste bud and dietary persuasion. Pizza crusts range from paper-thin to puffy and are made from just about any kind of dough: whole wheat, rye, sourdough—you name it. While a basic wheat crust will do for any pizza, you can choose a dough to better match particular toppings. Sauces can be savory, spicy, even sweet. Most cheeses are acceptable for pizza, and cheese may be absent altogether. Just about anything and everything in the way of vegetables, fruits, herbs, nuts, fish, and meat appear as toppings. Plain old pizza hasn't disappeared, but the word no longer depicts a dish; now it describes a versatile culinary concept.

Ironically, the broadened American definition of pizza has probably brought it closer to its actual roots. In Italy, this bread-based pie originated as a convenient means to a meal in bakeries or homes where bread was in the making, and regional circumstance determined the particular constellation of ingredients that came to characterize it. Though Naples unquestionably played an important role in pizza's history, I doubt this dish was ever limited to one strict formula. Depending on locality and season, Italian bakers of old likely improvised and adorned pizzas with ingredients at hand—perhaps walnuts, clams, artichokes, wild mushrooms, escarole, to name just a few. All that pizza requires is a bread dough crust baked with a topping of some sort. There's nothing heretical about trying out new flavor and texture combinations, and there are endless possibilities.

Here are some tips for creating new pizzas. While you can come up with lots of Italian variations, borrow ideas from other ethnic cuisines as well: for instance, tomatoes, eggplant or spinach, olives, and feta on a cracked wheat or sesame crust for a Greek-style pizza; colorful peppers, beans, pine nuts, avocado, and salsa on a cornmeal crust for a Mexican or Southwestern theme. Start with a rye or pumpernickel dough and add hearty ingredients such as mustard, sauerkraut, and tempeh, or, onions, mushrooms, potatoes, sour cream, and paprika. For a delectable dessert or brunch pizza, top a sweet dough with fruit and nuts. Just remember, a few carefully considered, coordinated toppings are generally preferable to "the works" in flavor and visual appeal. Refrain from oversaucing and arrange items artistically on top. Make an overall design or decorate halves or quadrants with different toppings.

Whatever your plan, your pizza will only be as good as the ingredients that go into it. While using top-quality oils, herbs, vegetables, nuts, olives, and cheeses may be the key to pizza success, that doesn't exclude leftovers as long as they're still fresh. It's handy to have pizza-size portions of tomato, pesto, and other sauces in the freezer. If thick enough, ratatouille, chili, and curries also make good pizza toppings.

Pizzas don't have to be round; you can make them oblong, square, or even in the shape of Texas if you wish. For a crisp crust, I recommend a baking stone or tiles and a super-hot oven. Blackened steel pans and pizza screens also promote crispness. Transfer your pizza directly from the oven to a wooden board and slice it with a razor-sharp cleaver or pizza cutter.

BASIC PIZZA

YIELD: 1 pizza—2 generous servings

PREPARATION TIME: 30 to 40 minutes to prepare; 10 minutes to bake

HERE'S A CLASSIC PIZZA—ONE OF THE SIMPLEST MEALS to make on a bread-making day. Use this recipe as a touchstone as you brainstorm for new combinations. Italian-type bread doughs are traditional, but any dough is a possibility—just set aside a piece of dough for pizza whenever you make bread. This recipe is a guide and is exceedingly variable, adapting to individual tastes and available ingredients. Add minced fresh herbs, such as basil, thyme, oregano, parsley, and rosemary; substitute other vegetables; include sliced olives or nuts. It's your show. The pizza recipes that follow this one provide examples of interesting combinations.

Cornmeal
12 ounces bread dough
1 1/2 teaspoons olive oil,
    plus extra for the pan
    and dough
1 small to medium-sized
    onion, sliced into
    thin rings
2 large cloves garlic,
    minced
1 medium-sized bell
    pepper, sliced crosswise
    into thin rings

1 cup sliced mushrooms
1/2 cup tomato sauce
    (page 273 or 274)
2 tablespoons finely grated
    parmesan, romano, or
    other hard Italian cheese
1 cup coarsely grated
    mozzarella cheese
Dried hot red pepper
    flakes to taste

If baking with a pizza stone or tiles, place them in the oven and preheat to 500°. Dust a wooden pizza peel or lightly greased 14- to 15-inch pizza pan with cornmeal.

On a lightly greased surface, roll the dough into a circle about 12 inches in diameter, depending on the crust thickness you prefer. Brush the dough lightly with olive oil, then transfer it to the peel or pan. Crimp the edge to form a slight lip.

Add the 1½ teaspoons oil to a skillet over medium heat. Add the onion and sauté for 2 to 3 minutes, until translucent. Add the garlic and continue sautéing, gradually adding the bell pepper and mushrooms. Cook briefly and remove the pan from the heat.

Spread the tomato sauce evenly over the dough. Arrange the sautéed vegetables over the sauce. Sprinkle on the grated cheese and scatter the mozzarella and red pepper flakes over the top.

Transfer the pizza from the peel to the stone or tiles in the oven, or place the pan on a low rack. Bake for 10 minutes, or until the bottom is brown and crisp. Slide the pizza onto a cutting board, cut it into wedges, and serve immediately.

Pesto Pizza

SOME BREAD DOUGH, LEFTOVER PESTO, A FEW TOPPINGS, and wow!—what a meal! I usually use an Italian or French dough for this pizza.

Cornmeal	*½ cup **Pesto** (page 267)*
12 ounces bread dough	*1 large plum tomato,*
1 teaspoon olive oil,	*thinly sliced*
plus extra for the pan	*Chopped chèvre or shaved*
and dough	*parmesan to taste*
1 small red onion, thinly	*1 tablespoon finely chopped*
sliced into rings	*parsley*

If you are baking on a pizza stone or tiles, place them in the oven. Preheat the oven to 500°. Generously dust a wooden pizza peel or lightly greased 14- to 15-inch pizza pan with cornmeal.

On a lightly greased surface, roll the dough into a circle about 12 inches in diameter, depending on the crust thickness you prefer. Brush the dough lightly with olive oil, then transfer it to the peel or pan. Crimp the edge to form a slight lip.

Notes

• For a dairyless pizza, omit the cheeses. Marinate 4 ounces of pressed, diced tofu in a mixture of 2 teaspoons lemon juice, 2 teaspoons olive oil, and 1 teaspoon minced garlic, and arrange it on the vegetables in place of the cheese. Or, top the pizza with marinated, cooked tempeh.

• Substitute **Roasted Red Pepper Sauce** (page 271) for the tomato sauce.

YIELD: 1 pizza—2 generous servings

PREPARATION TIME: About 30 minutes to prepare; 10 minutes to bake

Notes

• For a dairyless pizza, omit the cheese and top with marinated tofu, as described on page 313.

• Substitute **Watercress Pesto** (page 268) for the basil pesto.

YIELD: 1 pizza—2 generous servings

PREPARATION TIME: 10 to 15 minutes to prepare; 10 minutes to bake

Add the 1 teaspoon olive oil to a skillet over medium heat. Sauté the onion briefly, then remove the skillet from the heat.

Spread the pesto evenly over the dough and arrange the tomato slices on top. Distribute the sautéed onion over the tomato slices. Scatter on cheese as desired, and sprinkle the parsley over all.

Transfer the pizza from the peel to the stone or tiles in the oven, or place the pan on a low rack. Bake for 10 minutes, or until the bottom is brown and crisp. Slide the pizza onto a cutting board, cut it into wedges, and serve immediately.

MEXICAN PIZZA

RICE OR CORNMEAL DOUGHS ARE ESPECIALLY APPROPRI-ate for this pizza.

Cornmeal
12 ounces bread dough
Sesame or olive oil
1 cup **Refritos** (page 256)
¹/₄ cup salsa (page 270 or 271), plus extra for garnish

1 cup coarsely shredded Monterey Jack cheese (optional)
1 medium-sized ripe avocado
1 tablespoon lime juice
¹/₄ cup coarsely chopped cilantro leaves

If you are baking on a pizza stone or tiles, place them in the oven. Preheat the oven to 500°. Generously dust a wooden pizza peel or lightly greased 14- to 15-inch pizza pan with cornmeal.

On a lightly greased surface, roll the dough into a circle about 12 inches in diameter, depending on the crust thickness you prefer. Brush the dough lightly with olive oil, then transfer it to the peel or pan. Crimp the edge to form a slight lip.

Spread the beans over the dough. Spread the salsa on the beans. Sprinkle the cheese on top.

Transfer the pizza from the peel to the stone or tiles

in the oven, or place the pan on a low rack. Bake for 10 minutes, or until the bottom is brown and crisp.

While the pizza is baking, peel and thinly slice the avocado into lengthwise strips. Sprinkle lime juice over the avocado strips and fold gently with a rubber spatula to coat them with the juice.

Slide the baked pizza onto a cutting board. Arrange the avocado slices on top and sprinkle the cilantro over all. Cut the pizza into wedges and serve immediately. Pass additional salsa on the side.

INDONESIAN PIZZA

AN INDONESIAN SALAD ON TOP OF A RICE DOUGH CRUST!

YIELD: 1 pizza—2 generous servings

PREPARATION TIME: 30 to 40 minutes to prepare; 10 minutes to bake

1¹/₂ teaspoons tamari	12 ounces bread dough
¹/₂ teaspoon brown rice vinegar	1 cup **Spicy Peanut Sauce** (page 279)
¹/₄ cup plus 1¹/₂ tablespoons vegetable stock or water	2 to 4 tablespoons sliced green onions
1 (4-ounce) cake tempeh	¹/₂ cup thinly sliced Chinese cabbage
1 tablespoon peanut oil, plus extra for the pan and dough	¹/₄ cup thinly sliced carrot, lightly steamed
Cornmeal or rice flour	1 to 2 cups small broccoli florets, lightly steamed

Whisk together the tamari, brown rice vinegar, and 1¹/₂ tablespoons stock. Add the tempeh and marinate (refrigerated) for 30 minutes, or up to several hours or overnight. Drain, reserving any remaining marinade.

Heat the 1 tablespoon oil in a small skillet over moderate heat. Brown the tempeh on both sides. Add the ¹/₄ cup stock and cover the pan tightly. Steam until the liquid is almost gone. Add the leftover marinade and steam until the pan is dry. Cut the tempeh into small strips.

If you are baking on a pizza stone or tiles, place them in the oven. Preheat the oven to 500°. Generously dust a wooden pizza peel or lightly greased 14- to 15-inch pizza pan with cornmeal.

On a lightly greased surface, roll the dough into a circle about 12 inches in diameter, depending on the crust thickness you prefer. Brush the dough lightly with oil, then transfer it to the peel or pan. Crimp the edge to form a slight lip. Spread ½ cup of the peanut sauce over the dough. Sprinkle on the green onions and cabbage. Distribute the carrot, broccoli, and tempeh slices evenly on top. Drizzle the remaining peanut sauce over all.

Transfer the pizza from the peel to the stone or tiles in the oven, or place the pan on a low rack. Bake for 10 minutes, or until the bottom is brown and crisp. Slide the pizza onto a cutting board, cut it into wedges, and serve immediately.

Pizza à la Grecque

Sesame Bread (page 104) dough makes a great crust for this Greek-style pizza.

Yield: 1 pizza—2 generous servings

Preparation time: about 20 minutes to prepare; 10 minutes to bake

Kalamata olives are large dark Greek olives with a pronounced briny flavor—a welcome contrast to most California olives, which are rendered rather tasteless by extensive processing. Look for pitted kalamatas for convenience.

Cornmeal	4 cups loosely packed
12 ounces bread dough	fresh spinach leaves
1 tablespoon olive oil,	(4 ounces), finely chopped
plus extra for the pan	½ cup tomato sauce (page
and dough	273 or 274)
1 small red onion, thinly	½ cup crumbled feta
sliced into rings	cheese
1 clove garlic, pressed or	12 pitted Kalamata olives,
minced	sliced

If you are baking on a pizza stone or tiles, place them in the oven. Preheat the oven to 500°. Generously dust a wooden pizza peel or lightly greased 14- to 15-inch pizza pan with cornmeal.

On a lightly greased surface, roll the dough into a circle about 12 inches in diameter, depending on the crust thickness you prefer. Brush the dough lightly with oil, then transfer it to the peel or pan. Crimp the edge to form a slight lip.

Add the 1 tablespoon oil to a skillet over medium heat. Briefly sauté the onion rings and the garlic. Stir in the spinach and remove the skillet from the heat.

Spread the tomato sauce over the dough and top with the vegetable mixture. Scatter the feta and olives on top.

Transfer the pizza from the peel to the stone or tiles in the oven, or place the pan on a low rack. Bake for 10 minutes, or until the bottom is brown and crisp. Slide the pizza onto a cutting board, cut it into wedges, and serve immediately.

Pizza Primavera

Use a sourdough or yeasted French or Italian dough for this savory spinach- and herb-sauced pizza.

Cornmeal
Olive oil
12 ounces bread dough
1 cup **Italian Green Sauce** (page 272)
¼ cup finely chopped flat-leaf parsley

¼ cup chopped almonds
1 medium red bell pepper, thinly sliced into rings
Cubed chèvre, shaved parmesan, or coarsely grated mozzarella cheese to taste (optional)

Notes
• For a dairyless pizza, substitute marinated tofu (page 313) for the feta.

YIELD: 1 pizza—2 generous servings

PREPARATION TIME: about 20 minutes to prepare; 10 minutes to bake

If you are baking on a pizza stone or tiles, place them in the oven. Preheat the oven to 500°. Generously dust a wooden pizza peel or lightly greased 14- to 15-inch pizza pan with cornmeal.

On a lightly greased surface, roll the dough into a circle about 12 inches in diameter, depending on the crust thickness you prefer. Brush the dough lightly with oil, then transfer it to the peel or pan. Crimp the edge to form a slight lip.

Spread the sauce over the dough and sprinkle on the parsley and almonds. Arrange the pepper rings on top and scatter cheese over all.

Transfer the pizza from the peel to the stone or tiles in the oven, or place the pan on a low rack. Bake for 10 minutes, or until the bottom is brown and crisp. Slide the pizza onto a cutting board, cut it into wedges, and serve immediately.

REUBEN'S PIZZA

BUCKWHEAT OR RYE DOUGH MAKES AN APPEALING CRUST for this Old World pizza. Serve it with sautéed greens and dill pickles.

YIELD: 1 pizza—2 generous servings

PREPARATION TIME: 30 minutes to prepare; 10 minutes to bake

Cornmeal
12 ounces bread dough
1½ teaspoons sesame or
    other vegetable oil,
    plus extra for the pan
    and dough
1 (4-ounce) cake tempeh
¼ cup vegetable stock
    or water
½ recipe **Mellow
    Mustard Sauce**
    (page 280), uncooked

¼ cup finely chopped
    green onion
1 cup well-drained
    sauerkraut
1 small red bell pepper,
    thinly sliced
1 cup coarsely grated
    Swiss cheese (optional)
Paprika to taste

If you are baking on a pizza stone or tiles, place them in the oven. Preheat the oven to 500°. Generously dust a wooden pizza peel or lightly greased 14- to 15-inch pizza pan with cornmeal.

On a lightly greased surface, roll the dough into a circle about 12 inches in diameter, depending on the crust thickness you prefer. Brush the dough lightly with oil, then transfer it to the peel or pan. Crimp the edge to form a slight lip.

Add the 1½ teaspoons oil to a skillet over medium heat. Brown the tempeh on both sides. Add the stock and cover the pan tightly. Steam until the pan is dry. Remove the tempeh and slice it into short, thin strips.

Return the strips to the skillet and add the sauce. Cook over low heat, stirring occasionally, until the sauce thickens.

Spread the tempeh and sauce over the dough and sprinkle on the onion. Arrange the sauerkraut on top and scatter on pepper and cheese. Lightly sprinkle paprika over all.

Transfer the pizza from the peel to the stone or tiles in the oven, or place the pan on a low rack. Bake for 10 minutes, or until the bottom is brown and crisp. Slide the pizza onto a cutting board, cut it into wedges, and serve immediately.

Breakfast Pizza

ONCE, WHEN WE WERE CAMPING, I DREAMED THAT SOMEone came to the door of the tent in the morning and announced: "Here's your breakfast pizza!" The dream was so vivid that I was disappointed when I woke up and there wasn't a pizza for breakfast. A pizza like this one is just what I would have ordered. Serve it for breakfast or for any other meal. A pan works best for this because the uncooked filling is likely to spill over the dough as you manipulate a peel.

1 medium-sized red bell or pimiento pepper
1 medium-sized green bell pepper
Cornmeal
12 ounces bread dough
Olive oil
3 medium eggs
Freshly ground black pepper to taste

¹/₄ teaspoon sea salt
2 tablespoons minced green onions, chives, or garlic chives
1 tablespoon minced fresh basil leaves
1 teaspoon minced fresh tarragon or pericon leaves

YIELD: 1 pizza—2 generous servings

PREPARATION TIME: 30 minutes to prepare; 10 minutes to bake

Pericon, also called *sweet marigold,* is a culinary herb well suited to the hot, dry climate of the southwestern United States. Pericon's long, narrow, spear-shaped leaves have an intense anise scent and flavor and make a good substitute for tarragon. In autumn, the plant bears golden blossoms, which make attractive edible garnishes as well as bright spots in bouquets.

Roast and peel the peppers, as described on page 244. Cut them into thin strips.

• Vary the herbs in the filling, and, instead of or in addition to the pepper strips, lay on a thinly sliced plum tomato or lightly sautéed sliced mushrooms or zucchini. Add some grated cheese if you wish.

Preheat the oven to 500°. Generously dust a lightly greased 14- to 15-inch pizza pan with cornmeal.

On a lightly greased surface, roll the dough into a circle about 12 inches in diameter, depending on the crust thickness you prefer. Brush the dough lightly with oil, then transfer it to the peel or pan. Crimp the edge to form a ³/₄- to 1-inch lip.

Whisk the eggs with the black pepper, salt, green onions, and herbs. Pour this mixture onto the dough and arrange the roasted pepper strips on top.

Place the pan on a low rack in the oven. Bake for 10 minutes, or until the bottom is brown and crisp. Slide the pizza onto a cutting board, cut it into wedges, and serve immediately.

PISSALADIÈRE

THIS PROVENÇAL PIZZA ORIGINATED IN NICE. IT IS TRADItionally made without tomato sauce—simply dough smothered with seasoned, sautéed onions and decorated with anchovies and ripe olives. Though slightly different, this version preserves the spirit of the original dish.

YIELD: 1 pizza—2 generous servings

PREPARATION TIME: About 30 minutes to prepare; 10 minutes to bake

1 tablespoon olive oil, plus extra for the pan and dough	Cornmeal
	12 ounces bread dough
2 medium to large onions, thinly sliced	¹/₂ cup tomato sauce (page 273 or 274)
¹/₂ teaspoon minced fresh thyme leaves	10 to 12 pitted Kalamata olives, cut into slivers
¹/₄ teaspoon minced fresh rosemary leaves	

Add the 1 tablespoon olive oil to a skillet over medium heat. Sauté the onions for several minutes. Reduce the heat to low and continue to cook, stirring occasionally, until they are very tender and lightly browned. Stir in the herbs and cook briefly.

If baking with a pizza stone or tiles, place them in the oven and preheat to 500°. Dust a wooden pizza peel or lightly greased 15-inch pizza pan with cornmeal.

On a lightly greased surface, roll the dough into a circle about 12 inches in diameter, depending on the crust thickness you prefer. Brush the dough lightly with oil, then transfer it to the peel or pan. Crimp the edge to form a slight lip.

Spread tomato sauce over the dough, arrange the onions on top, and sprinkle on the olive slivers.

Transfer the pizza from the peel to the stone or tiles, or place the pan on a low rack. Bake for 10 minutes, or until the bottom is brown and crisp. Slide the pizza onto a cutting board, cut it into wedges, and serve.

Pronto Pizza

WHEN YOU DON'T HAVE YEASTED BREAD DOUGH BUT YEARN for pizza, this biscuit crust may be even quicker than sending out. Check the other pizza recipes for topping combination ideas, or create a new one. The most tender biscuits are made with pastry flour; the pastry and bread flour blend in this recipe provides an effective balance between tenderness and dough strength.

YIELD: 1 pizza—2 generous servings

PREPARATION TIME: 15 to 20 minutes to prepare; 10 to 15 minutes to bake

2 tablespoons olive oil, plus extra for the pan and dough
Cornmeal
Assorted toppings
$1/2$ cup milk or unsweetened soy milk
$1^1/2$ teaspoons lemon juice or vinegar
$3/4$ cup whole wheat bread flour
$3/4$ cup whole wheat pastry flour

$1/4$ teaspoon sea salt
$1/2$ teaspoon baking soda
1 teaspoon baking powder
$1/2$ cup tomato sauce (page 273 or 274) or other sauce, such as **Presto-Pesto!** (page 267) or **Roasted Red Pepper Sauce** (page 271)

Notes

- Omit the lemon juice and substitute $1/2$ cup buttermilk or yogurt for the milk or soy milk, or, omit the lemon juice and baking soda and increase the baking powder to $1^{1}/_{2}$ teaspoons.

If you are baking on a pizza stone or tiles, place them in the oven. Preheat the oven to 450°. Generously dust a wooden pizza peel or lightly greased 14- to 15-inch pizza pan with cornmeal.

Prepare and assemble all toppings.

Combine the milk and lemon juice and set the mixture aside to curdle. Whisk in the 2 tablespoons olive oil.

Sift together the flours. Measure out $1^{1}/_{2}$ cups and set the remainder aside for kneading. Sift the $1^{1}/_{2}$ cups flour with the salt, baking soda, and baking powder into a medium bowl. Make a well in the center and add the curdled milk mixture. Stir gently with a fork until a soft dough forms.

Turn the dough out onto a lightly floured surface and knead it a few times, adding more flour as necessary, just until the dough comes together and is not sticky. Form the dough into a ball, then roll it out into a 12- to 13-inch-diameter circle, about $1/4$ inch thick.

Lightly brush the dough with oil and transfer it to the peel or pan. Crimp the edge to form a slight lip. Spread the sauce evenly over the dough and arrange the toppings over it.

Transfer the pizza from the peel to the stone or tiles in the oven, or place the pan on a low rack. Bake for 10 to 15 minutes, or until the bottom is brown and crisp. Slide the pizza onto a cutting board, cut it into wedges, and serve it pronto!

Raspberry-Pear Pizza

Luscious and lovely to look at, this sweet pizza makes an unusual dessert, or breakfast or brunch dish. For the dough, try **Sweet Bread** (page 107) or **Apple or Pear Sauce Bread** (page 115).

Cornmeal

12 to 16 ounces bread dough

Walnut or other nut or vegetable oil

$^1/_4$ cup raspberry preserves (preferably fruit-sweetened)

1 tablespoon unsweetened apple juice

$^1/_2$ cup light toasted almonds, finely chopped

2 tablespoons whole wheat pastry flour

2 medium to large firm, ripe pears, peeled and cut into thin slices just before filling the pizza

YIELD: 1 pizza—6 generous wedges

PREPARATION TIME: About 30 minutes to prepare; 10 minutes to bake

Notes
• Substitute peaches for the pears.
• Substitute pecans or walnuts for the almonds.

If you are baking on a pizza stone or tiles, place them in the oven. Preheat the oven to 500°. Generously dust a wooden pizza peel or lightly greased 14- to 15-inch pizza pan with cornmeal.

On a lightly greased surface, roll the dough into a circle about 12 inches in diameter, depending on the crust thickness you prefer. Brush the dough lightly with oil, then transfer it to the peel or pan. Crimp the edge to form a slight lip.

Whisk the preserves and apple juice in a small saucepan and heat just to boiling. Simmer gently for several minutes. Remove from the heat and cover.

Thoroughly mix together the almonds and flour and spread this evenly on the dough. Arrange the pear slices, slightly overlapping, in a decorative pattern covering the entire crust.

Transfer the pizza from the peel to the stone or tiles in the oven, or place the pan on a low rack. Bake for 10 minutes, or until the bottom is brown and crisp. Slide

Bread-crusted Tarts

the pizza onto a cutting board and liberally brush it with all of the raspberry glaze. Cut the pizza into wedges and serve it immediately or after it has cooled somewhat.

SAVORY TARTS HAVE LONG BEEN ONE OF MY FAVORITE main dishes for dinner parties because they can be made before guests arrive and are attractive and easy to serve. Leftovers keep well too. Years ago, I began making them with bread dough rather than pastry crusts on days when I was making bread and eliminated half the work in the process.

I've found that bread-crusted tarts have just as much appeal as their pastry-crusted cousins. They are less rich, but this works to their advantage in these health-conscious times. Many classic main dish tart fillings, notably quiches, are loaded with eggs, cream, and cheese as it is; the extra fat in a pastry crust is "gilding the lily," as my mother was wont to say. Of course, you can cut down on richness in fillings too. Tofu sour cream, for instance, reduces fat and cholesterol without sacrificing a creamy texture and performs the binding function usually accomplished with eggs. Look through your recipe file and retrieve your favorite tart fillings to try with bread crusts.

When you're making bread and plan to make a tart, simply save out a piece of dough after it has risen at least once, preferably twice. If you're not ready to put the tart together, cover and refrigerate the dough. As the recipes describe, you'll shape the dough just as you would a pastry dough. Bread-crusted tarts are best when doughs and fillings are mutually enhancing: for example, rye doughs go especially well with things like onions, cabbage, mushrooms, and sour cream.

Cut tarts into large wedges for main dish servings or into small pieces for hors d'oeuvres or snacks. They can be made in square or rectangular pans as well as round ones.

Pizza Rustica

Pizza means "pie" in Italian, and this one, with a deep rich filling, is more like a pie as Americans know it. Like the other bread dough-crusted tarts to follow, this can also be made with a pastry crust. I like to serve it by candlelight with a crisp salad and a robust wine. Try a French or Italian dough for the crust.

YIELD: 1 (9-inch) tart—4 to 6 servings

PREPARATION TIME: 30 to 40 minutes to prepare; 30 minutes to bake

1 tablespoon kuzu powder
1 tablespoon Marsala
1 pound tofu, well pressed
³/₄ teaspoon sea salt
2¹/₂ tablespoons lemon juice
2 tablespoons canola or other light vegetable oil
1 tablespoon olive oil, plus extra for the pan and dough
1 medium-sized onion, finely chopped
2 cloves garlic, minced
¹/₄ to ¹/₂ pound mushrooms, sliced

Freshly ground black pepper to taste
1 to 2 tablespoons minced fresh basil, or 1 teaspoon dried
¹/₄ to ¹/₂ cup flat-leaf parsley, finely chopped
1 cup tomato sauce (page 273 or 274)
12 ounces bread dough
¹/₂ cup coarsely chopped, lightly toasted walnuts
1 large bell pepper, seeded and sliced into thin rings

Combine the kuzu and Marsala and set aside until the kuzu has dissolved.

Blend the tofu in a food processor fitted with the metal blade. Add the salt, lemon juice, and vegetable oil, and blend until the mixture is completely smooth.

Add the 1 tablespoon olive oil to a skillet over medium heat. Sauté the onion for about 3 minutes, until translucent. Add the garlic and mushrooms and continue sautéing until the onion is tender and the mushrooms no longer appear dry. Grind in black pepper and add the basil and parsley. Stir in the tomato sauce and bring it just to a simmer. Add the dissolved kuzu and cook, stirring, until the mixture thickens. Remove the mixture from the heat and allow it to cool somewhat.

Preheat the oven to 350° and grease a 9-inch pie plate. On a lightly greased surface, roll the dough into a 10-inch-diameter circle and brush it lightly with olive oil. Fit the dough into the pan and flute the edge. Sprinkle half of the walnuts on the bottom. Spread half of the tofu mixture on top, and then add half of the tomato-vegetable sauce. Arrange half of the pepper rings on top. Repeat these four layers, ending with the remaining pepper rings decorating the top of the pie.

Bake the pie for 30 minutes, then cool it briefly. Cut it into wedges and serve.

CABBAGE KUCHEN

YIELD: 1 (9-inch) tart—4 to 6 servings

PREPARATION TIME: 30 to 40 minutes to prepare; 30 minutes to bake

KUCHEN, GERMAN FOR CAKE, IS TRADITIONALLY MADE with yeasted bread dough rather than pastry dough. This filling goes well with many different doughs, but I especially like it with rye doughs.

1 teaspoon caraway seeds	4 cups finely chopped
1 teaspoon minced	cabbage
fresh dill weed, or	1/2 teaspoon sea salt, plus
1/2 teaspoon dried	extra to taste
1 1/2 teaspoons plus	8 ounces tofu, preferably
1 tablespoon light	(extra-firm) silken
vegetable oil, plus extra	1 tablespoon tahini
for the pan and dough	8 to 10 ounces bread dough
2 tablespoons lemon juice	1 teaspoon poppy seeds
1 medium-sized onion,	
finely chopped	

Toast the caraway seeds in a heavy-bottomed skillet over low to medium heat, stirring often. Grind the seeds to a coarse consistency with a mortar and pestle or spice grinder. If using dried dill, add it and grind again.

Add 1½ teaspoons oil to the skillet over medium heat. Sauté the onion for about 3 minutes, until translucent. Stir in the cabbage and cook for a few minutes, stirring often. Add the caraway and dill and sauté briefly. Add salt to taste. Transfer the mixture to a bowl and set it aside to cool somewhat.

Blend the tofu in a food processor fitted with the metal blade. Add the ½ teaspoon salt, the lemon juice, the 1 tablespoon oil, and the tahini, and blend until completely smooth. Fold this mixture into the sauté.

Preheat oven to 350° and grease a 9-inch pie plate. Roll the dough into a 10-inch-diameter circle on a lightly greased surface. Lightly brush with oil and fit it into the pan. Flute the edge just below the rim. Spread in the filling and sprinkle on poppy seeds.

Bake the pie for 30 minutes, until the crust is crisp and the filling is set; the point of a sharp knife inserted into the center should come out clean. Cool the pie briefly, then cut it into wedges and serve them warm.

Notes

• Omit the poppy seeds and lightly sprinkle paprika on top of the filling.

• Fit the dough into an 8-inch square pan rather than the pie plate.

• To make **Onion Kuchen,** follow the recipe, incorporating these changes: substitute 1 teaspoon cumin seeds for the caraway and omit the dill; omit the cabbage and increase the onions to 1 pound (weighed after paring and peeling), thinly sliced rather than chopped; add freshly ground black pepper to the onions and sprinkle paprika on top of the pie.

SPINACH TART

CREAMY, HERBED SPINACH FILLS THIS SAVORY BREAD dough tart. The filling alone makes a delicious pâté.

8 ounces tofu, preferably (extra-firm) silken

½ teaspoon sea salt, plus extra to taste

2 tablespoons lemon juice

1 tablespoon canola or other light vegetable oil

1 tablespoon tahini

1 tablespoon olive oil, plus extra for the pan and dough

1 medium-sized onion, finely chopped

2 large cloves garlic, minced

Freshly ground black pepper to taste

¼ teaspoon freshly grated nutmeg

1 tablespoon minced fresh basil

8 cups loosely packed fresh spinach leaves (8 ounces), finely chopped

¼ cup parsley, minced

8 to 10 ounces bread dough

YIELD: 1 (9-inch) tart—4 to 6 servings

PREPARATION TIME: 30 to 40 minutes to prepare; 30 minutes to bake

Notes

• Substitute ¹/₄ pound sliced mushrooms for half of the spinach; add them to the sauté along with the garlic.

YIELD: 1 (9-inch) tart—4 to 6 servings

PREPARATION TIME: 30 to 40 minutes to prepare; 40 to 50 minutes to bake

Blend the tofu in a food processor fitted with the metal blade. Add the ¹/₂ teaspoon salt, the lemon juice, vegetable oil, and tahini, and blend until the mixture is completely smooth. Set it aside.

Add the 1 tablespoon olive oil to a skillet over medium heat. Sauté the onion for 2 to 3 minutes. Add the garlic and sauté until the onion is tender. Stir in the pepper, nutmeg, basil, spinach, and parsley, and cook, stirring, just until the spinach is wilted. Cool the sauté briefly, then add it to the mixture in the food processor and pulse a couple of times to combine, but not purée, the two mixtures. Taste and add salt if needed.

Preheat the oven to 350° and grease a 9-inch pie plate. Roll the dough into a 10-inch-diameter circle on a lightly greased surface and fit it into the pan, fluting the edge just below the rim. Spread in the filling.

Bake the tart for 30 minutes, until the crust is crisp and the filling is set; the point of a sharp knife inserted in the center should come out clean. Cool the tart briefly, then cut it into wedges. Serve them warm.

HARVEST MOON

THE SIGHT OF THIS BRILLIANT ORANGE MAIN-DISH TART may set you to howling. Any strong bread dough works well for the crust, though I particularly like **Anadama Bread** (page 98) or an egg dough (page 112 or 168).

1 tablespoon sesame or other vegetable oil, plus extra for the pan and dough
1 medium-sized to large onion, finely chopped
1 medium-sized to large apple, peeled, cored, and finely chopped

Freshly ground black pepper to taste
¹/₄ teaspoon freshly grated nutmeg
1 to 1¹/₂ teaspoons minced fresh marjoram, or ¹/₂ teaspoon dried
¹/₂ to ³/₄ teaspoon minced fresh thyme, or ¹/₄ teaspoon dried

¼ to ⅜ teaspoon minced
   fresh rosemary, or
   ⅛ teaspoon dried
Sea salt to taste
2 cups mashed cooked
   butternut squash

3 medium eggs
⅓ cup lightly toasted,
   coarsely chopped pecans
12 ounces bread dough

Add the oil to a skillet over medium heat. Sauté the onion for about 3 minutes, until translucent. Add the apple, pepper, nutmeg, and herbs, and continue sautéing until the onion and apple are tender. Season with salt and remove the pan from the heat.

Blend the squash in a food processor fitted with the metal blade. Add salt to taste. Blend in the eggs thoroughly. Add the sauté and pulse briefly to combine, but not purée, the two mixtures. Fold in the pecans.

Preheat the oven to 350° and grease a 9-inch pie plate. Roll the dough into a 10-inch-diameter circle on a lightly greased surface. Brush the dough lightly with oil and fit it into the pan, fluting the edge. Spread in the filling.

Bake the tart for 40 to 50 minutes, until the crust is crisp and the filling is set; the point of a sharp knife inserted in the center should come out clean. Cool the tart for 20 to 30 minutes, then cut it into wedges and serve them warm.

Turnovers

THERE'S SOME TYPE OF STUFFED DOUGH IN JUST ABOUT every cuisine. The differences lie in the particular dough and filling and sometimes the cooking technique. Italians fold over and seal up pizzas and call them calzones. Spaniards and Latin Americans stuff yeasted or cornmeal dough with spicy mixtures of onions, peppers, and meat or fish. Eastern Europeans enclose seasoned kasha or chopped chicken livers in dough rich with chicken fat. Greeks wrap cheese, spinach, or meat fillings in fine, flaky phyllo dough. Russians fill their piroshki with hearty cabbage, chopped egg, or ground meat mixtures. Indian samosas are delicately crusted pyramids filled with superbly spiced vegetable medleys. And, long ago, Cornish pasties, baked turnovers traditionally filled with gravy-moistened leftover meat and potatoes and perhaps even a dab of jam in one end for dessert, were standard lunch pail fare for English miners.

Turnovers are baked, fried, or even steamed. I prefer baking to frying for health reasons, and because there are no greasy pans to clean up. I usually make turnovers when I'm already making bread, so it's most convenient to bake them at the same time. I've adapted some customarily fried items, such as Indian samosas or Latin American empanadas, and bake them.

I also use bread dough rather than specialized doughs for the same reason: It's available and therefore convenient. Save out what you need for the turnovers after the dough has risen at least once, preferably twice. Size turnovers to suit your meal plan: They can vary from tiny canapés to large half-moons. An egg wash or other surface treatment makes turnovers especially attractive.

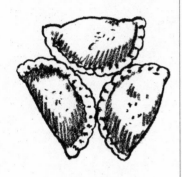

INDIAN TURNOVERS

INDIAN *SAMOSAS* ARE DEEP-FRIED TURNOVERS PREPARED from pastry dough and a spicy vegetable filling. Here is a less fatty, baked bread dough version. I like to use a cracked wheat dough for these.

YIELD: 4 large turnovers—4 servings

PREPARATION TIME: 30 to 40 minutes to prepare; 20 minutes to bake

1 large potato
1 tablespoon ghee or
    vegetable oil, plus extra
    for brushing the dough
1/2 teaspoon black
    mustard seeds
1 medium-sized onion,
    finely chopped

2 cloves garlic, minced
1 teaspoon finely grated
    fresh ginger
1 medium-sized carrot,
    thinly sliced
1 cup sliced mushrooms
3/4 teaspoon ground cumin

*¹/₄ teaspoon ground
   coriander*
Cayenne to taste
*1 cup shelled green peas
   or sugar snap peas*
1 teaspoon lemon juice

*¹/₂ teaspoon sea salt or to
   taste*
*¹/₂ cup **Tofu Sour Cream**
   (page 281) or yogurt*
1 pound bread dough

Notes

- For a shiny crust, brush the turnovers with an egg wash instead of with ghee or oil before baking.
- Sprinkle the turnovers with poppy or sesame seeds before baking.

Cut the potato into small dice and simmer it in water to cover until tender. Drain thoroughly.

Add the ghee or oil to a skillet over medium heat. Cook the black mustard seeds until they begin to pop. Add the onion and sauté for 2 to 3 minutes, until translucent. Stir in the garlic, ginger, and carrot. Add the mushrooms, cumin, coriander, and cayenne, and continue sautéing until the carrot is tender. Add the peas, potatoes, lemon juice, and salt, and cook briefly, stirring often. Stir in the **Tofu Sour Cream** or yogurt and remove the pan from the heat.

Preheat the oven to 400°. Grease a baking sheet or line it with parchment paper.

Divide the dough into 4 equal pieces. Roll each into a ball and cover these with a damp towel for a few minutes, until the dough has relaxed. On a lightly greased surface, roll one of the balls into a 6- to 7-inch-diameter circle. Spoon ¹/₄ of the filling onto the dough, fold it in half, and firmly crimp the edges together to seal in the filling. Transfer the filled dough to the pan. Make 3 more turnovers in the same manner. Brush the tops lightly with ghee or oil and prick them with a fork in two or three places to allow steam to escape during baking.

Bake the turnovers for 20 minutes, or until they are browned and crusty. For a softer crust, brush the turnovers lightly with ghee or oil again as soon as they come out of the oven.

PIROSHKI

YIELD: 4 large piroshki—4 servings

PREPARATION TIME: About 45 minutes to prepare; 20 minutes to bake

WHEN I STUDIED RUSSIAN IN HIGH SCHOOL, MY ENTHU-siastic teacher gave all of her students Russian names and introduced us to traditional Russian foods and folk dancing, as well as the language. This is where I learned to make *piroshki*, baked turnovers that are typically prepared from a rich pastry dough stuffed with chopped meat or hard-boiled egg and vegetables. Now I use bread dough to encase a hearty tempeh-and-vegetable filling. Rye doughs are particularly good for the crust.

1 teaspoon kuzu powder	*2 cups finely chopped*
1 teaspoon cold vegetable	*cabbage*
stock or water	*Freshly ground black pepper*
1 teaspoon caraway seeds	*to taste*
2 teaspoons plus 1	*2 to 3 teaspoons minced*
tablespoon vegetable oil	*fresh dill weed, or*
1 (8-ounce) cake tempeh	*1 teaspoon dried*
½ cup plus 2 tablespoons	*1 tablespoon mellow barley*
vegetable stock	*miso, or more to taste*
1 large onion, chopped	*1 pound bread dough*
1 small carrot, finely diced	*1 tablespoon beaten egg*
1 small turnip, finely diced	*mixed with a bit of water*
2 cups sliced mushrooms	*Poppy seeds*

Combine the kuzu and cold stock or water and set it aside until the kuzu has dissolved completely.

Toast the caraway seeds in a heavy-bottomed skillet over low to medium heat, agitating the pan frequently to keep the seeds from scorching. Grind the seeds to a coarse consistency using a mortar and pestle or a spice grinder.

Add the 2 teaspoons oil to a skillet over medium heat. Brown the tempeh on both sides. Add ½ cup stock and tightly cover the pan. Steam, turning the tempeh occasionally, until the pan is almost dry. Remove the tempeh from the pan and cut it into small pieces.

Add the 1 tablespoon of oil to the skillet over medium heat and sauté the onion, carrot, and turnip until they are almost tender. Stir in the mushrooms, cabbage, pepper, caraway, dill, and tempeh, and cook briefly, stirring often.

Whisk the miso and the 2 tablespoons stock with the dissolved kuzu until smooth. Stir this mixture into the sauté.

Preheat the oven to 400°. Grease a baking sheet or line it with parchment paper.

Divide the dough into 4 equal pieces. Roll each into a ball and cover these with a damp towel for a few minutes, until the dough has relaxed. On a lightly greased surface, roll one of the balls into a 6- to 7-inch-diameter circle. Spoon ¼ of the filling onto the dough, fold it in half, and firmly crimp the edges together to seal in the filling. Transfer the filled dough to the pan. Make 3 more piroshki in the same manner. Brush the tops with the egg wash and prick them with a fork in several places to allow steam to escape during baking. Sprinkle on the poppy seeds.

Bake the piroshki for 20 minutes, or until they are browned and crusty. Cool them briefly on a rack and serve them warm.

KASHA KNISHES

THESE EASTERN EUROPEAN BAKED OR FRIED SPECIALTIES traditionally consist of a nonyeasted dough and a potato, chicken liver, or kasha filling. In this variation, a crisp bread crust encloses a moist kasha, tofu, and vegetable filling. Rye doughs especially complement this filling, and doughs containing winter squash or sweet potato make for other good flavor combinations. Serve these knishes with sauerkraut and dill pickles.

YIELD: 4 large turnovers—4 servings

PREPARATION TIME: 45 minutes to prepare; 20 minutes to bake

1 teaspoon kuzu powder	1¹/₂ to 2 teaspoons minced
1 teaspoon cold vegetable	fresh dill weed, or
stock or water	³/₄ teaspoon dried
1 tablespoon vegetable oil	4 ounces tofu, mashed
1 medium-sized onion,	2 cups cooked kasha
finely chopped	(see page 19)
2 cloves garlic, minced	1 tablespoon dark miso
¹/₄ cup finely diced carrot	1 tablespoon tahini
¹/₄ cup finely diced turnip	1 tablespoon tamari
1¹/₂ cups sliced	2 tablespoons stock or water
mushrooms	2 tablespoons minced parsley
2 cups loosely packed,	1 pound bread dough
finely chopped kale	1 tablespoon beaten egg
Freshly ground black	mixed with a bit of water
pepper to taste	Poppy seeds

Combine the kuzu and the cold stock or water and set it aside until the kuzu has dissolved completely.

Add the oil to a skillet over medium heat. Sauté the onion for 2 to 3 minutes, until translucent. Continue sautéing, gradually adding the carrot and turnip. When these are almost tender, add the mushrooms, kale, pepper, dill, and tofu, and cook briefly, stirring. Stir in the kasha, cover the pan, and turn the heat to low.

Add the miso, tahini, tamari, and the 2 tablespoons stock or water to the dissolved kuzu and whisk until smooth. Stir this into the vegetable-kasha mixture, and remove the skillet from the heat. Add the parsley and let the mixture cool somewhat.

Preheat the oven to 400°. Grease a baking sheet or line it with parchment paper.

Divide the dough into 4 equal pieces. Roll each into a ball and cover these with a damp towel for a few minutes, until the dough has relaxed. On a lightly greased surface, roll one of the balls into a 6- to 7-inch-diameter circle. Spoon ¹/₄ of the filling onto the dough, fold it in half, and firmly crimp the edges together to seal in the filling. Transfer the filled dough to the pan. Make 3 more turnovers, brush on egg wash and prick them with a fork in several places to allow steam to escape during baking. Sprinkle on the poppy seeds.

Bake the knishes for 20 minutes, or until they are browned and crusty. Cool them briefly on a rack and serve them warm.

Empanadas de Picadillo

Empanadas are the Spanish and Latin American versions of turnovers. In Spain they are usually made with a yeasted dough and are baked. New World empanadas are commonly made with pastry doughs and are deep fried. *Picadillo,* a spicy filling for empanadas, is traditionally prepared with shredded meat, but tempeh is an ideal substitute. A corn-wheat dough is an especially good complement to this filling. You can also use the filling in tortillas (see pages 214–219) or in **Corn Crêpes** (page 210).

2 teaspoons plus 1 tablespoon olive oil

1 (8-ounce) cake tempeh

1 medium-sized onion, finely chopped

1 medium-sized bell pepper, finely chopped

3 medium-sized potatoes, cut into thin slivers

2¹/₂ teaspoons ground cumin

¹/₂ teaspoon ground cinnamon

¹/₂ teaspoon ground cloves

¹/₃ cup raisins

¹/₄ cup plus 1 tablespoon tequila

¹/₂ cup red salsa – see **Blender Hot Sauce** *(page 276)*

1 tablespoon dark barley miso

¹/₂ cup parsley, finely chopped

Sea salt to taste

1 pound bread dough

Add the 2 teaspoons oil to a skillet over medium heat. Brown the tempeh on both sides. Remove it from the skillet and cut it into small strips.

Notes
• Substitute other vegetables, such as parsnip, sweet potato, or cabbage, in the same proportions.

Yield: 4 large empanadas—4 servings

Preparation time: 45 to 50 minutes to prepare; 20 minutes to bake

Tequila is a clear, potent liquor made from a species of Central American century plant called *Agave tequiliana.*

Notes

• Add ¼ cup lightly toasted slivered almonds to the filling; stir them in after it has cooked.
• If you haven't any prepared hot sauce, add a pinch of cayenne to the sauté along with the other spices and add ½ cup chopped tomato.

Add the remaining oil to the skillet. Sauté the onion until translucent. Add the bell pepper and potatoes and continue sautéing until they are almost tender. Add the cumin, cinnamon, and cloves, and sauté briefly. Stir in the tempeh, raisins, the ¼ cup tequila, and the salsa. Cover the pan and cook over low heat for a few minutes, until the pepper and potatoes are tender.

Mix the miso and the 1 tablespoon tequila to a smooth paste. Stir this and the parsley into the tempeh mixture. Season with salt.

Preheat the oven to 400°. Grease a baking sheet or line it with parchment paper.

Divide the dough into 4 equal pieces. Roll each into a ball and cover these with a damp towel for a few minutes, until the dough has relaxed. On a lightly greased surface, roll one of the balls into a 6- to 7-inch-diameter circle. Spoon ¼ of the filling onto the dough, fold it in half, and firmly crimp the edges together to seal in the filling. Transfer the filled dough to the pan. Make 3 more empanadas in the same manner. Brush the tops lightly with olive oil and prick them with a fork in several places to allow steam to escape during baking.

Bake the empanadas for 20 minutes, or until they are browned and crusty. Cool them briefly on a rack and serve them warm.

MUSHROOM CALZONES

YIELD: 2 large calzones—2 generous servings

PREPARATION TIME: 45 minutes to prepare; 20 minutes to bake

ELBA'S ITALIAN KITCHEN WAS PERCHED AT THE TOP OF the steepest hill in Ithaca, New York. On Sunday evenings, Elba's offered large bread-crusted turnovers called calzones, filled with the chef's choice of ingredients—usually a delicate combination of spinach, onions, herbs, and soft cheeses. The original Elba's spirit lives on in these crusty, creamy, yet dairyless mushroom-stuffed crescents. You need a sturdy dough for this recipe: try a yeasted or sourdough Italian or

French. Calzone means "pants leg," so roll the dough into rectangles and prepare log-shaped turnovers if you prefer.

8 ounces tofu, preferably (extra-firm) silken	*½ pound mushrooms, sliced*
½ teaspoon sea salt, plus more to taste	*Freshly ground black pepper to taste*
2 tablespoons lemon juice	*¼ teaspoon minced fresh rosemary leaves, or ⅛ teaspoon dried*
1 tablespoon canola or other light vegetable oil	*½ teaspoon minced fresh thyme leaves, or ¼ teaspoon dried*
1 tablespoon tahini	*Cornmeal*
1 tablespoon olive oil	*1 pound bread dough*
1 large onion, finely chopped	
2 cloves garlic, minced	

Blend the tofu in a food processor fitted with the metal blade. Add the ½ teaspoon salt, the lemon juice, vegetable oil, and tahini, and blend until the mixture is completely smooth.

Add the olive oil to a skillet over medium heat. Sauté the onion for about 3 minutes, until translucent. Stir in the garlic and gradually add the mushrooms, pepper, and herbs. Continue sautéing until the onion is tender and the mushrooms appear moist. Allow the sauté to cool somewhat, then fold it into the tofu mixture and add salt to taste.

Preheat the oven to 400°. Grease a baking sheet or pizza pan with olive oil and dust it with cornmeal.

Divide the dough in half. Roll each half into a ball and cover these with a damp towel for a few minutes, until the dough has relaxed. On a lightly greased surface, roll one of the balls into a 9- to 10-inch-diameter circle. Spoon half of the filling onto the dough, fold it in half, and firmly crimp the edges together to seal in the filling. Transfer the filled dough to the pan. Make the other calzone in the same manner. Brush the tops with olive oil or spray on water for an especially crisp crust, and prick them with a fork in several places to allow steam to escape during baking.

Bake the calzones for 20 minutes, or until they are browned and crusty. Cool them briefly on a rack and serve them warm.

GREAT GREENS CALZONES

YIELD: 2 large calzones—2 generous servings

PREPARATION TIME: 45 minutes to prepare; 20 minutes to bake

THE FILLING FOR THESE CALZONES IS AN EMBELLISHED version of one of my favorite side dishes—sautéed greens and garlic. Mediterranean in concept, it is a subtly sweet combination. Use a basic wheat, cracked wheat, or Italian dough.

8 ounces kale or escarole
1 tablespoon olive oil,
    plus extra for brushing
    the dough
1 medium-sized sweet
    onion, finely chopped
4 cloves garlic, minced
1 tablespoon capers
2 tablespoons unsulfured
    golden raisins or
    currants

2 tablespoons chopped
    pitted Kalamata olives
2 tablespoons lightly
    toasted pine nuts
1/4 cup finely chopped
    flat-leaf parsley
Freshly ground black pepper
    to taste
Sea salt to taste
1 pound bread dough
Cornmeal

If you're using kale, strip the leafy portion off each stalk with a sharp knife. Finely chop the stalks and coarsely chop the leaves, keeping the two parts separate. Coarsely chop the escarole.

Add the 1 tablespoon oil to a large skillet over medium heat. Sauté the onion for 2 to 3 minutes, until translucent. Add the garlic and kale stalks and continue sautéing, gradually adding the kale leaves, until the onions and greens are just tender. Stir in the capers, raisins, olives, pine nuts, and parsley. Season the mixture with pepper and salt. Remove it from the heat and allow it to cool somewhat.

Preheat the oven to 400°. Grease a baking sheet or pizza pan with olive oil and dust it with cornmeal.

Divide the dough in half. Roll each half into a ball and cover these with a damp towel for a few minutes, until the dough has relaxed. On a lightly greased surface, roll one of the balls into a 9- to 10-inch-diameter circle. Spoon half of the filling onto the dough, fold it in half, and firmly crimp the edges together to seal in the filling. Transfer the filled dough to the pan. Make the other calzone in the same manner. Brush the tops with olive oil, or with an egg wash for a shiny crust, and prick them with a fork in several places to allow steam to escape during baking.

Bake the calzones for 20 minutes, or until they are browned and crusty. Cool them briefly on a rack and serve them warm.

YOU CAN ALSO ROLL OUT A DOUGH, SPREAD ON A FILLING, and roll it up. Leave the filled roll in loaf form or cut it into slices and bake them as separate buns. Cinnamon rolls are a classic example of the latter format. Loaves or buns filled with savory ingredients will work just as well as sweet ones and make unusual main dishes or partners for soups and salads.

As with other filled doughs, the dough for these should have at least one and preferably two rises before shaping. Then set it aside to rise again before baking. Match up doughs and fillings that have compatible flavors. Fruit and vegetable fillings usually need precooking and shouldn't be too liquid or contain large chunks. Fruit and nut butters, chopped nuts, seeds, dried fruits, minced herbs, and grated cheeses are all good possibilities for other filling ingredients.

Notes
- Add some feta to the filling.

Spiral Filled Doughs

CINNAMON SWIRL

YIELD: 1 loaf

PREPARATION TIME: 10 minutes to assemble; about 1 hour to rise; 40 to 50 minutes to bake

IN JUST MOMENTS, YOU CAN TRANSFORM A PLAIN LOAF OF bread into a spicy spiraled bread! Egg and sweet doughs are especially effective: Try **Challah** (page 112), **Sweet Bread** (page 107), or **Apple or Pear Sauce Bread** (page 115).

³/₄ teaspoon cinnamon
2 tablespoons date sugar
* or Sucanat*
1¹/₂ pounds bread dough
1 tablespoon melted butter
* or soy margarine, or*
* walnut or hazelnut oil*

¹/₄ cup raisins (optional)
¹/₂ cup coarsely chopped,
* lightly toasted pecans*
* (optional)*

Mix together the cinnamon and sugar and set aside. Grease a 9 x 5-inch loaf pan.

Roll the dough out into a 10 x 12-inch rectangle. Brush the dough with the melted butter, leaving a 1- to 2-inch border along one short edge. Sprinkle the cinnamon-sugar over the greased portion of the dough. Scatter the raisins and nuts on top. Beginning with the side opposite the unfilled edge, roll up the dough and pinch a seam to seal it. Place the roll, seam-side down, in the loaf pan. Cover it for about 1 hour, until the dough has risen and rebounds slowly when pressed. Toward the end of the rising period, preheat the oven to 400°.

Bake for 20 minutes, then lower the heat to 350° and bake for 20 to 30 minutes longer, until the loaf has browned, the sides are firm, and it sounds distinctly hollow when removed from the pan and tapped on the bottom. Brush butter on the crust to soften it, and cool the loaf on a rack.

Notes

• To prepare **Cinnamon Buns:** Leave one of the longer edges unfilled, roll the dough up toward that edge, and pinch it closed. Cut across the roll to form 8 equal pieces. Arrange these slices on their cut side in a well-greased baking pan, placing them close enough together so that they will rise up against one another. Cover the buns long enough for them to rise, until the dough springs back slowly when pressed. Bake at 350° for 40 minutes, or until the buns are browned and crusty.

• To make **Fruit Butter Buns,** substitute ¹/₂ cup **Pear Butter** (page 255) or another fruit butter for the cinnamon-sugar and proceed as for Cinnamon Buns.

STICKY BUNS

OCCASIONALLY ON WEEKEND MORNINGS, OUR FAMILY would have sweet rolls or coffee cakes of some sort, and this would start my parents reminiscing about Sunday mornings in Detroit during the war, when my dad would get up early and wait in line at Sanders Bakeshop to buy their famous sticky buns. Their sweet memories were the stimulus for these maple-pecan buns. **Date-Orange Bread** (page 116) and **Apple or Pear Sauce Bread** (page 115) are two especially good dough choices.

³/₄ cup lightly toasted,
  finely chopped pecans
¹/₄ cup maple syrup
1¹/₂ pounds bread dough

1 tablespoon unsalted butter
  or soy margarine, melted,
  or 1 tablespoon nut oil

YIELD: 8 large buns

PREPARATION TIME: 1 to 1¹/₂ hours to prepare and rise; 40 minutes to bake

Sprinkle ¹/₄ cup of the nuts on the bottom of a well-greased 9- to 10-inch glass or ceramic pie pan or comparable container. Drizzle half the syrup over the nuts.

Roll the dough into a 10 x 12-inch rectangle. Brush the dough with the melted butter, leaving a 1- to 2-inch border along one long edge, then brush on the remaining syrup. Sprinkle on the remaining nuts. Roll up the dough toward the unfilled edge and pinch a seam to seal it. Cut the roll into 8 equal slices. Arrange these on their cut side in the pan, placing them close enough together so that they will rise up against one another. Cover the pan for about an hour, until the dough has risen and rebounds slowly when pressed.

Preheat the oven to 350° and bake the buns for about 40 minutes, until they are browned and crusty. Run a metal spatula around the edge of the baked buns to loosen them, set a plate upside down on top of the pan, and invert the buns onto the plate, so that the sticky side is on top. Serve them warm.

Notes
• Substitute honey or rice syrup for the maple syrup and walnuts for the pecans.

PEANUT BUTTER SPIRAL BUNS

YIELD: 8 large buns

PREPARATION TIME: About 2 hours to prepare and rise; 40 minutes to bake

ADULTS WILL BE JUST AS ENTHUSIASTIC AS KIDS ABOUT these yummy buns. Try **Basic Whole Wheat Bread** (page 78) or **Sesame Bread** (page 104) for the dough. Like **Cinnamon Swirl** (page 340), you can bake this as a loaf rather than buns.

¹/₄ cup currants	¹/₂ to ³/₄ cup orange juice
1 teaspoon finely grated orange zest	1¹/₂ pounds bread dough
¹/₄ cup mild-flavored honey or maple syrup	¹/₄ cup toasted sesame seeds
²/₃ cup chunky peanut butter	¹/₄ cup toasted sunflower seeds
	Melted butter or margarine, or peanut or walnut oil

Combine the currants and zest in a bowl. Add the honey and peanut butter. Mix thoroughly, gradually adding the orange juice to achieve a spreadable consistency.

Grease a 9- to 10-inch round pie plate or baking dish.

Roll the dough into a 10 x 12-inch rectangle. Spread on the filling, leaving a 1- to 2-inch border along one long edge. Sprinkle on the sesame and sunflower seeds.

Roll up the dough toward the unfilled edge and pinch a seam to seal it. Cut the roll into 8 equal slices and arrange the slices on their cut side in the prepared pan. Let the buns sit, covered, for about 1 hour, or until the dough has risen and springs back lightly when pressed. Preheat the oven to 350° toward the end of the rising period.

Bake the buns for about 40 minutes, or until they are browned and crusty. Brush the tops lightly with melted butter or oil if desired. Cool the buns in the pan on a rack for several minutes, then turn them out and serve them warm.

Pizza Roll

Yield: 4 to 6 servings

Preparation time: 1½ hours to prepare and rise; 30 minutes to bake

These spiraled pizza slices are perfect for a buffet supper or picnic. Any strong dough works well for this roll, but I especially like to use an Italian dough or **Anadama Bread** (page 98). You can experiment with the basic format of this dish, using different savory fillings.

1 tablespoon olive oil, plus extra for brushing the dough

1 (4-ounce) cake tempeh

¼ cup vegetable stock

½ teaspoon tamari

1 medium red onion, finely chopped

4 cloves garlic, minced

¼ cup thinly sliced fennel bulb

2 cups sliced mushrooms (4 ounces)

1 teaspoon minced fresh basil

½ teaspoon minced fresh thyme

2 tablespoons finely chopped flat-leaf parsley

½ cup tomato sauce (page 273 or 274)

Freshly ground black pepper to taste

Sea salt to taste

Cornmeal

1½ pounds bread dough

Finely grated parmesan cheese (optional)

Coarsely grated mozzarella cheese (optional)

Add 1 teaspoon of the oil to a skillet over medium heat. Add the tempeh and brown it on both sides. Add the stock and tamari, cover the pan tightly, and cook until the pan is dry. Remove the tempeh and cut it into small dice.

Add the remaining 2 teaspoons of oil to the skillet over medium heat. Sauté the onion for about 2 minutes, then add the garlic and fennel. Gradually add the mushrooms and continue sautéing until the vegetables are tender. Stir in the tempeh, basil, thyme, parsley, and tomato sauce. Add pepper and salt to taste. Set the mixture aside to cool somewhat.

Lightly grease a baking sheet or line it with parchment paper, then dust it with cornmeal. If you are baking on a pizza stone, dust a baker's peel with cornmeal.

On a lightly greased surface, roll the dough out into a 12 x 12-inch square. Spread on the filling, leaving a 2-inch border along 3 sides. Sprinkle on cheeses if desired. Roll up the dough, starting with the unbordered edge, and pinch a seam. Fold in the ends and pinch them closed. Place the filled roll on the baking sheet, seam side down. Cover it for about 1 hour, until the dough rises.

Preheat the oven to 400°. Brush the top of the roll lightly with olive oil and pierce the top in several places with a long-tined fork. Bake the roll for 30 minutes, or until it is browned and crisp and sounds hollow when tapped on the bottom. Transfer it to a rack to cool to room temperature or slightly warmer. Cut the roll into 1- to 2-inch slices to serve.

Other Filled Doughs

YIELD: 1 coffee cake

PREPARATION TIME: About 1 ¹/₂ hours to prepare and rise; 40 minutes to bake

CRISSCROSS COFFEE CAKE

CRISSCROSS STRIPS OF DOUGH CONCEAL A THICK LAYER of spicy apple filling in this coffee cake.

1¹/₂ pounds firm tart apples (Pippins are good)
2 tablespoons maple syrup
¹/₄ teaspoon cinnamon
¹/₄ teaspoon freshly grated nutmeg

¹/₄ cup raisins
1¹/₂ pounds bread dough
2 tablespoons melted butter or soy margarine, or walnut or other nut oil

Peel and core the apples, and cut them into slices or chunks. In a covered saucepan set on a flame tamer over medium heat, cook the apples, stirring occasionally, until they are just tender. Stir in the maple syrup, spices, and raisins. Cool the mixture.

On a lightly greased surface, roll the dough out into a 12 x 15-inch rectangle. Brush the dough with 1 tablespoon of the melted butter. On the two long sides of the rectangle, make 3³/₄-inch cuts in the dough at 1-inch intervals. Spread the filling down the center of the dough, leaving 1¹/₂ to 2 inches of uncovered dough on all sides. Fold in the short sides first; then, beginning at one end, fold in the strips on the long sides alternately to form a chevron pattern. Cover the dough for 40 to 50 minutes.

Bake the filled dough in a preheated 350° oven for about 40 minutes. Place it on a cooling rack and immediately brush on the remaining melted butter or oil. Serve the cake warm or at room temperature.

Chinese Steamed Buns

STEAMED BREADS ARE TRADITIONAL IN THE NORTHERN region of China, but they are typically made with refined flour. This variation substitutes a whole wheat dough. I steam these buns in a double-tiered bamboo steamer set over boiling water in my wok, but you can use any steamer. Stuffed with a spicy vegetable and tofu filling, these rolls, dipped in a tangy sauce, make an unusual light dinner, lunch, or even brunch dish.

¹/₂ teaspoon kuzu powder

¹/₂ teaspoon cold water

1 tablespoon tamari

1 teaspoon roasted sesame oil

1 tablespoon **Hot Sherry** (page 235)

8 ounces tofu, well pressed and cut into small cubes

1¹/₂ teaspoons sesame oil

2 large green onions, finely chopped

1 clove garlic, minced

1 teaspoon finely grated fresh ginger

1¹/₂ cups thinly sliced bok choy or Chinese cabbage

1¹/₂ pounds **Basic Yeasted Whole Wheat Bread** dough (page 78)

1 tablespoon shoyu

1 teaspoon brown rice vinegar

Hot Chile Oil (page 345) to taste

Notes
• Add lightly toasted, coarsely chopped walnuts or pecans to the filling after it has cooked.
• Vary the fruit filling: use part or all pears or peaches (add or substitute allspice or ginger); add ¹/₂ to 1 cup fresh or frozen cranberries to the apples, and add 2 tablespoons more maple syrup; add fresh or frozen blueberries to the cooked apples.

YIELD: 6 large buns

PREPARATION TIME: 60 to 90 minutes to prepare and rise; 20 to 25 minutes to steam

....

Hot chile oil is simply oil flavored with hot peppers. It is commercially available or you can make your own. Put fresh or dried chile peppers or their seeds in a jar, add heated sesame, peanut, or other vegetable oil, and steep until the oil is well flavored. Of course, the more peppers you use, the hotter the oil will taste. Strain the oil and refrigerate it to forestall rancidity. Hot oil is used primarily as a flavoring, especially in Asian cuisines.

Shoyu, a full-flavored, mellow seasoning, is a naturally brewed, aged soy sauce made from soybeans, wheat, salt, and water. Add it near the end of cooking to preserve its flavor. See also **Tamari** (page 288).

....

Notes
• Add a few thinly sliced fresh or soaked dried shiitake mushrooms to the stir-fry.
• The **Sweet Potato and Apple** filling on page 299 is also a delicious stuffing for these buns.

Combine the kuzu and water and set it aside until the kuzu has dissolved completely.

Whisk the tamari, roasted sesame oil, and sherry in a medium-sized bowl. Fold in the tofu and marinate for 20 to 30 minutes, stirring occasionally.

Heat a wok or skillet, and add the sesame oil. Stir-fry the onions, garlic, and ginger briefly. Add the bok choy or cabbage, and continue stir-frying for a minute or two. With a slotted spoon, remove the tofu from the marinade and add it to the stir-fry. Cook briefly. Turn the heat to low.

Whisk the dissolved kuzu into the reserved marinade and pour it over the stir-fry. Cook, stirring, until the liquid thickens. Transfer the stir-fry to the marinating bowl and set it aside to cool.

Cut the dough into 6 equal pieces and form balls. Cover them for about 30 minutes. On a lightly greased surface, roll each ball into a 6-inch circle. Cover them until the dough relaxes.

Holding a circle in the palm of one hand, spoon $\frac{1}{6}$ of the filling into the center. Pleat the edge of the circle and pinch it firmly shut. Place it, pinched side down, on a lightly floured baking sheet and cover. Repeat with the remaining dough. Let the buns rise 30 to 60 minutes, or until they have just about doubled.

Arrange the buns in a steamer on squares of parchment paper or lightly greased waxed paper. Cover and steam the buns over gently boiling water for 20 to 25 minutes, until the dough is thoroughly cooked.

Whisk together the shoyu, vinegar, and hot oil. Serve the mixture in individual bowls as a dipping sauce for the warm buns.

THIRTEEN

Leftover Bread

Odds and ends of bread are almost inevitable in baking households. Enthusiastic bakers rarely wait to run out of bread before whipping up another batch, and who wants to eat up old scraps with fresh new breads beckoning? You can toss leftovers to the birds, but the birds are out of luck when it comes to any over-the-hill bread in my house, because I've found so many good uses for it.

One way to reckon with your perpetual baking impulse while avoiding waste is to keep an anticipated bread surplus fresh by freezing part of each batch as soon as it has cooled after coming out of the oven. This is especially effective for small items like rolls, English muffins, bagels, pita, chapatis, and tortillas. Slice loaves before freezing so you can take out individual servings. Having more than one kind of bread available is a definite asset when it comes to meal planning: Bread from a former baking may go particularly well with the soup you're making for lunch or the dish you're serving for dinner.

Still, sometimes you'll find yourself with bread several days old. First, are you absolutely certain this bread cannot be revived? If it's not too dry, reintroducing some moisture may do the trick. Refresh rolls by spraying them all over with water from an atomizer and heating them directly on the rack of a moderate oven. Voila! In several minutes they'll become almost just like their old selves, crisp-crusted and soft inside. Resuscitate whole or partial loaves or slices by wrapping them in a damp, unnapped towel and placing them in a covered casserole in a low to moderate oven for 15 minutes or so. Or, give the package a brief sauna in your steamer. Steaming also revives quick loaves, muffins, and flat breads. Most bread past its prime still makes great toast, and a brief stint in a moderate oven quickly crisps waffles and crackers.

Even though no longer restorable, truly passé bread is still a valuable resource. Some recipes, like French toast, require somewhat stale bread. Cubed, toasted, and seasoned dry bread is easily transformed into flavorful, textural garnishes for soups and salads. Diced bread may also function as a major salad ingredient, as in Middle Eastern fattouche and Italian bread salads, or lend substance to vegetable stuffings and bread puddings. Blend the rest to crumbs in a blender and keep them in your freezer. They have a multiplicity of uses, from breading vegetables, burgers, and croquettes, to contributing crunch to the top of stuffed vegetables, casseroles, and streusel coffee cakes, to becoming ingredients for pancakes, muffins, and loaves, such as the illustrious Eastern European black breads.

Follow the example of Latin Americans who never throw away a tortilla. Layer aged tortillas in casseroles or cut them into strips for a tortilla soup. You can easily make tortillas into chips for dips or bases for tostadas. Simply brush them, whole or cut into wedges, with a little oil and bake them in a moderate oven, just until they are crisp.

You can apply similar recycling principles to almost any leftover bread. I guess you could say this chapter is more about "getting out of" than "getting into" bread. It looks like we've come full circle, folks. Let the recipes inspire you.

French Toast

LEFTOVER BREAD MAKES BETTER FRENCH TOAST THAN does freshly baked French bread because it's less moist and fragile; porous yeasted breads work best. French bread makes excellent French toast; if it's a baguette, slice the loaf on the diagonal. Other good bread choices are **Challah** (page 112), **Apple or Pear Sauce Bread** (page 115), and **Poppy Seed Bread** (page 118). Also try using **Spiced Honey Bread** (page 108); omit the spices in the soaking mixture. Serve these crisp, golden slices of French toast with maple syrup or fruit butter, such as **Pear Butter** (page 255). See the notes below for a dairy-free, eggless version with a delicate spiced apple flavor.

Grated zest of 1 lemon
1/4 teaspoon freshly grated nutmeg
2 large eggs
1 cup milk or unsweetened soy milk

6 slices bread (about 1/2 inch thick)
Sesame or other vegetable oil

In a medium-sized bowl, combine the zest, nutmeg, and eggs, and whisk well. Gradually whisk in the milk. Pour into a shallow pan and arrange the bread slices in it. Soak the bread for about 10 minutes. Carefully turn the

YIELD: 2 generous servings

PREPARATION TIME: 30 to 40 minutes

Notes
• Substitute 1 teaspoon orange zest for the lemon zest and 1/4 teaspoon cinnamon for the nutmeg.
• For vegan **Apple-Cinnamon French Toast,** thoroughly blend 4 ounces tofu with 1 cup unsweetened apple juice and 1/4 teaspoon cinnamon, and proceed as with the egg mixture above. If you like, add 1/4 teaspoon freshly grated nutmeg. The finely grated zest of 1 orange is another tasty addition; juice the orange and combine the orange juice with apple juice to equal 1 cup.

slices over and soak until they have absorbed the egg mixture.

Heat a large skillet or griddle until water dripped onto the surface sizzles. Add a small amount of oil and tilt the pan to coat the bottom. Fry the slices until browned and crisp. Turn and cook the other side. Serve the French toast hot.

ITALIAN BREAD SALAD

TRY THIS TERRIFIC TUSCAN SOLUTION FOR LEFTOVER bread. The dry bread cubes soften somewhat as they sop up the pungent dressing. I like to serve this salad with a hot or cold puréed soup for a light summertime meal. You can prepare the salad a few hours in advance, but cut and add the tomato just before serving to preserve its flavor.

YIELD: 4 servings

PREPARATION TIME: 30 to 40 minutes

Notes
• Substitute an herbed vinegar, such as basil or tarragon vinegar, for the red wine vinegar. If you use basil vinegar, you may wish to decrease the fresh basil or substitute some minced fresh tarragon.
• Substitute sea salt to taste for the miso.
• Garnish the salad with freshly grated cheese, such as romano, parmesan, or grating ricotta—a solid, mild-flavored white cheese available at some cheese shops and Italian markets.

1 cup green beans, diagonally sliced into 1-inch pieces
1 medium-sized carrot, sliced
1 medium-sized bell pepper, sliced into thin strips
1 small red onion, sliced into thin rings
$^1/_2$ medium-sized cucumber, seeded if necessary and diced
2 cups $^3/_4$-inch bread cubes

4 cups torn mixed greens (lettuce, arugula, etc.)
$^1/_4$ cup loosely packed flat-leaf parsley, finely chopped
$^1/_2$ cup loosely packed fresh basil leaves, chopped
1 clove garlic, minced
Freshly ground black pepper to taste
3 tablespoons red wine vinegar
1 teaspoon dark miso
3 tablespoons olive oil
1 large tomato, cubed

Croûtes and Croutons

Croûtes are slices of toasted bread and croutons are cubes. To make croûtes, I brush sliced bread with olive oil, arrange the slices on a baking sheet, and bake them in a low to moderate oven until they are lightly browned and crisp. For croutons, cut slices into cubes before baking. Turn slices over and stir cubes occasionally during baking, and remain vigilant, because croûtes and croutons burn easily. Sometimes I flavor the oil with minced garlic and/or herbs before brushing the bread. To make croutons from already cubed bread, toss the cubes with oil and seasonings in a bowl before baking. You can also toast croûtes or croutons in an oiled heavy skillet on top of the stove. To make croûtes and croutons without any oil, simply bake the slices or cubes until they are crisp. If you want to flavor these, mix garlic, herbs, spices, orange or lemon zest, tamari, or whatever, with a small amount of liquid and brush slices or toss cubes with it before baking. To store croûtes or croutons, cool thoroughly and wrap them tightly, and refrigerate or freeze.

Float croûtes in soup or use them as crunchy bases for savory spreads to serve as appetizers or accompaniments for soups or salads. I especially like to spread **Roasted Garlic** (page 252) on olive oil–flavored croûtes. Croutons add interest to salads and provide a contrast in texture when used as a garnish for hot or cold puréed soups.

Steam or blanch the beans until they are just tender. Add them to a large bowl, along with the carrot, bell pepper, onion, cucumber, bread cubes, greens, parsley, and basil.

Whisk together the garlic, black pepper, vinegar, and miso. Slowly add the olive oil and whisk constantly to emulsify the mixture. Drizzle it over the vegetables and bread, and toss thoroughly. If you wish, cover and chill the salad for 20 to 30 minutes or up to several hours.

Add the tomato and toss the salad again. Serve it immediately.

FATTOUCHE

THIS IS A GOOD WAY TO USE UP LEFTOVER PITA. *Fattouche* means "moistened bread." To keep the pita from getting moist to the point of sogginess, though, add it at the very last minute. Include this salad in a buffet or serve it with soup for lunch.

YIELD: 2 to 4 servings

PREPARATION TIME: 30 to 40 minutes

Notes

• Add about ¹/₄ cup crumbled feta cheese.

YIELD: 4 to 6 servings

PREPARATION TIME: 20 minutes to assemble; 45 to 55 minutes to bake

1 pita (see page 225)
1 clove garlic, minced
Freshly ground black
   pepper to taste
2 tablespoons lemon juice
2 tablespoons olive oil
¹/₄ cup fresh mint leaves,
   minced
Sea salt to taste
4 cups freshly shredded
   greens

2 green onions, sliced
   lengthwise and finely
   chopped
¹/₂ medium-sized cucumber,
   diced
¹/₂ cup parsley, finely
   chopped
1 large tomato, cubed, or
   about 1 cup whole cherry
   tomatoes
10 to 12 Kalamata olives

Run a knife around the edge of the pita and separate it into two circles. Toast the bread until crisp in a 350° oven, then break it into small pieces.

In a small bowl, whisk together the garlic, pepper, and lemon juice. Add the olive oil very slowly while whisking constantly to emulsify the mixture. Stir in the mint. Season with salt.

In a large bowl, combine the greens, onions, cucumber, parsley, and tomato. Drizzle in the dressing and toss thoroughly. Add the crumbled pita and toss again. Serve the salad immediately, garnished with the olives.

BREAD PUDDING

TRANSFORM LEFTOVER BREAD INTO DELICATELY SPICED custard for dessert or breakfast. For an especially rich pudding, make it with leftover brioche or croissants—if you ever have any!

2 eggs
¹/₄ cup mild-flavored honey
¹/₄ teaspoon sea salt
¹/₄ teaspoon cinnamon
¹/₄ teaspoon freshly
   grated nutmeg

2 cups milk or unsweetened
   soy milk
¹/₂ cup raisins
3 cups ¹/₂-inch bread cubes

Preheat the oven to 325°. Grease a 9-inch round or 8-inch square ovenproof baking dish.

Whisk the eggs in a medium-sized bowl. Whisk in the honey, salt, cinnamon, and nutmeg. Gradually whisk in the milk. Stir in the raisins and bread cubes. Pour the mixture into the prepared pan and set the pan in a large pan of hot water. Bake the pudding for 45 to 55 minutes, or until a knife inserted in the center comes out clean. Serve it warm or chilled.

TORTILLA SOUP

THIS SOUP IS SORT OF AN ABUNDANTLY GARNISHED BUT liquid salsa enriched with tempeh and garnished with crisp corn tortilla strips.

1 (4-inch) poblano pepper	4 cloves garlic, minced
2 pounds ripe tomatoes	1 teaspoon ground cumin
1 to 2 tablespoons olive oil	1 teaspoon sea salt, plus
1 (8-ounce) cake tempeh	extra to taste
3 1/2 cups vegetable stock	4 corn tortillas
or water	1/2 cup loosely packed
2 medium-sized onions,	cilantro leaves, coarsely
chopped	chopped

Roast and peel the pepper as described on page 244 and transfer it to a blender.

In an ovenproof pan (with sides to catch the juice), broil the tomatoes, turning them occasionally, until they're charred on all sides. Blend them and their juice with the pepper.

Add 2 teaspoons of the oil to a pot over medium heat. Brown the tempeh on both sides. Add 1/2 cup of the stock, cover tightly, and cook until the pan is dry. Remove the tempeh from the pot and cut it into narrow strips.

Heat 2 teaspoons of oil in the tempeh pot and sauté the onions and garlic until the onion is translucent and

Notes

• Add about 1/2 teaspoon finely grated lemon or orange zest to the liquid mixture.
• Substitute maple syrup or Sucanat for the honey.
• Substitute chopped dates for the raisins.
• Serve the pudding topped with lightly toasted, chopped nuts.

YIELD: 4 servings

PREPARATION TIME: About 1 hour

Notes

• For a heartier soup, add a few tablespoons of cooked rice to each bowl.
• Garnish the soup with sliced ripe avocado.
• Substitute commercial tortilla chips or soft tortilla strips for the home-crisped ones.
• Poblanos vary considerably in hotness. If this is very mild or you prefer spicier foods, sauté a finely chopped jalapeño or serrano pepper along with the onion and garlic. Remove the seeds and membranes of the pepper to tone down the heat somewhat.

YIELD: 2 generous servings

PREPARATION TIME: 30 to 40 minutes

almost tender. Stir in the cumin and cook briefly, stirring constantly. Add the tomato/pepper purée, remaining liquid, and 1 teaspoon of salt, and bring to a simmer. Cover, reduce the heat, and simmer the soup for 20 to 30 minutes, stirring occasionally, until the flavors are well integrated.

While the soup is simmering, brush both sides of each tortilla lightly with olive oil, cut it into strips about 1/2 inch wide, and bake at 350° for a few minutes, until the underside is golden brown. Turn and brown the second side. Watch them, because they burn easily. Break the crisped tortillas into chips and set them aside.

Divide the tempeh strips among four bowls. Ladle in the soup. Sprinkle tortilla chips and cilantro on top, and serve the soup immediately.

MIGAS

IN SPANISH, *MIGAS* MEANS "CRUMBS"—IN THIS CASE, THE last crumbs of leftover tortillas. In this country, migas means seasoned scrambled eggs and tortilla strips—a popular item on Southwestern breakfast menus. Serve **Emilio's Salsa Verde** (page 270) or **Avocado Salsa Cruda** (page 270) alongside. Migas is a meal in itself, but for an even heartier one, add **Refritos** (page 256), rice, and **Whole Wheat Tortillas** (page 218) to the menu.

1 poblano pepper
3 large eggs
1/4 teaspoon sea salt, or to taste
1 tablespoon sesame, olive, or canola oil
1 medium-sized onion, chopped
1 clove garlic, minced

1 teaspoon ground cumin
1 medium-sized tomato, chopped
3 corn tortillas, cut into 1/2 x 1 1/2-inch strips
1/2 cup loosely packed cilantro, coarsely chopped

Bread Crumbs

Any kind of leftover bread, no matter how dry or stale, is "crumbable," and, of course, the type of bread you use affects the flavor and texture of whatever you use the crumbs for. When I have a few dry slices or crusts hanging around, I make them into crumbs before mold calls first dibs. Unless I have an immediate purpose in mind, I keep crumbs, soft or toasted, tightly wrapped in the freezer.

Tear or cut the bread into small cubes and blend them in a blender or a food processor fitted with the metal blade in batches. Stop occasionally to stir around the blade with a chopstick to loosen crumbs that become lodged there. Blend until the crumbs reach the fineness you desire. Either bag them for refrigerator or freezer storage, or first spread them evenly on a baking sheet and toast at 250° until they are dry and crisp. Cool crumbs thoroughly before wrapping them up.

Use bread crumbs to firm up the consistency and coat the outside of grain and bean burgers and croquettes (page 287), and to provide texture in pâtés (pages 262–267). Dip eggplant slices first into olive oil and then into crumbs, arrange them on a baking sheet, and bake for 15 to 20 minutes in a moderate oven until tender. These are good as is, sauced, or layered in a casserole. Dip green tomato slices into plain or herb-seasoned crumbs and fry them in a small amount of olive oil until fork-tender and lightly browned on both sides. Sliced vegetables or tofu may also be dipped in beaten egg and then coated with crumbs and fried. Mix crumbs with date sugar and spices for a streusel topping (see page 54), or use them as an ingredient in pancakes, muffins, and breads!

Roast and peel the pepper as described on page 244, and cut it into thin strips.

In a small bowl, beat the eggs with ¼ teaspoon salt.

Add the oil to a skillet over medium heat. Sauté the onion and garlic until the onion is just tender. Add the cumin and pepper strips, and sauté briefly. Stir in the tomato and cook briefly. Add the tortilla strips and beaten eggs, and cook, stirring, until the eggs are just set. Sprinkle on cilantro and serve the migas immediately.

BREAD CRUMB PANCAKES

YIELD: About 1 dozen 4-inch pancakes—2 generous servings

PREPARATION TIME: An hour or more to soak the crumbs; 15 minutes to prepare the batter; 5 minutes to cook each griddleful

BREAD CRUMBS SUBSTITUTE FOR PART OF THE FLOUR IN these delicate griddlecakes. The kind of crumbs you use will affect the pancakes' flavor; those I made from a heel of **Date-Orange Bread** (page 116) were especially memorable. To save time in the morning, soak the crumbs overnight in the refrigerator.

1 tablespoon lemon juice	1 tablespoon vegetable oil
1 cup milk or	1 egg, separated
unsweetened soy milk	$1/2$ cup sifted whole wheat
1 cup soft fine bread	pastry flour
crumbs	$1/4$ teaspoon sea salt
1 tablespoon maple syrup	1 teaspoon baking soda

Add the lemon juice to the milk and then pour the curdled mixture over the crumbs in a medium-sized bowl. Cover and set it aside until the crumbs are well soaked.

Whisk the syrup, oil, and egg yolk into the soaked crumbs.

Beat the egg white until it is stiff but not dry.

Sift together the sifted flour, salt, and baking soda. Gently stir this into the wet mixture, just enough to form a batter. Fold in the beaten egg white.

Drop generous tablespoons of the batter onto a hot, lightly greased griddle. Cook until the tops bubble and appear almost dry. Carefully turn and cook the second side. These pancakes are more fragile than some.

Serve pancakes immediately or keep them warm in a low oven.

Notes
• Add the grated zest of a small lemon to the wet ingredients and sift $1/4$ teaspoon freshly grated nutmeg with the dry ingredients.

CRUMB BUNS

YIELD: 10 muffins

PREPARATION TIME: 30 minutes or so to soak the raisins; 20 to 30 minutes to prepare; 20 minutes to bake

THESE ARE SOME OF MY FAVORITE MUFFINS, AND THERE are many ways to vary the basic recipe. Refer to the notes for some ideas. These muffins stay moist for several days.

1 1/2 cups unsweetened
    apple juice
1/2 cup raisins
6 ounces tofu
3 tablespoons sunflower
    or other vegetable oil
3 tablespoons maple syrup
1 cup soft bread crumbs

2 cups whole wheat pastry
    flour
1/2 teaspoon sea salt
1 teaspoon baking soda
1 teaspoon baking powder
1/2 cup lightly toasted,
    coarsely chopped pecans

Notes
- Substitute currants or chopped dried dates, apricots, prunes, or figs for the raisins.
- Substitute walnuts, almonds, or hazelnuts for the pecans. Rub the skins off of the hazelnuts after toasting them.
- Add 1/4 teaspoon each of cinnamon and nutmeg or other sweet spices.
- Add the zest of 1 orange or 1 lemon.
- Substitute orange juice for all or part of the apple juice.

Heat the apple juice just to boiling, pour it over the raisins, and soak them for about 30 minutes. Drain well, reserving the juice. In a blender or a food processor fitted with the metal blade, blend the tofu, gradually adding the reserved juice, until the mixture is thoroughly smooth.

Preheat the oven to 400°. Grease 10 muffin cups.

Whisk the oil and syrup in a medium-sized bowl. Whisk in the tofu mixture and stir in the raisins and crumbs.

Sift together the flour, salt, baking soda, and baking powder. Add this to the wet ingredients and stir gently, just until a thick batter forms. Fold in the nuts. Immediately spoon the batter into the muffin cups, filling them just to the top. Bake the muffins for 20 minutes, until they are browned and a tester inserted in the center comes out clean. Cool the muffins in the pan for a few minutes, then run a small metal spatula around each one and turn them out onto a rack.

Rustic Rye Bread

TOASTED FINE CRUMBS OF LEFTOVER BREAD COMBINE with whole grain flours to produce the rich, dark color of Eastern European peasant breads. This country rye follows that old tradition. It is moist and hearty, just right with a potato, beet, or cabbage soup.

YIELD: 2 loaves

PREPARATION TIME: 1 1/2 to 2 hours for sponge and dough; 5 to 6 hours for rising; 40 to 50 minutes to bake

Notes
- For an even more robust bread, increase the crumbs and rye flour to 2 cups each and decrease the wheat flour accordingly.
- For a stronger dough, substitute wheat flour for the rye flour.

3 cups spring water

¾ teaspoon active dry yeast

4½ to 5 cups whole wheat bread flour

1½ cups toasted fine bread crumbs

2 tablespoons blackstrap molasses (optional)

2 teaspoons sea salt

2 tablespoons corn or other vegetable oil

1½ cups whole rye flour

Heat ¼ cup of the water and cool it to lukewarm. Add the yeast and a teaspoon of wheat flour, cover, and set it in a warm spot to proof. Add 1¼ cups of the water and stir in 1½ to 2 cups of the wheat flour to form a thick batter. Cover and set it in a draft-free spot for about an hour, or until a sponge develops.

Meanwhile, bring the remaining 1½ cups water to a boil and pour it over the crumbs in a large bowl. Add the molasses, salt, and oil. Cover and set it aside until lukewarm.

Stir the sponge into the crumb mixture. Add 3 cups of wheat flour, a cup at a time, stirring well after each addition. Gradually stir in rye flour until a dough forms, pulling away from the sides of the bowl and balling up in the center. (If you don't add all of the rye flour now, add the remainder later as you knead the dough.) Turn the dough out onto a lightly floured surface and cover it for a few minutes. Wash, dry, and lightly grease the bowl.

Thoroughly knead the dough, adding flour only as necessary to keep it from sticking. Like other rye doughs, this dough tends to remain a bit tacky. When it is smooth and resilient, form it into a ball.

Place the dough in the bowl, cover, and set it in a draft-free spot for about 2 hours, until it has risen and a finger pressed into it leaves a depression.

Knead the dough a few times and return it to the bowl. Cover and set it aside for about 2 more hours, until the dough has risen again and does not rebound when pressed.

Divide the dough and shape it into loaves; I usually make round or oval ones. Cover these and set them in a draft-free spot for about an hour, or until the dough has risen and springs back slowly when pressed.

Slash the loaves and spray them with water or brush on an egg wash and sprinkle on seeds if you wish; I like poppy seeds on this bread. Bake at 400° for 20 minutes, then lower the heat to 350° and bake for 20 to 30 minutes longer, until the loaves have browned, have firm sides, and sound distinctly hollow when removed from the pan and tapped on the bottom.

Cool the bread thoroughly before slicing or storing it.

BEAN PREPARATION CHART

| BEANS (1 CUP DRY) | Regular Cooking | | Pressure Cooking | |
	WATER	PREPARATION TIME	WATER	PREPARATION TIME
Aduki	4 cups	1 hour	$2^3/_4$ cups	30 minutes
Anasazi	3 cups	2 to $2^1/_2$ hours	$2^3/_4$ cups	1 hour
Black turtle	4 cups	2 to 3 hours	$2^3/_4$ cups	1 hour
Chickpeas	4 cups	2 to 3 hours	$2^3/_4$ cups	1 hour
Kidney	3 cups	1 hour	$2^1/_2$ cups	45 minutes
Lentils	3 cups	45 to 60 minutes	$2^1/_2$ cups	25 minutes
Navy	3 cups	1 hour	$2^1/_2$ cups	40 minutes
Pinto	3 cups	2 to $2^1/_2$ hours	$2^3/_4$ cups	1 hour

DRIED BEANS

BEANS COME IN MANY DIFFERENT SHAPES AND sizes and have long been staples in most cuisines around the world. Beans are an excellent source of protein, particularly when consumed with grains. They are also rich in complex carbohydrates, vitamins, minerals, and fiber. Dried beans are economical and easy to store, and they have many culinary uses.

Cooked dried beans are often associated with flatulence and indigestion, but certain preparation techniques can minimize these effects. Soaking beans before cooking them enhances their digestibility and helps maintain their shape, which may be important if you're using them in a salad or another dish where their appearance counts. Add enough water so the beans will still be covered when they expand. If it is particularly warm, refrigerate soaking beans to prevent them from fermenting. An alternative soaking method is to bring the rinsed beans to a boil, turn off the heat, cover, and soak them for about two hours.

The sea vegetable kombu assists in the digestion of beans. Add a piece about 2 inches long for a cup of dry beans; it will have nearly disintegrated by the time they are done cooking. Extra minerals and other nutrients are a bonus. A bay leaf cooked with beans also promotes digestibility. Miso is another digestive aid and it augments beans' rich, full flavors. Add miso to taste, mixed to a paste with some bean cooking water, after beans are tender.

COOKING BEANS

ALWAYS SORT THROUGH DRIED BEANS OR PEAS to pick out any pebbles or other foreign matter; though somewhat tedious, this step may prevent a broken tooth. Rinse the beans to remove grit and dust, then soak them as described above. Drain the soaked beans, add fresh water to cover, and bring the beans to a boil. Skim off any foam that forms on the surface and reduce the heat to low. Cover and simmer the beans, checking occasionally to be sure there is enough water. Cook until the beans are tender. Do not add salt before they are thoroughly cooked or they won't soften. If you don't have difficulty digesting beans, cook them in their soaking water to preserve nutrients.

One cup of dried beans yields about $2^1/_2$ to 3 cups cooked. The chart shows the amount of water and cooking times for various kinds of beans. Older beans take longer to cook. Pressure cooking saves time and preserves flavor.

Index